Work with
Young People

Work with Young People

Theory and Policy for Practice

Edited by
Jason Wood and
Jean Hine

Los Angeles | London | New Delhi
Singapore | Washington DC

First published 2009

SAGE Publications Ltd
1 Oliver's Yard
55 City Road
London EC1Y 1SP

SAGE Publications Inc.
2455 Teller Road
Thousand Oaks, California 91320

SAGE Publications India Pvt Ltd
B 1/I 1 Mohan Cooperative Industrial Area
Mathura Road
New Delhi 110 044

SAGE Publications Asia-Pacific Pte Ltd
33 Pekin Street #02-01
Far East Square
Singapore 048763

Library of Congress Control Number: 2008934786

British Library Cataloguing in Publication data

A catalogue record for this book is available from the British Library

ISBN 978-1-4129-2884-7
ISBN 978-1-4129-2885-4 (pbk)

Typeset by C&M Digitals (P) Ltd, Chennai, India
Printed and bound in Great Britain by TJ International Ltd, Padstow, Cornwall
Printed on paper from sustainable resources

Mixed Sources
Product group from well-managed
forests and other controlled sources
www.fsc.org   Cert no. TT-COC-2082
© 1996 Forest Stewardship Council
FSC

CONTENTS

LIST OF FIGURES AND TABLES

THE CONTRIBUTORS

Derrick Armstrong is Dean of the Faculty of Education and Social Work and Pro Vice-Chancellor at the University of Sydney. He was co-director of the Economic and Social Research Council (ESRC) network investigating young people and pathways into and out of crime. Before this he jointly directed the national evaluation of the 'On Track' Crime Reduction Programme in the UK which was concerned with the role of multiple interventions in crime reduction for 6–12 year olds. His published work includes *Experiences of Special Education: Re-evaluating Policy and Practice Through Life Stories* (RoutledgeFalmer, 2003).

Jo Aubrey was global youth work manager at the National Youth Agency. Before that her doctoral thesis included analysis of the impact of globalisation on communities in Ukraine. She has also undertaken research work with children and young people in Central and Eastern Europe for UNICEF and the Department for International Development. She is currently a children's centre manager in Suffolk with a continuing interest in the development of education for globalisation.

Sarah Banks is Professor in the School of Applied Social Sciences, Durham University, UK and is co-editor of the journal, *Ethics and Social Welfare*. She has researched and published extensively in the field of professional ethics, particularly in relation to social, community and youth work, including *Ethical Issues in Youth Work* (editor, Routledge, 1999), *Ethics, Accountability and the Social Professions* (Palgrave 2004), *Ethics and Values in Social Work* (3rd edn, Palgrave, 2006) and *Ethics in Professional Life: Virtues for Health and Social Care* (with Ann Gallagher, Palgrave, 2008).

Thilo Boeck is a Senior Research Fellow in the Centre for Social Action at De Montfort University. He worked in Youth and Community Development in Peru, Germany and the UK which influenced his commitment to participative research. His current research explores social capital and community cohesion within a social justice and social inclusion perspective. He is currently the principal investigator on a participative research project funded by the Big Lottery Fund exploring the impact of youth volunteering on social capital and community cohesion. He is also working in partnership with the voluntary and statutory sector looking at community cohesion, involving local people in participative mixed methods research projects in Leicester and Leicestershire.

Jagdish Chouhan is a Senior Lecturer in Youth and Community Development at De Montfort University. He is responsible for postgraduate programmes in Youth Work and Community Development Work, and has interests and expertise in social exclusion, anti-oppressive practice and the theory and practice of work with young people, youth work and community development. He obtained his PhD at the University of Bradford in 1991 and his research on the 'Communication Environment of the Gujarati Community in Leicester' was part of a wider UNESCO debate on 'The Role of Information in the Realisation of Human Rights for Migrant Workers'.

Bernard Davies has been a teacher, a youth worker and a local authority youth officer, and has taught on courses for teachers, social workers and youth workers. In his work as an independent consultant he focuses mainly on youth policies and youth services. He is a visiting professor at De Montfort University, Leicester, and a trustee of 42nd Street, a mental health resource for young people based in Manchester, South Warwickshire YouthBank and the Muslim Youth Work Foundation. His publications include a three-volume of history of the Youth Service since 1939 (Youth Work Press 1999a, 1999b and National Youth Agency 2008).

Jennie Fleming is the Director of the Centre for Social Action at De Montfort University where she has worked for the past 10 years. Previous to this she has many years experience as a youth and community worker and a social worker. Jennie has worked on a wide range of research projects with young people – both large and small and is committed to working in a participative and empowering way.

Alan France is Professor of Social Policy Research at Loughborough University and is the Director of the Centre for Research in Social Policy (CRSP). Prior to this role, he was instrumental in establishing the Centre for the Study of Childhood and Youth at Sheffield University. He has published extensively on areas related to youth and citizenship, youth crime and risk, and youth policy including his most recent book *Understanding Youth in Late Modernity* (Open University Press 2007).

Jean Hine is Reader in Criminology at De Montfort University, Leicester. She has undertaken several major research studies about young people and crime, most recently as Director of the ESRC funded research network exploring risk and young people's 'Pathways into and out of Crime'. Her particular research interest is in the area of policy 'intervention' in the lives of young people in a variety of contexts, including education. She is co-editor of the *British Journal of Community Justice*.

Nicky Hudson is Senior Research Fellow in the School of Applied Social Sciences at De Montfort University. She is a sociologist with an interest in health, medicine, gender and ethnicity, and her previous research includes work with young people on issues of sexuality and teenage pregnancy. She is interested in the complexities of the research process and how it is shaped by the identities of those who carry out and participate in research.

Hazel Kemshall is Professor of Community and Criminal Justice at De Montfort University. She has research interests in risk assessment and management of offenders, effective work in multi-agency public protection, and implementing effective practice with offenders. She recently investigated pathways into and out of crime for young people as part of an ESRC funded network (with Boeck and Fleming). Hazel is the author of numerous publications on risk, including her most recent book: *Understanding the Community Management of High Risk Offenders* (Open University Press 2008).

Malcolm Payne is Head of the Youth and Community Division and Director of the Youth Affairs Unit at De Montfort University. He directs YAU's research programme including two major national projects for the Department for Education and Skills: the evaluation of the impact of youth work, and the study of the impact of the Connexions Service on young people at risk. Recently, he undertook, with colleagues, a review of transitions research to inform the Department's proposed 10 year youth strategy. Malcolm has written widely on aspects of youth work and youth policy.

Daniel F. Perkins is Professor of Family and Youth Resiliency and Policy at Pennsylvania State University. Prior to joining Penn State in 2000, he worked in the Family and Child Ecology Department at Michigan State and the Family, Youth, and Community Sciences Program of the University of Florida. His research area is family and youth resiliency and policy, with a focus on strengthening the capacity of families, young people, and communities to be partners in building strong families, fostering positive youth development, and creating caring, safe, and productive communities.

Mary Tyler is Principal Lecturer and Course Leader for the BA (Hons) Youth and Community Development in De Montfort University's Youth and Community Division. She is a qualified social worker and has Masters in Deviancy and Social

Policy and in Education Management. She worked in many roles with young people and communities before working at the National Youth Bureau (now the NYA) and the Open University. She teaches and acts as professional tutor for youth and community work students at undergraduate and postgraduate levels specialising in management teaching. She is co-author of the forthcoming book *Managing Modern Youth Work* (Learning Matters 2009).

Howard Williamson is Professor of European Youth Policy at the University of Glamorgan. He previously worked at the Universities of Oxford, Cardiff and Copenhagen, as well as being a practising youth worker for over 20 years. He has contributed to youth policy development in Wales, the UK and across the countries of the European Union and the Council of Europe. He has served on numerous government policy committees concerned with young people and was, until recently, a member of the Youth Justice Board. He was appointed CBE in the New Year's Honours 2002 for services to young people.

Jason Wood is Senior Lecturer in Youth and Community Development at De Montfort University. He is a qualified youth worker and has teaching and research interests in youth work, criminal justice, citizenship and social policy. He has recently completed a PhD study investigating young people and active citizenship. His other most recent research and publications have explored the community management of high risk offenders, including the ongoing development of the Multi-Agency Public Protection Arrangements (MAPPA) in the UK.

Tom Wylie was the Chief Executive of the National Youth Agency in England until 2007. He was born and educated in Belfast where he was a teacher and youth worker. He worked for the Scout Association and the National Youth Bureau and became one of Her Majesty's Inspectors of Education in 1979, managing the Inspectorate's Divisions responsible for youth and community work, for educational disadvantage and for curriculum. He has chaired or served on various governmental and EU advisory groups and committees of the Economic and Social Research Council, the Prince's Trust, and the Joseph Rowntree Foundation. He is now a trustee of several national voluntary youth organisations.

Scott Yates is a Senior Research Fellow in the Youth Affairs Unit at De Montfort University. He received his PhD in psychology in 2002, and his teaching and research interests span psychology, illness and disability, and youth studies. His recent research includes work on Foucauldian thought and discourse analysis, theorising subjectivity in learning difficulties research, youth identities and young people's career aspirations, the impact of recent social policy on the practical work of youth services, and the potential for youth work interventions with young people in hospitals.

Joe Yates is Criminology Subject Leader at Liverpool John Moores University. He has worked as a youth worker, social worker, youth justice worker and a youth offending team policy manager. His research interests relate to youth justice, social control and social policy responses to marginalised young people. He sits on the executive committee for the National Association of Youth Justice and is Director of the annual 'Social Work with Juvenile Offenders Symposium' hosted by the Inter University Centre in Croatia.

ACKNOWLEDGEMENTS

We want to extend a warm thanks to the contributors in this volume: they have all provided thought provoking insights, and this book is ultimately a reflection of their hard work. Our colleagues at De Montfort University have been incredibly supportive, with thanks especially to Hazel Kemshall for initial help and encouragement in developing the proposal. The team at SAGE Publications have demonstrated a welcome combination of patience and encouragement for this project so we are grateful to them for this. We say a big thanks to our families and friends for their emotional and oftentimes practical support. Finally to the anonymous reviewers whose comments led to a better version of this book, we are grateful for your time and help.

This book is dedicated to all those who continue to do meaningful work *with* young people: we genuinely hope this volume gives you further inspiration.

1

INTRODUCTION: THE CHANGING CONTEXT OF WORK WITH YOUNG PEOPLE

Jason Wood and Jean Hine

Introduction

The past ten years has been witness to significant expansion and change in work with young people. The field once occupied predominantly by youth services, social work and education now contains a wider network of agencies that seek to intervene in a young person's life. A qualified youth worker today is one who can be called upon to make a contribution to a number of agencies and organisations that, in many cases, did not exist ten years ago. In statutory youth offending partnerships and crime prevention teams, they work to prevent and reduce the reoccurrence of youth crime. In information, advice and guidance services, they undertake work to reduce the number of young people excluded from education, training or employment. Through various health initiatives, they work preventatively in reducing the various health risks that young people face. Positive activities and structured programmes of leisure, once the cornerstone of youth work, persist, but in a wide variety of contexts provided by a range of statutory, voluntary and private agencies. This broad range of work with young people frequently takes place in multi-agency contexts, where the disciplinary boundaries between professions are increasingly characterised as porous. As a result, the professional identity of a youth, health or social worker is somewhat under challenge as partnership becomes commonplace.

Many of the policy initiatives that have underpinned these changes have done so on the basis of a desire to improve things for all children and young people. In England, the *Every Child Matters* (ECM) framework offers five laudable outcomes for children and young people: being healthy, staying safe, enjoying and achieving, making a positive contribution and achieving economic well-being (DfES 2003). Similarly, the ambitions of the overarching *Youth Matters* and *Aiming High for Young People* strategies indicate both a desire to empower young people in the delivery of positive activities and for them to access high quality support in terms of advice and guidance (DfES 2005; HM Treasury/DCFS 2007). These positive messages are also evident at a European level: youth policy is governed by a commitment to advocating youth citizenship, promoting better participation and listening to the voice of young people (Williamson, Chapter 11).

However, such developments also invite wide-ranging criticism. The dominant message about young people is one of ambivalence: they are to be protected and improved through increased intervention, but simultaneously society must be protected from some of them. They are active participants in public life, yet are increasingly excluded from public spaces through dispersal and curfew measures. They are held up as responsible for making decisions, yet are often characterised as lacking the necessary skills to exercise this responsibility in an acceptable way. All of which results in young people being labelled in neat, dichotomous ways that do not necessarily reflect the complexity of young people's real lives and contextual circumstances.

At the same time as funding the expansion in the numbers of workers with young people, policy has also become more prescriptive, specifying how their work should be done and introducing a wide range of targets to be met by agencies delivering this work. Practitioners are increasingly required to demonstrate how their work results in accredited learning outcomes for young people. These targets are underpinned by an espoused commitment to evidence-based practice, though it is difficult to see the value of the evidence chosen. This is all the more surprising given the extent to which research and wider theory has increased understandings of young people over the past decade. The relationship between this growing body of research, much of it focused on young people, and the definitions and approaches found in policy is clearly not a strong as it could be.

This is a book about working with young people in this changing climate. It provides an opportunity for those who work with young people to consider the theoretical issues and wider theorising within which policy is formulated and their practice occurs. It considers some key theoretical and policy developments, and subjects them to a critical and timely review, inviting the reader to reflect upon the implications for the practice of working with young people.

Developments in theory and research

The study of youth and work with young people has seen advances in theoretical and empirical understanding over the past decade. Youth studies, itself a contentious area of research, has opened understanding of various aspects of young people's lives. Youth itself is an 'artefact of expertise' (Kelly 2003) which is subject to intensive interrogation and expert representations of 'education, family, the media, popular culture, (un) employment transitions, the life course, risks and so on' (Kelly 2003: 167).

Exactly what is meant by 'youth' is open to question (see Hine, Chapter 3), though central to the concept is the notion of it being a stage in life between childhood and adulthood. The period in the life course that is defined as 'youth' is as much a social construction as it is a period of individual change: Mizen defines youth as a 'socially determined category' (Mizen 2004: 5) and in this respect, it is little use to rely solely on individual biological markers as a frame for understanding youth. In very simple terms, the cultural, social and political contexts into which young people grow, invariably shape definitions of what is childhood, adolescence and adulthood.

Childhood is a contested and socially constructed period of the life course (Foley et al. 2001; James and James 2004). Like youth, childhood 'cannot be regarded as an unproblematic descriptor of the natural biological phase' (James and James 2004: 13). The experiences of a child growing up in the 1990s compared with that of those today will vary dramatically. Further complexity arises in any cross-cultural comparison of childhood, especially in the values ascribed to certain definitions of childrearing practices as compared to 'Western notions of what all children should aspire to' (Sanders 2004: 53). Such perspectives open up a challenge to claims of a neutrally defined 'normal' childhood since 'childhood as a social space is structurally determined by a range of social institutions and mechanisms' (James and James 2004: 213). These institutions and mechanisms reflect the dominant cultural and social adult expectations of childhood, either in response to the individual and collective behaviours of children or in the wide variety of macro determinates that influence the wider structure of society (James and James 2004).

Adulthood is also subject to social categorisation. What is meant precisely by adulthood is highly contested. Economic indicators would suggest full and continuous participation in the economy and the acquisition of property (Faulks 2000). Normative social indicators may include the formation of stable family units, characterised by the reproduction and socialisation of the next generation of children. Civil indicators would suggest political and civic participation. All of these claims though can be subject to dispute. For instance, if full economic participation and property acquisition are indicators of responsible adulthood, then the increase in uptake of higher education and its associated debt mean that many young people are effectively deferring the responsibilities of adulthood.

What is known for certain is that young people in late modern societies are characterised as leading immensely complex and fragmented lives. Their social identities are subjected to far-reaching, diverse and interconnected influences. These range from changing macro forces arising from globalisation (Aubrey, Chapter 4) and the risk society (Kemshall, Chapter 13), to more constant issues of social stratification relating to class, gender, race, disability, sexuality and so on (Chouhan, Chapter 6).

Two strands of recent research are worthy of exploration here since they have direct implications for the significant changes in work with young people over the past ten years. The first examines expanding knowledge about youth transitions in a markedly changing and complex world. The second undertakes to review the interplay of risk and resilience in young people's lives.

Changing, complex and extended transitions

Young people are frequently referred to as being in a state of transition, of moving between the life stages of childhood and adulthood: a stage termed adolescence or 'youth'. Age boundaries are often applied to this stage and are embedded in legislations related to education, voting rights and marriage, but in the modern Western world a range of economic and social indicators of adulthood are primary signifiers of the transition. In the discussion above, the idea that childhood and adulthood are problematic concepts was put forward. In any discussion around transition as a journey, one perhaps must accept some sort of a destination. For Coleman et al., adolescence is 'best understood as a complex transition between the states of childhood dependence and adult independence' (2004: 227). The extensive study of this transition period has provoked much recent empirical and theoretical interest, not least because of the complex changes associated with the risk society. Such research has been useful in considering:

- The interaction between personal capacity, biology and personality ('agency') and the systems and structures that influence young people ('structure').
- The ways in which institutions, social policies and systems intervene within a key stage of the life course.
- The ways in which other problems or situations emerge, particularly at the point of transition from education to employment. This is of particular interest to policy makers, often concerned with the interconnectedness of 'social exclusion'. (Bynner 2001: 6)

While there has perhaps always been a great deal of confusion over what constitutes arrival at adulthood (Coleman and Warren-Anderson 1992), transitions that were once understood to be linear are now recognised as fluid, changing and increasingly without a fixed end-point (Dwyer and Wyn 2001). Consequently, young people growing up in the modern world 'face new risks and opportunities' (Furlong and Cartmel 2007: 8) perhaps only glimpsed by previous generations. It certainly makes one's own reflections on childhood in many cases redundant.

Regarded as 'as important phase in the life cycle' (Furlong and Cartmel 2007: 34), the lineage from education to employment is one such example. Pathways from post-16 education are now beset by a range of further training opportunities, increased uptake at higher education and new uncertainty in traditional, skilled and unskilled labour (Furlong and Cartmel 2007). Government recognition that the nature of the labour market has shifted towards a 'knowledge economy' ultimately means that more young people are required to attend further and higher education and training for longer periods. Indeed, at the time of writing, developments in the UK suggest that the statutory school leaving age will rise to 18 from its current age of 16. One consequence of fragmented employment patterns and extended education is the changing relationship that young people have with their immediate families. In the UK for instance extended periods of financial dependency on parents and carers may mean home ownership takes place increasingly later on in the life course.

Key indicators for arrival at 'adulthood' are the acquisition of features that denote a shift from dependence on parents and family to independent living, including obtaining employment, forming a relationship and family, and moving into accommodation. These are the indicators chosen by Bynner (2005) in his description of 'capital accumulation' by young people. His findings show that across Europe there is a trend towards the achievement of the markers of adulthood coming at a later age now than previously, the concept of extended transitions, but he goes on to conclude that in the UK:

> … over the 24-year period examined, the most dominant feature was growing polarization between the advantaged and the disadvantaged. Emerging Adulthood was very prominent in the former, but the traditional accelerated routes to adult life were still as common as ever among the rest. (Bynner 2005: 377)

This work found that the social and economic changes leading to extended transitions for the majority of young people who are living in reasonable or affluent circumstances have not had the same impact on the lives of young people from more disadvantaged backgrounds. Involvement in extended education and training delays the onset of employment and the life features that depend economically upon that, but rates of such participation are lower for the more disadvantaged, with higher levels of early parenthood and early entry into work. The findings confirm the importance of addressing all the dimensions of youth identified by Hine (Chapter 3), particularly the historical dimension, as contexts change rapidly.

The focus on the notion of transition is accompanied by the view that young people are adults in the making, and thus do not have the awareness or competencies of adults. This view is informed by the dominant developmental perspectives of childhood presented by psychologists such as Piaget and Inhelder (1969). Children are seen to develop adult attributes gradually over their early and adolescent years in an additive and linear fashion, with normative age bandings identified as significant for the acquisition of particular competencies (the biological dimension in Hine, Chapter 3). Where children do not achieve these attributes by the prescribed ages this is deemed to be problematic and to signify the need for professional involvement and resolution. Where children perform better than, or not so well as, the system requires of them at particular ages, such as in education, this creates difficulties, both for the system and for the child.

It is argued that recent times have seen significant changes in young people's transitions, because the nature of the world in which they live has changed dramatically (e.g. Bynner 2005; Spence 2005). In this new world young people have greater opportunity but less certainty about their futures, requiring them to be more reflexive and make more reasoned choices about their futures (Beck 1992). At the same time, a range of social and economic changes have meant that transitions can be more difficult for young people to achieve and that this transitional phase of life is becoming longer and more complex (Valentine 2003), though as noted above, these changes have not affected all young people in the same way, with those from disadvantaged backgrounds tending to have different patterns of transition than those from more privileged backgrounds (Bynner 2005). At one time aspects such as class, gender, ethnicity and disability may have been more predictive of likely futures for young people, although these features are also likely to have masked wide ranging experiences of becoming adult. Thus the assumed commonality of experience of transition is increasingly being questioned in the era of individualisation, in parallel with increasing concern about the futures that young people will have.

Young people, risk and resilience

> Nowhere is the tension between the need to prevent risk and the necessity of learning to manage and take calculated risks more apparent than in the process of growing up from childhood to adulthood. (Thom et al. 2007: 1)

Certainly, young people are leading lives of increasing uncertainty and 'heightened risk' (Furlong and Cartmel 2007: 8) an idea located within the now well-rehearsed framework of the 'risk society' (Beck 1992). Life is literally prone to risks that once did not exist and 'people are seen to both cause risks and be responsible for their minimalisation' (Lupton 2006: 12). Whether these risks are the consequence of seemingly uncontrollable forces (such as global warming) or understood within the more localised or personalised experiences of the population (health related risky behaviours such as smoking, for instance), the overwhelming consequence is an increased feeling of insecurity and a desire for risk prevention and protection (Beck 1992; Kemshall 2002a; Furlong and Cartmel 2007). This 'culture of caution' (Thom et al. 2007) leads us ultimately to see risk through a negative lens.

The youth/risk dynamic is prominent in relation to young people's social activities and debates around youth welfare, criminal justice, employment and sexuality (Mythen and Walklate 2007). The expanding knowledge base about young people's personal and social risks is driven by research that gives increasing attention to young people as problems: sexual behaviour (Hoggart 2007), substance misuse and 'binge' drinking with grand but contested claims about alcohol misuse (see France

2007: 137–138), and the links between truancy and long-term social exclusion (Social Exclusion Unit 1998) are just three examples. This concern with risky behaviour drives a desire to predict it and stop it, using the idea of 'risk factors': literally what key determinants impact upon whether young people will grow up as integrated members of society, or as somehow deviant (Hayes 2002). This knowledge base has undoubtedly had strong influence on policy (Kemshall, Chapter 13).

This growing body of work also seeks to understand 'protective factors' and the idea of 'resilience' to address the question: what capacities do young people 'need' in order to ward off risk? Resilience is not simply located at the level of individual agency but is increasingly seen as a cultural and structural concept. Particular approaches to building resilience through community youth development (Perkins, Chapter 9) and social capital (Boeck, Chapter 8) demonstrate that to see young people as sites only of individual (in)capacity does little to address their wider social contexts: an issue further explored in the conclusion.

Developments in policy

Throughout history, youth policy has always responded to different political, public and social imperatives, since 'youth has always been under the microscope and of central concern to adults and the state' (France 2007: 1). The question of what to do with young people is beset by a curious mix of anxiety, fear, hope and aspiration and is always dependent on the changing social and political context in which young people are located: an ambivalence that can be found at the heart of policy messages about young people.

Key themes in policy development over the past ten years include the prominence of risk based social policy over traditional welfarist models. This includes an increasing emphasis on fostering conditions that promote 'self-reliance' and 'responsibility' (a theme discussed by Kemshall in Chapter 13 and Wood in Chapter 12). For young people in particular, there has been an increase in strategies designed to ward off social exclusion through the use of early intervention strategies. In some cases, the preoccupation with risk has led to a widening of the criminal justice net (Yates, Chapter 14). Services that were not traditionally classed as within the criminal justice arena find themselves increasingly contributing to outcomes related to the reduction of the risk of offending. What this means for competing paradigms (the value of social education, for example) is an interesting and ongoing debate, explored throughout this volume.

Another key driver has been the focus on child protection. High profile cases have inevitably always shaped social work and criminal justice policy; with media and public reactions leading often to a 'culture of blame' (Kemshall 2003). The failure by key child welfare and protection agencies to respond to seemingly obvious warning signs of abuse in a key case led ultimately to the formation of the Every Child Matters (ECM) policy framework. The five outcomes are now commonplace and can be found across merged children and young people's services, and even have close connection with the funding grants available to the voluntary sector.

Dealing with young people for what they might become

In any welfare system, resources are prone to economic rationalisation, and targeting offers a politically attractive option for addressing the most pressing social problems (Kemshall 2002a). The argument suggests that the more entrenched a difficulty becomes, the more costly and less effective interventions become. So policy responds by seeking to address early warning signs: the truancy, rather than the long-term exclusion from school; the cigarette smoking rather than the diseases that plague the individual in later life; the healthy eating of children in schools rather than the health consequences of obesity. The approach is often argued as commonsensical: if it is known that someone is more likely to do X, if they are displaying Y, then surely one should intervene? As former Prime Minister Tony Blair observed:

> Where it's clear that children are at risk of being brought up in disadvantaged homes where there are multiple problems, then instead of waiting until the child goes of the rails we should act early enough to prevent that. (Blair 2006 cited in The *Guardian*)

This emphasis on risk factors and precaution have ultimately led us towards a focus on the potential futures of young people via targeted policy and away from universal, open access welfare that deals with problems in the present (France 2008). Risk factors serve as 'targets' helping to identify 'populations at risk' (Schoon and Bynner 2003).

Early intervention is realised through a number of policy measures. All children and young people have access to universal education and health care, with minimum standards in both. But those children and young people who embody certain risk factors face greater levels of state intervention. Families in the most deprived communities in Britain are the targets of specialist, multi-disciplinary Children and Family Centres that seek to address the interconnected problems of health, education, child development and parenting. In criminal justice, the expansion of programmes of structured activity and the development of youth prevention services are targeted at those areas with higher crime rates in the hope that such programmes will divert potential offenders. Similarly, those young people Not in Education, Employment or Training (NEET) may find themselves subject to a raft of initiatives such as alternative curricula and dedicated personal advisers, both on compulsory and voluntary terms. The last ten years has seen a prioritisation of engagement in education, in whatever new forms it takes hold, including most recently through private enterprise seeking to offer alternative qualifications for those children most at risk of exclusion. Education merely becomes functional and not liberating (Chouhan, Chapter 6), seen solely as preparation for work (Armstrong, Chapter 7).

But a causal approach so often comfortable in science is not easily applicable to the understanding of human behaviours and relationships. Further, such 'pathological' approaches to individual motivation and risk taking do not tackle deeply entrenched structural issues: matters taken up by the contributors in this volume.

From entitlement to conditionality

A key theme in social policy has been the reframing of welfare from one of entitlement to one of conditionality (Dwyer 2004) putting at the centre the balance between individual rights and obligations. Increasingly, welfare is based on the 'something for something' society (Blair 1998) where the expected duties of the individual are more clearly prioritised. Welfare reform then is more than an economic imperative: it literally becomes a 'remoralizing' exercise, redefined as a system that encourages active participation of its citizens over passively dispensing compensation to those in need (see Kemshall 2002a: 111–112).

The theme of rights and responsibilities is then witnessed through a number of policy initiatives, and when seen in terms of a broader social framework can be applied to almost all aspects of youth policy. Rights in this case are often framed as a right to participate, with the UN Convention on the Rights of the Children often underpinning the rationale for encouraging the 'duty to consult'. Recent youth policy in the United Kingdom seeks to engage young people in the process of formulation, e.g. through *Youth Matters* consulting the views of nearly 20,000 young people. As Fleming and Hudson (Chapter 10) discuss, the more fully young people are enabled to participate, the more responsive and effective services can be in supporting young people.

Social responsibility is a more complex policy development. Obligations on young people are either quite specific (children will not truant, or they/their parents will face financial penalties) or rather more ambiguous (increasing 'respect', for instance). In whatever form they take, the desired moral and social behaviour of young people is increasingly determined by policy and instructed through education and welfare services. As Armstrong notes in Chapter 7, education policy ensures that each person has a place and knows that place and its boundaries. This is an important theme throughout the book and social responsibility is examined in relation to the youth service, criminal justice, welfare, education, active citizenship and broader social policy.

Implications for practice

The start of this chapter indicated that work with young people in the UK now offers a more diverse employment market driven by new and expanding policy intentions. This market includes housing authorities, the police, youth offending teams, health services, education, and welfare and guidance services. Much of the work is prescriptive and targeted, but creativity and diversity still flourish: practitioners do indeed seek to empower young people and develop meaningful relationships built upon increased trust (see for example, Yates' discussion in Chapter 15).

The guiding principles of youth work have in recent tradition been bound to those of informal education: an emphasis on voluntary association, starting from where the learner is at and encouraging them to reflect on their own experiences (Jeffs and Smith 2005) in order to engage in a process of moral philosophy (Young 2006). However, these principles are under challenge: how, for instance, to ensure voluntary association in a court ordered programme for young offenders? Or does a youth worker cease to be a youth worker when joining such a system? These matters are taken up in this volume, with discussions around principles and ethics (Banks, Chapter 5 and Chouhan, Chapter 6), and the purpose and expectations of work with young people (Payne, Chapter 18 and Tyler, Chapter 19).

What is clear from the changing knowledge and policy landscape is that those with a training in youth work can contribute much to these newer contexts, perhaps offering creativity in working within these new frameworks and changed agendas. They can play a significant role that re-examines the problems that young people present, and attempt to negotiate more holistic problem definitions and solutions. It is therefore important to see the picture as far from gloomy.

Practitioners are increasingly promoting ways of engaging young people in influencing and shaping their social worlds and many chapters illustrate practical ways in which this can be achieved. The increased attention to active citizenship and social capital offers a gateway to an alternative focus on young people as agents who can shape their social contexts with the support of trusted adults (Boeck, Chapter 8 and Wood, Chapter 12). This relies however on learning the lessons from research and practice where young people's views actively shape adult understanding of their worlds (Hine, Chapter 3 and Fleming and Hudson, Chapter 10). It also requires practitioners to restate their values and ethical positions so that these can act as lamplights in a complex and challenging set of environments – the notion of the principled pragmatist explored by Tyler in Chapter 19.

This book

The debate about the purpose, principles and practice of work with young people is therefore the subject of this book. Developments in theory, research and policy are critically examined and related to questions of practice. The key inquiries that guide this book include:

- What is known about young people, where does this knowledge come from, and to what extent has this knowledge changed?

- What is youth policy, what drives it and what does it seek to achieve?
- How can practitioners working with young people contextualise these developments in relation to professional work?

This volume offers a timely contribution to the debate. The contributors are all specialists in their respective fields, drawing on the latest research and practice to illustrate the debates about work with young people in changing contexts. Some of these arguments require outward thinking, in ways that require a reframing of understandings of both young people and youth work. Others invite a restatement of values, whether in commitment to working from where young people 'are at' or in recognising and challenging the inherent oppression and discrimination facing different social groups.

Any contribution to the debate will not cover all of the ground; nor should it try to. This volume reviews only some of the threads that together form the basis of modern work with young people.

Structure of the book

This book is organised into two sections. Part One (*Theory and Practice*) attends to some key aspects of understandings of young people, both in terms of their social construction and in the experiences they define themselves. Attention is also given to some key aspects of practice theory and how these apply to changing contexts of work with young people. Part Two (*Policy and Practice*) discusses key policy developments both in terms of policy drivers and the changing nature of services that work with young people. This necessitates attention to macro and local determinates, and how policy responds to complex social and personal issues.

Throughout the book, the authors make links to the practice of work with young people and reflective questions at the end of each chapter are designed to support the reader in relating the ideas to professional work and development. Reflective practice is an essential component of effective work with young people, and the questions are designed to stimulate only the beginning of what should be an ongoing interrogation and reflexivity.

Each part is preceded by a short introduction, and the concluding chapter critically reviews some of the key themes that emerge from this text.

PART ONE

THEORY AND PRACTICE

The lives of young people today are subject to complex challenges, as witnessed by the multifaceted theoretical frameworks that seek to explain their personal and social worlds. In Part One of this book, two authors address the ways in which knowledge of the 'youth question' has changed and developed in recent times. Alan France (Chapter 2) explores the changing conceptions of young people through an examination of the ways in which different disciplines have sought to define and explore how we understand 'youth' and the 'youth problem'. Taking a historical perspective he provides illuminating insights into how these ideas from the past have influenced current thinking about youth. Undoubtedly, this knowledge has grown and diversified radically over the past decade and France encourages practitioners to draw on inter-disciplinary knowledge to enhance understanding and work with young people. A key development in research over the past ten years has been to better understand the worlds of young people as they themselves define and experience it. Jean Hine (Chapter 3) examines some of these developments, questioning the limitations of 'evidence based policy' and arguing for more research grounded in the 'real lives' of young people. Such knowledge challenges many adult assumptions about the behaviour and experiences of young people.

Challenges to young people's lives emerge from numerous changes in the social and economic structure of wider society. The impact of globalisation, a theme introduced by Jo Aubrey (Chapter 4), is arguably greater for young people than for adults. It has broadened our understanding of the world around us through technological advances, and this brings with it a need to explore the exploitative elements of globalisation with young people.

At the heart of any profession is a commitment to professional ethics and values, and Sarah Banks (Chapter 5) draws on her extensive knowledge of the subject to establish the ethical standards and value positions that could/should underpin youth work in multi-agency environments and changing practice contexts. As Banks observes, such contexts offer the opportunity for practitioners to learn from other professional groups and to challenge established ways of doing things.

Inequality, exclusion, oppression and discrimination continue and persist through a range of social structures. These entrenched issues require attention to a key principle: anti-oppressive practice. Jagdish Chouhan (Chapter 6) offers a critical review of what constitutes anti-oppressive practice through an exploration of its key theoretical frameworks. In examining the personal, cultural and structural dimensions of oppression, Chouhan calls for a redefinition and adoption of empowering practices that encourage critical dialogue. Issues of inclusion and exclusion are further discussed by Derrick Armstrong (Chapter 7) as he undertakes a timely critical review of the role of education in modernity and post-modernity. He challenges contemporary conceptualisations of education policy and practice and calls for democratic education that supports young people in the critical questioning of social and political interests. For Thilo Boeck (Chapter 8) progressive youth work depends on participatory work that provides opportunities for widening young people's horizons and opportunities. Reviewing developments in social capital theory and its application to policy and practice, Boeck explores how young people's social networks can enhance or limit their opportunities to navigate risk. He calls for practitioners to distance themselves from seeing young people in terms of 'deficits' and enable them to escape the 'victim blame' culture. Instead, using a positive framework, practitioners can support the development of enhanced social capital to work with the needs and priorities of young people. Similar arguments are put forward by Daniel Perkins (Chapter 9) who critically reviews the adoption and promotion of community youth development in the USA. This approach works with young people in the promotion of their personal and environmental 'assets', emphasising the importance of capacity building of individuals and learning environments to foster positive development and engage young people with their communities.

Finally, the theme of understanding and acting upon the 'real worlds' of young people is revisited by Jennie Fleming and Nicky Hudson (Chapter 10). The authors conclude this section of the book by outlining the value of involving young people in all aspects of research. They provide a practical guide to participative research that will enable practitioners and researchers to actively engage young people as partners in the research process. The benefits go beyond their understanding of their peers: young people can develop skills, knowledge and self-esteem through the process.

2

CHANGING CONCEPTIONS OF YOUTH IN LATE MODERNITY

Alan France

Key arguments

- Understandings of youth, particularly the problematic behaviour of youth, have changed over time as the discourses and disciplines dominant in social science have changed.
- The dominant orthodoxy of this research maintained a perspective of deterministic youth who are a homogenous group, ignoring notions of diversity and difference.
- Newer research has challenged this through an exploration of subjectivity and identity and attention to 'difference'.
- In much social science the dichotomy of 'agency verses structure' has been rejected recognising that social life and choice is far more complex.
- Young people's voices are important and exploring influences, such as culture, history, and tradition as well as the emerging contemporary context and processes of social change all provide a more holistic understanding of their lives.

Introduction

Throughout history young people have been of fundamental interest to social scientists. Disciplines such as psychology, sociology, criminology, educational studies and

Table 2.1 Conceptions of youth over time

Time period	Social science influence	Influences and concerns	Impact
Early modernism eighteenth/ nineteenth century	Psychology and Positivist Criminology	– Enlightenment movement – Victorian Bourgeois Society – Anxieties over youth delinquency/ immoral behaviour	– Discovers 'adolescence' as natural stage – Constructs storm and stress as explanation of youth problem
Early twentieth century inter- war years	Positivist Sociology and Environmental Criminology	– Concerns over impact of urbanisation and youth delinquency	– Introduces influence of environment on behaviour – Youth culture as separate from adult culture
Post-war – 1960s	Functionalism	– Concerns over impact of the war on integration	– Constructs youth as a social institution – Age grading defined as natural order – Youth culture as alternative process of integration
1960s–1970s	Marxism and cultural studies	– Lack of class analysis to understanding social change	– Introduces notion of resistance to youth cultural studies – The importance of consumption to youth identities
Late modernity 1980s – present day	Feminism/post structuralism	– Failure of previous theories to understand diversity of youth – Impact of social change and growth of consumption	– The importance of young people's voice – Youth as agents – The central role of new technology and consumption

more recently, cultural studies have all had something to say about the activities of young people. This interest by social scientists has, in the majority of cases been focused on trying to understand and explain the 'youth problem'. As a result our understanding of youth and their activities has been historically structured by social science in particular ways (see Table 2.1).

These conceptions of youth are not theoretically neutral; they are influenced by the dominant ideas of the times in which they are conceived. Social scientists do not exist or operate in a political or social vacuum nor should we believe that theories are 'value free' and that social scientists are not influenced by the world around them. The first part of this chapter will chart the historical development of youth theories showing how different disciplines have constructed the meanings of youth. This discussion will highlight the key assumptions and influences that have shaped these meanings. The second part will turn attention to more recent developments in social science outlining the emergence of the 'new orthodoxy' and the influence of post-structuralism, drawing out major changes that have taken place in how social science is conceptualised and its impact on understandings of youth. The final section of this chapter will raise a number of core questions about this approach highlighting the lack of attention given to wider political and economic processes and the failure to recognise the embedded structural nature of the youth experience.

Modernism and the emergence of 'adolescence'

Modernity has been an economic and political project that not only re-structured and re-configured the ordering of society but also challenged traditional ways of thinking and understanding the social world (Giddens 1991). Modernity has its roots in the early seventeenth century and can be associated with:

- The introduction and expansion of industrialism and new ways of organising and producing goods and services.
- The establishment of capitalism as a form of ordering economic and social relationships.
- The rise of the modern state that expands its responsibilities and takes a central role in maintaining social order.

It was also the period of enlightenment when the belief in the political and 'rational' subject dominated. Science was given a central role in this process being seen as a major force in helping mankind master their environments. It is within this context that early theories of youth emerged in the new discipline of psychology. This new modernist orthodoxy formalised and justified youth as a universal stage of development in the life cycle and is defined as the stage of adolescence. This constructs the phase as a stage driven by internal influences (Springhall 1986). G. Stanley Hall (1904) was a critical contributor to this position; he was greatly concerned by the youth problems of delinquency and workless youth that seemed to exist in Victorian society. He saw adolescence as a 'second birth' and the early stages of man's higher nature. Adolescence was, to him, a natural stage of transition being influenced by biological and psychological processes. The 'youth problem' was then seen as a result of difficulties arising from the period of physical and mental transformation when the young move towards adulthood. This was defined as the stage of 'storm and stress' when the young were vulnerable to 'problematic behaviour' (Springhall 1986). Youth was then seen as '…a prisoner of its own nature' (Hendrick 1990: 103) and therefore not always in control of its actions. Hall's ideas were greatly influenced by the values of Victorian England and especially the post-Darwin movement that believed genes and genetics shaped the 'natural order'. An earlier version of this justified slavery, imperialism and colonial expansion (Griffin 1993) and was also used to explain differences between genders showing men to be superior to women (Dyhouse 1981). The adolescent 'problem' was then constructed as one of biology and psychology. Similar ideas dominated early developments in criminology where psychology was also greatly influential, especially the new emerging medical fields of psychiatry and mental health (Garland 2002). In this context juvenile delinquency was seen as a consequence of biology or a dysfunction of cognitive processes. For example, early criminologists proposed that criminality was a result of the 'pathological family' (Hollin 2002) suggesting genetic causes that were either located in individuals (i.e. the criminal gene) or were inherited from family (genetic dysfunction passed on from generations). Certain traits such as low intelligence, impulsivity and aggressiveness were claimed to be transmitted through genes.

The explanations of Hall and some of the early geneticists within criminology would not be given much credence today within social science, yet their influence cannot be underestimated. While the specifics may be rejected the ideas remain. Youth transitions, and especially 'problematic' transitions have become seen as a 'natural' phenomenon within theories of the life cycle. These have become strongly associated with developmentalism and scientific definitions that see the 'problem of youth' as a dysfunction of the body and mind. Evidence that supports these linkages between physical changes or genetic influence on behaviour remains elusive, yet the ideas developed in this nineteenth century social science remain a powerful influence in how youth is perceived and explained throughout modernity (France 2007).

The sociology of youth in modernism

Sociological approaches to our understanding of youth also had roots in concerns about the 'youth problem'. The Chicago School in America is recognised as the first major sociological analysis of youth and was concerned with causes of delinquency not through individual psychology but through the processes of social interaction with the urban environment of city life. The Chicago School left a major legacy in terms of theory by introducing the notion of 'culture' to the study of youth. For example, Shaw and Mackay (1942) introduced the idea of *cultural transmission* where criminal values in certain communities could be transferred across generations. While Sutherland (1939) constructed the notion of *differential association* where crime is not seen as being caused by personality but by association. It is the nature of the interaction where learning about motivations, techniques and moral justifications takes place.

From the 1940s onwards these ideas were developed further by functionalist writers such as Parsons. Functionalism has a major influence on the social sciences and shapes much of the thinking over questions of integration and how societies maintain social order. Parsons (1964) was greatly concerned about the problem of youth re-integration and how they were adapting to social changes taking place after the Second World War. Functionalists believed youth to be a 'social institution' that helped society function. Age grading was seen to maintain social continuity and acted to distribute roles, and make connections to other structural components of the system. It is here where individuals find self-identification and recognition of their place in society. The 'youth problem' was seen as a reaction to the tensions that were arising as society changed. As a result young people were seen to be creating their own *youth subcultures* as a mechanism of dealing with feelings of anomie (Parsons 1964). Yet while much of the theorising by subcultural theorists concentrated on a social set of explanations it took an 'oversocialised' and deterministic view of the delinquent seeing youth behaviour as a dysfunction of systems (France 2007). Young people were seen as passive and responding to the forces around them almost unquestioningly. There was no recognition that young people are social actors in these processes or that their behaviour can be defined differently in different contexts. This then becomes a form of sociological positivism (Muncie 2004).

Radical youth studies: politics of resistance

Most of the early studies of youth are American with the distinctive approach of British youth studies not taking root until the 1960s. This explanation of youth is more radical as it was influenced by the developments and social theorising taking place in British society. It is a historical moment when the political consensus of 'welfare capitalism' that emerged after the war was showing tensions. Arguments that class was 'dead' were being challenged as evidence of a growing 'embourgeoisement' between classes remained unsubstantiated (Goldthorpe et al. 1968). This was also a time of substantial change when youth became a site of major concern to politicians and social scientists. Throughout the 1950s and into the 1960s there was a growing awareness about the emergence of the 'teenager' and in particular of youth groups such as 'mods' and 'rockers' that challenged the status quo. Concerns were also raised over the growth of new radical political youth activities such as the peace movement, 'ban the bomb' marches and the rise of new feminism, that were challenging to the orthodoxy of modern society.

As both a reaction and a reflection of these events three major developments in social science took place. Firstly, a crisis existed in British criminology in that theorising failed to evolve. Much of criminology remains focused on the positivist ideas of measurement and improving the administration of criminal justice (Griffin 1993). In response a group of criminologists made a significant break from the mainstream orthodoxy creating a 'new deviancy theory' that radicalised how deviance was to be theorised. This sees the growth of labelling theory and class analysis in criminology. A second development comes through the Birmingham Centre for Contemporary

Culture (CCC). They saw the analysis of the youth question as a political project (Griffin 1993) and were interested in how young people 'used' subcultures as a response to their economic and social conditions. Much of this early work focused on the politics of resistance and how young people were 'resisting' social changes taking place in their lives (see Hall and Jefferson 1975). A final development was in educational research. Through ethnography this approach was embedded within class analysis and questions of resistance. Hargreaves (1972) for example saw the creation of an 'anti-social' culture as a cause of educational failure while Willis (1977) in his classic study of *Learning to Labour* saw the 'counter-school culture' not as a consequence of educational failure but a 'cause' that socially reproduced their position in the labour market.

By the early 1980s youth research had become a major force in the social sciences, but significant concerns were also being raised about its limited focus on understanding young people's lives. The radical approaches in the 1960s and 1970s did little to challenge the commonsense assumptions of determinism. While they remained silent on biological determinism they did reinforce a social determinism that saw transition as a 'normal' part of being young albeit a social one. They could also be criticised for 'over-reading' the activities of the young without listening to what they had to say (McGuigan 1992). Similarly, while they rejected the 'storm and stress' model of psychology they continued to theorise young people's lives as 'a social problem'. For example, the work of CCC concentrated on trying to explain young people's subcultural activities as a form of resistance or what Cohen and Ainley (2000) called the 'storm and dress' model of explaining youth behaviour. Much of this early work also concentrated on the more spectacular and public forms of activities. CCC concentrated on those subcultural groups that dominated media interest such as 'mods' and 'rockers' giving no attention to 'ordinary kids' or their 'ordinary lives' (Brown 1987). This also tended to romanticise behaviour that for other groups was problematic.

One final yet significant limitation was that most youth research focused on the activities of young white working class men or what Griffin (1993) calls the 'malestream' approach to youth research. Feminist writers were quite rightly critical of this approach but this was not just about the lack of attention to the lives of young women, but also a failure to recognise racial and cultural differences. The dominant orthodoxy of these more radical approaches to the study of youth and their activities therefore created a perspective of youth as homogenous, ignoring notions of diversity and difference (France 2007).

The 'new' orthodoxy in youth theorising

By the time we reach the 1990s strong arguments are being put forward for the expansion and development of youth research that addresses these limitations discussed above (Griffin 1993). Simultaneously, major structural and cultural changes are taking place in late modernity that indicate youth is changing (France 2007). This gives rise to new developments and interests within social science. At the heart of these are attempts to shift the focus from 'youth as a problem' to that of 'the problems of youth' and much contemporary research starts to give a stronger focus to exploring the impact of social change on young people's lives. Questions of subjectivity and identity and the importance of difference dominate much youth research analysis. This new approach also widens the methodological focus of youth research. Mainstream social science still remains dominated by quantitative and 'neo-positivist' approaches, yet new approaches, influenced by feminism and educational studies, emerged that advocated the importance of listening to the voices of the young. These developments have significant influence in re-conceptualising youth into a 'new' orthodoxy creating new ideas and forms of analysis of the youth.

Subjectivity and identity

Theories of youth had been dominated by perspectives that saw youth identities being either biologically or socially determined. The 'new orthodoxy' suggests that the notion of identity construction is a subjective process that cannot be 'read off' as predictive (Bennett 2005). Recent theorising recognises that old dichotomous models of social identity (biology versus social) are unable to understand the complexity of social life or the diversity of influences that shape the social processes of identity construction. As a result identity is seen as a negotiated process where individuals have 'agency' or control. These developments have also been influenced by theories that suggest that in late modernity life is becoming more individualised. Life is seen as more uncertain and therefore needs to become a 'biographical project', where individuals have to plan and navigate their own career and lifestyle directions (Beck and Beck-Gernshein 2002; Kemshall, Chapter 13). For example, in late modernity school to work transitions have collapsed. They have been replaced with more diverse, extended and broken transitions, which see the youth phase extended in age (France 2007). In this context young people have to make more individualised choices and are unable to rely upon traditional ways of transition. This growing individualisation is also seen in the cultural activities of the young. Youth culture is seen as being more creative and innovative and less collective in its nature (Bennett 2005). Technology, such as computers, MP3 players, DVDs and mobile phones and other forms of consumption, is creating opportunities for the young to construct new cultural identities that cut across old class based divisions (Bennett 2005). Young people take commodities and technology and use them to help shape their own identities through forms of symbolic exchange (Willis 1990). Identities can be in flux and changing dependent upon social context. New technology is allowing young people to be more creative and help them form new identities.

The importance of 'difference'

In late modernity the 'new' orthodoxy has also been interested in questions of 'difference'. This has its roots in the feminist movement of the 1980s and in particular the work of Angela McRobbie. Writing about the girl's magazine *Jackie* she demonstrated how girls not only resisted dominant notions of femininity, but also appropriated them by giving them new meanings and significance (McRobbie 1980). Other examples show similar processes taking place in areas such as shopping (McRobbie 1994), advertising (Nava and Nava 1992) and the Internet (Davies 2004). More recently the cultural phenomenon of 'girl power' is seen as an indication of girls having more autonomy. Its 'arrival' was credited to the Spice Girls and it is being seen as the 'new feminism' where girls are seen as being '…feisty, ambitious, motivated and independent' (Aapola et al. 2005: 26).

Debates about differences in gender have also been influenced by the 'masculinity turn' (Collier 1998) where the notion of learning about how to be a boy is important. Schooling is seen as a critical site where young boys learn about being a man (Frosh et al. 2002). Boys are seen to negotiate and construct themselves either in line with dominant discourses ('hegemonic' masculinity) or in opposition to them. Being masculine and heterosexual requires young men to distance themselves from women, femininity and gay males, because they have to maintain the superiority of heterosexuality to continue the process of control and domination (Frosh et al. 2002). Much of this debate has focused on the 'crisis in masculinity' suggesting that in late modernity social changes in labour market transitions, educational achievement, and social integration, are causing young men major problems (France 2007).

Issues of racial identities in social science research have also been seen as important in debates about difference. While there has been a growing political concern over questions of social integration, educational achievement and crime amongst ethnic groups of young people, youth research has shown how the 'mixing' of different ethnic cultures in late modernity is creating 'new ethnicities' (Back 1996). While their lives may be full of racism and disadvantage, many young people from black and Asian backgrounds are able to be creative and innovate within and through their own culture. Again it is in the area of consumption and new media where these opportunities are seen to emerge. New technologies in the music industry for example are creating ways of expanding and sharing varied and diverse ethnic cultures. The global world is a world of diverse cultural practices that can be transported, via new communication mediums, between the first and third world (Gilroy 1987, Aubrey Chapter 4). Identity formation is therefore a process of negotiation, where 'new ethnicities' are actively produced, consumed and transformed by young people themselves through different cultural practices such as dress, styles, listening to music, and watching television. Ethnic youth are then recognised as both producers and consumers of their own culture, which is shaped by the interplay between local and global forces (Back 1996).

The political economy of consumption and the commodification of youth in late modernity

The 'new' orthodoxy in youth studies and the strong 'cultural turn' instigated by post structural social science has had a major impact on our conceptualisation of youth. Not only has it broadened our knowledge base but also brought new ideas and theories that have highlighted the 'agency' of the young, their creativity, and their innovation. But such an approach is not without its problems. While it advocates 'agency as autonomy' it gives little recognition to the importance of other processes. Limited attention is given to wider shaping processes such as the political economy of consumption or to the embedded nature of structural factors. While the innovativeness of some aspects of youth activities is difficult to deny we cannot divorce these processes from production or capitalist relationships (Frith 2004). For example, the sphere of consumption may have become more important in young people's lives but it cannot be separated from production. Consumption is a fundamental aspect of capitalist social relations, in which not only is labour replenished, but also gives rise to a whole host of new consumption pursuits, which have involved the further commodification of social life.

One such example can be found in the notion of 'girl power'. What can be missing from this analysis is recognition of the powerful influence and control of the cultural industries. It constructs girl power as non-political and can encourage girls to think about 'being a girl' in cultural rather than political ways (Taft 2001). In this way girls are disempowered, as it does not challenge the powerful political structures that shape the everyday lives of girls. It also portrays girlhood as a white middle class way of life where personal responsibility and individualism are valued above collective action, seeing citizenship through consumption (Aapola et al. 2005). Girl power is big business providing access into a teenage market that has over £1.3 billion of spending power (Mintel 2003). The cultural industries are not interested in empowering girls but in capturing their spending power. Tying girls into brand loyalties and creating skilled consumers is important to the industry and while we might want to recognise that girls are astute consumers and producers of their own culture the industry is also highly-skilled at marketing and producing desires (Russell and Tyler 2002). Modern day notions of youth are being commodified as a way of marketing consumption and selling new diverse products.

Similar processes are evident around other cultural activities of the young. For example, youth night-time leisure activities have also become highly commodified. Hollands and Chatterton (2003), in their study of night-life in the northeast of England, show the influence of the brewing industry in shaping the night-time activity of the young.

New bars, nightclubs, themed nights and the introduction of music venues alongside the rebranding of alcoholic drinks has led to a restructuring of urban leisure. This is not driven and shaped by the new cultural activities of the young but by an industry keen to make large profits out of young people's leisure and cultural pursuits (Hollands and Chatterton 2003).

Agency vs structure

As we saw above the 'new' orthodoxy has provided analysis of youth that not only recognises but also prioritises the importance of agency. Notions of 'individualisation' and 'choice' have dominated analysis of youth in late modernity, yet questions of structure and especially class structure cannot be discounted. As history has shown British society is dynamic in reproducing, even in times of major social and political change, class divisions (Byrne 2005). These tend to be entrenched in geographical regions where local circumstances shape life chances (MacDonald and Marsh 2005). Evidence in the area of school to work transitions, education achievement, post sixteen education take up, and the usage of new digital media all show that class remains an important factor in shaping young people's present and future trajectories (France 2007). Similar patterns exist between genders in that working class girls are less likely to enter higher education than their middle class counterparts (Walkerdine et al. 2001).

Yet in much social science the dichotomy of 'agency versus structure' has been rejected recognising that social life and choice is far more complex. One attempt to address how young people's choices seemingly are being more individualised yet also remain highly structured has turned to the notion of 'structured individualism' (Furlong and Cartmel 1997). In selecting career pathways and routes young people will draw upon their own resources. The types available are linked to their class position, and are seen to limit how they might be able to take up opportunities compared to their middle class counterparts (Ball 2003). The notion of 'choice' and 'opportunity' creates a sense of false reality for the young, in that they believe they are able to take control of their own lives yet in reality it remains limited. This 'epistemological fallacy' creates a feeling for young people that they have influence over their lives and are able to negotiate pathways as though they have real opportunities (Furlong and Cartmel 1997).

Others within the social sciences have tried to 'bridge this gap' by drawing more upon the notions of 'culture'. Bourdieu (1991), for example, argues that a person's economic, social and cultural capital shapes tastes, lifestyles, accents, cuisine and social networks. Class is then defined through a set of social relationships and the deployment of such resources. Important in this is a person's 'habitus'. This is constructed over time and reflects historical knowledge and understanding and local tradition about 'how things are done'. It acts as a framework of reference for young people and helps inform them of how they need to operate in their own worlds. Recent theorising in youth studies has drawn upon these ideas to help understand the processes of identity construction and to help understand the complexity of the relationship between 'structure' and 'agency'. Much still remains unknown about these processes and problems remain (Devine and Savage 2005) for example, class tends to be regulated to a set of social practices that marginalise the economic context and the influence of capital production in shaping social life (Crompton and Scott 2005). This being said these developments within youth studies have restated the importance of questions of structure into any analysis of young people's life chances. Individualism as 'autonomy' or as a 'free floating' process acting outside of structural contexts cannot be accepted. Notions of production and class have to be included in analyses of young people's lives.

Conclusion

Understandings of youth, particularly the problematic behaviour of youth, have changed over time as the discourses and disciplines dominant in social science have changed. Such change continues, and the study of youth has radically altered since the mid-1990s providing new insights and understandings of youth as a stage in the life course. This is a positive move that has provided new opportunities to capture and understand the complex lives that young people are living in late modernity. The rejection of theories that locate the questions (and solutions) in either disciplinary 'silos' or dichotomous models of analysis opens up new ways of thinking about how different factors influence how young people live their lives and also become adult citizens. The return of class to this discussion within social science is also important for the study of youth. It reengages debates of structure and readdresses the imbalance of individualisation that has been a recent dominant force in social science thinking. But the good news is that this is not a return to traditional debates of class analysis. It is recognised that individuals are social actors and make a contribution to their own lives and that their voices are important in helping us understand these processes. Exploring influences, such as culture, history, and tradition as well as the emerging contemporary context and processes of social change, is a step in the right direction to getting a better and more holistic understanding of young people's lives.

Reflective questions for practice

- **Reflect on the young people you work with. To what extent are their 'choices' shaped or influenced by wider structural forces or social processes? Can you identify these?**

- In reading research articles for your studies, can you identify what disciplines underpin the research?
- In what ways does the research represent young people? Does this representation take account of their subjective interpretation of their social lives?
- In what ways does this research help you to understand 'difference' in young people's lives?

Further reading

France, A. (2007) *Understanding Youth in Late Modernity*, **Buckingham: Open University Press.** This book shows how the ideas of past political action, in conjunction with the diverse paradigms of social science disciplines, have shaped modern conceptions of the youth question.

Kehily, M.J. (ed.) (2007) *Understanding Youth: Perspectives, Identities and Practices*, **London: Sage.** Drawing on recent research and the insights of young people the book provides a clear and comprehensive overview of youth in late modernity.

3

YOUNG PEOPLE'S LIVES: TAKING A DIFFERENT VIEW

Jean Hine

Key arguments

- Most policy understandings of the lives of young people are based on adult perceptions and interpretations, which often have little cognisance with children's perceptions and understandings of their lives.
- Policy and positivist research tend to categorise young people and deal with them within those specific categories, ignoring the complexity of young people's lives.
- A growing body of research is exploring young people's understandings of their lives and of their behaviour, revealing a quite different view to that from research undertaken from a more positivist 'adult' perspective.
- Research and practice needs to be holistic, multi-disciplinary and about understanding the contexts of young people's lives in order to build on their strengths.

Introduction

Working with young people (a term that avoids the negative connotations of the word 'youth', about which more later) usually refers to working with older children and young adults. Those who do this are frequently working with young people who on the one hand are deemed to be vulnerable in some way, or on the other, are identified as being a problem to others: this is the classic troubled/troublesome dichotomy

(Hoghughi 1978; Worral 1999). Where this work takes place in a statutory context that work is constrained and increasingly prescribed by policy makers, with such constraints becoming common in the voluntary sphere too (Wylie, Chapter 17). These policies and the guidelines that accompany them are based on particular understandings about young people. These understandings are influenced by current theories (France, Chapter 2) about appropriate or 'normative' behaviours and the reasons for inappropriate or problematic behaviour: theories that are underpinned by an understanding of the lives and actions of young people from an adult perspective.

Policy, in respect of children and young people in particular, is promoted as being informed by 'evidence' – research and statistics that identify the most 'effective' ways of responding to that problematic behaviour. Much of this research also takes an adult-centred view of young people's lives with its normative notions of what young people should and should not be doing at various points in their lives, usually related to aspects of age.

Increasingly the concerns around children and young people are framed in terms of their future and what they might become, and policy is linked to research and procedures which enable prediction and the identification of those who are most 'at risk' of becoming a problem in the future. This occurred at the same time as the increasing acknowledgment of the rights of children and young people (United Nations 1989) and facilitation of their participation and consultation about policies that affect them (e.g. DfES 2001). The depth of this consultation and its impact on policy makers is, however, open to question.

The premise of this chapter is that there are many false assumptions within this model. Those who work with or develop policies for young people need to take a different view and look at young people's actions from the perspective of young people themselves. Examination in this way often reveals that behaviours that appear irrational or unwelcome to adults can have a reasonable explanation and meaning from the perspective of the young person. It is argued that an understanding of this perspective would facilitate the development of policies and practices that better engage with young people and that this in turn would produce more desirable outcomes for both adults and young people. It does however require a different research approach to provide insights that inform the delivery of more relevant and effective work with young people.

This chapter examines the concept of youth and policy understandings of young people before arguing for taking an alternative view of young people and their behaviour.

The concept of 'youth'

While the word has been in existence for a very long time (*The Oxford English Dictionary* suggests c.1100), the term 'youth' specifically did not enter the modern

English policy agenda until the early part of the twentieth century (Davies 1999a). The start of a 'youth' service is identified as 1939 with legislation to establish local youth committees with representation from a range of voluntary organisations providing activities and services for youth. Interestingly most of the titles of these organisations did not contain the term 'youth', having alternatives such as girls, boys, lads, young women, young men (Davies 1999a: 7). Now the term is at the heart of much policy such as Youth Matters (DfES 2005) and is included in the names of official bodies such as Youth Justice Board and Youth Courts.

The importance of a shift in language about children and young people should not be under-estimated. The understanding of the power of language that originated with feminism spilled over into a range of topics including discourses about children and young people. Arguably the most significant of these were the changes in criminal justice in relation to young people introduced by the Criminal Justice Act (CJA) 1991, which signalled a shift in responses to the problematic behaviour of young people – the so-called 'punitive turn' (Hallsworth 2000) – and the term youth becomes more synonymous with young people involved in problem behaviours. The CJA 1991 Act replaced the Juvenile Courts that dealt with the offending of under 17-year-olds with Youth Courts that incorporated 17-year-olds within their remit. It also introduced the notion of 'maturity' into sentencing, allowing for those who were deemed to be more 'mature' to be sentenced by adult court. However there was little evidence that this option was used by sentencers and it was soon removed. Evaluation of the changes (O'Mahoney and Haines 1996) revealed some increase in the severity of sentencing. These changes occurred at the same time as the government was promoting a more punitive approach to offending generally, epitomised by Michael Howard's famous claim that 'prison works' (Howard 1993). The CJA 1991 also formally introduced multi-agency working as responsibility for the servicing of these courts shifted from Social Services Departments (SSD) to SSDs and the Probation Service. The move to multi-agency working, and the shift from a welfare approach for responding to juvenile offending to a justice/punishment approach to responding to the offending of 'youth' was reinforced by the CJA 1998 with the introduction of Youth Offending Teams and a new framework for the sentencing of young offenders.

The change in the use of language has accompanied changes in understandings about youth and young people, which paradoxically are both positive, acknowledging potential strengths in young people (DfES 2006), and negative as in much of the media hype about 'youth crime' and policy responses to it. It has been argued that the introduction of the term 'youth' was a valuable political ideological tool that identified a social problem and provided a focus for reports, legislation and sanction (Brown 2005). The term has become linked with negative aspects of young people, such as criminal and anti-social behaviour, so that when these issues are raised it is frequently young people that come to mind rather than the adults who are the perpetrators of most crime and anti-social behaviour. In contrast, adults are generally portrayed in a positive

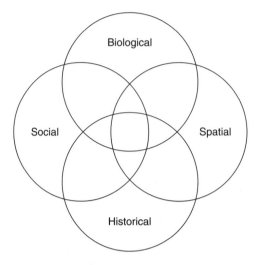

Figure 3.1   Intersecting dimensions of youth
Source: Based on Spence 2005

light: as Brown puts it, 'rarely do we imagine middle aged people as corporate or white collar criminals, embezzlers or orchestrators of sleaze in politics' (2005: 6).

The historical dimension to understandings of youth is important. It is one of four dimensions identified by Spence (2005), namely biological, social, historical and spatial. In this model the circumstances of individual young people or groups of young people can only be understood in the context of the melding of these four dimensions. This can be represented visually as in Figure 3.1.

The *biological* dimension addresses the physical characteristics of the individual, such as their size and appearance. There are expectations of what young people will look like at particular ages, though these may vary, particularly by gender. For instance height is a key characteristic, and young people who are over- or under-tall for their age will experience youth differently to those who match general expectations. Another physical characteristic is the onset of puberty, though the significance of this has diminished in Western societies. Biologically, psychological theories contain expectations of the acquisition of particular cognitive and emotional abilities within specific age bands.

The *Spatial* dimension relates to the geography of the individual, whereby 'youth' as a concept is understood differently in different places. These can be as distant as being a young person in a rural village in India and a young person living in an English city, or as near as a young person living in an affluent neighbourhood in that English city and one living in social housing in a nearby deprived neighbourhood in the same city. The physical space that they inhabit will substantially affect their experience and even the timing of their 'youth' (see Wood and Hine, Chapter 1 for a discussion of transition).

The *Historical* dimension considers the fact that understandings of 'youth' vary at different times in history within the same place. This is certainly true of the UK, as Spence describes some of the changes that have been apparent since pre-industrial Britain (Spence 2005: 50–52). At different times in history children and young people have been seen very differently, and the balance of the importance between the other three dimensions has varied. For instance, it is argued that the industrial and techno-logical changes linked to the growth of factories, and social changes related to the labour movements of adult males led to legislation that limited the employment of young children and enabled the introduction of universal education (Brown 2005).

The *Social* dimension is arguably the most important, relating as it does to the social and economic position within which young people live (for a more detailed discussion see Hine and Wood, Chapter 20). Young people's lives and their expecta-tions thereof are substantially shaped by the key social structures and institutions around them (e.g. family, school, employment) and in the accompanying economic position. Some aspects of this are taken up in various chapters in this volume, such as Armstrong (Chapter 7), Boeck (Chapter 8), Perkins (Chapter 9).

The crux of this approach is that to understand young people it is necessary to consider not only each of the four dimensions but also how they inter-relate and impact. For the purposes of this chapter this means consideration of youth for young people living in modern England (there is variation between different parts of the UK). Here there are many broad similarities of context for young people, such as the education system and criminal justice policies, but there are also important differ-ences between sub-groups that will relate more directly to their social and economic position (the spatial and the social).

> The here and now in which young people live is not just about being young, but about a whole range of personal and social circumstances and issues which can be equally, if not more important than age. (Spence 2005: 55)

Understandings of children and young people have changed substantially in the last quarter of a century, with ongoing acknowledgement of the active agency of young people. In parallel with this has been a shifting policy agenda that enables participa-tion by young people, and with it addresses questions of rights and responsibilities.

Participation, responsibilities and rights

Since the 1970s a growing academic interest in the sociological concept of 'child-hood' has resulted in significant changes in understandings of this life phase (James et al. 1998) which in turn has led to different possibilities and expectations of young people in terms of participation, responsibilities and rights. The inter-relation of these themes was highlighted by Morrow, arguing for a change of perspective about children and young people:

> The social construction of childhood dependency, based as it is on conceptions of children as developing objects, and therefore as incompetent and irresponsible, precludes us from acknowledging the extent to which children are capable, competent, and have agency and responsibility in their own lives. (2005: 260)

These rights were reinforced in 1989 by the UN Convention on the Rights of the Child, which proclaimed that the well-being of the child was more important than the wishes of adults, and that children had specific rights, the most important of which was the right to be consulted in decisions that affect them. These developments acknowledge the child/young person as an autonomous human being, albeit within substantial structural constraints. As such, UK policy now acknowledges the importance of seeking the views of children and young people in decisions that affect them – the participation agenda (DfES 2001).

The punitive rhetoric of the New Labour Government that came to power in 1997 took up the mantra of rights, but juxtaposed it with the notion of responsibilities (Blair 1999). The ability to act 'responsibly' is an inherent aspect of transition from childhood to adulthood, with young children being seen as having very little or no responsibility for their actions, gradually increasing to the adult having full responsibility for decision making and actions. It is fundamental to the criminal justice system whether an individual can be held to be responsible and punished for their actions. In relation to children and young people this came to the fore in debates about changing the age of criminal responsibility. The Criminal Justice Act 1998 lowered the age of criminal responsibility in the UK from 14 to 10, with children as young as this being deemed to understand the difference between right and wrong and thus be accountable for their actions. This very much fits with the general 'responsibilisation' thesis (Rose 1996a) whereby government increasingly expects citizens to 'self-regulate'. This is very apparent too in the 'Respect' agenda and approaches to anti-social behaviour by young people, extensively discussed by Joe Yates in Chapter 14.

There has also been concern among politicians about the lack of participation by young people in formal political processes, particularly that they are less likely to vote in national and local elections than older people (Furlong and Cartmel 2007). However this should not be seen as young people not having an interest in politics, as research with young people has shown substantial interest in political and current issues (Hine 2004; Wood, Chapter 12). It is rather that the political values of young people are different and they demonstrate their political involvement in different ways, for instance by involvement in issue related groups, such as the environment, or by using their consumer power, such as buying 'fair trade' products (Furlong and Cartmel 2007).

Policy perspectives

Policies tend to be developed around the notion of an idealised child, the normative model which identifies what young people should and should not be doing and what they need for them to become 'normal', notions of which change over time. This view of the child assumes a passive recipient of services and policy initiatives. Paradoxically the rhetoric attached to the modern participation agenda does not appear to have impacted upon the commonly held view that young people have limited understanding and that adults know best. These idealised children and young people are valued for their 'becomings' and need care and protection and preparation for adulthood. Where young people do not match this idealised view they are perceived to be a potential challenge to social order and 'intervention' is necessary to address the problem. The assumption is that intervention is always and necessarily a good thing and the negative consequences of intervening unnecessarily are not acknowledged. The agency or professional they are in contact with will determine whether they are identified as being troubled or troublesome (Hoghughi 1978). Whichever label is attached to them they will be increasingly surveilled, either for their own safety or for the safety of others. The control and surveillance of young people is now greater than at any time and their freedoms are diminished by legislation for safety and security, often introduced in the name of protecting children from harm. Knepper argues that social policy in general has become increasingly criminalised in the last few years, by which he means that 'social welfare issues have been redefined as crime problems' (2007: 139). He warns, 'when the goal of crime reduction is stirred into the rationale for social policy, it tends to become the sole or most important justification' (2007: 140).

Despite statements to the contrary, social policy increasingly presents a singular view of young people as dependent on their parents for financial and social support, as in need of schooling and qualifications to prepare them for work and for adulthood, and importantly as both the source of many current social problems and being the bearer of potential future problems: as, essentially, hostages to fortune. Youth and childhood are stages of life increasingly interfered with and managed by policy, be it in terms of health, education, youth justice, or social benefits.

> It seems then that children (the inhabitants of *childhood*), as 'beings', are too valuable in terms of human capital to be given any say in shaping their own lives. Rather they are to be possessed in order to maximise their potential as investments in *our* future. (Hendrick 2003: 253, italics in original)

Adults in all societies look to their younger generations to care for them as they move into old age and infirmity, be that in different ways. In modern British society the well-being and comfort of the older generation depends fundamentally on the economic well-being of younger individuals and of the state. The recent pensions crisis is in part related to an awareness that the balance between the generations is changing, with a much larger and growing older generation in need of support from a shrinking young economically active generation (Pensions Commission 2006). The possibility of these future adults being economically inactive and therefore taking from the economic pot rather than contributing creates greater demands and expectations of the younger generation and a requirement for them to have a productive and unproblematic adulthood.

Dichotomised lives

Policy tends to function on the basis of identifying young people as belonging to a specific category and deal with them within those categories or boxes, this despite a rhetoric and understanding that young people's lives are often a complex mix of issues requiring multi-agency working. These boxes tend to be dualistic and separate young people in ways that do not match the real world, for example they are an offender or they are a victim, they are a truant or they are not, they are in need of protection or not, they are troubled and vulnerable or they are troublesome and a threat. In reality these categories are never as simple as this, nor are they necessarily mutually exclusive. These views of young people are based on Western middle class norms of a linear path to adulthood, a path which does not acknowledge gender, ethnicity or disability, nor the reality of young people's lives (Evans and Furlong 1997).

This model is fuelled by a particular model of research. This research is positivist in nature, searching for causal patterns in young people's lives, and particularly aiming to identify the factors that allow the prediction of those young people most 'at risk' of problematic futures. Such research is quantitative and uses statistical procedures that work best with binary categories. It is a methodology that requires an over-simplification of the real world, and in the process crudely ignores features which are difficult to measure and categorise, or not identified as statistically significant by the statistical procedures. These approaches are seeking general broad patterns and cannot take account of nuanced and subtle aspects of young people's lives, aspects which may nonetheless be particularly important. The work often uses false dichotomies. While this research depends in large part on the involvement of young people as participants and providers of the data, the framing of the data and its understanding is adult centred, and the understandings of young people themselves are not seen as relevant. This approach has its roots in the rise of the 'scientific method' and social science, and 'a powerful alliance in the construction of youth and its regulation was made between social and scientific discourses and social "reform"' (Brown 2005: 17).

This approach to research invites methodological and moral criticisms: it relies on statistical correlations and probabilities that turn into policy certainties. It assumes the nature of data is unproblematic. For instance, research has identified poor parental supervision as a risk factor for offending (Farrington 1996; Beinhart et al. 2002). In this research, assessing 'parental supervision' becomes questions to young people about how often their parents know where they are and what they are doing. This assumes that if the parent does not know it is because the parent is not supervising the young person appropriately. This conceptualisation ignores the role of the young person in letting the parent know where they are and what they are doing – it is not unusual for young people to avoid telling their parents, or to tell them something different to what they actually are doing. Parental supervision is a social construct, and as such we need to know how others construe this concept to be able to understand its relevance and how it might be addressed in practice.

This type of research fits a policy model that pathologises young people with a deficit approach – if the young person does not fit the normative model there must be something wrong with the young person and intervention is necessary to address that deficit and achieve a better fit. This approach overestimates and overemphasises the problems of young people, and in particular the problems of the most marginalised groups of young people. It does not acknowledge that children and young people develop in different ways and different roles depending on the context of their lives.

An alternative perspective

Despite the participation agenda, about which there is some scepticism (see Wood, Chapter 12; Davies, Chapter 16), most understandings of the lives of young people are based on adult perceptions and interpretations, which often have little cognisance with young people's perceptions and understandings of their lives. Until relatively recently this adult perspective has been taken for granted and very little questioned. There has however been a growing body of theorists in turn arguing that this is dangerous. For instance Dwyer and Wyn argue that 'the experience of a past generation is accepted as "normative"' (2001: 205) which belittles the value of young people's current experience: young people continue to be 'the object of intensive adult scrutiny and concern' (2001: 202). This call for a different understanding requires different types of research, and theory building that actually involves children and young people (e.g. Ungar 2004; Fleming and Hudson, Chapter 10).

> the need to give 'active voice' to young people about the dramatic social and economic changes they have been subjected to is unmistakeable in the light of the increasing disparity between the propaganda of policy and their own experiences of outcomes. (Dwyer and Wyn 2001: 195)

Research aimed at understanding young people's perspectives has been popular in the past (Parker 1974; Willis 1977) but became less common with the decline of interest in youth subcultural theories. More recently a growing body of research is exploring young people's understandings of their lives and of their behaviour, revealing a quite different view to that from research undertaken from a more positivist and 'adult' perspective. It is discovering that actions that appear irrational or inexplicable to outside, and particularly adult, eyes, can be understood and explained as perfectly logical by the young person. Exploring young people's understandings shows how behaviour seen as undesirable by adults may be performing a useful function for the young person. Thus for instance truanting from school can be a young person's strategy to avoid being bullied (Gleeson 1994).

Ungar (2004) takes the view that young people's behaviour is generally purposeful, and that problematic behaviour can usually be understood as doing the best that can be done in difficult circumstances. He gives examples of a range of studies which demonstrate this. For instance, defiant behaviour by young people is frequently seen as negative, and yet this has been shown to produce better outcomes for a young person than 'passive victimage'. He found that:

> vulnerable youth … found through their delinquent and disordered behaviours the same health resources (self-esteem, competence, meaningful involvement with their communities and attachment to others) as their more stereotypically resilient peers. (Ungar 2004: 354)

These understandings are important as they suggest why some approaches to working with young people may not be successful, and at the same time identify potentially critical components of practice from the voices of young people. These voices identify that the 'how' of intervention and practice is more important for effective work than the 'what' of what works evaluations (Lyon et al. 2000; Hallet et al. 2003; Hine 2006; Yates and Payne 2006). Such research is also important because it critically presents an understanding and interpretation of young people's behaviour, particularly their problematic behaviour, that is different to that presented by policy and media. For instance, McCulloch (2006) found that group identity was related to feeling safe in groups with friends as opposed to a policy view that a group of young people must be a threat to order. Young people's friendship groups are frequently presented in a negative light, as leading young people into problematic behaviour, and yet young people's perspectives show that friends are an important source of support for young people in difficult times (Mullender et al. 2003; Hine 2006).

Research with young people shows that they accept the responsibilisation thesis. A study of young offenders in prison (Lyon et al. 2000) found that these young people placed an emphasis on self-determination, choice and responsibility, with most believing that they had had a choice not to offend. Many had had to struggle to survive in difficult and disrupted circumstances, and a number felt seriously let down by adults who could have cared for them or helped them. Once they had become involved in the cycle of offending it was very hard to get out. Many young people spoke of being scared, humiliated and depersonalised on reaching prison. Above all, young people wanted to be treated with respect and taken seriously by professional adults. Research by Hazel et al. (2002) had similar findings. Offenders described their criminal activity as a rational choice, but they underestimated its seriousness and the likely consequences. According to their own accounts of their contact with the criminal justice system, they soon realised what was expected of them, and assumed the appropriate submissive role. The young people felt they lost control over what they were saying and found that police interviews could be verbally and physically intimidating. 'The interviews unveiled high levels of confusion, isolation and resentment, none of which provide a useful basis for changing behaviour among young offenders' (Hazel et al. 2002: 14).

Interviews with young people involved in relatively minor offending (Hine 2007) show how children can become criminalised for behaviour that has no criminal intent. Young people who live in disadvantaged areas are more likely to receive a criminal record because of the way in which their behaviour is identified and formalised. These children are more likely to be in public areas in their neighbourhoods; these neighbourhoods tend to have more crime and thus are more heavily policed. These two factors mean that the behaviour of young people is more likely to be seen by the police, and when it is it is frequently construed in terms of criminality and addressed formally by means of arrest, charge and sanction (McAra and McVie 2005).

Many young offenders are known to have been excluded from school, and yet the way in which these two factors interact is little understood. Berridge et al. (2001) found that permanent exclusion from school tended to trigger a complex chain of events which served to loosen the young person's affiliation and commitment to a conventional way of life. They experienced a loss of time structures, a changed relationship with parents and siblings and the erosion of contact with pro-social peers and adults. Association with similar young people resulted in heightened police surveillance and a re-casting of identity. The research participants described how truanting was a result of conflict with teachers, 'boredom', or to be with friends. Young people are frequently given labels by the adult world and have little opportunity or power to resist those labels. When they attempt to do so in aggressive ways, often the only way in which they know how to gain attention, this is seen as reinforcement of the label that was applied (Hine 2006). These young people can find themselves in a Catch 22 situation with apparently no way out.

Conclusion

This chapter has presented some of the issues surrounding the current approach of much policy and research, arguing that it presents a distorted and often negative view of young people's lives. A growing body of research exploring young people's understandings of their experiences presents a different picture, one that acknowledges the strengths of young people. This research focuses on concern for young people in their here and now rather than the future they may become. It acknowledges that young people's lives are not lived in isolation from the large scale structural and social changes occurring around them, nor from the impact of these changes on the lives of adults: youth, childhood and adulthood have to be understood as relative concepts that each influence the other. It also acknowledges the limitations of considering young people's lives from one discipline or perspective – young people experience their lives holistically, and researchers and policy makers should attempt to understand and address it so:

> ...developing an understanding of youth which is based on the reality of young people's lives requires the researcher to take an approach that moves beyond 'discipline' boundaries ... to focus more on the connections and links between different aspects of young people's lives. (Wyn and White 1997: 3)

Working with young people should be about more than breaking out of individual agency silos into multi-agency working. It should also be about seeing young people in the round, understanding the context of their lives, and acknowledging and building on their strengths in ways that are appropriate to help them make the most of that context in an increasingly complex world.

Reflective questions for practice

- **What challenges do young people face today that are different from when you were growing up? What experiences are similar?**
- **Consider any 'problematic behaviour' of young people you work with. What is usually called upon to explain this behaviour? What labels are used?**
- **Do young people offer different explanations and labels for their behaviour?**
- **How might research that takes into account the views of young people help you in your practice?**

Further reading

Brown, S. (2005) *Understanding Youth and Crime: Listening to Youth?*, **2nd edn, Maidenhead: Open University Press**. Provides an interesting and detailed discussion of the historical development of understandings of young people and the relationship of this with policy.

Prout, A. and Hallett, C. (eds) (2003) *Hearing the Voices of Children: Social Policy for a New Century*, **London: Routledge Falmer**. A collection of papers addressing the question of children's voice and social policy, which provides many examples of research that does include the voices of children and young people and offer the 'different view' of their lives.

4

GLOBALISATION AND GLOBAL YOUTH WORK

Jo Aubrey

Key arguments

- Globalisation is a social process that explains the greater interconnectedness of the world, evidenced through changes in communication and technology, trade, politics, culture and the environment.
- The negative consequences of globalisation include the dominance of Western cultural and consumerist ideals over other traditional cultures.
- Globalisation has significant impacts upon young people, not least in terms of the impact of increased consumerism. Branded goods are similar the world over and are specifically targeted at young people.
- This results in setting aspirations for young people about how to look, and what to wear. In turn, this can have negative consequences for body image and individuality.
- Youth work can no longer be confined to the local or national context, it needs to address the global community and the inequalities at a global level that manifest themselves locally.

Introduction

This chapter will examine how globalisation influences and impacts on young people, and how youth workers and other professionals can best support them to develop a critical understanding of the global dimensions in their lives. It will begin with an introductory theory base for understanding the main themes of globalisation. It will then examine in some depth the cultural aspects of globalisation, specifically in relation to young people. It will conclude with an examination of the role of youth work and the use of informal education to critically explore with young people how their lives and their communities are interconnected with forces that have their roots at a global level, how they are able to embrace the positive aspects and also to challenge the negative effects of globalisation for themselves as individuals, their communities and the wider world.

Globalisation

The world is interconnected as never before. With internet and communications, people thousands of miles away can be contacted within seconds. Decisions that are made and actions that are taken in one part of the world, have a direct impact on people and communities thousands of miles away, and the young people with whom we work will feel its impact in many spheres of their lives.

This phenomenon has become known as globalisation, the social process by which 'the constraints of geography on economy, political, social and cultural arrangements recede, in which people become increasingly aware that they are receding' (Waters 2002: 5). Literally, it is the process with which the world has become smaller and more interconnected and its chief characteristics can be broadly divided into four areas:

- Communication and information technology
- Global trade
- Politics
- Culture

Each are now discussed in turn.

Communication and information technology

Thinking back to the early 1990s, the internet was in its inception stage. When studying at university in 1995, this author had access to four computers with internet access. At universities today, libraries are fully equipped with instant access to the internet. There are internet computers in campus cafes and opportunities for e-learning and teaching, and specialist internet chatrooms where you can discuss course work with fellow students or attend a virtual seminar with your tutor. This is not even scratching the surface: virtual networks, such as Facebook or Myspace are now everyday communication tools for much of the population.

The internet has grown and developed over a period of ten years. An illustration of just how quickly it has become commonplace can be found in the United States and the introduction of the radio. It took 40 years for the radio to gain an audience of 50 million. Comparatively, the same number was using computers after only 15 years and after the introduction of the internet, it took only four years for the same amount of people to be regularly using the internet.

Media communications have also developed rapidly within a limited period. News reporting provides a useful demonstration of this. During the Iraq War journalists became 'embedded' with military units in that country and were able to report on the news as it was happening. It was possibly the first conflict where the 'action' could be broadcast live. Similarly when the terrorist attacks of 9/11 occurred, it is estimated that a billion people across the world saw the second plane hit the south tower in real time (Giddens 2002: xii).

Global trade

When eastern European communist economies collapsed at the beginning of the 1990s, the world moved further towards becoming one single capitalist market place. International free trade laws ensure that multinational companies are able to trade across national boundaries. In order to maximise profits and to ensure low prices for consumers, they tend to establish their factories and manufacturing plants in countries where the workforce is cheapest, exploiting the poorest of the world who are struggling to meet even the most basic of needs (DEA 2005). The majority of these transnational, or multinational companies (TNCs and MNCs) are based in the USA. Giddens (2002) argues that the global trade is the business of rich northern countries to the detriment of southern countries. Aside from the huge gaps in wealth, some of these companies sell harmful products to countries in Africa that are banned or heavily controlled in the rest of the world. These include destructive pesticides, poor quality medical supplies, and cigarettes with very high levels of tar and nicotine. This, he concludes:

> Creates a world of winners and losers, a few on the fast track to prosperity, the majority condemned to a life of misery and despair ... rather than a global village, one might say this is more like global pillage. (Giddens 2002: 16)

The UK too has experienced the impact of global trade over the last few years. A decision made in China impacted on communities in the West Midlands when the Rover Plant in Birmingham was closed. Similarly, Peugeot's car manufacturing plant in Coventry saw thousands of redundancies when its French management decided that it would be cheaper to manufacture their cars elsewhere. At the time of writing this chapter, over 1000 jobs with a large insurance company are to be lost in the east of England because a call centre is to be relocated in India, where cheaper wages ensure that high profits are maintained.

Politics

During the 1980s the Cold War saw two superpowers jostling for power on the world stage. After the collapse and fragmentation of the Soviet Union, the United States has become the world's only remaining 'superpower'. Many now refer to it as a hyperpower because it is the most economically dominant nation state in the world, with a powerful military position. The global dominance of American values and culture have brought about a clash of values and beliefs that is reflected in the war on terror and increased levels of racism and islamophobia in western countries. Almost a decade before the attacks on the World Trade Centre, Barber (1992) described this clash as 'Jihad versus McWorld' where western culture attempts to permeate the furthest corners of the world, but is being resisted by peoples who are seeking to undermine American political and cultural dominance. These groups of people have declared their own war against political globalisation, permanent uniformity and integration into McWorld and, as such:

> International relations have sometimes taken on the aspect of gang war – cultural battles featuring tribal factions that were supposed to be sublimated as integral parts of large national, economic, post-colonial and constitutional entities. (Barber 1992: 8)

Culture

The notion of a McWorld draws us neatly into a discussion concerning the global dominance of Western and American culture. McWorld:

> Represents an American push into the future ... pressing nations into one homogeneous global culture, one McWorld, tied together by communications, information, entertainment and commerce. (Barber 1992: 34)

The film industry and the news media are dominated by American companies. Even Britain's reasonably successful film industry relies on US production and distribution corporations. The Disney Corporation, for example, has huge transnational broadcasting power, and owns media initiatives across the globe. It has introduced Disney cartoons to China and India and is aggressively attempting to 'disnify' the globe with a whole range of media products, theme parks and merchandise. When the film *Mulan* was released in 1998, it was an active attempt by Disney to permeate the Chinese market through the release of a film that was loosely based on the folklore story of a Chinese heroine. The story was sufficiently Disnified. The traditional story was changed to include the usual stereotypes and a happy ending where boy and girl sing a romantic song together and disappear into a warm sunset, cheered on by a few misty-eyed mice wearing clogs and waistcoats! The film was a hit in Taiwan, Hong Kong and other

Asian markets. However, at the time of writing, the Chinese Government has still not given its permission for a mainland theatrical release for *Mulan*.

Many academics argue that the global dominance of Western products (of which Disney is a prime example), their advertising and the values attached to them, are having a devastating impact on indigenous communities, gradually eating away at local traditions world wide (Rantanen 2005). Wertheim (2002) uses strong language to illustrate this:

> American fast food culture, pop music, films and television infect the cultural body of other nations ... This pattern of viral replication repeats itself the world over, with American pop cultural norms, choking out and stifling native flora and fauna. (in Sardar and Wyn Davis 2002: 104)

Globalisation and young people

> Globalisation isn't about what's out there, remote and far away from the individual. It is an in here phenomenon too, influencing intimate and personal aspects of our lives. (Giddens 2002: 12)

In 2004 the National Youth Agency created a web survey to assess youth worker attitudes to global youth work. Over 150 youth workers responded with roles ranging from youth workers, youth work managers, volunteers and principal youth officers. Seventy per cent of those who responded felt that youth workers recognised the importance of work with young people around global youth work, but as many admitted that they did not have the knowledge or tools to be able to raise the issues with confidence. The first part of this chapter has introduced some of the characteristics of globalisation. This section will examine some of the ways in which young people feel the impact of a globalised world, and how their lives are now intricately and irreversibly connected to the global dimensions that have been discussed above. Globalisation and its impacts are wide and far reaching, and the focus here is specifically on culture and young people as consumers, issues that affect the majority of young people regardless of wealth.

Young people as consumers

Consumerism is a prominent feature of a capitalist society. Consumption keeps the money flowing and generates wealth. In order to keep people buying, fashions and needs change, fuelling our desire to purchase new goods:

> Our desires are recycled, reinvented and even invented in relation to new products, the endless pursuit of the new, which fuses the thrill of invention and with the status awarded innovations and newness in most of the world. (Westwood 2002: 82)

All over the world young people recognise the golden McDonalds archway and the red and white Coca Cola logo. Nike trainers and other sports labels are sought after and bought by image conscious young people of many nationalities. While their parents look different, young people in Sydney, Cairo, Glasgow and Tokyo not only all look similar, they listen to the same music, eat the same food, and drink the same branded drinks (Rantanen 2005). The products that are marketed to young people do not stop at fast food and clothing, but also include computer games, toys, film, cinema and television and mobile phones.

Many of these branded goods are marketed solely to attract the younger consumer, with no equivalent products specifically aimed at adults. McFadyen (1992: 1) calls this 'global youth marketing' and argues that such is the perceived spending power of young people, companies who market goods that will attract them are considered recession proof and, as such, are television's most affluent and treasured advertising customers. Euromonitor, an organisation that measure market trends, published a report in 2003 called *Marketing to Teenagers*. The report anticipates a 'robust adolescent market' and goes on to predict that 'pester power' and peer pressure make it unlikely for the teen market to experience any serious fall in revenue.

Young people are being exploited through global marketing and advertising strategies levelled only at them. Youth workers and teachers are all too familiar with young peoples' passion for branded goods, and the teasing and bullying that often occurs when they spot cheap supermarket trainers, or designs that have gone out of fashion.

The importance of self-image and body image are as important as the products themselves. Magazines specifically aimed at young men and women are full of such images. Glossy photographs of airbrushed models don the covers and many of the articles include how to look better, feel better and get slimmer to attract men or women. The message is that you are simply not good enough, handsome enough or beautiful enough. Emblazoned across the pages are advertisements for all the products that you might need to look like the model on the front cover. Connell argues that these magazines are nothing more than:

> Commercial attempts to create disgust with bodies as they are now, and the offer of commercial remedies in the form of diets, exercises regimes, fashion and cosmetic surgery. The rise of the men's fashion magazines and the marketing of fitness products to men suggest this dynamic is becoming more explicit and more universal. (2000: 93)

Over the past few years, there has been a growth in the diagnoses of eating disorders among both young men and women. Young women are at particular risk of both anorexia nervosa and body dysmorphic disorder, a disabling condition that simply means an overwhelming disgust with one's own body. A recent article in the *Independent* suggests that:

> There is now concern amongst experts that the current media obsession with ultra skinny celebrities could be pushing our natural tendency to be self-critical towards diagnosable neurotic disorder. (Feinmann 2006)

The obesity debate continues and with it a more distorted image of what is a healthy weight and what is not. In America the BMI (body mass index) has been lowered to the extent that George Clooney and Brad Pitt now fall into the obese category! The global diet and beauty industry is worth billions per year. If people are constantly made to feel insecure about their bodies, it is likely to be worth far more in the future.

Implications for youth work

In the early 1990s the Development Education Association (DEA) was pivotal in developing an area of youth work education that deals with globalisation, they named it global youth work and defined it as:

> Informal education with young people that encourages a critical understanding of the links between the personal, local and global issues. It seeks their active participation in bringing about change towards greater equity and justice. (DEA 2005: 23)

Global youth work is sometimes misunderstood to be a new form of development studies: the learning about other countries and cultures and raising awareness of the situation of people living in poverty in the 'developing' world. As Sallah (2008) notes:

> It is often the case that a lot of youth workers ... still look at global youth work from [the] perspectives of 'we have to save those poor souls'; 'it makes us feel bad and we have to help them'. (2008: 6)

Such thinking is rooted in colonial and missionary history: it does little to foster critical awareness of the reasons for global inequality. Related to this issue is the claim that 'charity begins at home'. Youth workers have argued that the young people with whom they work often live in deprived circumstances and have enough to worry about without being asked to enter into a discussion about globalisation. However, as this chapter has argued, through the economic process of globalisation, *all* young people are at risk of being exploited, and youth workers are in a unique position to enable young people to develop critical thinking skills that allow them to challenge the images that tell them what they should buy, what they should look like and who they should be.

Youth work can no longer be confined to the local, or even national context, it needs to address the global community and the inequalities at a global level that manifest themselves locally. This is the process of 'work with young people that starts from the everyday experiences and critically links their personal, local and national realities to the global' (Sallah 2008: 6). It relies on raising awareness and consciousness with the aim of transforming this into action. Such educational approaches are common in the anti-oppressive practice of youth workers (Chouhan, Chapter 6). However, as Chouhan also points out before we can involve others in such a process, we must be aware of ourselves. In this mould, the reader is invited to consider the impact of globalisation on their own life with this short activity.

Box 4.1   Acting personally, thinking globally

Take a short break from reading this book. Think back over the day you have had so far. Make a list of all the things you have done since you woke up this morning. This might have included making a cup of coffee, taking the bins out, driving to work or university, reading a book and so on.

Now consider how these everyday activities might have a global dimension. For instance, you may have woken up to the sound of an alarm clock (*where was it made?*) with the latest news bulletin about oil prices *(global communications delivering news of global trade issues)*. As you made your coffee, were you aware of where the coffee came from and the price paid to the farmers who harvested it? What did you throw in the bin this morning, and how might this contribute to global environment concerns about waste and recycling? As you travel to work, you may very well feel the impact of global prices in oil and again, be a contributor to global issues about the environment. What advertising caught your eyes on the way to work, and what might this say about how you should look and behave?

Even this simple exercise reveals our increasing interconnectedness with the world, and also shows how straightforward it can be to link the personal and The global. As research has shown young people are concerned about all kinds of international and global issues (UNICEF 2003, Save the Children 2004, DEA 2005) and as such, youth work should embrace this interest or ignore a whole dimension of the lives and interests of those they work with.

Further youth work training is also needed to enable youth workers to be able to explore the issues with young people confidently. In England, The National Youth Agency has now changed its validation requirements to ensure that universities and college offering professional youth work qualifications incorporate global dimensions on curricula. The current government, and its relevant departments are also keen that both the formal and informal curriculum in schools, includes learning around international and global issues. Resources are increasingly available to facilitate effective global youth work (see, for example, Sallah and Cooper 2008).

Conclusion

Globalisation has come from nowhere to being everywhere. (Giddens 1999: 7)

Youth workers, their managers and those who develop youth work curricula, can often be under the impression that global youth work is a whole new theme that has to be squashed into what is already a packed curriculum. However, as a profession, youth work has always had a commitment to principles of anti-discriminatory practice that run through both curriculum areas for young people and training courses for youth workers at all levels. Similarly, global issues can be woven into the curriculum in the same way. The key to global youth work, as with any youth work, is that it begins where young people are at, and within a climate of globalisation and interconnection, where they are at will normally have a global dimension.

Reflective questions for practice

- **What are the most pressing global issues being reported on in the news at the moment? How might these global concerns be related to personal, local or national issues?**
- **What techniques could you use to encourage young people to develop their awareness of the connection between the personal, local, national and global?**
- **This chapter has talked about the impact of globalisation on body image. How are young people affected, and in what ways can you challenge these problems?**

Further reading

Sallah, M. and Cooper, S. (eds) (2008) *Global Youth Work: Taking it Personally*, **Leicester: National Youth Agency**. A very useful and engaging practical manual that introduces globalisation theory and offers a wide range of global youth work activities and tools to use in work with young people.

Sernau, S.R. (ed.) (2008) *Contemporary Readings in Globalization*, **London: Sage**. An introductory reader to globalisation. The readings have been selected from numerous well respected journals as well as from the popular press. The journal articles have been edited to make them more 'user friendly' for the undergraduate student.

5

ETHICS AND VALUES IN WORK WITH YOUNG PEOPLE

Sarah Banks

Key arguments

- Youth work is guided by a set of professional ethical beliefs about what is regarded as valuable or worthy.
- Ethical codes of conduct tend to focus on ethical principles (how we should act) rather than on moral qualities (what sorts of people we should be) but both are equally important in professional ethics.
- Ethical principles are open to interpretation, and may often conflict with each other in the everyday practical situations encountered by youth workers. This can lead to workers experiencing ethical problems and dilemmas, in having to weigh up which principles to prioritise.
- Inter-professional settings bring into tension different ethical priorities, but can also serve to encourage youth workers to reflect on their own professional identities and values more closely.
- There are no easy right answers to ethical questions about individual needs and the common good, but these questions need to be repeatedly asked, especially in the increasingly inter-agency approaches to work with young people.

Introduction

In common with many occupations in the welfare and caring field (medicine, nursing, teaching, social work), youth work is often described as 'value-based' and by its very nature is fraught with ethical issues and dilemmas. This chapter will first discuss what is meant by 'value-based' and 'ethical', before moving on to explore what the values of youth work might be and what kinds of ethical challenges arise, particularly in the context of inter-agency and inter-professional working with young people. It will conclude with a discussion of the extent to which all practitioners with young people can or should operate from a common value base.

Youth work as value-based

This book is about work with young people, which suggests it covers practice with young people that we may call 'youth work' (performed usually by qualified youth workers with an informal educational purpose) as well as other types of work with young people (performed by other professionals or unqualified volunteers with a range of purposes – from leisure to punishment). In examining the values of work with young people, the chapter will focus mainly on youth work. There is not space to enter the debate here about whether and in what sense youth work is a 'profession' or even a distinct occupational group, but the adjective 'professional' (as in 'professional values') will be used to mean relating to purposive work that is undertaken within the framework of an occupation (see Banks 1996, 2004a for more detailed discussion of the nature of professions).

To describe youth work as 'value-based' suggests that at the heart of the occupation there is a set of ethical beliefs about what is regarded as worthy or valuable. Of course, the subject matter of values may be political, cultural, aesthetic and religious as well as ethical, and these areas overlap, but this chapter will focus specifically on ethical values. Ethical matters are concerned with human (and animal) welfare or well-being. Broadly speaking, ethics (as an area of study) covers questions such as: 'What counts as right action?' or 'How should we live?'. Ethical values may take the form of general principles (for example, 'respect people's rights to make their own choices') or qualities of character ('being respectful'). Professional ethical values have a more specific focus on the context of the professional practice. So, for example, one of the ethical principles of youth work identified in the statement of values and principles from The National Youth Agency (2004b: 4) is: 'Respect and promote young people's rights to make their own decisions and choices'.

It is important to note that 'values' is a highly contested concept and is used in many different ways. This chapter is concerned with ethical values in a professional context, often referred to in the literature as 'professional values' (Banks 2001a). These are sometimes distinguished from the 'personal values' that people hold across their life in general (for example, 'eating animals is wrong') and societal values that are part of the context in which professions and professional practice are constructed and valued (for example, 'promote democratic participation in civic life'). Clearly these are artificial distinctions. 'Professional values', which develop as a shared set of beliefs amongst members of an occupation about right action and good character in a professional context, are formed out of and feed into a dynamic and changing relationship between the values people bring to the job (their motivation and commitment to do this type of work) and societal norms and demands (for care, control, punishment, for example), a point illustrated by Payne in Chapter 18.

Youth work in the UK developed from charitable and philanthropic activities of individuals and voluntary organisations in the latter part of the nineteenth century (see Wylie, Chapter 17). It grew in the twentieth century as part of state welfare systems premised on societal values about people's duty to care for one another; the promotion of a more equal distribution of goods; and the enhancement of collective well-being through building individual moral character and self-reliance and controlling deviant and unruly behaviour (Jeffs 1979; Davies 1999a). As youth work gradually became recognised in the UK from the mid-twentieth century as an occupation with specific training and qualifications, more explicit statements of shared professional values were produced. The statements produced by the Council for Education and Training in Youth and Community Work, and a series of Ministerial Conferences on youth work in the 1980s and 1990s were particularly influential, identifying the core purpose of youth work as the promotion of education, equality of opportunity, empowerment and participation (National Youth Agency, 1990).

Professional ethical values in youth work

Written statements of professional values can be found in textbooks, guidelines for education and training and codes of ethics or conduct (see, for example, Banks 1999; Community and Youth Workers' Union 1999; Jeffs and Smith 1999a; Banks 2001a; National Youth Agency 2004b, 2005). These statements reflect the social and political climates of the places and times of their devising and the motivations and commitments of the current and past members of the occupational group. They are also designed to influence and challenge prevailing societal norms and values and to develop, enhance or define the value commitments of individual practitioners. In this sense, they can be seen as a meeting point for societal and personal values. The values included and their definitions vary. They tend to focus more on ethical principles (how we should act) rather than on moral qualities (what sorts of people we should be). This is probably because it is easier to define and measure behaviour or action than character traits, but both are equally important in professional ethics.

The statement of values and principles of the English National Youth Agency makes the following statement about the nature and purpose of youth work:

Youth work is informed by a set of beliefs which include a commitment to equal opportunity, to young people as partners in learning and decision-making and to helping young people to develop their own sets of values. (2004b: 1)

This is a very general statement, the content of which is open to interpretation. The commitment to 'equal opportunity' signals work that at the minimum tries to avoid prejudice and discrimination and at its most radical may be concerned with changing the balance of power and wealth in society, as discussed by Chouhan in Chapter 6. 'Partnership' with young people also indicates a concern with equality of power in the youth work relationship, while the use of terms like 'learning', 'decision-making' and 'develop' reflects youth work's core purpose as informal educational work with young people as they move into adulthood. 'Helping' is a term often avoided in such statements of professional values, as it can have connotations of paternalism and charity. However, it is a useful reminder of the caring relationship that lies at the heart of youth work. In order genuinely to 'help' a young person we may need to empathise, be sensitive to their needs and concerns and offer some support, whether moral or practical. Helping is often associated with giving.

The National Youth Agency (2004b) statement then lists four ethical and five professional principles for youth work, which are clearly meant to guide workers in reflecting on questions about: 'what ought I to do as a youth worker?' and 'what kind of person should I be as a good youth worker?' The four ethical principles are listed below in italics, to which further elaboration is added, making brief connections with some ethical theories and traditions. The five professional principles are here subsumed into 'professional integrity', which could be regarded as an overarching moral quality or virtue.

1   *Treat young people with respect, valuing each individual and avoiding negative discrimination.* This principle is often linked with the ethical theory of Immanuel Kant, an eighteenth-century German philosopher, who based his moral philosophy on the ultimate principle of 'respect for persons' (Kant 1964). However, there is also emphasis in many other moral philosophical and religious traditions on human dignity and worth. In the case of youth work, this principle is about regarding each young person as worthy of attention, regardless of what they have done or who they are. It is also about not treating young people as objects or as a means to someone else's ends. Young people are often stigmatised, and may be subject to unnecessary and degrading treatment, simply because of their youth and lack of political and economic power (Hine, Chapter 3). Youth workers, therefore, often have to work hard to implement this principle, especially in the context of work with other professionals who may prioritise other values (for example, public welfare and safety).

2   *Respect and promote young people's rights to make their own decisions and choices, unless the welfare or legitimate interests of themselves or others are seriously threatened.* For Kant, being a person meant being capable of rational thought and self-determined action, so it logically follows that respecting persons entails respecting their rights to make their own decisions. However, young children, people who are severely ill or who have learning disabilities, for example, may not be judged capable of making 'rational' choices. What counts as 'capable' and 'rational' may depend on the seriousness of the decision to be made, which is why the second part of the principle is important (which relates to threats to the well-being of the young person in question or others). For youth workers,

making a professional judgement about how much freedom of choice to allow a young person in the context of work with a group may be a delicate one. But this principle reminds workers that young people's participation in decision-making about their own lives, group activities or policy matters is important and should not just be respected, but also actively promoted. This links with the educational purpose of youth work, and a concern to help young people develop their own sets of values, as noted earlier.

3 *Promote and ensure the welfare and safety of young people, while permitting them to learn through undertaking challenging educational activities.* This principle is more consequentialist or utilitarian in tone. That is, it is looking to the consequences of our actions and the outcomes for young people – reminiscent of the principle of utility, which suggests that the right action is that which promotes the greatest amount of good (Mill 1972). Of course, it raises the question of what counts as 'welfare' and who judges what is good for young people. These are issues that have to be debated with the young people themselves. But the addition of the phrase about permitting young people 'to learn through challenging educational activities' is a reminder that a cautious parentalist approach to ensuring safety should be balanced with the need and right for young people to learn through making mistakes and taking risks.

4 *Contribute towards the promotion of social justice for young people and in society generally, through encouraging respect for difference and diversity and challenging discrimination.* This is an important and complex principle, which embraces the concept of equality as well as justice. It is about treating people and distributing resources fairly, challenging unwarranted differential treatment (for example, exclusion from activities on the basis of skin colour), while paying respectful attention to diverse religious and cultural identities and differentiating when appropriate. It is also about working towards greater equality of outcomes for everyone in society, including young people. This entails youth workers being critically aware of the nature of oppression and oppressive attitudes, actions and structures and having the competence and ability to identify and challenge these.

5 *Act with professional integrity.* The five professional principles that have been summarised under the moral quality of professional integrity include being honest and open in dealings with young people, taking care not to exploit relationships, recognising boundaries between personal and professional life, taking account of multiple professional accountabilities, maintaining skills and competence required for the job, fostering ethical debate and working for conditions in employing agencies so that the ethical principles are upheld. While placing all these statements under the broad banner of 'professional integrity' may be stretching the concept somewhat, they are all related to practitioners being aware of what it means to be a good professional and being committed to the professional ethical values as a whole (Banks 2004b). The notion of there being certain qualities associated with being a good youth worker has resonances with the virtue ethics of Aristotle, the ancient Greek philosopher, and more recent moral philosophers (Aristotle 1954; MacIntyre 1985; Hursthouse 1999; Swanton 2003). While only professional integrity is covered here (often conceived as an overarching moral quality or competence), clearly there are other moral qualities that would be highly valued in the youth worker, such as: trustworthiness, honesty, care (including empathy and moral sensitivity) and courage (see Banks and Imam 2000).

In trying to elaborate briefly on each value, it becomes clear that one of the problems with such lists of values is that they are open to interpretation. What counts as 'respect'? What do we mean by 'welfare' or 'social justice'? Furthermore, the principles may often conflict with each other in the everyday practical situations encountered by youth workers. For example, promoting young people's safety and welfare may mean refusing to let them make their own decisions (for example, to climb without a rope up a rock face). In some agencies or settings, one principle may tend to have priority (for example, a youth counselling service may stress respect and autonomy, while a youth offending project may place more emphasis on welfare and safety). This can lead to workers experiencing ethical problems and dilemmas, in having to weigh up which principles to prioritise. In inter-agency and inter-professional working, not only may practitioners interpret 'respect' and 'welfare' variously and give them different priority, they may not even share the same professional values. For example, health professionals (often qualified nurses) are generally employed in youth offending teams, alongside social workers, youth workers and others. The stated ethical principles of nursing (Nursing and Midwifery Council 2004), while placing great emphasis on treating people with respect and promoting their autonomous decision-making, do not mention 'social justice'. This does not mean that nurses do not care about social justice, simply that in their day-to-day practice, their first and most direct concern is the care of the individual patient.

Ethical challenges in practice

This chapter will now look at a case example taken from an interview with a youth worker, Tom, who was asked to describe his work in a youth offending team, with a particular focus on ethical issues and problems. Names of people and places have been changed in order to preserve anonymity. As far as possible Tom is quoted in his own words, to enable analysis of what he is saying in this interview about his professional values and the ethical issues in his work. This example has been chosen as it highlights some of the ethical challenges for youth workers operating in multi-agency and inter-professional settings, and also illustrates how a youth worker gives an account of himself as a committed and responsible practitioner. Inter-professional settings can serve to encourage youth workers to reflect on their own professional identities and values more closely, as they are working daily with people from other professions (see Banks 2004a, for a more in-depth discussion of ethical issues in inter-professional working).

'I'm in very big trouble at the YOT': Tom's case

Tom is a qualified youth worker who has been working in a youth offending team (YOT) for over a year. The YOT covers two local authority areas (a large town and a rural district) and is a partnership between several agencies – local authority children's services, education, probation, health and police. YOTs were set up in England in 2000 with the aim of reducing offending by children and young people through offering a more targeted and holistic service (see Yates, Chapter 14 for discussion about these developments). They have to work within a national framework for undertaking assessments of young people, with targets set for reductions in youth offending, monitored by the Youth Justice Board. In many teams one or more youth workers may be employed – particularly to undertake 'preventive work' with young people.

Tom was the only youth worker in this YOT and reported finding the work extremely challenging. He was currently involved in working with young people who had been given a 'final warning'. Tom commented about his work as follows (italics are used where emphasis has been added):

> I have great problems with the final warnings. It's a 12-week programme and in that time you go in, you make your assessment, and then you look at working with the young person and their family around creating an intervention package. And that's how it works. I mean, *I have a problem around the ethics of it in the first place*, because of the actual way the final warning system is set up … The young person is arrested and asked … well, they're given the opportunity to plead guilty: 'You plead guilty'. That's the option they've got: plead guilty. If you say 'no, I'm innocent', then you get charged and sent to court. If you say 'yes, I'm guilty' … the whole thing opens up for you and you can go down this wonderful line … This great youth work …
>
> We have 10 days in which to interview them and put in this 'agreed' package of intervention. Between receiving the arrest form and doing the actual interview, we have access and apparently we have rights to the young person's medical records. We speak to their GP, their school, social services, any other services they've ever been involved with, and if necessary we can use social services to look at their parents. So *we get a whole raft of their life in a big file* and we walk in the front door and sit down in their living room and ask the questions we already have the answer to …
>
> The final warning is about saying to a first-time offender: 'We're going to try and help you not offend again.' There's a nice bit and there's a big stick. The big stick being: 'We're on your case. We walk in with this big file and we know everything about you. You can't lie to us. We know you don't go to school. Your mam and dad didn't know you didn't go to school, but they do now, because I've just mentioned it. You take drugs. Well, your dad didn't know that, but we know that because you've been arrested previously for having a miniscule amount of cannabis'. So the whole life of this person is then laid open to all and sundry, *so there's a big dilemma there* …
>
> The biggest issue about final warnings for me is they're *a blanket approach to youth offending*. When you look at statistics, something like 78 per cent of all first-time offenders do not reoffend, without any intervention. So I've just taken … that's 78 per cent of people's personal lives and laid waste to them, because that's what I've got to do to get to the other 22 per cent …

> So the intervention package is supposed to be for 12 weeks. I'm in very big trouble at the YOT, because I've got cases that are nearly a year old now. And I keep trying to explain, this is about *the youth work dilemma* thing, I keep trying to explain that *I'm about the process of trying to get this young person from here to somewhere.* Going in rattling at them for 12 weeks is going just to produce nothing, because when I shut the case and walk away in 12 weeks' time, they will fall off the perch again and get themselves in trouble and then they've got three offences going to court, and *I can't justify that myself to myself …*
>
> What's happened now is I've moved out of final warnings, *I don't do them any more, because I'm too uncomfortable.* Although I've still got these cases that I'm finishing off, I'm not prepared to hand them over. I'm not prepared to close them until I think the young people are in a stable enough situation to let them go and move on, on their own.

Choice and justice in the final warning system: 'I have a problem around the ethics of it in the first place'

Tom questions whether it is right that only those who admit their guilt are given the chance to participate in a programme of youth work activities. He implies that the 'option' that young people have about whether to admit guilt or innocence is hardly a true choice, since if they wish to avoid going to court, then they have to admit their guilt. Furthermore, those who claim innocence and go to court cannot avail themselves of the benefits of youth work. Regardless of whether we think Tom's judgements about the ethical basis of final warnings are correct, clearly what he is doing is giving an ethical evaluation of the whole system. Implicitly his comments raise questions about the nature of choice (what counts as 'genuine choice') and about justice as fairness (some of those young people who claim innocence may also benefit from youth work, but they do not have the chance).

Respect in information gathering and sharing: 'we get a whole raft of their life in a big file'

Tom speaks of gathering a mass of information about the young people with whom he is going to work. This reflects the emphasis in recent UK policy on sharing information between professionals and agencies in order that young people do not have to give the same information repeatedly to several practitioners and agencies and to ensure that all relevant information is gathered so that practitioners can work effectively (DfES 2003, 2005). This could be argued as being about respecting young people (not over-questioning them) and a concern for their welfare. Certainly a significant impetus for the development of systematic information-sharing has come from child abuse cases when it was felt that practitioners from different agencies were not working together effectively and sharing what they knew (see Laming 2003).

Yet Tom is also aware of the negative impact of this concern with information, commenting: 'we get a whole raft of their life in a big file'. It is as if the rich and complex life of an individual young person has been encapsulated in a file: who the person is becomes identified with a file. This can result in a depersonalising effect, a failure to respect the young person as a person (rather than a set of records). The file also gives power to the worker, who walks in knowing 'everything about you' and 'the whole life of this person is then laid open to all and sundry'. Tom doesn't use the term 'confidentiality', but clearly he is concerned that personal information is being passed around not just between professionals, but also to parents. He says the information is given to 'all and sundry'. While this is obviously an exaggeration, it indicates that he feels the process to be intrusive and perhaps disrespectful of young people's rights to confidentiality. He says; 'so there's a big dilemma there'. He does not elaborate at this point in the interview, but from a later conversation it is clear that he means there is a dilemma about how much or little to reveal. He later speaks of being circumspect himself about how much he tells the school about the nature of a young person's offence, as well as being careful what he says to parents. Yet he knows he must tell other agencies some details of what he knows, in return for their sharing of information with him. The development of such systems for information gathering and sharing between practitioners and agencies is contributing to the growth of what some have termed a 'surveillance society' (Foucault 1977; Garrett 2004; Parton 2006), where not only do young people feel the intensity of the integrated professional gaze, but practitioners themselves may feel trapped by a net of procedures and protocols.

Impersonality in the standardised approach: 'a blanket approach to youth offending'

One of the problems for Tom, it seems, is that he does not feel he can fit the work he judges he needs to do with individual young people into the prescribed format. Not only is there a standardised reporting procedure, but the allotted time (12 weeks) is not enough for many young people, in his view. While recent policy developments emphasise the need to target individuals and work with them to meet their specific needs, Tom actually cannot do this, as the framework within which he is operating does not allow him enough freedom. This is an example of the growing tension between policies that claim to devolve decision-making to local areas and individual residents or service users, while at the same time there is increasingly centralised target setting and accountability mechanisms (see Banks 2004a: 149–178 and the tensions discussed by Yates in this volume, Chapter 15). Tom wants to give attention to the particular circumstances of each young person's life and to have room to use his professional discretion and judgement about how he should work with young people and for how long. Yet Tom's refusal to close his cases means that the YOT records do not show any outputs or outcomes for the young people with whom he is working. This causes problems for the YOT manager, as it looks like the team is being inefficient and ineffective, since the work that Tom has done has not been measured or accounted for.

Welfare and education in good youth work: 'I'm about the process of trying to get this young person from here to somewhere'

Tom appears to have a vision about what he should be doing, linked to what he thinks good youth work is. He says he tries to explain what he is doing: 'this is about the youth work dilemma thing'. He is not very explicit about what he thinks 'the youth work dilemma thing' is, but from what he says next, we can guess that he may be concerned to adopt an informal educational approach, to respect young people, work at their pace, enable them to develop, grow and change in ways that are sustainable. He will need time to build a relationship of trust with a young person, to allow for set-backs and mistakes. As a youth worker, he is not interested in 'quick fixes' – his work should be more long term and the effects more lasting.

Professional integrity: 'I don't do them [final warnings] any more, because I'm too uncomfortable'

Finally we learn, towards the end of the extract, that Tom has stopped working on final warnings. His explanation is that he is 'too uncomfortable'. If professional integrity is about holding on to the values of one's profession (especially in the face of adversity), then Tom is demonstrating this quality here. He says that he can't justify *to himself* (this suggests he is using an internal mechanism as a yardstick, such as his conscience) walking away from young people after 12 weeks when he knows they are not ready. The 'self' that he is referring to seems to be the self in the role of professional youth worker. Some readers might question the strength of Tom's commitment to youth work values, for while he is not prepared to compromise on how he does the final warnings work, he is prepared to give it up completely, knowing someone else will do it. However, elsewhere in the interview Tom recounts a whole series of struggles he has undergone in the YOT to get the team to recognise what youth work is (that it is not simply leisure activity), which indicates that he has been fighting battles on a number of fronts. He reports at the end of the interview that he has received requests from local schools for him to work with groups of young people at risk of exclusion, which he feels is more truly preventive work and can utilise his skills and values as a youth worker to much better and more comfortable effect.

Conclusion

This example was not chosen specifically to illustrate problems youth workers find working in YOTs, nor indeed should this case be regarded as typical. Rather, the aim was to show a youth worker talking about how he makes sense of his professional ethical values and handles ethical issues in his work in an inter-professional team. To some readers Tom may appear rather intransigent or misguided in his strategy for bringing about change in the YOT and the youth justice system generally. However, some of the issues raised may lead us to reflect on the nature of the core purpose and values of youth work in comparison with other occupational groups working with young people.

In inter-agency and inter-professional settings an opportunity is provided for practitioners to learn from each other, to challenge their established values and ways of doing things, and constantly to revise notions of 'good practice'. This does not mean that youth workers should become interchangeable with police officers or social workers, otherwise their vital and distinctive contribution is lost, as was the case with Tom in the YOT. However, it does bring opportunities for debate about what counts as good outcomes for young people and how these can be achieved. The work that Tom was doing on final warnings will be passed on to another member of the team – perhaps a social worker or police officer. It may seem less uncomfortable for them as they are more used to time-limited interventions within prescribed assessment frameworks. Yet we would still expect these practitioners to show young people respect, treat them fairly and to be committed to achieving lasting outcomes. The kind of debate that Tom's experience could have engendered in the team might have been about what counts as respecting young people and how does it relate to and how important is it compared with, say, discouraging their offending behaviour? Colleagues might question whether Tom's long-term approach might encourage dependency, and point out that if he gives too much time to just a few young people, then he is denying others the chance of potentially valuable work.

There are no right answers to these questions, but they are questions that need to be asked repeatedly. We would expect that values about respecting and promoting young people's choice and well-being would be shared by all professionals working with young people. But how this is achieved may vary according to the setting and the extent to which practitioners see themselves as particular types of professionals whose values are located within a wider context of a core purpose of the work. In youth work this core purpose is about informal education. This means a good youth worker will be more concerned with promoting autonomy and sustainable relationships than, perhaps, one of their social worker or police colleagues might be, whose core purpose is social welfare or public order.

Reflective questions for practice:

- **Professional values guide our work as practitioners. Can you make a list of the core professional values that are important to you?**

- Do you make use of a professional code of conduct in your work, and if so, how do you use it?
- Think about Tom's work and consider your own role in a multi-agency context. What aspects of work in these situations might make you feel uncomfortable?
- How might you defend or assert your own professional values in such situations?

Further reading

Banks, S. (ed.) (1999) *Ethical Issues in Youth Work*, **London, Routledge.** This edited collection has chapters by different authors covering a range of value conflicts and dilemmas for youth workers, including issues relating to confidentiality, religious conversion, social control, sources of funding and participatory research.

Banks, S. (2004) *Ethics, Accountability and the Social Professions*, **Basingstoke, Palgrave Macmillan.** This book examines the ethical implications of recent changes in the organisation and practice of the social professions (social, youth and community work). It discusses the nature of professions, professional ethics and includes specific chapters on inter-professional working and the challenge of new accountability requirements (targets, outputs, procedures and proformas).

Boss, J. (2007) *Ethics for Life: A Text with Readings*, **3rd edition, New York, McGraw-Hill.** This book gives useful background on various ethical theories and is written in a clear, practical style. It includes readings, photographs/drawings of key thinkers, biographical details and discussion of religion and cultural relativism.

Acknowledgements

I am grateful to the youth worker whose interview provided the case example, and to many other social professionals whose interviews have contributed to my understanding of the ethical challenges in the work. This chapter was commissioned and written during 2005–6.

6

ANTI-OPPRESSIVE PRACTICE

Jagdish Chouhan

Key arguments

- Anti-oppressive practice is a key principle of work with young people, and involves critically understanding and acting upon the power differences and inequality present at personal, cultural and structural levels.
- Key thinkers in sociology have analysed how oppression is maintained through structures and the social processes of socialisation and internalisation.
- These processes are underpinned by dominant views of what constitutes 'natural', 'normal' and 'desirable' social structures and behaviour.
- The role of practitioners is to engage in dialogue with young people and their communities, enabling and achieving a level of critical consciousness to challenge oppression.
- In order to do this, practitioners need to understand who they are and the process of how they come to think and feel the way they do about 'others'.

Introduction

> 'We need to be the change that we are
> seeking in the world we live'.
>
> Mahatma Gandhi

A key principle of youth and community development work is tackling oppression and discrimination, working towards anti-oppressive practice to bring about equality and social justice in society (FCDL 2003; National Youth Agency 2004). A distinction is made here between anti-oppressive practice, concerned with an awareness of power differentials, challenging wider injustices in society and working towards a model of empowerment and liberation; and anti-discriminatory practice which challenges more specific acts of discrimination operating within society's legal framework (Dalrymple and Burke 2006; Young and Chouhan 2006). Anti-oppressive practice requires that practitioners have an understanding of oppression and power, commitment to empowerment and the ability to reflect, critically analyse and change their practice. (Young and Chouhan 2006: 26)

This chapter will explore how values and belief systems are acquired and impact on the professional engagement of youth workers and community development workers. Inequality and oppression are social constructs and when an individual accepts these ideas as natural, commonsense and right, they have internalised this oppression and those in a position of power do not need to resort to external controls to gain conformity and compliance from those who do not have power. Oppression will be analysed in relation to Thompson's (2006) Personal, Cultural, Structural (PCS) model and Dalrymlple and Burke's (2006) model of empowerment. Development of Thompson's model will show ways in which professionals, as agents of change, can challenge oppression and injustice.[1] The chapter draws heavily on the author's experience of racism from a Black, male, youth and community development work perspective.

Understanding oppression, discrimination and anti-oppressive practice

Anti-oppressive practice is based on the understanding and belief that:

- society creates divisions and people also divide themselves;
- some groups of people, whether consciously or unconsciously, believe that they are superior to other groups of people in society; and
- such beliefs are embedded deep within structures and institutions, in culture and in relationships with each other.

Critical thinking and analysis is essential for practitioners to work in an anti–oppressive way. They must explore their own value base and power position but also:

- Identify and challenge assumptions
- Recognize the importance of the social, political and historical context of events, assumptions, interpretations and behavior
- Imagine and explore alternatives
- Exercise reflective skepticism towards claims to universal truths or ultimate explanations. (Brookfield 1987 cited in Young 2006: 81)

The significant social divisions in society are based on class, race/ethnicity, gender, age and disability, and form the basis of social structure, 'the "network" of social relationships, institutions and groupings – which play an important role in the distribution of power, status and opportunities' (Thompson 2006: 21). Understanding oppression means understanding the differing levels at which it operates. Acts of discrimination and oppression do not operate in isolation but within the context of culturally assumed consensus within a broader framework of social structures and institutions. Such circumstances and conditions are maintained by oppression, socialised and internalised, and then normalised through the 'taken-for-granted-ness of everyday life' (Berger and Luckmann, 1967), where ideas and beliefs become 'common-sense' and 'natural'. Young and Chouhan argue:

> This includes invalidation (e.g. women's experiences and opinions do not matter), denial (e.g. lesbians and gay men do not exist), and de-humanization (e.g. of Black people and people with disabilities). Misinformation about the nature, history and abilities of different groups of people are then used to justify their continued mistreatment. Highly significant among such misinformation are two underlying assumptions: That difference necessarily implies relations of superiority/inferiority. That biology provides legitimate justification for discrimination. (2006: 22)

Differences in society are therefore used to exclude certain people and groups by those in a position of power at all levels in society, with science sometimes being used to justify this position.

Oppression also becomes conditioned so that, to a greater or lesser extent, people believe the lies, myths and misinformation about themselves and others in society, often acting on these beliefs and behaving according to the stereotype of, for example, how a Black person or a woman is supposed to behave. This process can then become what Merton (1957) describes as a 'self-fulfilling prophecy', further entrenching the belief. For example, it may be internalised and accepted that inequality is 'natural' and 'normal', that power should not be distributed evenly and that it is acceptable for one group in society to enjoy more of the benefits that come with it in terms of prestige and material privileges than another group. The acceptance and acting out of this idea in reality is called oppression, which Thompson describes as:

> Inhuman or degrading treatment of individuals or groups; hardship and injustices brought about by the dominance of one group over another; the negative and demeaning exercise of power. Oppression often involves disregarding the rights of an individual or group and is thus a denial of citizenship. (2006: 40)

Freire offers a more concise definition of oppression, 'Any situation in which 'A' exploits 'B' or hinders his or her pursuit of self-affirmation as a responsible person is one of oppression' (1996: 37).

Table 6.1   Features of Thompson's PCS model

Personal	• Beliefs, attitudes and behaviour. • Ideas which people have about themselves and others which they accept are 'true'. • A tendency to respond in a particular way when encountering certain people or situations. • How people regard and/or treat others.
Cultural	• Assumed consensus about what is true, right, good, normal. • Commonly accepted values and codes of conduct.
Structural	• Structures and institutions within society which act to perpetuate social divisions, prejudice and discrimination.

Oppression is not about the misuse of personal power by an individual, or personal instances of discrimination, prejudice and inequality but about a system of deeply ingrained attitudes and practices which permeates and filters through society. It is about the collective power and ability of some groups in society to exclude, deny, control and define other groups and those people who belong to those groups (Young and Chouhan 2006). Multiple oppressions cross cut and interrelate, further disadvantaging and affecting certain groups and individuals in society. The Black feminist bell hooks eloquently describes this experience in relation to Black women, 'at the moment of my birth, two factors determined my destiny, my having been born Black and my having been born female' (1981: 12).

Oppression is the result of power differentials that exist in society. These differences favour groups that are categorised as white, heterosexual, male, upper/middle class, able-bodied, and adult. This informs discrimination, which Thompson defines as:

> Unfair or unequal treatment of individuals or groups based on an actual or perceived difference; prejudicial behaviour acting against the interests of those people who characteristically tend to belong to relatively powerless groups within the social structure (women, ethnic minorities, old or disabled people and members of the working class). Discrimination is therefore about social formation as well as individual or group behaviour. (2006: 40)

Two models can be used to understand how oppression operates and can be challenged: Thompson's (2006) PCS model and Dalrymple and Burke's (2006) model of empowerment.

Thompson's PCS model identifies three embedded and interconnected levels of oppression: Personal, Cultural and Structural. The features of each level are presented in Table 6.1.

For Thompson (2006: 26–28), the 'Personal or psychological' level represents the individual's internalised thoughts and actions that are taken for granted as being right and 'normal' and is a result of experiences gained through interactions with others. The 'Cultural level of shared ways of seeing, thinking and doing' are 'the interests and influences of society', the shared thoughts and feelings of what is accepted as right and normal within different groups. The C level acts as a form of social control and brings conformity to society's norms, and 'comic humour acts as a vehicle for transmitting and reinforcing this culture.' The Structural level is 'the network of social divisions and power relations so closely associated with them … and the ways in which oppression and discrimination are institutionalized and thus "sewn in" to the fabric of society' (Thompson 2006: 28).

In this model the P level exists within the C level, which in turn is embedded within the S level. Individual thoughts and actions (P level) are influenced by the culture in which individuals live (C level), acting as an immediate form of external social control. These culture(s) exist within, and are determined by wider society (S level). Thompson's PCS model shows how oppression filters through all aspects of society affecting thoughts and behaviour.

Dalrymple and Burke (2006: 119) offer a similar model for analysing the process of empowerment and personal growth. It has three concentric circles representing empowerment at different levels: feelings, ideas and activity, which relate to biography, changed consciousness and political activity respectively. This model is a positive approach which emphasises the notion of empowerment and its importance in the relationship between the practitioner and the young person. A relationship in which the committed practitioner starts from where the young person is at in terms of their needs and rights, supporting them and tackling their oppressed position to redress the imbalance of power. This position is very much in line with Freire's, *Pedagogy of the Oppressed* in which he argues that 'a pedagogy of the oppressed people … must be forged with, not for the oppressed' (1996: 30).

> The process is one that is interlinked but also occurs at any or all of the levels at any one time. The process is ongoing. Change at the level of feelings will affect the level of ideas as self awareness develops. This enables mobilization at the level of action, which in turn affects one's biography at the level of feelings, as inevitably change has occurred. This is a continual process. (Dalrymple and Burke 2006: 120)

The mutual processes of change within each level reciprocate and influence one another.

Practitioners have a moral, legal and professional obligation to carry out their duties in an anti-discriminatory way. Dalrymple and Burke (2006) argue that practitioners need to work within the 'system' and the law in an anti-oppressive way to promote practice that is beneficial and supportive to clients. However, legislation can itself be oppressive and disempowering, functioning as an ideological tool that maintains the position and interests of certain groups. Where legislation is changed or introduced to reduce oppression it can be slow to take effect:

> Ingrained attitudes based on historical social practices do change only slowly, and therefore laws may promote lip service to the principle of equal treatment and token gestures towards implementing it, without resulting in any fundamental alterations in the economic and social structures of society. (Carter 1988: 140)

Oppression occurs wherever there is an imbalance of power and the process of socialisation and internalisation will uphold these oppressive conditions. Doyle (1997) suggests that there are four main prerequisites for oppression to operate:

- Where a person or people in a position of power misuse their power.
- Where the oppressed are objectified by the people with power.
- Where collusion operates either knowingly or unknowingly resulting in silence.
- Where the abused or oppressed is entrapped or accommodated, i.e. where they have gone through a process of blame and despair through to identification with the abuser/oppressor and compliance with what they are experiencing. (1997: 8–15)

Oppression creates the illusion that the dominant world view is the only one that exists. Having unwittingly assimilated society's dominant values, internally validating them and making them our own, they guide and direct behaviour and actions towards other people (Dalrymple and Burke 2006). Experience of oppression will determine what is internalised and thereby define what it means to be different. This experience and knowledge is then used in relationships with others. People from oppressed groups have the choice of adopting the values of the oppressor or challenging and fighting back (Ward and Mullender 1991), creating two ways that this internalised oppression can manifest itself: assuming a 'victim' role by acting it out or by acting it out on others in the form of mistreatment of one group by another, for example, the mistreatment of bisexuals by lesbians (Sydney Bisexual Network 2000). This conflict among subgroups within a community further isolates and divides people who identify and belong to these subgroups and communities, thereby maintaining the status quo (Jackins 1979).

The acceptance of their subordinate position, of inequality and oppression is referred to as internalised oppression and means that those in positions of power do not have to use external controls to achieve compliance from those without power. For example, patriarchal Western societies produce and perpetuate images of women as passive, emotional, caring and intellectually inferior. The creation and acceptance of traditional roles such as motherhood and domestication for women becomes easier as they are seen as 'natural', 'normal' and acceptable, a 'taken for grantedness' of everyday life (Berger and Luckmann 1967). At all three levels of the PCS model, values, attitudes, beliefs and institutions create a deep seated bias against women, thereby allowing men to dominate in society.

Thompson's structure and culture play an important role in ensuring and maintaining oppression through ideology. Indeed, for Thompson (2006), ideology is the 'glue' that binds the three levels together and 'acts as the vehicle of cultural transmission between the P and C levels'. He goes on:

> it is ideology which explains how the C level reflects, maintains and protects the S level by presenting social divisions as 'natural' and 'normal' and thus desirable ... the relationship between the levels is an ideological one, a reflection of the meeting point of the idea of power and the power of ideas. Ideology is not an abstract force ... Indeed, it is in and through human action that ideology comes into being. (2006: 36)

Ideology at structural, cultural and personal levels

Structural level

Marx was primarily concerned with class oppression which he saw as operating at an economic structural level within capitalist societies (Haralambos and Holborn 2004). The bourgeoisie owned the means of production and therefore dominated society, while the proletariat sold their labour to survive. By paying the proletariat less than the value of what they created, the bourgeoisie were able to exploit the proletariat, creating surplus value which they kept themselves. This process would increase the divisions between the two groups and therefore the wealth and dominant position of the bourgeoisie would remain. For Marx, the notions of 'ruling ideology' and 'false consciousness' were key in understanding how class oppression of the proletariat was maintained.

Ideology was the process whereby the bourgeoisie were able to successfully perpetuate and entrench their political beliefs and ideas at all levels, which justified and maintained oppression and therefore the status quo. The role of the state was important and integral in this process but the state was also controlled by the bourgeoisie, to maintain and promote their ideas and interests (Edye 2002). An analogy can be drawn between the idea of false consciousness and Berger's (1966) idea of internalisation in that both refer to a situation in which groups accept and believe a set of ideas, beliefs and relations as 'normal' and 'natural', rather than see the reality, which for Marx was the oppressive capitalist system.

Antonio Gramsci took Marx's ideas further; he also saw the bourgeoisie's use of the role of the state as crucial in maintaining oppression and the status quo. However, he saw the state as being divided into two, 'political society' and 'civil society'. Political society was largely made up of institutions whose force could be used to repress any challenges and maintain the status quo. Such institutions include the police, the army and the legal system. Civil society was made of institutions that were largely private and separate from the state such as the mass media, the church, political parties and trade unions. Gramsci did not see the structures of society as inevitable and natural, but institutions which were developed and designed to maintain the capitalist order. The capitalist social order would be maintained by preparing people for their roles in society, once they had been instilled with capitalist ideas, morals and thinking (Haralambos and Holborn 2004).

One criticism of Marxist theory is its lack of examination of forms of oppression other than class, e.g. race and gender and the lack of attention paid to the lived experiences of specific groups and their oppression. However, some Marxists have argued that these other forms of oppression are really another manifestation of class exploitation and Black people are really part of the proletariat, with some arguing that they represent an 'underclass' (Giddens, 1973). This is another way in which the bourgeoisie maintain their dominant position, by creating racial divisions between Black and white people thereby creating a weakened working class. Similarly, Beechey (1986); Castles and Kosack (1973) and Chouhan (1991) suggest that the role of women and migrants in the labour market needs to be examined within a context of international capitalism, arguing they are part of a reserve army of labour that the capitalist system can call into the labour market when there is a shortage of white working-class men in the system (Haralambos and Holborn 2004).

For many traditional Marxists, the liberation of the proletariat would come when they are conscious of their own oppressive condition and exploitive situation, and could see how the dominant ideology of capitalism was contradictory to their interest and position. In becoming aware of the reality of their situation, the proletariat would reject capitalism and unite as a group to oppose it. Although such an analysis is useful in understanding oppression and power relations, it presents real challenges. Making changes at the structural level may be difficult, particularly in mobilising and developing change in practice. That is not to say that practitioners who are in a position of power at this level do nothing, only that it may be limited and difficult, requiring broader and more strategic thinking and planning. For example, practitioners can work with young people and the local community to facilitate a campaign and lobby their local councilors, MPs and the media to generate an awareness of the need for community facilities in a local area. Practitioners need to ensure that they make the link between the practical realities of peoples' personal lives and the structural context in which they live.

Gramsci argued that the bourgeoisie would be able to maintain ideological control for much longer through consent. That is, by offering limited concessions to soften the perceived exploitation and experience, the proletariat would remain loyal to the capitalist system (Edye 2002). Gramsci acknowledged that as a consequence alternative and countervailing ideas may develop, and introduced the notion of hegemony, to describe how the bourgeoisie gained full support from society. Hegemony is the relation of domination, by consent and not coercion, of one group over another through political and ideological leadership (Simon 1991). Through manipulation and the use of the mass media, the dominant group is able to achieve full hegemony, when subordinate groups resign themselves to a particular social order through consent rather than force (Bilton et al. 1996). In British society the hegemonic group is white, adult, male, upper/middle class, heterosexual and able-bodied.

Gramsci argued for the creation of 'organic intellectuals' from the working classes who would engage not only in consciousness raising but also consciousness transformation. The role and development of the working-class intellectual was critical in the creation of a counter hegemony. For practitioners, the battle and struggle for concepts and ideas leaves open the opportunity for the creation of an opposition and therefore the development of an alternative discourse (this will be discussed further below).

The operation and process of ideology is important to Thompson's structural level because it is here that the dominant values of society are enveloped and woven into institutions. The dominant ideas, beliefs, actions and ways of practicing become fused and part of the structural organisation of society, around which a system of social control is built (Edye 2002). When a part of 'human activity has been institutionalised ... this activity has been subsumed under social control' (Berger and Luckmann 1995: 73).

Freire (1996) argues that institutions at a structural level, such as education, play a crucial role in the development of the child in society. The learning and socialisation here will be internalised and shape their ideas and beliefs. He argues that education needs to move away from the 'banking concept', where education is simply about a process of 'depositing' information into the student's mind, where they learn facts and figures which are then regurgitated as and when needed. The 'banking concept', of education is very much a 'functionalist' approach, a form of social control, ensuring that people are socialised with the dominant ideology, trained to fit into the requirements and needs of society (Parsons 1964).

Freire argues that students also need to understand 'why?'. The process of understanding the world through 'problem posing' and questioning the validity of information received is crucial to achieving a point of 'critical consciousness' in students. The role of practitioners is to engage in dialogue with young people and their communities, enabling and achieving a level of critical consciousness with them so that they have the tools to transform their own world and thereby an opportunity to challenge oppression.

Cultural level

If ideology is about the communication of ideas, then clearly language and other forms of communication play a crucial role in constructing and maintaining discriminatory and oppressive forms of practice (Thompson 2006). Theories that provide an analysis and understanding at a cultural level offer an opportunity to change and challenge dominant and oppressive ideas. The importance of understanding structural oppression is its emphasis on the control of ideas at the cultural level. Culture is a mechanism for encouraging acceptance of the social order without criticism. This is achieved through the positive portrayal of the accepted hegemony and the negative portrayal of those that deviate from this norm. Coercive power is not necessary to maintain hegemony, which can be achieved simply by, for example, the dominant values being expressed by watching TV (Macionis and Plummer 1997: 119).

Foucault challenged Marx's analysis of social class in maintaining the dominant position of the bourgeoisie. He was critical of Marxists believing they held 'absolute truth' compared to the ideas of the ruling class, arguing that no single system of thought held absolute truth outside of how knowledge and ideas are represented through language. Foucault analyses power at a cultural level and introduces the notion of 'discourse' to highlight cultural codes (stories, images and representations), where language is structured through a system of meanings, shaping aspects of social life and acting as a vehicle of social processes. Discourses are powerful and play an important role in the socialisation process of an individual's knowledge, and are based on dominant ideologies. Fook (2002) argues that language does not operate in a vacuum and is not neutral but is part of the social world, acting as a bridge between the personal and the social. Therefore, the very words that we use can unintentionally be oppressive, constructing and maintaining oppressive and discriminatory forms of practice. Helene Cixous argues that Western societies have built up an oppressive discourse in which women are perceived to be inferior to men. Women are seen to be 'passive', about 'nature' and the 'heart' whereas men are about 'activity', 'culture' and the 'head' respectively (Cixous and Clement 1996: 63). She argues that gender discourses usually split men and women into binary opposites with men occupying a powerful position of strength and control, while women are seen as dependant, irrational and in a negative way (Edye 2002).

For Foucault, discourses are created and developed at the cultural level and at any one time, there would be many discourses being contested and claimed as knowledge and truth by its members. The more *accepted* a discourse becomes, the more powerful a force it is. To illustrate, Foucault (1967) examined the discourse of madness, arguing that at a particular point in history, it came to be seen as a form of 'sickness'. Once this definition had come to be accepted as knowledge and 'true' it led to a number of social practices, particularly those involving the medical professions, with institutions then being developed to treat this 'sickness'.

Foucault's analysis of discourses provides practitioners with an understanding of how ideas are developed and contested at the cultural level and therefore the possibility of developing a resistance or countervailing discourse which offers an alternative view to the dominant discourse. Perceived 'truths' can be challenged and reduced to social constructs. With new social interactions constantly occurring, there is an opportunity to determine meaning and thereby challenge and change the dominant values, belief systems and inevitably the structures which uphold them.

Personal level

Understanding oppression at a the P level needs examination of how prejudice and discriminatory ideas develop through social interaction, shared cultural beliefs and social practices at a structural level.

Social constructionists believe that reality is socially constructed (Berger 1966; Berger and Luckmann 1967). They emphasise the important link between individual interactions and wider social structures and how the two work together. This is different to Marxism (focusing on structure) and Symbolic Interactionism (focusing on individual action).

Societies are formed over time and within a geographical area through social interaction. Through interaction individuals map and categorise the world around them and thereby collectively develop a consensus and a collective, subjective interpretation of reality. The mechanism and process by which humans transfer an understanding of society and the world to individuals is called socialisation, largely seen as primary and secondary socialisation. Primary socialisation is the critical stage that takes place in early childhood when the child is interacting with family members. Secondary socialisation takes place throughout life and in wider society.

Socialisation is the process whereby the individual develops their identity and becomes integrated and part of a social group, learning group culture and the roles they will be acting out. It is through socialisation that we learn who we are and what we should think, do and feel. Bilton et al. (1996) suggest that although society shapes our knowledge, it also has an element of control over our behaviour. Social constructionists believe this to be 'the process whereby "natural", instinctive forms of behaviour become mediated by social processes' (Bilton et al. 1996: 200).

Having been socialised within a specific group or environment, internalisation is the mechanism by which the external social world with its messages and meanings is integrated into the individual's consciousness (Berger 1966). Through this process the individual believes and accepts what is learnt as being 'true', 'natural', 'normal' and 'proper'. The values held by the group become identified and part of their self. An individual, by accepting and conforming to society's dominant values and beliefs, will be given certain rewards, feel included and have a sense of security of their place in the world. Society frees individuals from understanding and questioning the world themselves and from the difficult and troubling responsibility of making certain decisions about their role within it. It is perhaps because of the rewards and benefits that come from conforming to society's dominant values and beliefs, that for the most part, most people will not be critical of society, allowing the process of internalisation to carry on unconsciously, as emphasised in Berger's *Invitation to Sociology:*

> Only an understanding of internalization makes sense of the incredible fact that most external controls work most of the time for most of the people in society. Society not only

controls our movements, but shapes our identities, our thoughts and our emotions. The structures of society become the structures of our own consciousness. Society does not stop at the surface of our skins. Society penetrates us and envelops us. (1966: 140)

An analogy can be drawn between Emile Durkheim's notion of 'collective conscience' (Haralambos and Holborn 2004) and Berger's suggestion that 'society becomes the structures of our consciousnesses'. Both would perhaps argue that effective socialisation occurs when:

We think we are acting independently and autonomously ... in fact our journeys through life are biographically structured, by norms and values which existed before us and will continue to exist after we have left. (Bilton et al. 1996: 200)

Behaviour, the way individuals interact and relate to others is also socially constructed. Where individuals have not complied with 'pressures' of conformity, other external controls and sanctions may then be applied. This may include anything from the 'benefits' society gives being withdrawn, or the threat of it, through to physical violence. Eric Fromm argued that the pressure and power for humans to conform is so enormous that individuals accept and adopt wholly the personality presented to them by cultural patterns:

The discrepancy between 'I' and the world disappears and with it the conscious fear of aloneness and powerlessness ... the price he [sic] pays, however, is high; it is the loss of his [sic] self. (Fromm 2001: 159)

The importance and need for human beings to 'belong' is further emphasised in Clarke's (1996) analysis where he argues that individuals search for 'significance', 'security' and 'solidarity' in their relationship with others. Freire noted that oppressed people preferred the 'security of conformity' because they were 'fearful of freedom', having 'internalised the image of the oppressor and adopted his [sic] guidelines' (1996: 29). The notion of change may also bring with it fears and anxieties as we are challenged to move out of our 'comfort zones' into unknown territory, a point taken up by Boeck in Chapter 8.

Internalisation can have a detrimental and negative effect on the individual. For example, an individual can lead a 'false' life, accepting the role that society expects and not taking personal responsibility of who they are and their actions, accepting values and attitudes that have a detrimental impact on themselves and the lives of other people. For example, Davies agues that is it almost impossible for gay, lesbian or bisexual people growing up in British society not to have internalised negative messages about their sexuality (Davies and Neal 1996: 55).

To challenge oppression at the P level, practitioners need to understand who they are and the process of how they come to think and feel the way they do about 'others'.

Empowerment and the reflective practitioner

In recent years, the term empowerment has become a fashionable word that has been hijacked and interpreted differently by many people. For instance politicians emphasise 'welfare consumerism', individual rights, participation and a form of community development that Gilchrist (2003) argues allows the state to implement initiatives locally. For youth and community development workers, empowerment is about the collective working and struggle of groups towards a universal need (Ward and Mullender 1991), and challenging and breaking down barriers that prevent justice and equality (Friedmann 1992). O'Brien and Whitmore define empowerment as:

> An interactive process through which less powerful people experience personal and social change, enabling them to achieve influence over the organizations and institutions which affect their lives and the communities in which they live. (cited in Morley 1991: 14)

For Barry (1996), empowerment is about participative engagement which brings about and results in people gaining control and being able to influence issues that impact on their lives. It is about moving people and communities away from dependency. Empowerment, like oppression, is linked to power and control. Ward and Mullender define power as:

> the capacity not only to impose one's will, if necessary against the will of other parties, but also to set the terms of the argument, including at the national and international level. (1991: 23)

Dalrymple and Burke list a number of principles and assumptions that underpin work that is genuinely empowering. These include working collaboratively and inter-professionally, acting as agents of change, developing informal social networks, participation, a level of awareness, experience affirming efficacy, effective use and access to resources, a dynamic and eclectic approach to problem solving, advocacy, and written agreements and charters (2006: 110–111).

Practitioners need to enable and support people to understand the connections between their position and lived experiences and the reality of structural inequalities that impact on them (Dalrymple and Burke 2006), but also be aware that empowerment as a concept is not without its limitations. Gomm (1993: 133) suggests four different notions of empowerment: 'liberating', 'helping', 'disabling' or 'brokerage' relationships, the last two of which are abusive relationships. He highlights the paradox of empowerment:

> To empower oneself, to seize power, is a perfectly logical idea, and we don't need the word 'empowerment' to express it. To empower someone else, implies something which

is granted by someone more powerful to someone less powerful: a gift, made from a position of power… people who say they are in the business of empowering rarely seem to be giving up their own power: they are usually giving up someone else's and they may actually be increasing their own. (1993: 137)

Conclusion

Practitioners need to be aware of the specificity and interconnectedness of oppressions and how they impact on people's lives, and to challenge discrimination, inequality and injustices at all levels. Ideas, thoughts and opinions are created and develop within social structures and processes which are influenced by history, politics, economics and other social factors (Everitt et al. 1992). Where possible, new and alternative discourses should be created and developed to challenge the existing status quo, critically challenging taken for granted assumptions about the world, being clear about value positions and presenting issues in an open, accountable and transparent way. Reflecting on and evaluating practices can ensure that actions have relevance and achieve the desired change for the individuals and groups being worked with. The reflective practitioner is one who recognises:

Ethical dilemmas and conflicts and how they arise (for example through unequal power relationships with users; contradictions within the welfare state; society's ambivalence towards the welfare state…). They are more confident about their own values and how to put them into practice; they integrate knowledge, values and skills; reflect on practice and learn from it; are prepared to take risks and moral blame. There is recognition that personal agency and values may conflict and that the worker as a person has moral responsibility to make decisions about these conflicts. (Banks 2001b: 140)

Reflective questions for practice

- **Taking the author's suggestion that practitioners 'need to understand who we are', reflect on your own personal views, prejudices and stereotypes of different identities. Why do you think you hold these views, and how are they reinforced?**
- **Do these views influence why and how you work with young people?**
- **How do you explain the differences in the life chances and opportunities open to different groups of young people you work with?**
- **In what ways do you seek to challenge inequality and oppression?**
- **How does this practice fit with the models of empowerment suggested in this chapter?**

Further reading

Thompson, N. (2006) *Anti-Discriminatory Practice,* **4th edn, Basingstoke: Palgrave.** A useful companion that introduces the PCS model as a theoretical framework for anti-oppressive practice, and explores oppression in relation to different social groups.

Thompson, N. (2003) *Promoting Equality,* **2nd edn, Hampshire: Palgrave Macmillan.** Extends the PCS model to explore strategies for challenging oppression.

Note

1 Specific dimensions of oppression will not be addressed as the reader can explore and pursue these on their own at a later stage: race and ethnicity (Husband 1987; Skellington 1996; Solomos and Back 2003; John 2006; Kundnani 2007), gender (Moore 1994; Richardson and Robinson 1997; Connell and Messerschmidt 2005), sexuality (Jackson and Scott 2004; Fish 2006), and disability (Oliver 1996; Swain et al. 2003; Barnes and Mercer 2005), class (Roberts 2001; Davies 2005b; Garrett 2007) or age (Bytheway 1995; S. Thompson 2005).

7

EDUCATING YOUTH: ASSIMILATION AND THE DEMOCRATIC ALTERNATIVE

Derrick Armstrong

Key arguments

- Education has served as a process of assimilating chaotic and delinquent youth into the desired social and economic norms characteristic of modernity.
- Special education has served the interests of the mainstream sector by removing troublesome children, and the interests of professional groups whose 'specialist' identities were legitimated by the continuing existence of the system.
- The labelling of individuals or sections of the community as 'needy' carries with it the implication that they lack the power and/or resources to be self-determining. It reinforces the social power of those who are in a position to define the needs of others.
- One of the biggest challenges for practitioners is developing a democratic practice based upon a critical questioning of the social and political interests that inform and are served by educational policy and practice.

Introduction

Education systems have increasingly provided explanations for social and economic inequality (Finch 1984). An education system may fulfill the function of providing a vehicle for advancement within a meritocracy, yet it also serves as a tool for defusing political dissent by promoting the notion that the privileged deserve to be there. This chapter argues that the thrust of educational policy and reform has consistently been focused upon the assimilation of 'problem' youth, rather than upon their exclusion. Assimilation has opened up opportunities at different times for some young people but education has also operated in ways that emphasise its role in the management of 'troublesome' youth and in the maintenance of social order. Whether or not this central role of the education system is challenged in post-modernity is debatable. In large part, theorists of post-modernity as a libratory movement have not sufficiently taken account of the relations of power and social interests within which education systems are embedded.

This chapter describes how the transformation from pre-modern to modern times was characterised by the paradoxical relationship between the individual and society and the 'problem' of social order. Resolution of that problem was sought in a rationalist model of the social world in which a natural order of progress unfolded through the assimilation of difference within a homogenous society. This hegemony was only seriously challenged with the collapse of the post-war compromise in the 1980s that ushered in a radical break with the past. The fragmentation of order and the decline of civil society not only created the diversity of individualism but also required it. From that point on, social and educational policy were no longer concerned with compensation and assimilation but concerned instead with the policing of moral boundaries and risk management. The chapter ends with reflections on a democratic future for education.

Rationalism and the contradictions of modernity

The question of how to secure a stable social order within which diversity could flourish as a catalyst for renewal was to become a central concern of modernity. Rationalism provided modernist society with both the means of its realisation and the mechanism for controlling the unpredictability of the social diversity that threatened to undermine it. A rational conception of humanity implied both the exclusion of irrationalism from human affairs together with the possibility of rehabilitation, treatment or correction. In pursuit of these dual ends the specification of difference through observation, classification and regulation quickly became the hallmarks of modernity.

Zygmunt Bauman has argued that what is distinctively modern is the concern with order and the fear that unless some action is taken, order will dissipate into chaos.

> What makes it [chaos] so disorderly is the observers' inability to control the flow of events. ... In a modern society, only the vigilant management of human affairs seems to stand between order and chaos. (Bauman 1990: 182–183)

Yet, Bauman also argued that this rationalist ideal is not only an impossible ambition to realise but also highlights the contradiction which 'resides in the very project of *rationalization* inherent in modern society' between society and the individual.

Assimilation and the policy contradictions of education

A belief in the rational ordering of the world and therefore in the possibility of manipulation of the world by rational action, increasingly informed an interventionist social policy agenda during the nineteenth and twentieth centuries. The 'vigilant management of human affairs' focused upon the identification and classification of those human attributes that threatened the rational model of 'man'. Yet, in identifying and classifying these attributes, the aim was not to cast those who held them out of society. Unlike the leper colony of the pre-modern world, and the 'ship of fools' (Foucault 1967) at the beginning of the modern world, the chaos that threatened the rational ordering of things was to be disarmed, treated and assimilated within the realm of reason. Education became centrally concerned with the management and assimilation of a chaotic and delinquent population of youth.

Modernism was based upon an assumption of a society that defined the parameters of rational behaviour and sought to neutralise or absorb difference through mechanisms of inclusion. Exclusion operated on the margins of the accepted social order, not as a central defining process of social relationships. It was a mechanism for managing chaos that *for the moment* could not be understood and could not be rehabilitated within the prevailing social order. Exclusion represented an admission of the failure of the project of modernity and for that reason the violence of its response could be extreme. The thrust of the modernist project was towards assimilation. Social progress was embodied in the successful incorporation of difference within a reality that was fairly homogenous and therefore unchaotic. The assimilation project of modernity extended across all areas of social life. It formed, for example, a cornerstone of the policy of empire. Similarly, it was central to the introduction and expansion of a system of universal education towards the end of the nineteenth century. The 'chaos' of national and tribal differences was assimilated into the order of empire in just the same way as working class youth (demonised for the 'chaos' and disorder of their lives) were assimilated into socially useful labour by the inclusivity of the factory and the school.

Throughout the twentieth century, education was at the cutting edge of the modernist project of assimilation. The refinement of procedures for testing and measuring children's abilities and performance created possibilities for maximising the effectiveness of schooling as a system for maintaining social control and perpetuating social roles and rewards.

Post-war reform and its contradictions

The years following the end of the Second World War witnessed wide-ranging social reform. Education was at the centre of the reform movement. Education was a key to change in society, both for reformers who saw it as the catalyst and vehicle for realising the aspirations of the masses, and for those at the forefront of the new economic revival who saw it as the means of preparing a skilled and motivated workforce.

Post-war educational reform can be understood as an attempt to engineer a society in which the needs of all citizens were addressed through schools which were designed to meet their different needs. Society may be highly differentiated but the engineering of social reform continued to be framed by the boundaries of a homogeneous social order. Each person has a place and knows that place and its boundaries. Education, rather than excluding the child from participation in society, in fact located the child and provided opportunities within society. Yet this process of inclusion did nothing to challenge the nature of this social order as one within which diversity must be assimilated and therefore controlled. The 'inclusive' character of these reforms is suggested by what McCulloch has described as 'education as a civic project'.

> 1944 could be read as the high-water mark of education as a civic project in this country. Educational reform was seen not only as a means of achieving equality of opportunity, but also as a way to enhance citizenship. This project involved a strong sense of the power of education to foster social solidarity and cohesion. (1994: 93)

However, McCulloch goes on to argue that although the reforms of the 1940s pursued a strongly civic goal, they lacked the means to achieve it, contradicted as it was by the tripartite divisions of 'academic', 'technical' and 'vocational' education that lay at the heart of the 1944 Act. It has been widely argued that the 1944 Education Act was a compromise, and a compromise that diverted the education policy agenda away from a transformatory politics.

The introduction of compulsory post-elementary education established the principle that all children are educable and therefore that their educational needs should be met within the school system. This was a profoundly inclusive policy but it also had consequences that encouraged the growth of separate forms of education for different types of child. While the Act introduced the principle of 'education for all', it organised this universal education on the basis of a differential understanding of children's 'academic', 'technical' and 'vocational' educational needs. The tripartite system therefore was incapable of challenging the hierarchies of social and economic power and privilege embedded within it. The tripartite system of education introduced by the 1944 Act, despite reformist ambitions, had ultimately been concerned with engineering a cohesive and inclusionary social system which maintained power in the hands of dominant social interests. The expansion of a fourth stream of separate special education for those who could not manage in, or would not be managed by, the secondary modern sector, was similarly concerned with including all sections of the child population, even the most troublesome, within a single differentiated but interrelated system. However, by the 1960s a new surge of reform was challenging the inadequacies of the 1944 Act.

The struggle to sustain educational reform

The comprehensive education reforms of the 1960s implicitly challenged the logic of separate systems for different types of child. Inclusion in a single system of education was demanded as a human right together with equal access to educational opportunities for progression. By 1970, comprehensive schools had triumphed. However, although they had succeeded in discrediting and supplanting the secondary modern schools, the outcome was one in which the grammar school and the secondary modern school 'were yoked together under a single label, but the resilient traditions of differentiation remained as active as ever' (Galloway 1985: 29).

By the 1970s, there existed a large and costly system of special educational provision outside of the mainstream school sector that largely catered for 'troublesome' children with learning difficulties and behavioural problems. Yet, as Tomlinson's (1981) study of the assessment of children identified as 'educationally subnormal' showed, the procedures for categorising educational needs in terms of 'handicap' were often the product of different and competing professional interests. Assessments tended to be based on assumptions that were rarely made explicit by professionals. These were derived from professionals' perceptions of their own roles and interests rather than from any 'objective' assessment of the child's needs. The system of categorisation served in practice to reinforce the 'expertise' of professionals while operating as a bureaucratically convenient, if crude, mechanism for rationalising the redistribution of resources encouraged by the civic project of the 1944 Act. Special education had assumed a logic of its own in which it simply served the interests of the mainstream sector by removing troublesome children and the interests of professional groups whose 'specialist' identities were legitimated by the continuing existence of the system.

The politics of 'need'

The Warnock Committee, set up in 1974 in response to a growing disenchantment with the 1944 framework, was to have wide-ranging influence upon the subsequent development of special educational policy and practice. The Warnock Report has to be seen within the overall context of an attempt to construct a more rational framework for identifying and dealing with children failing in the mainstream school system, but, for the first time, it recognised schools as a context within which children's educational needs might be created. This is significant because it implies that the educational needs of a child may vary according to factors occurring within the school attended.

The 'discovery' by the Warnock Committee of 18 per cent of children within mainstream school with 'special educational needs' can be seen as reflecting concern about the academic failure of large numbers of children within the mainstream sector and a critique of the school system. This discovery was revealed in the wake of the raising of the school leaving age to 16 and at a time when there was a growing crisis of youth unemployment accompanied by concerns about delinquency and social disaffection. In the context of an enforced extension of compulsory education for young people who neither wanted it nor benefited from it, together with restricted employment opportunities, the educational label of 'special needs' conveniently legitimated the educational and socio-economic disadvantages experienced by young people. It embodied an ideology of individual failure (be it failure of the child or of the school) that delegitimated any discussion of 'inclusion' in the context of a wider political critique of the social relations within which education policy is framed and contested. In this respect, the Warnock Report can best be understood in relation to the collapse of the post-war social compromise.

The regulation of failure

Regulation theorists have argued that the institutions of the state are underpinned by modes of regulation which institutionalise conflict and confine it within certain parameters compatible with the maintenance of social order. The intervention of the state in education thus became a central feature of state formation in the late nineteenth and early twentieth centuries. The social compromise of 1945 lay in the preservation of the dominant values of capitalism. It did so through the creation of mechanisms to alleviate the social cost endemic in the incoherence of economic individualism. These mechanisms included the partial regulation of markets through the intervention of the state, and the regulation of social disadvantage through the welfare state. Whereas liberal individualism had represented rights as asserted always in defense of private interests, welfare rights were acknowledged as legitimate claims on the state to support those people who were most disadvantaged by capitalist forms of production and distribution (see Wood, Chapter 12 for a brief discussion about welfare rights and citizenship). However, the justification for such intervention was not primarily moral. Rather, it lay in attempts to correct and improve upon the market in order to optimise the allocation to choices through the 'Pareto principle', which maintains that improvements in the social condition of one individual which do not make others worse off, are ethically neutral. The provision of welfare benefits is, in theory, a form of insurance to which all members of society potentially have access.

Needs theory has had a central place within the welfare rights discourse and been a significant feature of the development of special education systems across Europe since 1945. There was an assumption that educational needs could be accurately assessed by reference to some assumed minimum or norm that then legitimated the redistribution of 'social' wealth. Significant deviations from the norm would be identified as indicative of 'special' needs requiring the allocation of compensatory resources. Thus, needs theory retained the focus upon the individual that was characteristic of pre-war liberalism, while advocating the role of the state as the protector or guardian of citizens against the anarchy of private interests. The role of social democracy was to regulate competing individual interests while providing a cushion of support for those whose needs were marginalised by the social outcomes of this competition. This view of social democracy assumed that the state is neutral, yet such a representation is deeply problematic.

The society in which we live is one where production for profit remains the basic organising principle of economic life, requiring the disciplining of labour power to the purposes of capital accumulation. This in turn gives rise to contradictions in the regulatory role of the state in social and economic life. The viability of the welfare state lay in the provision of a context that supported the accumulation of capital. However, welfare policies exposed the contradictions between the political role of the state in legitimating the accumulation of capital and the economic consequences for the capitalist system of the appropriation of surplus value by the state.

The Warnock Committee's proposal that almost 20 per cent of children would have special educational needs at some point in their school lives highlights the contradictions within and between the political and economic domains of capital accumulation in four ways:

> *First*, the identification of almost 20 per cent of children with special needs represented a logical extension of post war policies supporting the inclusion of marginalised children under the protection of the welfare state. It was one of the policies that comprised the post-war social contract between capital and labour, facilitating the continued accumulation of capital.
> *Second*, it was the outcome of political agitation for humanitarian reform that was independent of the interests of capital accumulation. In other words it reflected the discontinuities and contradictions between the political interests of capital and the constitution and policies of the state.
> *Third*, this recommendation legitimated the rising youth unemployment of the 1970s resulting from economic downturn and the crisis of capital accumulation. It presented a policy solution to growing concerns about how the consequences of economic crisis were being reflected in delinquency and social disaffection among young people.
> *Fourth*, it turned attention toward mainstream schools and the inadequacies of curricula and pedagogic practices, proposing an alternative special educational discourse based upon school reform and inclusion within the mainstream school.

In advocating a policy of inclusion the Warnock Committee, whether intentionally or not, was responding to the rapidly changing political and economic agendas of the late 1970s. This agenda was famously initiated by James Callaghan's Ruskin College speech, which demanded new systems of flexibility, accountability and, most of all, cost-effectiveness from educational services.

The logic of replacing categories of handicap with a general and relativistic concept of special educational needs would be to move towards curricular responses, yet the Warnock Report opted for an organisational and bureaucratic response of individual identification. The upsurge in statements of special educational needs in the 1990s, particularly for 'moderate learning difficulties' and 'emotional and behavioural difficulties', suggests that struggles around these questions impact strongly upon the construction of policy as practice. In practice, categories are frequently recreated both as a resource management mechanism by local education authorities and as a tool for prizing additional resources out of the system by schools and, increasingly, by organised parent groups. The fundamental role of categorisation as a tool for managing resources is ignored in the Warnock Report.

The politics of 'inclusion'

By the 1980s, a new era had begun in which much of the responsibility for Britain's alleged lack of industrial competitiveness was laid squarely at the door of those who had championed the post-war civic project. Education as a vehicle for advancing social justice had given way to 'personal choice' theories. These celebrated the rights of the individual and the role of education as a commodity to be traded in the market place and to be employed as social capital (see Boeck, Chapter 8). An emphasis upon 'professional judgement' was clearly out of step with the criticisms of teachers and schools that climaxed with the 1988 Education Reform Act. At the time, advocates of a more integrated system of education saw this viewpoint as supporting reform of mainstream schools to make them more inclusive, which it may indeed have been. It was certainly quite explicitly opposed to child deficit notions of learning difficulties. Moreover, it did go some way towards recognising the importance of the relationship between power and needs. Yet, it failed to fully acknowledge the powerful role of professional interests in defining needs. In the absence of effective mechanisms for protecting the child's interests where that interest might be in conflict with those of more powerful groups, a child-deficit model of needs was inevitably perpetuated. The labelling of individuals or sections of the community as 'needy' carries with it the implication that they lack the power and/or resources to be self-determining. It reinforces the social power of those who are in a position to define the needs of others.

A new discourse centred on the failure of schooling highlighted the ideological ground upon which debates about education would be focused from that time to the present day: the changing relationship between education and the economy. This approach reinforced the centralisation of control over education in the hands of government together with the expansion of surveillance and control. The birth of the 'audit society', in which economic accountability reconceptualised the social purpose of schooling, opened the doors to cost-benefit analyses as the measure of educational outcomes and the value and effectiveness of schools. Ironically, it also pushed the 'inclusion debate' into the mainstream of policy pronouncements. In his foreward to the government's 1997 Green Paper on special education, the Secretary of State for Education, David Blunkett, argued that the underlying principle of inclusion is that of improving achievement:

> Good provision for SEN does not mean a sympathetic acceptance of low achievement. It means a tough-minded determination to show that children with SEN are capable of excellence. Where schools respond in this way, teachers sharpen their ability to set high standards for *all* pupils. (DfEE 1997: 4)

It is particularly interesting that the language used to talk about 'inclusion' in the Green Paper is that of the market (the salability of achievement) rather than of the social inclusion of difference and diversity.

A political programme for social and economic inclusion centred upon the value of educational achievement in the market place resurrected the human capital theory of education and training and did little to challenge the inequalities that underpin the exclusion of those with limited exchange-value in the market place of employment. Human capital theories of education do little to advance the interests of young people and adults with learning difficulties who are increasingly excluded from the labour market. Moreover, the policy rhetoric of inclusion disguises the financial imperatives that are reigning in the redistribution of goods and services according to 'need'. In other words, the irony here may be that 'inclusive' education becomes the rhetoric that legitimates the withdrawal of an inclusive, if imperfect, system of social welfare.

Educational ideologies and the reconstruction of educational purpose

Wilfred Carr and Anthony Hartnett, in their book *Education and the Struggle for Democracy,* argued that in a society which takes democracy seriously, issues about the ways in which teachers are themselves educated will always be central to the public educational debate (1996: 195). On the other hand, as these authors also noted, part of the ideological strategy of the political right is the creation of widespread public concern about teacher education through the adoption of a rhetoric of 'teaching quality', 'professional competence' and 'good practice'. By doing so, the problems of society are defined in ways that presume the inadequacies of the school system in meeting the new forms of society that have emerged and are articulated in the ideologies of neo-liberalism. The pedagogical model underpinning the neo-liberal educational ideology is fundamentally anti-democratic because it denies legitimacy to educational debate about the form and content of education. It constructs an ideological model of educational value and purpose that is then to be implemented as a technological project. Educational debate is prejudged by the ideology of neo-liberalism. Teaching is represented as a value-free technical activity. 'Good practice' becomes no more than a 'bureaucratically framed specification of competencies and skills' (Carr and Hartnett 1996: 195). In the absence of professional autonomy grounded in developing their students' capacity for democratic deliberation, critical judgement and rational understanding, teachers 'quickly become neutral operatives implementing the "directives" of their political masters and mistresses' (Carr and Hartnett 1996: 195).

The place of education in any society and the competing pedagogies through which particular outcomes are pursued are constituents in the history and contestation of democracy. Education systems are contextualised by their histories and the struggles that have formed and shaped their role, but they are also given meaning by their futures and the aspirations that we have for the kind of society that we want to achieve. In the modern world, education systems are central to the contestation of political and social values. Educators, as citizens, are participants in those struggles. In this process the meaning of democracy is emergent and evolving. Pedagogy is political in the sense that it may be democratic, reflective, critical, participatory, tolerant and non-hierarchical, or it may be authoritarian, based upon received meaning, uncritical applications of knowledge, certainty about 'standards', and belief in competencies as the measure of the 'good' citizen. But education cannot be defined in terms of an unremitting pursuit of ideological interests. That is a contradiction.

What is schooling for?

The crisis of purpose in education is a worldwide crisis, but it also reflects a wider process of redefinition of the character and role of the state. The neo-liberal critique of education claims that traditional, state controlled systems have lacked both the flexibility and the will to respond imaginatively to the challenges of the new times in which we live. Education systems are seen as part of the bureaucracy of post-war welfare idealism gone wrong; one element in an egalitarian utopia that has atrophied on the one hand into a dependency creating system of pity, and on the other hand into a system that stifles opportunity and initiative by the imposition of mediocrity. It is argued that public education no longer demonstrates 'fitness for purpose' because the purpose towards which it directs its energies is located in a world that no longer exists and is based on an ideology that is no longer relevant. What so animates neo-liberal politicians is their belief that the education system is holding society back while unproductively consuming considerable, potentially wealth creating, resources.

The modern discourses of 'accountability', of 'standards', of 'choice and diversity', are central both to the re-conceptualisation of purpose in education and to the management of youth through the school system. This trend is not limited to schools, and is seen increasingly in youth services (Davies, Chapter 16) and other forms of work with young people under the guise of 'managerialism' (Tyler, Chapter 19). What is happening is, in part, an attempt to reign in what is seen as a burgeoning state bureaucracy. It is about a disinvestment in the state; a refusal to see the role of the state as being to provide educational opportunities and support as a right. This reflects a belief in self-help as well as a belief that the state is a self-reproducing bureaucracy that diverts resources from the creative and wealth-producing sectors of society into systems of administration and welfare support that reinforce the dependency of the poor on those same bureaucracies. For neo-liberals this is not simply a commitment to the interests of the rich over the poor. Nor does it entail a lack of interest in the poor. It follows instead from the view that the position of the less advantaged is best improved by giving more entrepreneurial members of society the freedom to generate wealth, which necessarily, through increased employment opportunities, will filter down to the less well off. The second strand to the neo-liberal argument, however, is that in breaking the dependency of low-income groups on welfare they too will become more entrepreneurial and wealth generating members of society. What stands in the way of this goal is the state itself, or at least that element of the state bureaucracy that works against the interests of the market.

Yet the state, in fact, retains considerable power and authority within the neo-liberal world. As Andrew Gamble (1988) has argued, what characterises modern government is the project of creating a free economy and a strong state. In other words, minimalist state involvement in the social sphere contrasting with a strengthening of the capacity of the state within the parameters of the authority that it continues to assert. This is evident in arenas of international affairs and internal security. Paradoxically, the power of the state is also evident within those very domains, such as education, that are attacked for their interference with the freedom of the market. In this respect the authority of the state is used to reduce the influence of those groups who stand outside the neo-liberal project – trade unions, teacher organisations, political opponents.

The centralisation of power within the state apparatus increasingly involves the state in the regulation of its institutions and agencies whilst at the same time deregulating the context within which they operate. Diversity of provision is encouraged, private schools are advantaged over public schools, universities are deregulated and forced into self-privatisation in the face of funding cuts and moves towards a free market for providers. Simultaneously, the state is busily enhancing its control over the declining public sector. Schools face greater regulation and control over what can be taught and how. Likewise, universities are shackled by the interference of government in their operations.

Conclusion: education as a democratic practice

The challenges are immense. It is insufficient merely to propose alternative models of education that are more enriching or inclusive. One of the biggest challenges is that of developing a democratic practice based upon a critical questioning of the social and political interests that inform and are served by educational policy and practice. To be critical is to take risk, but questioning what the powerful would have us believe must be at the heart of any aspirations we have towards a democratic society. To question the institutionalisation of dominant ideas by the application of scientific method is to conceptualise the educational process as democratic, but also places those engaged in this work in a highly political realm. This is not to say that the practice of educators is political in an ideological sense. Quite the reverse: it would be equally anti-democratic to simply oppose dominant ideas. Education as a democratic activity requires critical dialogue with all ideas, practices and structures. Antonia Darder has referred to this as a creative and often intuitive process that:

> helps teachers discover new ways of being with their students in the classroom and new ways of introducing experiences that can effectively assist students to connect more deeply with their own critical capacities, in order to explore the world and understand themselves more fully. (2002: 93)

This requires that the skills of dialogue be placed at the centre of the learning process.

Paulo Freire believed that intuition and dreaming are necessary elements of a pedagogy committed to critical human development. The world is shaped in communion with history. This approach to pedagogy is familiar to teachers. Teaching is after all a creative art. Its success depends upon the creation of a learning context in which there is synergy between those mutually engaged in the processes of learning and teaching and connects with the experiences brought to the learning encounter by all those involved. To define teaching simply in terms of the transmission of knowledge is to be uncritical about what and how knowledge is constituted. It is also to disembody learning from the processes of human dialogue, both in the present and with the past. Learning always involves a revisiting and a reconstitution of the truth through critical dialogue. Teaching strategies are most effective when they arise from the critical capacity of teachers to listen to their students and engage actively with the process of learning. The creativity of teaching lies in this constant critical interaction with the learner in the interrogation of truth and the exploration of what Raymond Williams (1989) called 'the possibilities of common life'.

Participation and dissent are central to democratic life and the possibilities of common life. For educators these possibilities are revealed through dialogue with students and in dialogues with the communities of policy and practice with whom they work. They centre upon an exploration of the relationship between everyday experiences and attempts to build an understanding of the world and of practice through dialogical reflection and critical generalisations (Chouhan, Chapter 6). It cannot simply be concerned with the accumulation and transmission of knowledge and competencies; it is an educator's duty to interrogate what is meant by knowledge and how it is formed and to understand the limits of competency. Educators are engaged in a process of human inquiry that makes them human. As Freire and Macedo argued, 'For apart from inquiry, apart from the praxis, individuals cannot be truly human. Knowledge emerges only through invention and reinvention, through the restless, impatient, continuing, hopeful inquiry human beings pursue in the world, with the world, and with each other'(1998: 69).

It is by dreaming this future that we can begin to understand our responsibilities and through the questioning of truth recognise our lives as unfinished.

Reflective questions for practice

- **Reflect on the educational systems that young people are involved in. What are these designed to prepare them for?**
- **In what ways are young people segregated in the education system?**
- **How are the needs of different young people identified, and what action is taken as a result?**
- **In what ways can you develop a 'democratic practice' in your own educational work with young people?**

Further reading

Freire, P. (1996) *Pedagogy of the Oppressed*, **London: Penguin.** This classic text critically reviews the purpose of education, drawing on the author's own experience as an adult educator working with the Brazilian poor.

8

SOCIAL CAPITAL AND YOUNG PEOPLE

Thilo Boeck

Key arguments

- Young people engage with others through a variety of associations forming many different types of networks. Social capital encapsulates the differences in these types of networks.
- Social capital is seen as a social resource that can give access to opportunities, education, the labour market, and can lead to collective efficacy. It is thus often seen as matched to policy concerns.
- Alignment with policy concerns can fail to recognise how social capital is influenced by the stereotypes of an area and assumptions made about its residents and young people.
- Using the analogy of 'harbour', 'setting sail' and 'navigation', we can understand how young people move between closed, 'static' networks to more open, 'dynamic' networks.
- Young people have to be recognised as valid and valued contributors to social capital, and practitioners need to facilitate environments where they can enhance and nurture dynamic social capital.

Introduction

Working with young people poses some fundamental questions, not only about our own world view, principles and values but also about the way in which we relate to young people and how we perceive their position in our society. We also cannot ignore the policy environment or the aims and objectives of the organizations we are working with. The social capital debate is one which will have a direct impact on our organisations, funding opportunities and on our practice. This will ultimately have a direct impact on the lives of young people and how practitioners will interact with them.

Practitioners, organisations and students face dilemmas in finding a compromise between apparently conflicting forces within their work (a theme discussed by Tyler in Chapter 19). Quite heated debates are often generated between people who seem to come from similar perspectives, but disagree strongly when it comes to addressing both the practices and the fundamental question of 'what is our task and role as youth workers?'.

Practitioners with vast experience often challenge this author: 'It is easy for you to speak about transformative action, about tackling the root causes of discrimination and social injustice ... but if you are there out in the field, you will see that reality is different: constantly battling for funding, restrictive policies and the ever changing field of government policies and priorities.'

If these concerns and questions sound familiar, this chapter might contribute to disentangling some of these questions in relation to the enhancement of social capital, and give pointers to how we can use current thinking and policy priorities in order to work in a transformative and participative way which gives young people the opportunities and tools to navigate the ever changing demands of daily life.

The outline of the chapter is as follows:

1 *What is social capital?* Explores the concept of social capital and its relevance to young people's lives
2 *Why is it important?* A look at some of the current issues about young people and why social capital is seen as important. The section concludes with a critical reflection
3 *How can you enhance social capital?* This section highlights some of the underlying principles for the enhancement of social capital and looks at some practice implications

What is social capital?

Young people engage with others through a variety of associations forming many different types of networks. Sometimes each of these networks has different sets of norms, trust and reciprocity. Social networks are not only important in terms of emotional support but also crucial in giving people more opportunities, choice and power (Boeck et al. 2006). However, there can be significant differences between the types of networks people have, not only in quantity but also in quality. The concept of social capital can encapsulate these differences.

Social capital is a complex and varied phenomenon (Field 2003) and because of this debates on its meaning and how it can be explored or measured are still rife

(Halpern 2005). Another factor which quite often adds to the confusion is that the concept of social capital is being used in all sorts of arenas, without much clarity about its implications for policy and practice development. Most definitions revolve around the notion of 'social networks, the reciprocities that arise from them, and the value of these for achieving mutual goals' (Baron et al. 2001: 1). As such social capital is seen as a set of relationships and interactions that have the potential to be transformative (Weller 2007). Taking this into account we might define social capital in the following way:

Defining social capital

Social capital is a resource that stems from the bulk of social interactions, networks and network opportunities that either people or communities have within a specific environment. This environment is characterised by a commonality of mutual trust and reciprocity and informed by specific norms and values.

There are different types of social capital which are important in different situations, or moments in our life. These types are shaped through:

- The types of networks (similar or diverse, outward or inward looking).
- Specific and shared norms and values.
- The type of community (location, interest, identity, faith, etc.).
- Power and economic resources.

Adapted from Boeck et al. 2006

Many authors tend to make a distinction between different types of social capital: bonding, bridging and linking. *Bonding social capital* resides in family and friendship relationships, and peer groups that provide a sense of belonging in the here and now. *Bridging social capital* is, as it sounds, about creating links with people outside our immediate circles. These networks can be very important for broadening our opportunities and horizons. Putman (2000) considers the distinction between bridging and bonding to be of crucial importance, highlighting what he considers to be some of their consequences: 'Bonding social capital is … good for "getting by" but bridging social capital is crucial for "getting ahead"' (Putnam 2000: 23; see also Field 2003). Thus, bridging social capital is seen to generate broader identities and reciprocity, whereas bonding social capital bolsters our narrower selves. This reflects Granovetter's (1973) writings about the 'strengths of weak ties' which are said to have a strong cohesive power and positively influence mobility opportunity. *Linking social capital* is about access to influential others and power structures (Woolcock 2001).

Only recently, research attention has begun to focus on young people and social capital (Raffo and Reeves 2000; Holland 2005; Holland et al. 2007; Schaefer-McDaniel 2004; Morrow 1999, 2001, 2004; Weller 2007). In this setting the ideas about social capital have been applied to young people's friendship and socialising networks formed in their neighbourhoods, schools, leisure and interest groups, as a way of examining whether these are helpful in enabling young people to move on in their lives and access jobs, training and education, or whether they act to hold them back and deter them from trying new things. A key theme within these studies has been the 'extent to which young people access and/or generate social capital and exhibit agency in its acquisition and deployment' (Holland 2005: 2). This body of work draws (and expands) on the work of Putnam (2000) and Coleman (1997) with a special focus on Bourdieu's (1986) work and acknowledges the inter-relationship between social capital and wider structural factors in society. As such he has influenced researchers in questioning how underlying issues of race, class and gender impact upon individual social capital and the diverse ways they utilise this as a social resource in their everyday lives (Holland et al. 2007). It distances itself from an approach which treats urban youth as threats to civil society or views young people as passive consumers of civic life. This is embedded within a critical awareness of the systems and institutions that promote or hinder progress toward social equality and respect for human dignity (Noguera 2005).

This chapter will focus on social capital from a social justice and social inclusion perspective, embedded in ideologies of democratic empowerment and change that are sensitive to children's and young people's rights and civil liberties (Chawla and Malone 2002: 129). As such social capital is seen as a *social resource* (Holland et al. 2007; Weller 2007) that can give access to opportunities, education and the labour market and can lead to collective efficacy. Traditionally these social resources have been viewed as a quality of adult social networks that may provide benefits to adults and children (Spilsbury and Korbin 2004: 193). This chapter will look at how these social resources are a quality of young people's social networks.

Other perspectives place stress on social capital as the 'glue' of society. For example, Putnam's (2000) notion of social capital as a community asset – which has heavily influenced New Labour's social policy – emphasises civic engagement as in membership of local non-governmental organisations. Norms of reciprocity and trust among community members seem to focus on the maintenance of the social system, specifically cohesion and social order, and thus aim for integration into mainstream society. Within this analysis, values provide general guidelines for behaviour and they are translated into more specific directives in terms of roles and norms (see Armstrong, Chapter 7 and Wood, Chapter 16 for examples of similar policy approaches).

Both perspectives have much to contribute but also might lead to further stigmatising some groups of young people, labelling them as 'anti-social' or 'a nuisance' if they do not conform to certain types of social capital. A careful exploration of young people's own perspectives of values, norms and views of society is needed, a theme evident in Hine's discussion around understanding the real worlds of young people (Chapter 3).

A perspective which tries to integrate the above perspectives can be described through the analogy of 'The Harbour, Setting Sail and Navigation'. To illustrate some application to young people's lives, the author draws on his recent research that investigated young people and social capital.[1]

The 'Harbour' can be a safe space, but for many young people it can be a place where they feel trapped. The social capital is more static and young people tend to interact with other, similar young people. Networks are based upon their immediate locale of the street, local park and home and are characterised by a strong sense of belonging (Boeck et al. 2006; Hine and Kemshall 2006; Morrow 2002a). Previous research such as that by Morrow (2004) and MacDonald and Marsh (2001) has noted that networks of family, kin and peers emerged as important aspects of their analysis of youth and youth transitions. Morrow identifies place and neighbourhood as influencing 'how or whether young people were able to access the relationships that are so important to their sense of belonging' (Morrow 2004: 216). As one young woman indicated in our study around social capital:

> we are all alike, because we like to go out and have a good time together ... We know the same people, we hang around the same area, we like the same things, we like the same ... clothes. I don't know, some people I can trust, some people I can't.

The neighbourhood is a place to socialise but paradoxically young people often do not feel that they belong to the neighbourhood, but rather feel quite detached from it. Within this, 'a sense of safety' and 'knowing other young people who hang around these places' seemed to be interlinked (see also Morrow 2004). Tight bonded networks were often small and static in nature.

Worms asserts that close observation of tenement housing reveals a labyrinth of discrete but active sociability networks:

> Locked in a form of social exile, inhabitants fall back on the immediate vicinity to create primary sociability networks indispensable for personal and social identity ... Networks of sociability between neighbours help solve daily practical problems or defend against outside threats. ... (2004: 161–162)

This might lead to a protective/narrow trust, which is more inward looking and reciprocity is characterised by an immediate or even no sense of return. Within this environment there is a danger young people's outlook on life can become restricted and often less optimistic, with a feeling that their own actions (agency) will have little impact on their life course.

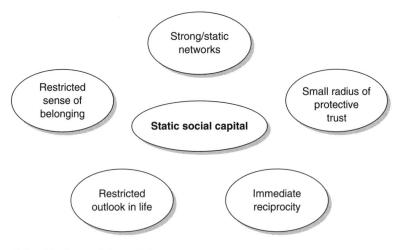

Figure 8.1   Static social capital

Q: What do you think you'll be doing in a year's time?
A: F*** knows.
Q: Next week?
A: Dunno. Slopping out.

(Young man, interview 11)

This can be referred to as static social capital (Boeck et al. 2006). However important it might seem to be for the individual ultimately it seems to diminish self and group efficacy (to act/be different). Quite often these young people tend to be 'risk averse' in the sense of being unable or unwilling to take the risk to leave their present situation, immediate network and locale.

Figure 8.1 draws together some of the individual and social aspects which define 'static social capital' i.e. 'the Harbour'.

To 'Navigate' means that young people have the resources to interact with different groups of other young people and adults: they draw from a more dynamic social capital. Within these different networks some young people show a more complex diversity, especially within groups from different places such as the school, the local area, interest groups or identity groups:

I have different friendship groups, like college friends, friends from work, friends from your old school, things like that.

(Young man, focus group 10)

The diverse networks are varied and dynamic in nature and young people engage in a varied range of activities with more choice in how to spend their free time.

> Different groups … Different family and friends, different roles in each one … You speak to them differently you treat them differently, family and friends…
>
> (Young man, focus group 10)

Trust is more about feeling comfortable with each other and a sense of camaraderie. Reciprocity is characterised by generalised and positive sense of return.

> It's the trust in the sense that you have to trust them (friends and other people) in such a way to get forward in life, if you don't trust them you won't move forward, do you know what I am saying?
>
> (Young woman, focus group 12)

> We are allowed to do what we want as long as it is within reason, there aren't any restrictions on what we can do, parents trust us more.
>
> (Young man, focus group 9)

Friends are more diverse within the family and school environment. This combined with a more supportive neighbourhood environment and seeing themselves as part of the school community and other alternative communities and groups, creates the necessary field for young people to develop bridging social capital.

Class is still highly relevant when it comes to the access of these diverse resources. Some studies (Evans 2002; Noguera 2005; Walther et al. 2005 Holland et al. 2007) suggest that for young people from poorer backgrounds the access to different 'leisure activities', opportunities to travel and having a diverse access to different groups is still denied through their class position. The networks of some young people from more affluent backgrounds were widespread, consisting of various local points of intensification. This enabled them to access diverse networks in terms of social space and territory. There are examples illustrating that by tapping into the social and cultural capital of their parents, young people can establish a countrywide network which they realised through the contacts of their parents. For other young people the networks expand through belonging to interest groups (such as music and sport). Consequently, Walther et al. state that 'for transitions to work, it is crucial that the socio-spatial structure of networks extends beyond the immediate context of everyday life and contains exit options from social origin' (2005: 225).

The following figure draws together some of the individual and social aspects which define 'dynamic social capital' i.e. 'Navigation'.

To be able to move between 'being at the harbour' and 'to navigate' plays a key part in young people's lives, not only in terms of their well-being but also in the creation of new opportunities and identities. As such social capital helps us to

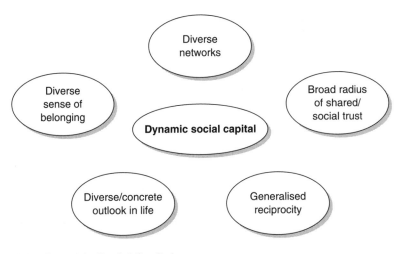

Figure 8.2   Dynamic Social Capital

understand the social context within which youth transitions occur and how the agency of young people is bounded 'by the surrounding opportunity structure' (MacDonald and Marsh 2001: 383).

Why is it important?

One of the emphases within government policy for children and young people is to enhance their social capital to prevent them encountering problems such as poverty and crime and to improve educational achievement, by encouraging volunteering and civic participation (ONS 2003). Essentially, the (re)integration of young people into normative social structures has been seen as a question of improving their social networking and life chances – the development of their social capital. Within this broader perspective the inclusion of young people in decision-making and organisational structures has been one of the central themes of policy on children and young people of the Labour Government (see DfES 2003). Government schemes have also begun to encourage young people's involvement in the community (explored in Davies' Chapter 16).

The next sections explore some links between social capital and current policy priorities. While there are overlaps between the sections the first section which refers to cohesion is embedded in a perspective which looks at social capital as 'the glue of society'. The other sections –'risk taking'/crime, employment and inclusion – are embedded in a perspective which looks at social capital as a 'social resource'.

Young people and 'cohesion'

Research originating within the voluntary sector and based on a youth work perspective has often been based on concepts of young people's capacity to form strong social networks, and the influence of youth work approaches on young people's ability to contribute to community capacity (Cutler and Frost 2002). The voluntary youth sector's approach to social capital is rooted in the parallel concept of 'community cohesion' which became a focus of discussion in the aftermath of the rioting which swept through inner city communities in Leeds, Oldham, Burnley and Bradford in the summer of 2001. As Denham (2001) and Cantle (2001) have noted, the principal (but by no means, the only) participants in these riots were young people under 25. It was subsequently posited in a number of Government reports that part of the reason for the sudden breakdown in law and order in those towns and cities had been a breakdown of Denham's concept of community cohesion: or respect for core social values, reciprocal rights of community members and the identification of common goals in spite of religious and cultural differences (Denham 2001). There is strong evidence to suggest that youth work can help to build social capital within heavily segregated communities. Thomas' (2003) research with white and Asian young people in Oldham explores their feelings about community cohesion in their neighbourhoods, and comes to the conclusion that youth work is a strong force for the formation of social capital among otherwise marginalised young people, and can overcome some of the problems brought about by the conditions of space and place in communities.

'Risk taking' and crime

Research has found that desistence from offending and heroin use was aided by the support of family members and partners and the leaving behind of earlier social networks that encouraged crime and drug use (see for example, Webster et al. 2004).

'Risk pathways' and offending are linked to notions of 'static' or 'dynamic' social capital. Boeck et al.'s (2006) study suggests that young offenders or those 'at risk' are typified by their static social capital (i.e. strong bonds to a limited group, a protective and narrow radius of trust, a restricted sense of belonging and a less optimistic and often fatalistic outlook in life). Static social capital might be the context within which to take risks (e.g. commit crime), but paradoxically it restricts the capacity to take risks associated with 'moving on', or to negotiate the risks associated with normal life transitions.

A focus on social capital as a resource and as the social context within which people negotiate everyday life would involve paying attention to locale, peers, networks, and the social resources to which people have access. Work with 'at risk' people would need to strengthen resilience by enabling them to enhance 'dynamic' and bridging social capital.

Creating access to employment

There seems to be significant evidence of how social networks can create access to employment Field (2003). Half of young people in Spain in a 1996 survey had entered work thanks to family and friends; a study of young people who had grown up in the German Democratic Republic, found:

> that the individual's education played a more important role than the father's resources in finding work; nevertheless, nearly half of their sample had found work through informal channels, and in these cases it was often important to possess strong ties with highly prestigious contacts. (Field 2003: 51)

Raffo and Reeves (2000) found that the young people who draw on a more localised static social capital were:

> unaware of how to find work through agencies, job centres or even through friends and family. Their main avenues for hunting down jobs were highly localized, informal and linked to previous experiences of finding part-time work, i.e. local shop windows. (2000: 157)

Even in those cases where young people have access to multiple social resources within a restricted location, similar dynamics were found (Raffo and Reeves 2000; MacDonald and Marsh 2001; Walther et al. 2005). Young men in particular who restricted their contacts to those within their own neighbourhood or their own youth cultural scene reported that they found their networks a positive resource for finding jobs or apprenticeship posts. However the impact of these networks for finding jobs was limited, gaining access mainly to temporary work and assisting in the shops of relatives (Walther et al. 2005: 230). These very rarely lasted longer than a year and more often than not were part of a rapid sequence of temporary low-paid jobs (Raffo and Reeves 2000) interspersed with lengthy periods of idle unemployment.

Social exclusion/inclusion

MacDonald and Marsh (2001), have found that whilst connections to local networks could help in coping with the problems of 'social exclusion' and generate a sense of 'inclusion', paradoxically they could simultaneously limit the possibilities of escaping the conditions of 'social exclusion'. This might constrain horizons and lead to a pathway of restricted choice, restricted power to do otherwise, and restricted opportunity (Kemshall 2002; Boeck et al. 2006). Holland et al. (2007) highlight that many young people value bonding social capital during their transition phases as an important mechanism to bridge across into new networks and opportunities. Some, however, recognised their bonding networks as highly constraining, tying them into their community. While the networks allowed them to 'get by', they stifled individual progression and social mobility. For some, then, there was a strong desire to bridge, or 'move out' with education as a means to 'escape from the bubble' (Holland et al. 2007).

An example is that of sectarian communities in Northern Ireland. Some of the young men in Holland et al.'s (2007) study were totally embedded in the sectarian Northern Ireland youth culture, and all their social capital came from that association and those networks. This bonding social capital can provide young people with a strong sense of belonging, security and safety but also with few opportunities for interactions with other people including peers, that could help to generate new, informal and practical knowledge to start the process of dealing with the constraints in their lives and thus gain access to material, cultural or social resources.

Be critical!

One of the concerns about the policy focus on social capital is that it can be perceived as having a strong 'normative' element linked inevitably to political ideology. Social capital can be used within a neo-liberal agenda to provide subtle ways to regulate young people within communities through informal control and sanctions (Halpern 2005) and trying to achieve harmonisation and integration in society; thus, the enhancement of social capital could become part of a subtle regulation (Forbes and Wainwright 2001; Muntaner et al. 2000; Green 2002).

Quite often the debate on social capital which sees it as the 'glue of society' fails to recognise how social capital is influenced, among other facets, by the stereotypes of an area and assumptions made about its residents and young people. This might be reflected in the portrayal by government policy, the media, local policy, power structures and community services (see Boeck et al. 2001). Evers (2003: 15) asserts that social capital has not yet been 'linked systematically with the topics of power and inequalities; sometimes it even seems to divert our attention from their impact'. DeFilippis writes that social capital is a 'flawed concept because it fails to understand the issue of power in the productions of communities and because it is divorced from economic capital' (2001: 781). While this criticism is important, it is not valid for all models of social capital (e.g. Bourdieu 1986; Erben et al. 1999; Portes and Landolt 2000; Morrow 2001).

How can you enhance social capital?

The enhancement of social capital is a process which has to be embedded within young people's lives. Thus empowerment in the form of added social capital becomes a central theme within progressive youth work. As Chawla and Malone (2002: 129) put it, actual empowerment requires 'the appropriation of power by young people beyond just knowledge of the source of their disempowerment to opportunities to engage in activities to change their situation'. Young people have to be recognised as valid and valued contributors to social capital. It is about creating with young people environments where they can enhance and nurture dynamic social capital. Integral to this is the creation of opportunities and opening up new spaces where they can contribute authentically to the ongoing policy development and social and physical planning of their neighbourhoods and cities.

Setting sail

The notions of 'harbour' and 'navigation' have already been explored. This section explores how, as practitioners and policy makers we can support young people to 'set sail'.

'Setting sail' is about *enhancing dynamic social capital*. This is one of the factors (among economic, political, cultural) that will give young people power to support their ability to navigate the challenges everyday life presents them.

> Because it's different, you get sick of the same place. If I was to stay round my house, because I've been round mine all my life you just say oh God, I want to get away, I want a change, I want to get away from this, I want to meet new people so you just go away. See new people, meet them, say hello, get their numbers and meet up again sometime.
>
> (Young man, interview 17)

This is not about 'avoiding' risks but about having the resources to cope, manage and make informed choices in their lives.

> I don't think that I've got to a point where everything is closed off and the end of the line, there are end of line signs written all over the place. I think there are things that are closed now that weren't before, but it's not terminal, it doesn't stop quite as much, the sidings on some of the lines don't work whereas they would have done before, now they don't so you've got less options but still a big range, there's still a lot of them. It's not like there's only one option and that's it.
>
> (Young man, interview 6)

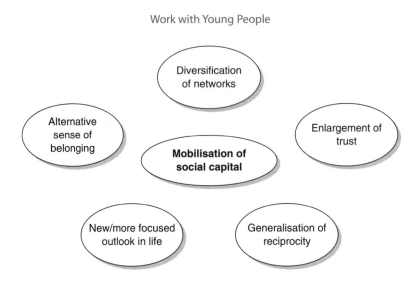

Figure 8.3   The mobilisation of social capital

It is about working with young people and not for them so they can set sail and have *more power and opportunities* in their lives.

> If you have got something to look forward to you are more willing to do it ain't you? If you ain't got nothing to look forward to there is nothing to live for is there? If you ain't got nothing there for you, no family, no job, no education no anything…

(Young woman, focus group 10)

Figure 8.3 shows some of the individual and social aspects which contribute to the 'mobilisation of social capital' i.e. 'Setting Sail'.

Young people need to have the possibility and the freedom to create, change and influence events within their life transitions. This personal and individual engagement is influenced but not determined by existing structures (Evans 2002) and is shaped by the experiences of the past, the chances present in the current moment and the perceptions of possible futures. The dynamic social capital can contribute to create the social sphere in which agency is nurtured and young people can act upon their rights as creators and critical citizens who have *power*: being able to have their voices heard, and have a part in decisions that affect them.

What can practitioners do?

Progressive youth work is about working with young people in participative ways to provide the opportunity to widen their horizons of what is possible. They support

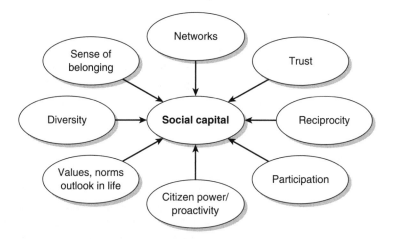

Figure 8.4   Social capital framework

young people to break out of a demoralising and self-perpetuating narrowness of vision, introspection and 'victim blaming' induced through poverty, lack of opportunity and exclusion. As such it is important to be aware of the structures of society and make them transparent to young people. It turns the spotlight round from people as a problem in themselves, to the problems they encounter, and enables them to see opportunities to develop a much wider range of options for action and change (Arches and Fleming 2006).

The enhancement of social capital has to distance itself from the 'deficit' and 'blaming the victim' approaches. It has to be based on a commitment to young people having the right to be heard, to define the issues facing them, to set the agenda for action and, importantly, to take action on their own behalf. Empowerment, participation and capacity release are core elements for the enhancement of social capital. Practitioners should recognise that while using – and sometimes being part of – the structures set up by the government, one is still able to be critical and able to promote structural, political and cultural change (see Chouhan, Chapter 6).

Through work with young people, adult volunteers and practitioners, and based upon existing research, a multi-faceted framework of social capital as a heuristic device for research, evaluation and practice has been developed (Boeck and Fleming 2005). This framework contains the key features of social capital and those factors which were seen as related to social capital or which might influence the enhancement and development of social capital (i.e. sense of belonging, outlook in life and power; Morrow 2002a: 138). The above framework has been adapted by many organisations to shape and inform their work with young people and communities.

Conclusion

By way of a conclusion, some of the areas within the social capital framework which might be useful for policy and practice development are highlighted here. In line with an empowering approach these questions and actions should be explored with young people in order to understand and integrate their perspectives, needs and priorities.

Reflective questions for practice

- **Diversification of networks:** Enhance networks of support and interaction. Discuss with young people, who is supporting them? Who is important to them? Explore ways for young people to meet and interact with new people and groups, different from their immediate locale of street, school and family.
- **Enlargement of trust:** Explore with young people who they trust and the meaning of trust. Work towards establishing strong trusting relationships within safe environments. Do they only trust a small number of people? How will they be able to take the risk to trust new people?
- **Generalisation of reciprocity:** Do they feel that they give and never get anything back? Do they always expect an immediate return? Do they feel that it is worth contributing to their groups, communities, society? Work with young people in participative ways to engage with others, work towards change in their neighbourhoods, communities or other groups. Encourage them to do things with other people.
- **New, more focused outlook in life:** How do they see their future? Do they think they can influence their future? This is about working with them in building their self-confidence, relating it to new networks and new trusting relationships. Work with young people to discover their skills and thus enhance their aspirations by encouraging them to take the risk of change.
- **Alternative self and sense of belonging:** How do they see themselves? As active or passive? If they feel trapped work on building up resilience, setting positive goals with a sense of achievement. Can they see themselves differently from how they are now?
- **Community effect:** What are the required community processes to nurture reciprocity and shared norms and values between young people and their communities? What contribution (benefits) does young people's community involvement make to the community of which they are members? Is this being recognised and valued by the community? To what extent does participation enhance the social capital of young people and the communities which they are part of?

- **Young people and organisations: What are the different relationships which young people form with and within organisations? What is their relationship with adults? Participative ways of working with young people should be nurtured. Power imbalances should be challenged.**

Further reading

Field, J. (2003) *Social Capital***, London: Routledge.** A useful introduction to social capital, through the theoretical underpinning of the subject, the empirical work that has been done to explore its operation, and the effect that it has had on policy making.

Note

1 The quotes from young people and analysis within this section are taken from the project, 'Young People, Social Capital and the Negotiation of Risk' which was part of the ESRC Network: 'Pathways into and out of Crime: Risk Resilience and Diversity' Grant number: L330253001.

9

COMMUNITY YOUTH DEVELOPMENT

Daniel F. Perkins

Key arguments

- **Community Youth Development (CYD) creates environments that encourage positive relationships between young people, peers and adults and enables young people to shape their own development, and that of the community.**
- **CYD relies on the natural process of youth development, is proactive and strengths based, uses intentional, planned activities and engages young people in their communities.**
- **Young people need opportunities for: positive relationships, the building of skills and competences, and for meaningful engagement in their own and the wider community's development.**
- **The model incorporates the six 'Cs' of: competence, confidence, connection, character, caring/compassion and contribution.**
- **Youth practitioners have a critical role to play in the promotion of the six 'Cs', and ultimately in the promotion of personal and environmental assets.**

Introduction

Youth development is a process that occurs as young people interact with all levels of their ecology and the systems within those levels, including the other people in their environment, such as family, peers, other adults, and members of their communities. This can lead to either positive or negative developmental and behavioral outcomes. Over the last century, the theoretical frameworks of the social sciences (e.g. psychology, sociology, and human development) have been dominated by deficit and risk thinking, often concerned with the 'youth problem' (France, Chapter 2). Indeed, complex and expensive services and programmes have been developed to address pathology and its symptoms (Benson 2003). While not misguided, the deficit-reduction paradigm may have unintentionally enhanced the over-professionalisation of care and civic disengagement (Benson 2003) certainly in evidence in specialist education, for instance (Armstrong, Chapter 7). This view has led to the belief that young people are characterised as problems to be managed or fixed (Wood, Chapter 12; Kemshall, Chapter 13). Within this framework the focus of our efforts is prevention.

While it is important to diminish the risks that face children and young people, this chapter presents a theoretical framework that postulates a two-prong strategy to reach the goal of providing an atmosphere that fosters fully functioning young people. The first and most explicit strategy involves the *promotion* of personal and social assets of young people (i.e. physical development, intellectual development, psychological and emotional development, and social development; see Table 9.1) as outlined in the seminal book sponsored by the United States' National Research Council and the Institute of Medicine (Eccles and Gootman 2002). The second strategy involves an implicit goal that *prevention* of risk behaviors among young people and decreasing of risk processes in their environment are necessary if we want young people to be fully functioning. However, while this second strategy is important and necessary, it is insufficient without simultaneously addressing the first strategy.

The Community Youth Development framework is derived from the resiliency research and positive youth development theory that emerged in the United States during the 1990s. This framework involves a shift away from concentrating on problems to concentrating on strengths and competencies for active engagement. To foster positive development from a community youth development framework requires supports and opportunities for skill and competency development and the utilisation of those newly acquired skills for the betterment of one's community. This chapter presents a theory of developing an exemplary young person; a young person who is healthy and who is 'thriving' (Lerner 2004). Lerner defines a thriving young person as:

an individual who – within the context of his or her individual set of physical and psychological characteristics and abilities – takes actions that serve his or her own well-being and, at the same time, the well-being of parent, peers, community, and society. (2004: 4)

A major premise of the community youth development framework is that young people can and should be actively engaged in their own development and the development of the world that surrounds them. Thus, thriving as defined by Lerner is considered an outcome of the community youth development framework.

Table 9.1   Personal and social assets that facilitate positive youth development aligned with six Cs of Community Youth Development

Asset category (Cs of positive youth development)	Individual assets
Physical development (competence)	Good health habits Good health risk management skills
Intellectual development (competence)	Knowledge of essential life skills Knowledge of essential vocational skills School success Rational habits of mind – critical thinking and reasoning skills In-depth knowledge of more than one culture Good decision-making skills Knowledge of skills needed to navigate through multiple cultural contexts
Psychological and emotional development (competence, confidence, character, caring/ compassion)	Good mental health including positive self-regard Good emotional self-regulation skills Good coping skills Good conflict resolution skills Mastery motivation and positive achievement motivation Confidence in one's personal efficacy Planfulness – planning for the future and future life events Sense of personal autonomy/responsibility for self Optimism coupled with realism Coherent and positive personal and social identity Prosocial and culturally sensitive values Spirituality or a sense of a 'larger' purpose in life Strong moral character A commitment to good use of time
Social development (connection, caring/ compassion, contribution)	Connectedness – perceived good relationships and trust with parents, peers, and some other adults Sense of social place/integration – being connected and valued by larger social networks Attachment to prosocial/conventional institutions, such as school, church, non-school youth programs Ability to navigate in multiple cultural contexts Commitment to civic engagement

Source: Adapted from Eccles and Gootman (2002). Reprinted with permission from the National Academic Press © 2002, National Academy of Sciences.

Community youth development

Community youth development is defined as purposely creating environments that provide constructive, affirmative, and encouraging positive relationships that are sustained over time with adults and peers, while concurrently providing an array of opportunities that enable young people to build their competencies and become engaged as partners in their own development as well as the development of their communities (Perkins and Borden 2003). Coined by the Nation Network for Youth (Hughes and Curnan 2000), the *community* youth development framework builds on the *positive* youth development framework by including engagement as a principal component. A community youth development framework is employed to move beyond keeping young people *problem free* and *fully prepared* to *fully prepared and engaged* (Pittman et al. 2001). Thus, a premise in the community youth development framework is that besides being 'fully prepared', young people need to be engaged by adults as partners in their own development and in the development of their communities. This framework emphasises that young people are resources whose development can be fostered in ways that both serve them and society in mutually beneficial ways (Roth et al. 1998; Lerner 2004).

Practitioners in partnership with young people have a critical role in providing direction to the community youth development framework. From a practitioner's point of view, employing a community youth development framework means including young people as *partners* in programme planning or community mobilisation efforts to create environments that link young people with adults in positive *relationships*, and also provides new opportunities for young people to develop *skills*.

There are four parts to the community youth development framework:

1   the natural youth development process;
2   the strengths-based approach;
3   utilisation of intentional programmes or organisations (Hamilton's *Youth development: a definition in three parts* as cited in Lerner 2004) to build capacity; and
4   the engagement of young people in their community.

Each of these is now discussed in turn.

First, youth development is a *natural process* in the same way as child and adolescent development is a natural process. Youth development is the natural unfolding of the potential inherent in the human organism in relation to the challenges and supports of the physical and social environment. People can and do actively shape their own development through their choices and interpretations. Development lasts as long as life, but youth development enables individuals to lead a healthy, satisfying, productive life, as young people and later as adults, because they gain the competence to earn a living, to engage in civic activities, to nurture others, and to participate in social relations and cultural activities. The process of development may be divided into age-related stages (e.g. infancy, childhood, adolescence, and smaller divisions of these stages) and into domains (notably physical, cognitive, social, emotional, and moral).

Community youth development involves a *proactive approach* where there is active support for the growing capacity of young people by individuals, organisations, and institutions, especially at the community level. This framework is rooted in commitment to enabling all young people to achieve their potential. It is characterised by a positive, asset-building orientation, building on strengths rather than categorising young people according to their deficits. However, it recognises the need to identify and respond to specific problems faced by some young people (e.g. substance abuse, involvement in violence, and premature parenthood). The most important manifestation of community youth development as a philosophy or approach is the goal of making communities better places for young people to grow up. Youth participation is essential to the achievement of that goal.

Those programmes and organisations that are youth development-centered have as their core an *intentional set of activities* that foster young people's growing capacity. Youth development programmes are inclusive; participation is not limited to those identified as at risk or in need. They give young people the chance to make decisions about their own participation and about the programme's operation, and to assume responsible roles. They engage young people in constructive and challenging activities that build their competence and foster supportive relationships with peers and with adults. They are developmentally appropriate and endure over time, which requires them to be adaptable enough to change as participants' needs change. Youth development is done with and by young people. Something that is done to or for young people is not youth development, even though it may be necessary and valuable. Programmes to prevent or treat specific problems stand in contrast to youth development approaches. However, problem-oriented programmes may incorporate youth development principles by acknowledging participants' strengths and the wider range of issues they must cope with. They can also give participants a strong voice both in the choice to participate and in the operation of the programme.

Ultimately, a community youth development framework manifests itself as a *contribution to something greater than oneself*. Thus, if we are talking about youth programmes, youth voice and participation is required in every step of the programming process (e.g. planning, implementation, and evaluation). Youth voice and participation are critical to fostering young people's capacity and sense of cohesion in the community. Therefore, within a community youth development framework, young people are fully invested in their community and are empowered as full partners to provide direction, insight, energy, and efforts around problem-solving for the community. Young people are full contributors to their community and are called upon to employ the skills and competencies that they are currently developing.

Indeed, young people have a right and a civic responsibility to participate and contribute to their communities. Active participation in the community is viewed as essential to the positive development of young people and ultimately to the success of communities and institutions (see Wood, Chapter 12). Youth participation involves learning and work that is woven throughout the community, not just in specific projects (Pittman 2000). If engaged as partners, young people can be powerful change agents for the betterment of their community. It is engagement in the community that represents the fourth leg of this stool known as community youth development. Pittman summarises this point in the following quote:

> We will have to work carefully in this country to identify or create the public ideas that underpin a sustained effort to bring all young people into civic, social, and economic arenas of their communities as lifelong learners, workers, and change agents. We must recognize that this public idea, like any stable platform, must have at least three legs: one leg in policy, one in public opinion and values, and a third in organizational practice. We could argue for the importance of a fourth leg in youth culture, for this idea must resonate with young people, tap into their resources, and unleash their potential. (2000: 35–36)

Community youth development means promoting processes that provide *all* young people with the core components needed for successful development and engagement in their communities, regardless of their level of risk. The core components include: (1) opportunities for positive relationships with peers and adults; (2) opportunities for skill building and competency development; and (3) opportunities for meaningful engagement and voice in one's development and their community's development.

Core Component 1: Opportunities for positive relationships

The role of caring adults in the lives of young people cannot be overstated. Since the first studies in resilience, caring relationships with non-parental adults have been found to be an essential element for young people beating the odds against adversity (Perkins and Borden 2003). Of course the role of parent(s) or carer(s) is critical to the positive development of young people; however, the socially toxic and chaotic environment that surrounds our young people cannot be addressed by families alone. Caring relationships with non-parental adults provide a frame of reference and a learning tool for how one is supposed to act. Non-judgemental love and mentoring are the characteristics of these caring relationships.

Rhodes (2002) found in her analysis of the Big Brothers/Big Sisters program (youth mentoring designed to help young people achieve their potential (see www.bbbs.org) that length of time is also an important factor to consider. Relationships between mentor and youth mentee that were less than six months in nature tended to inflict more damage than good on the young person. When less than six months, the relationship contributed to a lack of continuity and stability in the young person's life. Moreover, Masten (2001) found that these relationships seem to be most needed during times of transition such as the transition into high school. Caring relationships with non-parental adults, according to the report from National Research Council and the Institute of Medicine provide, 'an environment of reinforcement, good modeling and constructive feedback for physical, intellectual, psychological [and emotional], and social growth' (Eccles and Gootman 2002: 96).

Given the goal of the community youth development framework is to foster the successful development and engagement of young people in their communities, a core component is opportunities to build positive supportive relationships with adults and peers. Such opportunities are important for establishing pro-social norms. Pro-social norms are standards of interacting with others in a positive behavioural climate that actually reinforce those norms for behaviour, facilitating positive peer relationships, and taking the initiative in encouraging and rewarding their peers and in fostering cohesion through shared routines, practices, and norms.

Core Component 2: Opportunities for skill building and competency development

In order for young people to become competent and contributing adult members of society, they need opportunities and support *now* as young people, to develop their personal and social assets (see Table 1, Eccles and Gootman 2002). These assets are the building blocks of development likely to promote successful passage through adolescence and facilitate optimal transition into the next phase of life. Thus assets increase the likelihood that a young person is headed along a possible trajectory toward finding a meaningful and productive place in one's cultural ecology. There are four general categories that assets fit into: physical health, cognitive development, psychological and emotional development, and social development. These personal and social assets are more simply stated as the 'five Cs' identified by Lerner and his colleagues (Lerner 2002, 2004; Lerner et al. 2000). These include (1) competence in academic, social, emotional, and vocational areas; (2) confidence in who one is becoming (identity); (3) connection to self and others; (4) character that comes from positive values, integrity, and strong sense of morals; and (5) caring and compassion. Each of these 'Cs' represents a cluster of behaviours that community youth development practitioners seek to promote through their youth development programmes (e.g. see Villarruel et al. 2003).

Promoting the five 'Cs'

The promotion of the first C, *competence*, involves goals of enhancing a participant's social (interpersonal skills such as communication, assertiveness, and conflict resolution), academic, cognitive (e.g., logical and analytic thinking, problem solving, and decision making), and vocational competencies.

Fostering adolescents' *confidence*, the second C, includes goals relating to improving adolescents' self-esteem, self-concept, self-efficacy, identity, and belief in the future.

Promoting the third C, *connections*, encompasses developing and strengthening adolescents' relationship with other people and institutions such as faith-based institutions and schools.

The fourth C, *character*, involves increasing self-control, decreasing engagement in health compromising (problem) behaviours, developing respect for cultural or societal rules and standards and a sense of right and wrong (morality), and spirituality.

The fifth C, *caring and compassion* has goals of improving adolescents' empathy and identification with others. In a study of youth programs by Roth and Brooks-Gunn (2003), programmes that focus on the five Cs were more effective in improving competence, confidence, and connections among participants.

Adapted from Roth and Brooks-Gunn 2003

Within a community youth development perspective, there is a sixth C, contribution (Pittman 2000; Perkins et al. 2003; Lerner 2004). By contributing to their families, neighbourhoods, and communities, young people are afforded practical opportunities to make use of the other five Cs. Without the sixth C, young people can be akin to ships in the harbour, they are safe, but that's not what ships are built for (as Boeck suggests in Chapter 8). Community youth development is not about insulating but about strengthening young people. It is a lot harder for young people to succumb to pressures of their environment when they have been given supports and opportunities to develop and use their skills. Young people with support and skills are less likely to break under the pressure, rather they are more likely to learn and grow from challenges through the enhancement of their social capital (Boeck, Chapter 8). These young people are more likely to make the healthy choices. Adults and society cannot totally protect young people from stress and challenges; eventually they will encounter them. Thus, it is better to prepare young people by providing them opportunities to develop skills necessary for successful adulthood. Finally, competence, in and of itself, is not enough – skill building is best achieved when young people are confident of their abilities and are called upon to contribute to their communities. The development of confidence, commitment, caring, character, and connection are essential.

Core Component 3: Opportunities for meaningful engagement and voice

There are many developmental benefits gained through engagement with one's environment. Opportunities for participation, contribution, and engagement enable young people to address developmental needs such as sense of generosity and mattering, sense of mastery, and sense of belonging (Brendtro et al. 1990; Eccles and

Gootman 2002). When a young person is efficacious, that is, when a young person has an opportunity to feel competent doing things that make a real difference in their social world, a sense of mattering is created (Eccles and Gootman 2002). Moreover, a sense of mastery is developed through participation in flow-producing experiences (Csikszentmihalyi 1997).

Flow experiences encompass high levels of goal-directedness, concentration and intrinsic motivation. Through these *flow* activities or experiences, young people engage in a discovery process about their skills, talents, and interests because they have opportunities to problem-solve, make decisions, and work with others. Autonomy-granting activities are often flow experiences and as such they are engaging, challenging, and interesting and promote a range of competencies and skills. The power of autonomy-granting activities comes from the 'voice' and 'choice' that young people are afforded within the school, youth work, and community contexts. These autonomy-granting activities also foster a sense of belonging and ownership.

Resilience research and youth development research has found that opportunities to contribute or to 'matter' within one's context are linked with successful outcomes in adolescents (Eccles and Gootman 2002; Villarruel et al. 2003). Young people involved in making contributions are reframing their self-perceptions as well as other adult's perceptions of them, from being a problem to be solved and a receiver of services to being a resource and provider of services (Bernard 2004). By engaging in acts to help others, young people gain a sense of generosity and self-worth, as well as an opportunity to overcome the egocentric thinking so prevalent in adolescence (Werner and Smith 1992). Providing them with opportunities to contribute is an explicit core component of a community youth development framework. According to the Carnegie Council on Adolescence (1995) report, one of the most powerful strategies for enriching the lives of young people is to enlist their energies in improving their own homes and communities.

Conclusion

Community Youth Development is a model for working with young people that promotes their personal and social assets as a means of preventing their risk behaviours and decreasing risk processes in their environment. This model incorporates the six 'Cs' of competence, confidence, connection, character, caring/compassion and contribution. Youth practitioners have a critical role to play in the promotion of the six Cs, and ultimately in the promotion of personal and environmental assets (see Table 9.1). These assets have an important role in preventing young people's engagement in risk behaviours and mitigating or eliminating risk factors and processes. In order to be effective, practitioners must be intentional and deliberately focused on capacity building by shaping environments and the learning opportunities to foster positive development within young people (Walker et al. 2005).

In the United States, youth practitioners utilise the community youth development framework in structured environments designed to help guide young people's development. The needs of young people grow more complex as they approach adolescence, and public commitment to supporting their development tends to weaken as they grow older. The 'developmental imperative' for young people addresses this state of affairs by suggesting that young people need and deserve:

1   early and sustained investments *throughout the first two decades of life,*
2   supports *throughout their waking hours;* and
3   investments that help them achieve *a broad range of outcomes.* (Tolman and Pittman 2002: 21–22)

The community developmental imperative calls on us to consider the full range of young people's time as crucial to ensuring positive youth development.

Reflective questions for practice

- **Try mapping the six 'Cs' against your own programmes of work with young people. In what ways do you support young people to develop these asset categories?**
- **Who are the trusted adults in a young person's life, other than their parent(s) or carer(s)?**
- **How do you support the development of positive relationships between young people, and between adults and young people?**
- **How do you involve young people in the development of the wider community?**

Further reading

Villarruel, F. A., Perkins, D. F., Borden, L. M. and Keith, J. G. (eds) (2003) *Community Youth Development: Practice, Policy, and Research,* **Thousand Oaks, CA: Sage.** This book focuses on positive methods for youth development that are rapidly supplanting the traditional deficit-oriented, problem-reduction approaches. Each chapter contributes to an overall understanding of the 'how' and 'why' of community youth development.

10

YOUNG PEOPLE AND RESEARCH PARTICIPATION

Jennie Fleming and Nicky Hudson

Key arguments

- Participatory research is about including stakeholders and users in all aspects of the research process, not just as data providers. It is considered an ethical and professional way to carry out research and links with many current themes in youth work.
- Young people can be actively involved at all stages of the research process, but this will present different challenges to the researcher.
- The extent to which young people are involved can be thought of as a continuum that ranges from 'tokenism', 'consultation', 'collaboration' through to 'user-led' research. Meaningful approaches can have many benefits.
- The benefits for young people include raised political and social skills, self-esteem and the capacity of young people to influence services.
- The benefits for research and organisations include the use of different perspectives, access to marginalised groups and a more effective distribution of resources.

Introduction

There is a plethora of research about young people, much of which involves them in the role of data provider or respondent. Traditionally, 'participants' or 'respondents' have been excluded at crucial design and analysis stages of research, with their involvement often perceived as irrelevant, especially in a positivist model of research. Research agendas are traditionally set, and evaluation exercises conducted, without consultation with these groups, a problem exacerbated among those who are perceived as being 'hard-to-reach' and often marginalised in other arenas of social life. Young people, particularly those who may be vulnerable or disadvantaged, have, as a result of this tradition, largely been silent in research in any other capacity than as data provider.

A growing body of expertise seeks to challenge the persistence of this asymmetrical relationship between those who carry out research and those who are 'researched', and instead suggests that young people can and should contribute to research. This chapter provides an overview of some of these debates and offers some guiding strategies for carrying out effective research which actively engages young people. Examples are drawn from existing literature and from a range of projects carried out with young people by one of the authors, but the principles will apply to participative research with other marginalised groups (for example see Culley et al. 2007).

This chapter will provide a brief overview of the benefits, challenges and dilemmas of carrying out effective participatory research with young people. Engaging young people in the processes of academic and practice-based research is crucial to ensuring that research is reciprocal, inclusive and ethically sound. Research should aim to be relevant to intended audiences and potential 'users' and this cannot be successfully achieved if key stakeholders are not included at all stages.

The case for including young people

The involvement of 'users' in research, evaluation, and policy and practice development is a relatively recent phenomenon. Over the past decade there has been a growing emphasis on encouraging users to become involved in and responsible for the implementation, development and evaluation of the services with which they are engaged. It has been suggested that this change has been driven by wider social and political forces, such as a move to more market-led and consumer approaches to service provision advocated by the New Right, and subsequently developed by New Labour in their 'third way' approach to welfare provision, and the move towards 'self-advocacy' as enshrined in human rights legislation (see Beresford 2002).

At the same time, there has been a corresponding and related increase in emphasis placed on those who carry out research and evaluation to embrace the participative approach. Including 'users' or research 'participants' in the research process has become and is continuing to be considered an ethical and professional way to carry out research (BSA 2002). Researchers, and practitioners – who are increasingly also engaged in research and evaluation – need to be aware of the impact of the research on 'participants' and also aware of the need to carry out research which is user-focused and socially located within the perspective of the groups for whom the research will have most impact.

The case for involving young people more fully in research has been made convincingly elsewhere (see for example Kirby 1999; Smith et al. 2002). It has been argued, for example, that young people have a right to take part and to have their views listened to (France 2004). Including young people can also bring new perspectives to the research and can address issues of power between researchers and researched, and between young people and adults. Participation also recognises and values young people's skills and experiences (Fleming and Ward 2004: 165).

What is research?

The term 'research' can be used as a catch-all phrase for information gathering and analysis of different kinds. The processes involved in research, audit and evaluation for example, can be very similar; often being carried out with the objective of meeting different aims and of producing different outputs. Bryman (2004: 277) suggests that evaluation is the 'study of the impact of an intervention', whereas research has been defined as 'a process of systematic investigation of a subject for the purpose of adding to the body of knowledge about that subject' (Wilson et al. 2000: 3).

Evaluation then, has a more specific aim in terms of its goal of assessing the impact or value of a specific system or programme. Research, on the other hand has a broader objective, which is to generate understanding of a phenomenon, and may or may not have an evaluative element. For the purposes of clarity in this chapter, references to 'research' relate to the broader definition and elements of the process may be applicable to other forms of data collection exercises, including evaluation.

The research process is a cyclical and iterative one, with distinct but often overlapping stages. It is always important for researchers to identify the key stages involved in any study, but it becomes particularly pertinent when carrying out a piece of participative research, to identify the stages in which to involve young people.

Box 10.1   Key stages of the research process

- identifying topics
- prioritising
- commissioning
- designing research (including ethics)
- managing research
- collecting data
- analysing and interpreting data

- presentation of findings
- dissemination
- evaluating
- acting on the findings

Adapted from Hanley et al. 2000: 15

These stages are not discrete (nor are they exhaustive), but it is important to recognise that the different stages will often feed into one another, for example, analysing data may lead one to make the decision to collect further data. Managing the research may lead to ethical dilemmas which were not considered at the planning stage and may require further reflection by the research team. Involving young people at one or all of these stages is possible and each will present different challenges for researchers and practitioners. Identifying the stages at which to involve young people may depend on a number of factors, including their level of interest, the time scale, available resources, who is funding or commissioning the research, and the theoretical position of the researchers. The level of involvement of young people needs to be meaningful for those involved and will depend, among other things, on the choices of the young people themselves.

Participative research: a continuum

The levels of engagement and participation of young people (or any social group) in research can usefully be viewed as a continuum. Ladders (e.g. Hart in Badham and Wade 2005: 10) or continuums of involvement highlight how involvement can take different forms and how there can be varying degrees to which participants can truly 'participate' in research (Hanley et al. 2000; Kirby 2004; McLaughlin 2006a, b). This chapter uses an adapted version of the continuum given by Hanley et al. (2000: 9) that covers four points on the spectrum: tokenism, consultation, collaboration and finally, user-led research.

Box 10.2   A continuum of involvement in research

Tokenism is an addition to Hanley et al.'s model (2000) that is all too common in research work with young people. Tokenism is defined as 'the policy or practice of making only a symbolic effort' (Merriam-Webster's Online Dictionary). This means that there is no real attempt to involve young people and to give them some influence over the research or evaluation, but lip service might be paid to the notion of their involvement.

(Continued)

(Continued)

Consultation is the practice of asking for a specific population or groups' views and perceptions, perhaps of the substantive issue, as well as accessing their views about the design of the research. This level of involvement may come at the beginning of the research (and often does) but may also come at subsequent stages, depending on the design of the study.

Collaboration is more purposively a partnership between the researcher or practitioner and the young people. In this approach, the research often remains researcher-led, but a two-way relationship is fostered in which the young people play an equal role and are often actively involved at all stages of the research process.

User or young people led research is where the young people themselves are fully engaged in and in control of the research, which only involves professionals or adult researchers if they are invited by the young people.

Adapted from Hanley et al. 2000

The following discussion of each category on this continuum offers examples of both published research and unpublished research of the authors.

Tokenism

'Tokenism' in research is prevalent but not advocated! It is important that youth work practitioners are aware of this sort of practice so they can recognise it when they see it, can challenge it and can help people see how they can be more participative. Tokenism is not participation; young people have nothing to gain from it and indeed it can be counterproductive as young people are likely to quickly realise that their opinions and involvement are not really valued and become disenchanted not just with this project, but with other opportunities for participation and research. It has few benefits, for researchers and young people alike, however it can give the appearance of participation and could falsely legitimise the research with some audiences.

Consultation

Consultation can be one of the least participative models in the continuum (other than tokenism) since it often requires minimal involvement by young people. Consultation largely involves asking people for their views, which may or may not be influential in the final research process (Kirby 2004).

An example of consultation with young people in research (Fleming 2003) is an evaluation of a national youth work project where the commissioners were keen for it to be an external evaluation from a university, as they felt this would be taken seriously by others. At the start of the project a consultation day was held with a group of young people where, through a series of exercises and discussions, they gave their input into the sorts of areas that needed to be explored, what methods would work best and advised about language and best approaches to young people. These were used to inform the design of the research and the questions asked. After a period of information collection a workshop was run at the organisation's conference for young people, which was designed to involve them in the analysis and interpretation of the information collected. Again, through a series of exercises, the young people made a significant contribution to the development of the findings that were written into the final report.

Such substantial consultation offers young people the opportunity to have some influence over the research, and their perspectives can be included into various stages of the research. It has the advantages of ensuring some involvement in a project that otherwise would be determined by the agendas of the adults and that could miss important points. However, the participation and influence of young people can be limited, as the agenda is ultimately set and developed by the researchers. In such a model there is limited scope for developing reciprocal relationships between the young people and the adult researchers from which all parties could benefit. There is little potential for young people's empowerment in this model, and once again as young people see their involvement is limited, albeit slightly more than with tokenism, it has the potential for disenfranchisement from this and future research. In the example given above, the young people had a very strong influence on the design and focus of the research, as well as the analysis of data, however as Kirby (2004) points out young people are often asked their views, but too frequently their views do not actually influence decisions. As Wood (Chapter 12) notes, consultation by itself can often fail to identify the issues that have real consequence for young people.

Collaboration

There are many examples of collaborations between young people and adults in research; many involving young people as co-researchers alongside adults. Kirby defines collaboration as that which 'involves the active, on-going partnership with young people in research and the development of services' (Kirby 2004: 10). Smith et al. (2002), write of a collaborative project with young people to find out about the health needs of socially excluded young people. In this example, young people made choices about the questionnaire design, practical arrangements, and the conduct of interviews. Smith et al. suggest that the young people 'over-ruled the professional researcher on a number of matters' (2002: 192).

In another example of collaborative research, Badham (2005) describes a collaborative national consultation with disabled children and young people, including some with severe and multiple impairments: 'Ask Us!'. To ensure the participation and involvement of the children and young people in the whole consultation process, part of the funding available was allocated to provide training and payment to young disabled people as researchers. In total 48 disabled young people across the country were researchers during the consultation. In each area a small group of young disabled people were approached to become researchers. The responsibility for the level of participation and involvement of young researchers in local consultations was left with individual projects to organise. The projects worked differently with each local group of young researchers. Some involved young researchers in the planning stage through to the production of the final output (which was a CD), others elected to give researchers specific tasks as part of the consultation, while one employed young researchers in the role of experts and advisors to the project. A common approach taken with all the young researchers was to offer in-house training in communication and interview techniques along with training in the use of the digital camera, video and audio recorders. Offering young people training as part of their involvement can be an added benefit both for researchers, in terms of the quality of work, and also for the development of the young people's skills (see Badham 2005 for further discussion).

Fleming's work with The Centre for Social Action (CSA) at De Montfort University has included a large number of collaborative research and evaluation projects with young people. Examples include: community consultations in collaboration with young people investigating how to improve the area's local estates for young people (Guinness Housing Trust 2000), and the evaluation of a local authority Teenage Pregnancy Prevention Strategy, where young people were trained and supported to be paid peer evaluators (Teenage Pregnancy Prevention Partnership Board 2001).

A further example of collaboration with young people is the evaluation described in the previous *consultation* section (Fleming 2003). The initial project was an evaluation based on a consultation approach. However, in a subsequent piece of follow on work, young people were key partners in an evaluation which followed a *collaborative* model. This constituted a second evaluation of the national youth project, which was conducted once the 'external evaluation' had been completed by the CSA. The commissioners asked the CSA to work with a group of young people to support them in undertaking their own further evaluation. The young people volunteered from projects around the UK and attended two residential weekends where they received training including such topics as research processes, ethical considerations, and different methods to collect information. The training also included input into the research design. In the process of the training they made decisions about what questions they wanted to ask and how best to do this. The young people designed a session to use with other young people and an interview for adult workers. The evaluation session that the young people developed as a result had a short questionnaire, and a range of interactive exercises that enabled young respondents to give their views and opinions. The young people then carried out national consultation with other projects and travelled the country to consult with others involved in local projects to get their views and opinions. Once all the information collection had been completed, the team came together for a final residential, where they analysed all the information. Ultimately they produced a DVD of their findings that was sent to all the projects in the network.

These examples show the range of collaborative research that is possible. While they have very different foci, they share a number of things in common. Most importantly, all are based on the assumption that by involving young people in the research, the relevance of the research process and findings to the participants will be increased, thus allowing for an exchange of knowledge and skills between young people and researchers.

The above examples recognise the value of involving young people in all stages of the evaluation, including the analysis of the data, an area from which they have traditionally been excluded. Collaboration opens up new possibilities by including them at this important stage (Hanley et al. 2000; Jones 2004). Young people undoubtedly gain personally from their involvement in research, both in terms of knowledge and skills, as well as the satisfaction that they are having an impact, as demonstrated by the following quote from a young researcher, 'Ultimately I enjoyed running the sessions, enjoyed being in control, being prepared – it was a positive, empowering experience' (Researcher's notes).

However, there are also challenges for researchers who use the collaborative approach. The agenda is often, to some extent, set by others; which was indeed the case with the evaluation of the Teenage Pregnancy Prevention Strategy (Teenage Pregnancy Prevention Partnership Board 2007). The young people joined the project once the first phase had taken place. The parameters were largely set by the local authority but the young researchers did have some considerable ability to influence the phase of consultation with other young people. For major, funded pieces of research it is often after the funding has been secured that young people are involved, so it is important to recognise that they may have missed out on developing the initial design and being involved in integral processes such as designing information leaflets, as in the case of the teenage pregnancy evaluation where these had had to be done early to allow time for ethical review.

In a collaborative approach, care needs to be taken to share power and control over the process; young people may need help to obtain and understand all the information they need to make informed decisions about the project.

Young people led research

There are few research projects which adopt an approach which goes to this stage of the continuum of participation with young people. Kirby suggests that this level of involvement, where young people actively control the research process, might be interpreted as:

> research where the locus of power, initiative and subsequent decision making is with ... young people, rather than older adult researchers. It does not mean young people undertake every stage of the research, or that 'professional' researchers are necessary excluded from the process altogether. (2004: 10)

Much has been written about adult service user involvement in research (see for example Turner and Beresford 2005), however projects which are wholly young people-led are noticeable by their absence in the literature. Nevertheless there are some examples of young people having the power, initiative and responsibility for decision making in the research, once it has gained funding. An example of this approach is a project investigating the impact of volunteering on young people and their communities (CSA 2005: 8). In this project, which is currently underway, a core group of young people form the project steering group and meet on residential trips throughout the course of the project, making decisions about the research design, analysis, reporting and dissemination processes. Young volunteers will be trained as researchers and have an active role to play in the development of information collection methods.

It is also important to remember that all research does not have to be large scale, receive funding, and take a lengthy period of time. There are examples in a recent publication (Berdan et al. 2006) where young people undertook small research projects in class. Lori Farias writes that: 'students choose their own cause, research it, create a plan of action to positively affect the cause, act upon it, reflect on their progress, and present their entire project to the class' (2006: 51). In a second example, Chinwe Obijiofor writes of young people investigating landfills in their community (2006: 43).

Young person led research has many advantages, and links with many themes that are central to current youth work: citizenship; civic engagement; participation; empowerment and seeing young people as social actors rather than objects of study (James and Prout 1998; see also Hine, Chapter 3 and Wood, Chapter 12). It places them clearly in control of the research, and while they may call on research 'expertise' from others, it is their interests and questions that are being explored in ways they think are the most appropriate. Young people are in control of the entire process and their perspectives dominate the research in this approach.

Challenges to actively involving young people in research

Research which includes members of social groups who are traditionally excluded from such processes can present challenges. Practical complexities, such as the need for additional resources, both financial and in terms of extra time and support for young people, need to be accounted for. For some young people, other life experiences may interrupt the research process, which may be new and unfamiliar territory. Researchers need to allow for such eventualities and build contingency and flexibility into research timescales.

Including young people also raises key methodological issues. Research which involves young people may not be taken seriously by adult audiences and researchers need to make research and dissemination processes transparent and robust. It is also important to note that membership of any social group is fluid and constantly changing and re-negotiated. As Alan France and Jean Hine (Chapters 2 and 3) argue, 'young people' as a category can ignore very real diversity and a shared age may not be the only significant social signifier. The suggestion that by 'matching' researchers and participants we can get at accounts which are more valid and that there will be more 'rapport' between participants, has been questioned (Culley et al. 2007) and therefore the methodological reasons for including young people in research should be clear at the outset.

Benefits of involving young people in research

Despite the dilemmas and challenges of involving young people in research, there are significant benefits for young people, researchers, and the research itself, provided it is done in a professional and effective manner (McLaughlin 2006a, b). In particular, authors have pointed to the political and social benefits of including young people. Kirby suggests that participatory research is about achieving democratic participation and social justice for children and young people, which includes involvement in 'institutional decision-making processes' (1999: 1). Links have also been made with young person led research and their rights under the United Nations Convention on the Rights of the Child (Checkoway and Richards-Schuster 2003: 23), particularly Articles 12 and 13 which set out that children have the right to say what they think should happen in their lives and that they have the right to receive and to share information (UNICEF undated). Checkoway and Richards-Schuster go on to suggest that being involved in community-based research prepares young people for 'active participation in a democratic society' (2003: 23).

Young people will be able to offer different perspectives. Practitioners may be expert in their field, but that does not imply the ability to see all the perspectives on that area of interest. Young people can offer valuable insights that adults might not perceive or would otherwise misinterpret (Hine, Chapter 3). Smith et al. give examples of how the young people in their project used their own experience to shape the information collected (2002: 199). As a follow on from this, young people can help to ensure that research doesn't just measure outcomes that are identified and considered important by professionals, as illustrated in Yates' discussion around the importance of multi-faceted issues in work with young people (Chapter 15). The involvement of young people can therefore help to ensure that money and resources are not wasted on research or services that have little or no relevance to their lives.

Young people may be able to help the involvement of their peers for research projects. They may find it easier to make contact with people who are often marginalised, such as young people from black and minority ethnic communities or gay and lesbian young people. They can create more young people friendly ways of asking for information.

Experience of the authors and of other writers recognises that young people's involvement in research, done well, can help empower young people. McLaughlin suggests that young people can gain in the areas of self-esteem and confidence, employability, citizenship, experience of work, remuneration and ownership of the research process and findings (2006a, b).

Good practice in involving young people in research

Young people or service user led research is often the preferred approach for service user groups that have become disillusioned with mainstream research approaches which they found to have disempowering effects on their lives and few positive outcomes (Beresford and Evans 1999, O'Sullivan and D'Agostino 2002). However, as Hanley et al. point out:

> different types of involvement will be appropriate for different research projects …
> [and] … in any single research project, you might consult, collaborate with, and ask consumers to lead in different stages of the project. (2000: 11)

New Opportunities Fund (2003) suggest an approach which seeks to maximise the involvement of young people in both a project and its evaluation, which implies involving young people at every stage and ultimately leads to more valuable research outcomes, an approach the authors endorse and advocate. Young people should be encouraged to think about research and how they can influence it. Researchers and youth work practitioners undertaking research projects and evaluations should always consider how they can maximise the involvement of young people in the research they are planning, and involve them from as early as possible in the process. However, whatever the involvement of young people is in research, there are some common aspects of good practice.

> **Box 10.3   Good practice pointers for young people's active involvement in research**
>
> *Clarity*
> Be clear about the purpose of the research. Young people need to be clear about what they will be doing and to understand any limitations to their involvement and influence. Everyone must have enough information to make an informed decision about their involvement.
>
> *Choice*
> Do not make assumptions about what young people will and won't be able or want to do. Ultimately, their involvement and what form it takes must be young people's choice.
>
> *Training and support*
> Enabling young people to take part through safe, ethical and inclusive practices needs careful planning. Researchers also need to ensure appropriate support and training are in place for the level of involvement young people have chosen.
>
> *Recognition*
> Recognition of their contribution in the form of payment, certificates, rewards and accreditation opportunities can be given, and ensuring that young people have feedback on the impact of their involvement is crucial.

As with all types of research, it is vital that there is the opportunity to act upon findings and for young people to see whether things have changed as a result of their involvement in research. With the 'Ask Us' project the young people not only had an input into how and what the research was about, but also presented their findings to local and national government and gave evidence to the Committee on the Rights of the Child (Badham 2005).

Conclusion

This chapter has offered some suggestions and examples from the practice and experience of the authors and others working with young people in research. There is a strong case for the inclusion of young people in research, both in terms of creating an inclusive and participative project, but also in terms of the benefits to the young people themselves who can be given the opportunity to gain skills, knowledge and self-esteem through this process. It also fits closely with the current youth work agenda of encouraging greater levels of active citizenship for young people (Wood, Chapter 12).

In order to involve young people in research effectively, it is important that researchers and practitioners reflect on and constantly strive to develop and improve practice (Smith et al. 2002: 191). As part of this process, all research with young people should include reflection and evaluation of research processes as well as the involvement of the young people themselves. This process of reflection might usefully include a consideration of what can be done to make research and evaluation interesting and relevant to young people; research does not have to be boring! Perhaps most importantly, reflection on research should include thoughts about what comes next; it is important to consider the young people themselves and what happens once the research is completed.

Reflective questions for practice

- In what ways are young people 'actively involved' in the design, implementation and evaluation of your service?
- At what level of the continuum used in this chapter would you plot the involvement of young people?
- Considering the involvement of young people in your own research projects, what benefits might this bring?
- What challenges do you think you might face, and how could you overcome them?

Further reading

Denscombe, M. (2003) *The Good Research Guide: For Small-scale Social Research Projects*, **2nd edn, Buckingham: Open University Press**. An excellent introduction to the basics of social research. It provides clear and understandable summaries of research strategies, approaches and methods for information collection and data analysis.

Fraser, V., Lewis, S., Ding, S., Kellett, M. and Robinson, C. (eds) (2004) *Doing Research with Children and Young People*, **Buckingham: Open University Press**. Introduces the key considerations in carrying out research with children. It discusses issues that can arise and will help in the planning and carrying out of research with children.

Save the Children (2000) *Young People as Researchers: A Learning Resource Pack*, **York: Joseph Rowntree Foundation**. Training exercises to help young people understand what is involved in a research project and to enable to them to develop the necessary skills and knowledge to do so.

PART TWO

POLICY AND PRACTICE

The past decade has been witness to a growth and diversification of dedicated youth policy both in the UK and Europe. Whether in the 'discovery' of new youth problems, or in the changing composition of services that work with young people, the priorities and messages that drive youth policy hold considerable challenges for practitioners.

In the opening chapter of this section, Howard Williamson (Chapter 11) examines the broad context of European youth policy and its impact in the UK, describing its history and the extent to which it presents a coherent and integrated attempt to support and develop young people. He argues that youth policy in the European Union reflects that of the UK: it is imbued with 'paradox and contradiction'. This paradox and contradiction is signalled by various 'mixed messages' about young people. On the one hand they are seen as participative and responsible citizens, on the other as potentially dangerous or risky individuals. These themes are explored in the next two chapters.

The beginning of the twenty-first century has seen substantial policy commitment to the idea of 'participation' by young people in a range of guises. This has been most evident in the agenda to foster active citizenship in young people, a discussion taken up by Jason Wood (Chapter 12). Citizenship education in its current form in schools is not without difficulties and Wood argues that those who work with young people in all contexts can make a more significant contribution by understanding and acting upon the social contexts in which young people find themselves. Arguably one of the key policy drivers over the past decade has been the prioritisation of 'risk'. As Hazel Kemshall (Chapter 13) determines 'youth and risk are increasingly intertwined'. Youth policy has been 'risk driven' with increasing emphasis on the use of 'risk factors' for early identification, problem prediction and preventive intervention. However, the personal capacity of young people to influence their social worlds cannot be overlooked and, as Kemshall argues, personal biography might yet triumph over risk prediction.

A thread apparent in all of the chapters is the increase in targeted interventions that seek to address particular problems or challenges that young people face. Two of the domains where these issues are most acute are youth justice and information, advice and guidance services. Joe Yates (Chapter 14) explores the emergence of the new youth justice powers that locate youth policy increasingly within the context of crime control. In doing so, he invites us to identify the limits of an 'anti-social behaviour paradigm', particularly in terms of the challenges it presents for professionals working with young people. Scott Yates (Chapter 15) reflects on evaluation of the work of the Connexions service in England and identifies good practice principles that can be applied to information, advice and guidance work with young people. Young people's lives are filled with complexity and so too is the impact that good quality advice work can have: it is multi-faceted in its nature and dependent on the relationship between trusted adult and young person.

What of the implications of all these changes for more general and traditional youth work? Both statutory and voluntary sectors have felt the impact of policy developments over the last decade, both sectors having been concerned with the positive development of young people in different ways. The Youth Service in England has a long history of providing youth work in universal, open-access contexts. Bernard Davies (Chapter 16) builds on his early historical analysis of youth services by examining the key policy developments since 1997 that have impacted upon the traditional 'home' of youth work. Increased targeting and a drive towards specialist interventions has radically reconfigured the purpose of the youth service, and he posits that the incorporation of the youth service into the new Children's Services in fact lead to its permanent demise. Tom Wylie (Chapter 17) meanwhile reviews youth work in the voluntary sector, arguing that it has flourished in this domain due to substantial political support and funding. This support for voluntary provision seems likely to continue, yet this may be at the expense of state providers and limit creativity and diversity within the sector.

These policy developments pose real questions for the occupational identity and principles of youth work, an issue that Malcolm Payne (Chapter 18) engages with critically. As Payne argues, youth workers are employed in ever diverse and challenging contexts that lay open so-called 'pure' tenets of practice to interrogation. He discusses what these policy developments mean for the occupational identity of youth work and its claimed distinctions. Mary Tyler (Chapter 19) concludes this section by considering the role of the youth worker in this diversified occupational context and the competing tensions that can arise for those working with young people. Drawing together the inter-woven threads of policy, ethics and practice, Tyler argues for 'principled pragmatism' that is clear about the purpose and nature of practice and realistic about what can be achieved. The result is that youth workers can claim their practice is both authentic and legitimate in supporting young people.

11

EUROPEAN YOUTH POLICY AND THE PLACE OF THE UNITED KINGDOM

Howard Williamson

Key arguments

- Key developments in European youth policy include: the First World Congress of the Ministers of Youth of the United Nations, the European Youth Programmes, the Council of Europe courses on transnational issues, the European White Paper on Youth, and the Youth Pact.
- A synthesis of different youth policies revealed dramatic differences and strong similarities across the nations, and offers an ideal type for conceptualising youth policy.
- Despite being a well-resourced country, the UK has patently failed to engage with that wider European debate and it rarely conceives of an overall framework of 'youth policy'.
- Expressing a willingness to be subjected to a Council of Europe youth policy review may see the development of more rational and integrated youth policy and practice.

Introduction

This chapter examines the emergence of a 'youth policy' framework at a European level and considers the extent to which the United Kingdom passes muster in relation to what is slowly being established as some kind of European ideal. The UK has a poor track record in contributing to that broader European debate and continues to punch well below its weight. Moreover, despite its considerable financial and human resources, it appears to perform weakly in combating pathologies in young people and extending their opportunities and life chances.

There are many similar challenges facing countries across Europe in relation to young people: education and (un)employment, sexual (ill-)health and substance misuse, family support, offending and exclusion. The scale of such challenges is, however, likely to be different, as is the political will, economic capability and professional capacity to address them. There is, therefore, no blueprint or magic bullet, but there is a range of concepts, structures, domains, cross-cutting issues and underpinning support mechanisms that arguably require reflection and attention if the best possible youth policy is to be established in the circumstances that prevail.

Youth policy developments in Europe: a brief history

'Youth policy' at a European level, even just a decade ago, was hardly recognisable. It was a concept still in the making. Its antecedents, however, lie much further back, first in the student unrest of 1968 and second in the fall of communism in 1989.

Following *les evenements* in France in 1968 the Council of Europe opened its European Youth Centre in Strasbourg, which became the location for a range of training courses on issues such as human rights, democracy, tolerance and intercultural learning. This was the first indication of provision specifically for young people at a European level. It would be more than 30 years later that a European Union with 25 member states and a Council of Europe with 46 member states would join forces on a 'youth' agenda – incorporating attention to the training of youth workers, youth research and youth policy. Both institutions were dramatically smaller then and, certainly in the youth field, there was little interaction between them (see Chisholm 2006).

There were also, however, other players in the early days of European youth policy development. Lauritzen and Guidikova (2002) have mapped 'official' developments in the youth field, starting with the declaration by the United Nations in 1985 of the International Year of Youth and its three governing themes: peace, participation and development. In 1989 the United Nations produced its Convention on the Rights of the Child and 1992 saw the publication of the European Charter on the Participation of Young People in Municipal and Regional Life (CLRAE 1992). There were various resolutions of the Council of Ministers of Youth within the Council of Europe and the final text of the First World Congress of Ministers of Youth of the United Nations, which met in Lisbon in 1998. Once they have listed such developments Lauritzen and Guidikova make the following cogent observation:

These texts are what people make of them. Even if there is no army behind them to make sure they are followed to the letter, why would youth ministers and authorities, NGOs, and parliaments agree on them when they have already decided to ignore them afterwards. (2002: 373)

In other words, however much the sceptic might allege that much of this is high-level rhetoric, it does still reflect some level of political intent. And ultimately, at the Youth Ministers' meeting in Bucharest in 1998, there was a resolution defining 'The Youth Policy of the Council of Europe':

- Help young people meet the challenges facing them and achieve their aspirations.
- Strengthen civil society through training for democratic citizenship, in a non-formal educational context.
- Encourage young people's participation in society.
- Support the development of youth policies.
- Seek ways of promoting youth mobility in Europe.

By this time, the European Union had already initiated its youth programmes: Youth for Europe (1992–1999), the 'YOUTH' programme (1999–2006), and now the 'Youth in Action' programme (2006–2013). These have included youth exchanges, youth initiative projects, study visits by youth workers, and the European Voluntary Service programme (EVS).

The Council of Europe has continued to run a range of courses on a host of transnational issues, governed by its principles of human rights, democracy and tolerance and its practices of co-management. During the mid-1990s, it ran a huge anti-racism campaign across Europe under the banner of 'All Different, All Equal'. A second compaign with the same name was launched in St. Petersburg in September 2006 and culminated in Malmo, Sweden in October 2007 (see Swedish Ministry of Integration and Gender Equality 2007).

These developments therefore comprise some of the building blocks that slowly gelled into a more comprehensive view of 'youth policy'. Initially, there were separate – and quite distinctive – pathways being followed by the two European institutions, but slowly this work has converged and there is now, increasingly, a shared agenda being followed, notably on account of an integrated partnership agreement between the European Commission and the Council of Europe that has been operational since May 2005. Nevertheless, at the end of the 1990s, rather different youth policy foci were in train.

The European Union: recent progress

In December 1999, the European Union – initially an area of economic co-operation but increasingly concerned with social integration – announced that a White Paper on Youth was to be prepared. There followed a series of consultations with governments, young people and – significantly – youth researchers. The rules concerning

EU levels of 'competence' and principles of 'subsidiarity' meant that the scope for a White Paper on youth policy was heavily circumscribed. It could not, for example, directly address issues such as formal education or employment, nor could it require member states to act on its propositions.

The White Paper (European Commission 2001) was launched in November 2001. Its four paramount themes are participation, information, voluntary services and a greater knowledge and better understanding of youth. Each theme has been pursued by what is known as the 'Open Method of Co-ordination', which culminates in the estab-lishment of common objectives, agreed by the Ministers for Youth. These are, in essence, standards to which all member states of the EU should aspire and ultimately achieve.

The other important youth policy development within the European Union has been the European Youth Pact. This was established in 2005, mid-way through the 'Lisbon Strategy' which, in 2000, proclaimed the intention that by 2010 the European Union would be the most competitive and dynamic knowledge-based economy in the world. The Youth Pact calls for urgent action in response to demo-graphic change (the 'generational contract') and emphasises the need to give young people a first chance in life and the skills to contribute to competitiveness, growth and social cohesion. In short, it underlines the view that the Lisbon strategy needs the support of young people to succeed – and for this to materialise, member states need Action Plans delineating how they are going to do this. The Youth Pact, in effect, broadens and deepens the EU's policy focus on young people, through includ-ing 'the fields of employment, social cohesion, education, training, mobility, as well as family and professional life' (Council of the European Union 2005). Indeed, reporting on the Pact, the European Youth Portal (www.europa.eu.int/youth) com-ments that 'This is the first time that youth policy has featured so visibly at EU level'. By the end of 2008, the European Commission was embarking on new plans for 'youth policy' over the next decade, including attention to issues such as the impact of the internet, youth violence, and public images of young people.

The Council of Europe: recent progress

The Council of Europe – essentially a pan-European inter-governmental organisation concerned with human rights and democracy – may have held its Youth Ministers' Conference in 1998 that set out a resolution on the 'youth policy' of the Council of Europe (see above), but the flesh for those bones started to be produced a year earlier. In 1996, the government of Finland had proposed that the Council of Europe should embark on a process of reviewing national youth policy. Finland offered to be the first country for such an international review and an embryonic process was established. The country concerned would produce a national youth policy report, and the Council of Europe would compose a review team that would visit the country on two occasions before producing an international report based on its findings. There would then be an international 'hearing' at a meeting of the co-managed Joint Council of the Council of Europe Youth Directorate comprising the inter-governmental committee on youth (the CDEJ) and representatives of youth organisations across Europe (the Advisory Council).

The objective of this process was threefold: to provide a critical eye on the country concerned, to provide ideas and lessons for other countries within the Council of Europe and – most significantly for this chapter – to start to construct some shared parameters within which a European level 'youth policy' might be considered.

The Finland review took place in 1997 and there have, since then, been a further 16 completed reviews. This has built up a body of knowledge about numerous principles, policies and practices in relation to young people across many cultural and political contexts, which were first 'synthesised' after the first seven reviews (Williamson 2002). A second synthesis report on the 'second seven' countries to be reviewed (Williamson 2008) has added to the structure and content of the youth policy framework advanced by Williamson in 2002 (see below), as well as reflecting on the efficacy of the ways in which the reviews are currently conducted.

More recently, through the partnership arrangements now in place between the European Commission and the Council of Europe, there has been a series of research seminars convened by the Youth Directorate but focusing on key issues of concern to the Commission, including some of the themes of the EU White Paper (see, for example, Hoskins and Williamson 2005; Colley 2006). Whatever the substantive focus of these seminars, academic youth researchers and policy analysts have undoubtedly contributed to the overarching fourth pillar of the White Paper – that is, the greater understanding and knowledge of youth.

Building a 'youth policy framework'

A reading of the material emerging from the first seven Council of Europe international reviews of national youth policy produced the first attempt at a transversal, inter-sectoral youth policy framework that could – perhaps should – be a guiding model across Europe. That synthesis report (Williamson 2002) was completely grounded in the seven national and seven international reports on Finland, the Netherlands, Sweden, Romania, Spain, Estonia and Luxembourg – a reasonable spread of European countries with very different traditions, cultures and contexts. It revealed some very dramatic differences (such as in policy approaches to substance misuse) but also some very strong similarities (such as the policy commitment to education and lifelong learning). It did not set out a blueprint for youth policy but it did suggest an 'ideal type' in relation to the conceptualisation of youth policy, structural questions, principal domains, cross-cutting issues, and foundation stones for effective practice. The model would necessarily require, indeed demand, adaptation according to particular circumstances but it has, so far, stood the test of time and informed the international reviews that have subsequently taken place (of Lithuania, Malta, Norway, Cyprus, Slovakia, Armenia, Latvia, Hungary and Moldova). Of course, those reviews have produced new issues and ideas (such as the influence of the church or the role of the army), but the original framework for thinking about 'youth plicy' remains largely intact.

The framework asks first how a country conceptualises the idea of 'youth' and the idea of 'youth policy'. There is then the question of what constitutes the overarching umbrella for 'youth policy': legislation, structures and budgets to make things happen. Supplementary questions relating to this infrastructure are concerned with whether or not approaches are enabling or restrictive, relationships between ministries, and mechanisms for the operationalisation of strategic visions. Within these overarching considerations are questions about the role of youth organisations and the National Youth Council, if it exists. The answers to these, and more, questions provide a map of the terrain on which youth policy is positioned and provide some very real clues about its likelihood of reaching the young people at whom different strands of policy may be directed.

Those strands are themselves located within different policy domains, often predominantly but never exclusively within (formal and non-formal) education and the related fields of training and employment. Beyond these, however, are the domains of health, housing, social protection, family policy and child welfare, leisure and culture, youth justice, and national defence and military service. All have a bearing on the lives of young people and may promote or constrain their prospects and possibilities.

There are, moreover, a range of issues that cut across, indeed cut *through*, these policy domains. These include questions of participation and citizenship, of combating social exclusion and promoting inclusive practice, and of the provision of youth information. There are further, related, cross-cutting questions to do with multiculturalism and minorities, mobility and internationalism, safety and protection, and, fundamentally, equal opportunities. All of these issues merit both empirical inquiry and more conceptual debate within the framework of any youth policy.

Finally, there are foundation stones that promote and produce better policy and practice. These include the commissioning and use of youth research, the training of professional practitioners who work with young people, and the dissemination of good practice. Without such approaches in place, youth policy development and implementation can end up being a somewhat hit and miss affair, and more likely to be subject to changes in the political wind and the vagaries of political whim.

This, then, is the current framework within which deliberations at a European level take place on the idea of 'youth policy'. After delineating some of the broad trajectories in youth policy in the United Kingdom, some of the 'tests' that are applied to youth policy in the European context will be focused on in the context of the UK.

Youth policy in the United Kingdom

At the time of the inception of the new Labour government in May 1997 it was a relatively easy task to map out the broad framework of what might be considered as 'youth policy'. There were mainline strategies across the territory of education and training (schooling and youth training programmes), leisure-time activity (the youth service), provision for young people with 'special needs', and responses to young people in trouble. Much of that 'youth policy' had been around for some time (even if there were occasional 'branch-line' new initiatives), delivered by time-honoured institutions and professional groups such as the careers service, national voluntary organisations (like the YMCA, Save the Children or the NSPCC), social workers and the police (see Davies, Chapter 16 and Wylie, Chapter 17).

Since the late 1990s, however, the pace of policy change has speeded up. The proclaimed evidence base was the changing complexity of youth transitions (Furlong and Cartmel 1997; Barry 2001) which demonstrated that while factors such as the fragmentation of the class structure and the emergence of 'globalisation' have produced far greater opportunities for many young people than ever prevailed before, they have also produced a corresponding risk and vulnerability for a significant minority of young people. That risk manifests itself in what is generically referred to as 'disengagement' or 'social exclusion', which can mean many things but is often concerned with educational drop-out and underachievement, health risk and substance misuse, homelessness and criminality (see Jones 2002).

There has, therefore, been a prima facie case for reviewing the framework and content of British youth policy, and certainly to consider mechanisms of intervention which might potentially renew opportunity and inclusion, rather than intentionally or inadvertently push young people further to the edge, through a process of 'blaming the victim' (see Williamson 1993). That was at least the rationale when the incoming new Labour government set up the Social Exclusion Unit (SEU), the de facto Ministry of Youth according to Coles (2001), given its significant, if not exclusive, focus on youth issues: truancy and school exclusion, homelessness, teenage pregnancy, non-participation in education, training and employment, and the education of children in care. Indeed, it produced a seminal analysis of the social condition of young people in one of its Policy Action Team reports (Social Exclusion Unit 2000a). Yet even by the time PAT 12 reported in March 2000, the landscape of youth policy was already a complex array of initiatives across policy domains and across the age range (see Social Exclusion Unit 2000a: 105).

We also need to recognise that the devolution settlements of the late 1990s have produced increasingly different 'youth policy' trajectories in Scotland, Wales and Northern Ireland. Wales, for example, rejected the model of the Connexions Service in England and opted for its own 'flagship' policy for supporting young people in Wales, *Extending Entitlement* (National Assembly for Wales 2000). Devolution has added to difficulties in understanding youth policy in the United Kingdom, but the pace of change has remained inexorable. Initiatives (such as the Children and Young People's Unit in England) have often been scrapped after just a few years, despite being planned initially for the 'long run'! (see Williamson (2005) for a full exposition of the detail of youth policy development in the UK at the turn of millennium). As a wealthy western European democracy (at least ten times richer, pro rata, than some of the new EU member states), the UK should have the wherewithall to serve its young people well.

Subjecting youth policy in the UK to the European 'test'

The best way, of course, for the UK to learn from European youth policy development, as well as to contribute to it, would be for it to participate in the Council of Europe international review process. In the absence of that process, some tentative conclusions are offered as to how the UK might 'stand up' to that kind of scrutiny if ever it were to happen. Space precludes moving systematically through each and every policy domain and cross-cutting theme; instead, the five 'Cs' of youth policy reflection (Williamson 2002) will be invoked, and pertinent illustrations offered accordingly. These five 'Cs' refer to questions of coverage, capacity, competence, co-ordination and cost.

Coverage

The UK, unlike many other countries, performs well in ensuring geographical 'reach'; the regional disparities that can exist are usually far less pronounced than those that prevail elsewhere in Europe. The UK also advances specific policy affecting young people right across the spectrum of public policy: notably, education, training, health, housing and criminal justice – and all points in between. However, perhaps surprisingly, it still often fails to reach effectively those young people most specifically targeted by particular initiatives. The prime example, is that of 'status zer0' youth (Istance et al. 1994) or 'NEETs' (Social Exclusion Unit 1999) – those not in education, employment or training – whose numbers have remained stubbornly intractable despite huge resources and special measures being dedicated to their re-engagement and re-inclusion. It is generally felt in research and professional corners that this policy failure has been the result of absurd political expectations – targets and time-scales that can only be achieved by focusing effort and energy on less hard to reach populations of young people. The application of inappropriate targets is well known to engender 'perverse behaviour' (Adebowale 1999), the 'cherry picking' of easy candidates for intervention, or, as Victor Adebowale once remarked, 'hitting the target, but missing the point'.

Capacity

In terms of capacity, the UK also has a commendable infrastructure for the delivery of youth policy. Despite occasional reorganisations, it has mechanisms of delivery from central, through regional (and devolved), to local government, as well as the possibility of using quasi-governmental structures (in, for example, health services) and the experience of established voluntary organisations and youth NGOs. Thus there is no particular bureaucratic reason for failing to transform youth policy aspiration into grounded practice; it is more a question of where best to position the responsibility for new initiatives. This is a luxury that is the envy of many other countries that do not have such traditions of governance and service delivery.

Competence

A similar point prevails in relation to competence. In many domains of youth policy, there has been a long tradition of professionalisation – with both full and part-time routes to achieve qualifications, and often both academic and competence-based routes. The UK is awash with reviews of training, the setting of occupational and quality standards, and the assessment of competence. This contrasts firmly with other nations that have relatively few strands of professional practice within youth policy domains. Even Norway, with its distinctive commitment to young people (see Williamson 2004), provides only very modest opportunities for training in youth work, while countries such as Latvia are quite desperate to draw on the ideas that inform the practice of the youth justice system for England and Wales. Whether or not, in the UK, the curricula available to those training for various forms of work with young people remains appropriate and up-to-date is another matter; the learning and development structures are clearly in place.

Co-ordination

Ever since the late 1980s (see, for example, ACOP 1989) it has become increasingly apparent that UK 'youth policy' remains poorly co-ordinated, with little communication between different government departments. It was this 'silo mentality' that the Social Exclusion Unit was meant to tackle and break down, but there is little evidence that much has changed. The need for effective channels of communication has become ever more essential, given the proliferation of policy initiatives, but rarely does it appear that one arm of government knows what another is doing. That problem has worsened since devolution, for there are now parallel horizontal communication imperatives (across each of the two levels of governance, on non-devolved and devolved youth policy issues) as well as the need for vertical communication and co-ordination between them. This has become, perhaps, the most severe obstacle to ensuring that youth policy retains an internal coherence throughout the UK, even if different parts of the UK elect to establish some-what different priorities and procedures.

Cost

Finally, in terms of budgets, the UK, despite the political pleading of scarce resources, is a wealthy state. Some of its youth policy initiatives, such as the New Deal for Young People, have cost more than the state budgets of the smaller new members of the European Union. The central budget for youth justice is huge and this does not take account of expenditure at the local level. The UK also has first-class human resources (that produces the 'competence' discussed above). With the exception of the Nordic countries and some other western European neighbours, no country spends more of its public resources indirectly and directly on young people.

Overall, then, the United Kingdom looks well positioned to both reflect and shape thinking about 'youth policy' across the Europe of which it is a part. This looked even more likely when a dedicated Minister for Young People was appointed in 1998. Yet the UK has patently failed to engage with that wider European debate, it rarely conceives of an overall framework of 'youth policy' (and instead dwells on component parts), and real practice that might make a dif-ference to real lives is often submerged under the weight of political rhetoric and bureaucratic inertia. The words, soundbites, philosophy and vision are com-mendable: every young person should have 'the best start in life' (DfEE 2000a), or a 'flying start' (Welsh Assembly Government 2003); 'Every Child Matters' (DfES 2003) and 'Youth Matters' (DfES 2005). Indeed, the latter two documents share a vision that all young people should benefit from five core outcomes aris-ing from a range of practice: being safe, staying healthy, enjoying and achieving, making a positive contribution, and achieving economic well-being. No one can argue with that. But ensuring that those furthest away from realising such posi-tive futures are reached and supported is the acid test of effective youth policy, and many commentators in the UK (Coles 2001; Jones 2002; Mizen 2004) suggest that a combination of civil service inaction, professional entrenchment, inflexible targets and performance management, and an absence of real political will have produced greater social division among young people in the UK, not improved social cohesion. More advantaged young people soak up the resources; more excluded young people remain detached from processes of access and inclusion.

The story is, of course, much the same in many other countries. Youth policy is a complex and challenging task, but the UK, with its voluntary sector and training traditions, its public resources and its structures of governance, should be a leader in the field. It is not, and instead displays a level of incompetence across a range of policy domains and in relation to particular social groups of young people that should be a cause for considerable embarrassment.

Conclusion

UK youth policy swings from conceptualising young people as valued citizens, through suggesting a sense of their vulnerability, to perceiving them as villains. Simultaneously it promotes their participation *and* demonises their allegedly 'anti-social' behaviour. But the UK is not alone in taking this stand: youth policy in most countries is imbued with paradox and contradiction. What seems to be important is that policy strives to establish some level of cross-sectoral congruence, one that preferably is positive and opportunity focused, within the human and financial resources at its disposals. This is where the UK disappoints for it is without doubt one of the best resourced youth policy contexts in the whole of Europe – with both financial allocations and trained personnel at its disposal. Quite how it therefore manages to sustain, among other pathologies, such low levels of numeracy and literacy, high levels of substance misuse, teenage pregnancy and youth crime, and low levels of post-16 educational participation is something of a mystery. These are not residual policy problems, but significant policy challenges (see Education Committee 1998), demanding concerted political effort. Joining up its thinking on youth problems, challenges and possibilities would be a start. Expressing a willingness to be subjected to a Council of Europe youth policy review might further expose the 'tyranny of policy momentum' (see Hyman 2005) that obstructs the development and consolidation of more rational and integrated youth policy and practice.

Reflective questions for practice

- **Reflect on the diagnosis of UK youth policy in this chapter. Why do you think it fails to support those who are the most excluded?**
- **What areas of youth policy impact upon your work with young people?**

- How are the issues that this policy seeks to address different or similar to wider European concerns?
- Try comparing the work that you do with a similar project in another European country. What might be the similarities and differences in the approaches used and the outcomes achieved?

Further reading

Williamson, H. (2002) *Supporting Young People in Europe: principles, policy and practice*, **Strasbourg: Council of Europe Publishing**. – provides a critical and useful overview of the policy developments referred to within this chapter.

Williamson, H. (2005) 'Young people and social inclusion – an overview of policy and practice', in M. Barry (ed), *Youth Policy and Social Inclusion: Critical debates with young people*, **London: Routledge**. – a chapter in an edited collection that examines the changes in UK youth policy since 1997 with thoughtful and reflective critiques.

Williamson, H. (2008) *Supporting Young People in Europe: Volume 2*, **Strasbourg: Council of Europe Publishing**. – elaborates on the first volume by identifying new challenges and issues facing young people and a critical reflection on the process of international reviewing of national youth policy.

12

EDUCATION FOR EFFECTIVE CITIZENSHIP

Jason Wood

Key arguments

- Citizenship has a long history, but since 1997 a new focus on linking communitarianism and citizenship has been evident in UK youth policy.
- Communitarianism is a political interpretation of citizenship that attempts to balance rights and responsibilities, and social obligations with individualism.
- Citizenship education, targeted at addressing young people's deficits, is an attempt to strengthen the political, social and moral responsibility of individuals. In this form, it can be interpreted as a method of social control.
- Despite its problems, citizenship education can be a process for empowering young people and practitioners are encouraged to adopt the principles of 'effective' citizenship as opposed to mere 'active' citizenship.

Introduction

The past decade has seen unprecedented concern to promote young people's skills, knowledge and values associated with active citizenship. Significant policy developments such as the teaching of citizenship in schools, a programme of post-16 citizenship education and the prominent civil renewal agenda have all set out to establish a consensus on what capacities young people should demonstrate in order for them to qualify as 'active citizens'.

What does active citizenship mean and how is it understood in contemporary social policy? This chapter reviews the common theoretical and policy framework within which citizenship education is located, including a brief introduction to the developments in citizenship education.

In drawing on current research and exemplars of good practice, the chapter concludes with a set of principles and characteristics that can guide those who work with young people outside of formal education in developing citizenship education that is meaningful and effective, beyond mere activity alone.

Understanding citizenship

The idea of citizenship has been with us in Western political and philosophical thought since the birth of Greek city states. At its most basic level, citizenship concerns the status associated with membership of a particular community (and in many cases, the state). It is this status that brings complexity to the definition, in questions around what rights and obligations should be associated with membership. Other authors have examined these questions in detail (for useful introductions, see Lister 2003; Heater 2004). In brief, citizenship can be understood by examining two broad traditions – the liberal perspective and the civic republican tradition.

Stemming from seventeenth-century political thought, the liberal political perspective favours a legal model of citizenship that recognises and promotes individual rights and guarantees these in law. It is essentially in favour of 'natural equality' among full members, and sees the state as performing a minimal function. The influence of British sociologist T.H. Marshall (1992 [1950]) on our understanding of how citizenship rights are conceptualised cannot be understated. As Lister notes, 'most modern accounts of citizenship take as their starting point Marshall's celebrated exposition' (2003: 16). Written in the period following the Second World War, Marshall's work tied together an unequal economic system (capitalism) marked by continuing class divisions and inequalities, with a set of common duties and rights that would mediate the impact of such conditions. As Marshall said: 'we are not aiming for absolute equality' (1992: 92) rather, an equality of status. Marshall proposed three interconnected sets of rights for all citizens: civil rights, political rights and social rights (see Marshall 1992: 8; Lister 2003).

The focus on rights in its liberal form has enabled minority groups to claim access to equal rights – the 'extension of citizenship' (Faulks 2000: 3), evident in movements based, for example, on 'race', gender, disability, class and sexuality. Key moments in history, even very recently point to a continuing debate about assuring an egalitarian citizenship definition. Arguments about civil partnerships and marriages for gay and lesbian couples are a case in point. This perspective sees citizenship as an ideal with benefits only available to some, ultimately becoming more universal.

While the liberal models of citizenship have had most influence on the development of British citizenship, it is in the civic republican traditions that have a longer heritage. Citizenship can be first traced back to the city states of Athens and Sparta during the fourth and fifth centuries BC. Citizens were characterised by involvement in public duties within the 'polis' (city state). Public participation entailed common commitments to civic duty in governing and defending the state (Heater 1999, 2004; Faulks 2000). In this definition, the citizen was 'constituted as political actor' (Lister 2003: 25) with values such as the 'submission of individual interest to that of the common good' (Lister 2003: 24).

The question of what makes a citizen is extensively discussed in Aristotle's *The Politics* through a series of deliberations about the constitution, the state and the role of the public. The translator notes that Aristotle 'is inclined to think of citizen as a kind of species and to look for the marks by which it may be recognised' (Aristotle 1992: 167–168) and this is an accurate description of the ways in which Aristotle examines the constituent parts of the 'citizen proper'. Book three of *The Politics* is headed 'how should we define the citizen' and recognition that 'there is no unanimity, no agreement as to what constitutes a citizen' (Aristotle 1992: 168). A citizen is bound to the constitution and is therefore defined against what state he [*sic*] lives in. Being born into membership is not in itself the defining feature since being 'resident in a place [does not] confer citizenship: resident foreigners and slaves are not citizens' (p. 169).

It is possible however to determine the 'citizen proper' (or perfect citizen, 'without defect'):

> What effectively distinguishes the citizen proper from all others is his participation in giving judgement and in holding office. Some offices are distinguished in respect of length of tenure, some not being tenable by the same person twice under any circumstances ... Others such as members of a jury or of an assembly, have no such limitation. (Aristotle 1992: 169)

The notion of obligation, according to Aristotle was one of political participation. Serving office in city states was the best example of how a citizen could demonstrate political and civil responsibility. There are of course other forms of general obligation that can be qualified as citizen responsibility, most obviously the obligation to work. Marshall had identified this and there is little doubt that while welfare services were in most cases universal, variable market rights can be considerably altered if the work obligation is not met (Marshall 1950; Faulks 2000).

The communitarian perspective

By the time New Labour was taking power in the UK, the validity of welfare states was challenged from above by globalisation, the influence of Europe and wider questions about the viability of the state. The triumph of capitalism meant that traditional ties and social relationships were also being challenged by greater levels of individualisation (Giddens 1998a). Governments faced a test: how to instil moral and social obligatory connections between individuals while at the same time trumpeting wealth generation and individual consumerism? For the then Prime Minister Tony Blair, the challenges of the new world indicated a need to 'define a new relationship between citizen and community' (Blair 1993: 11). The basis for a 'modern notion of citizenship' (Blair 1993: 7) was linked to two important threads: economic effectiveness in respect of providing welfare 'opportunities' (Morrison 2004) and new forms of social cohesion in terms of a renewal of civic and civil life. It is in the last of these two that communitarianism gains ground.

Whereas traditional liberal perspectives suggest an individualisation of citizenship (a private, legal guarantee) and the civic republican almost entirely on participation (in the political community), the communitarian perspective attempts, at first sight, to bring balance emphasising both rights and responsibilities. Communitarian citizenship is often discussed with a rhetoric of responsibility to others (Lister 2003) with rights coming as a condition of the exercise of these duties, and located at the community level.

Communitarian definitions of citizenship emphasise the importance of 'community' in realising this balance between rights and responsibilities (Etzioni 1993; Tam 1998). Community has gained significant weight in recent political history. New Labour in particular is responsible for recasting it as not merely a 'soft and romantic' concept, but as a 'robust and powerful idea' (Mandelson and Liddle 1996: 19). For Blair, community 'acknowledges our interdependence; it recognises our individual worth' (2000) capturing both the need for individualism and social bonds. As a narrative, it enabled Blair to distinguish Labour from the previous Conservative administration particularly in attempting to define key ideological differences and to stress loyalty to the left-wing roots of the party (Goes 2004).

David Blunkett, in his role as Home Secretary, also utilised community as a key instrument of social change (see Blunkett 2003a, b). Blunkett accepted that communities have changed in their function and that we now rely on them for 'basic order, decent behaviour; the socialisation of the young into community norms' (2003a: 14), things that 'generally come unstuck in disadvantaged communities' (ibid). Thus the task of government is to build community capacity to make local decisions in order to promote ownership over social order.

Both Blair and Blunkett represent community as an ideal, and these views mirror those of many communitarians who:

> *begin* with the concept 'community': community is a valuable thing and the theoretical and practical problem these communitarians try to tackle is, crudely, how to get it, and how to secure it once it has been got. (Frazer 1999: 42)

Communitarianism is argued to resolve a central dilemma for governance in advanced liberal democracies: how to manage complex and diverse groups, together with the myriad of social and moral problems they present and face, in an age when individualistic choice and freedoms are seemingly paramount. Rose (1999) has argued that this complex balance between freedom and the need to regulate behaviour, coupled with the state's failure to tackle entrenched social problems has led to a process of 'government at a distance'. Members of society are 'activated' and encouraged to address difficulties through a process of 'responsibilisation' and 'autonomisation' (Rose 1999). They become active citizens charged with self governance and if problems persist, the allocation of blame is directed at those who 'deserve' it (Rose 1999; see also Kemshall, Chapter 13 and Yates, Chapter 14).

Rose (1999) suggests that the principal site where this governance occurs is a 'third space', that of 'community'. Seen as outside of the big institutions that can be termed intrusive, this more detached and natural place forms an extension of government. Indeed, as he argues:

> What is happening here is not the colonization of a previous space of freedom by control practices; community is actually instituted in its contemporary form as a sector of government. (Rose 1999: 175–176)

In these idealised, politicised communities, members and professionals undertake to regulate and monitor social behaviour. In practice, this is evident through increasing civil measures for tackling anti-social behaviour and fostering respect on the one hand (Yates, Chapter 14) and the drive towards 'active citizenship' and civil renewal on the other.

Communitarian citizenship therefore depends upon the activation and responsibilisation of young people for tackling their individual and social problems. How might citizenship education be seen to contribute? Two key problems were cited as justification for the introduction of citizenship education in the recommendations made by the Advisory Group on Citizenship (AGC) in 1998. These were the political literacy of young people, and wider concerns about anti-social behaviour.

The report draws on studies that have indicated low levels of 'public issue discussion' in schools and low and declining levels of voting behaviour among the 18–24 age group (see AGC 1998: 15). This position reflects claims that 'young people are estranged from conventional politics and are becoming increasingly politically apathetic' (Wallace 2003: 243). For many commentators, an entrenched apathy among the age group is evident (Wilkinson and Mulgan 1995) with some going so far as to label young people as a generation who, by default, care little about anything other than themselves (Pirie and Worcester 2000). This argument is perhaps too simplistic to warrant serious endorsement, especially when countered by the increasing evidence drawn from research that actually takes into account the views of young people. For instance alienation, a decline in trust (Mulgan and Wilkinson 1997) and cynicism and scepticism (Wring et al. 1998) are often cited by young people as causes for disengagement.

Kimberlee (2002) identifies a significant counter-argument in the literature that she terms the 'alternative value' discourse. This approach concerns 'the new politics', where young people are less likely to engage in traditional or conventional party politics in favour of issue-led campaigns, such as environmental work. Evidence suggests that young people's participation in these movements has actually increased in recent years (Roker et al. 1999). Across Europe for instance, there is very real evidence of young people's involvement in high levels of political activism, especially in resistance movements or challenges to government rule (Wallace and Kovatcheva 1998; Machacek 2000).

If political illiteracy is deemed to be a major problem for the demonstration of active citizenship, it is in the social and moral behaviour that a very real crisis is perceived. Young people have long been subjects of adult anxiety in relation to their criminal or anti-social activity (Kelly 1999; France 2007), and as a result the objects of 'moral panic' (Jeffs and Smith 1999b). Public perceptions of dangerous youth are magnified through 'amplification by the media' (Furlong and Cartmel 2007: 119), reinforcing a dominant perspective that young people and risk are increasingly intertwined (Kemshall, Chapter 13). Young people thus become the targets of ever-greater state interventions designed to control their behaviour. These 'powerful narratives of risk' loom large in attempts to regulate youth identities (Kelly 2000: 303). A combination of lower levels of public tolerance for incivility together with an increase in the fear of young people (Young and Matthews 2003) serve to disguise the reality of a general decline in youth related criminal activity (Furlong and Cartmel 2007). Such fear reproduction effectively stigmatises young people further, resulting in yet more surveillance and regulation (Kelly 2003; McKenzie 2005) and a perverse consequence is of a vicious circle, 'Society … becomes increasingly fearful, suspicious of youths, which in turn means they are more closely supervised by the police than any other age group' (McKenzie 2005: 194).

The two justifications for citizenship education frame an individual as *sans* appropriate knowledge, *sans* acceptable values and as a consequence, lacking the necessary qualities of a future citizen. Firstly, there is the issue of a democratic deficit. This problem is not seen in terms of a failure in governing systems at a structural or societal level. Rather, the problem is located within the individual's capacity to participate as an effective citizen. Secondly, whereas once crime and anti-social behaviour may have been seen as symptoms or causes of structural disadvantage, they are now rooted in a moral underclass discourse (Levitas 2006) that identifies the individual as culpable for engaging in morally or socially irresponsible acts. Thus, young people are seen as problems to be managed, moulded and reformed rather than as active citizens who can think and make decisions about issues that concern them (Gewirtz 2000). Consequently, citizenship education becomes, 'focused around imparting information about moral obligations and students' responsibilities towards society' (Cunningham and Lavalette 2004: 258).

Citizenship education in schools

It was the publication of the *Excellence in Schools* White Paper in 1997 that rejuvenated the idea of citizenship education. Professor (now Sir) Bernard Crick, the founding member of the Politics Association, was appointed by the then Secretary of State for Education David Blunkett with the remit to provide advice on 'effective education for citizenship in schools'. The appointed Advisory Group on Citizenship (AGC) made recommendations aiming at 'no less than a change in the political culture of this country' (AGC 1998: 4). The recommendations were subsequently adopted near verbatim, with the Citizenship Order enacted in 2000, requiring all schools to teach citizenship as part of the national curriculum from September 2002. In doing so, they should seek to work within three broad learning objectives:

- **Social and moral responsibility**: Pupils learning from the very beginning, self-confidence and socially and morally responsible behaviour both in and beyond the classroom, towards those in authority and towards each other.
- **Community involvement**: Pupils learning about becoming helpfully involved in the life and concerns of their neighbourhood and communities, including learning through community involvement and service to the community.
- **Political literacy**: Pupils learning about the institutions, problems and practices of our democracy and how to make themselves effective in the life of the nation, locally, regionally and nationally through skills and values as well as knowledge – a concept wider than political knowledge alone.

To date, the delivery of citizenship education in schools has been characterised as 'uneven, patchy and evolving' (Kerr et al. 2004). Critical success factors include:

- Clear, coherent and broad understanding of citizenship education;
- Supportive school ethos and values system;
- Senior management support;
- Positive relations between staff and students;
- The employment of a dedicated and enthusiastic citizenship co-ordinator;
- A range of delivery approaches within regular time slots.
  (Kerr et al. 2004: 2)

Additionally, the active involvement of young people in schools and the wider community provided an opportunity for learning and *experiencing* active citizenship

(Kerr et al. 2004: 2–3). Such opportunities depend on student interest, the teaching staff's involvement in the wider community and the school ethos (ibid: 5).

Citizenship education post-16

In 2000, Crick was again requested to chair an advisory group with a remit to examine the feasibility of delivering citizenship education for 16–19 year olds. The advisory group recommended to the Secretary of State, that:

- citizenship should be acknowledged as a Key Life Skill and should be given its proper place alongside the six Key Skills identified already
- an entitlement to the development of Citizenship – of which, participation should be a significant component – should be established which would apply to all students and trainees in the first phase of post-compulsory education and training, and
- all such young adults should have effective opportunities to participate in activities relevant to the development of their Citizenship skills, and to have their achievements recognised. (FEFC 2000: 7)

The learning outcomes are described in the initial advisory group report (FEFC 2000: 14–18) covering the already well-established themes evident in the earlier work of the AGC (1998). Principally, any citizenship programmes should have a number of key concepts at the core of attributes they wish to develop in young people, namely: participation, engagement, advocacy, research, evaluation, empathy, conciliation, leadership, representation and responsibility (FEFC 2000: 15). These concepts would be ideally placed in the context of a number of roles that citizens play, ranging from 'consumer' to 'worker' (ibid.).

A number of studies have attempted to provide an evaluative contribution to the emerging initiatives designed to develop a citizenship curriculum for the 16–19 age bracket, bolstered by a number of formal pilot schemes. There is recognition that citizenship education, having only arrived formally in 2002, is still relatively embryonic and prone to being under-researched (Gearon 2003). Impact measures are thus difficult to measure in newer pilot projects. Nonetheless, some initial research provides illumination on the developments of citizenship education.

A three year evaluation of the post-16 citizenship development projects established by the government in 2001 found that the most effective citizenship programmes are those which combine knowledge and understanding with action, termed 'political literacy in action' replacing mere political knowledge (Nelson et al. 2004: 2). The active involvement of young people in making decisions about their learning (ibid.) together with evidence of negotiation with young people of the key issues to be explored were cited as critical success factors (2004: 6). Such practice is aided by critically reflective learning environments that depend on a variety of experiential learning experiences, together with the use of relevant current events and useful resources (ibid.). While educational programmes that worked in partnership with national organisations, local charities or community agencies were considered 'best practice', such examples:

> tended to be underdeveloped, with little interaction ... and some larger organisations reporting that they found it difficult to find suitable opportunities for community linking and activities for all their young people. (Nelson et al. 2004: 5)

Here, small youth work projects were advantageous due to their unusually high staff to young person ratio, resulting in greater opportunity for community integration (ibid.).

Craig et al. (2004) suggested that the most successful citizenship provision was characterised as having flexible, but rigorous frameworks for delivery with a clear definition of citizenship. This was complemented by an enthusiasm and commitment from senior managers and staff delivering programmes, with the active involvement of young people in decisions about their learning (Craig et al. 2004: 1).

Towards 'effective citizenship' education

The problems with communitarian citizenship are readily identified, even with a cursory review offered in this chapter. It has the tendency to romanticise communities, and institute these as sites of governance without due regard to the power differences that exist in neighbourhoods. Citizenship education, in this mould, becomes nothing more than a programme of addressing a young person's individual political, social and moral deficits. Actually, as recent research shows young people identify 'strongly with their city and/or local neighbourhood' (Osler and Starkey 2003: 252; see also Wood 2008) and already engage in a wide range of behaviours that are suggestive of 'compassion, respect for differences, and a willingness to work with others' (Giroux 2003: 140). These acts of citizenship are wide ranging, and not easily defined in neat policy categories of what it means to be a good citizen (Lister et al. 2002; Wood 2008). Citizenship education offers the opportunity to build on these experiences, but also to recognise that such an enterprise needs to do more than 'activate' young people: they must be supported to be effective in shaping and influencing their social worlds.

What then are the key characteristics of effective citizenship, and how might practitioners' work facilitate its development? The first distinction is the difference between what Faulks (2000) has termed 'thin' and 'thick' citizenship. Thin citizenship is characterised by a rights privileged, passive independence that suggests freedom through 'choice'. Thick citizenship, on the other hand, is characterised by mutual interplay between rights and responsibilities, an interdependence between citizens and an emphasis on civic virtue as the path to freedom. It is dependent not only on the individual exercising her/his active citizenship behaviours but the wider civic

Table 12.1 Differences between active and effective citizenship

Active citizenship	Effective citizenship
Thin	Thick
Personal rewards	Collective rewards
Individual behaviour	Community behaviours
Political awareness	Political change
Tokenistic	Realistic
Deficits	Opportunities
Prescribed	Negotiated

community also accepting a 'shared responsibility for our common future' (Osler and Starkey 2003: 252). To work towards such ethical goals however requires a commitment to the further characteristics outlined in Table 12.1.

There has been much interest in the personal rewards gained from active involvement in voluntary work and other initiatives through structured activity. Indeed, many of the key governmental campaigns and policy initiatives underpinning volunteering drives have emphasised a 'rewards' approach (see for example *Youth Matters*). However, this limits the purpose of the active citizenship experience to a narrow set of individualised gains. Such rewards and accredited outcomes tend to lead only to short-term, specific 'acts' of structured citizenship rather than a comprehensive change in thinking, values and ongoing behaviour (Wood 2008). Instead there is an opportunity to emphasise a *wider reward gain* for the whole community. This means arguing that communities *benefit* from the active engagement of young people in public life, not least through better inter-generational relationships.

The goal of educators may indeed be to support individual knowledge, skills and attributes but we must also take an active role in shaping *community behaviours*. Communities can be hostile places where young people can be targeted and excluded. Practitioners need to engage in a process of 'conflict resolution', ensuring that the wider community develops a healthy respect for its younger members: the notion of reciprocity (Fitzpatrick 2005; Ungar 2007). For example, Norfolk County Council developed an effective pilot programme that involved young people in a scheme designed to overcome the mutual mistrust and poor relations between young people and the community police. With a recognition that 'young people are an intrinsic part of the communities in which they live' (Ronan and Cooper 2005: 10), the 'Young People as Police Trainers' programme led to better relationships, and more effective strategies for tackling anti-social behaviour including an increase in non-punitive measures. Here, the focus was less on young people's behaviour and more on the attitudes of the police and the wider community.

Citizenship educators must also think about strategies for effective, *political change*. Many laudable attempts at encouraging political literacy are limited to short term, high profile events. In schools, evaluative studies lament the absence of 'political literacy in action' envisaged by the AGC report (Kerr et al. 2004). In its current form, citizenship education may do little to address the 'crisis in politics' (Storrie 2004) and does not address the fundamental structural problems inherent in the democratic deficit. A longer term, effective engagement would require a systematic review of how political institutions demonstrate responsiveness to young people's needs as a norm, rather than in the guise of short term consultation. In Norfolk, a 'menu' of approaches to involving young people in decision making has been commended for its efforts. Two notable examples include:

- The establishment of a 'young person's scrutiny group' that has ensured that all local decisions impacting upon young people are effectively 'reviewed' by a panel involving extensive youth-led consultation.
- A formal recognition that not all young people will want to engage in the formal local authority democratic structures, particularly those who are 'hard to reach'. Here, workers should approach such tasks with innovation as is the case with another Norfolk initiative, 'Life Swap', where young people who face systematic difficulties, and local councillors, share insights into their lives in order to foster better understanding and dialogue (see www.lifeswap.org.uk).

Indeed, such strategies avoid the common issue of tokenism, evident in much local authority consultation. For example, in a study of rural Connexions services, we found that standardised models of consultation had been applied in order to fulfil the requirement of 'talking to young people'. In this case, rural issues were overlooked and consultation was not followed up (Wood 2003). The other end of such an approach is to overstate the possibility of political change. Here, the experience of Warwickshire's Youthvoice is worth drawing on. Their approach is grounded in a *realism*. Young people frequently lobby central government departments to advocate on behalf of their peers. As part of these interventions, they expect to be disappointed sometimes, and reflect upon this as an important learning process about the limitations of one's own involvement in democracy.

Almost all research about citizenship education focuses on the deficits inherent in young people. Rather, we should instead recognise that young people possess skills and knowledge that should be built upon. For example, Roker and Eden (2002) suggest that young people across the country are involved in social action of varying degrees and that participation is representative across a broad range of ethnic and social backgrounds. Working from an opportunities perspective enables us to adopt a 'social action' approach to work with young people, asking: what is already known and acted upon? How do young people already engage in social action? What are the existing barriers? Asking such questions enable us to better locate citizenship opportunities in the context of the localised experience of young people.

The characteristics of effective citizenship rely on a cornerstone feature of youth work practice: *negotiation* between practitioners and young people. This takes place across a number of levels: in the issues that are most important to young people; the methods that should be employed to deliver citizenship education and; the roles that young people play. In each of the evaluative studies conducted on the various citizenship programmes (from formal education through to youth work at post-16), an emphasis on negotiated learning is seen as a critical success factor yet, unsurprising it is rarely prioritised in formal education (Craig et al. 2004; Kerr et al. 2004; Nelson et al. 2004). Prescriptive citizenship, in the form of standardised teaching of knowledge alone with limited impact, is prone to be undervalued and in fact, as we have seen, leads to limited evidence of consequent action.

Conclusion

Citizenship education has gained impetus over the past decade, with all suggestions that a political consensus is now grounded in terms of what is expected from young people in the way of social, moral and democratic behaviours. Those who work with young people outside of formal education can make a significant contribution based upon a longstanding commitment to increasing participation and fostering democracy. This, however, requires a move in both purpose and method towards an 'effective citizenship' education: a more sustainable, negotiated process that will have greater impact upon communities and institutions. Such an approach requires a restatement of the values inherent in youth work: respect for young people, voluntary association, negotiation of issues and advocacy of young people's place in their communities. It requires a negotiation of 'the theory and practice of what it means to be a citizen' (Coffey 2004: 49). Only with such commitments can citizenship truly reflect a 'whole community' approach, with young people valued as critically engaged members of both political and public space.

Reflective questions for practice

- Think about the young people that you work with. What sorts of socially and politically 'responsible' behaviour do they already engage in?
- What is the relationship between young people and the wider community like?
- Are there any tensions? How could you go about challenging some of the problems that exist?
- Try applying the principles of effective citizenship to your own work with young people – how would you compare them to your practice?

Further reading

Heater, D. (2004) *Citizenship: The Civic Ideal in World History, Politics and Education*, **Manchester: Manchester University Press**. A comprehensive introduction to the core aspects of citizenship, with chapters ranging from the origins and history, through to the 'feeling of citizenship'.

Invernizzi, A. and Williams, J. (eds) (2008) *Children and Citizenship*, **London: Sage**. A very useful and accessible edited collection of chapters exploring the theoretical, policy and legislative contexts of children's citizenship.

Lockyer, A., Crick, B. and Annette, J. (eds) (2003) *Education for Democratic Citizenship: Issues of Theory and Practice*, **Aldershot: Ashgate**. Reviews theoretical and practical issues of citizenship education including: the problems of teaching citizenship in an anti-political culture, issues of gender and 'race', the political status of children and the teaching of controversial issues.

For practical ideas about planning, implementing and evaluating post-16 citizenship programmes, see the extensive Qualifications and Curriculum Authority website at: www.qca.org.uk/post16index.html

13

RISK, SOCIAL POLICY AND YOUNG PEOPLE

Hazel Kemshall

Key arguments

- Youth policy is increasingly directed towards young people who are 'at risk' or a risk to others.
- This has led to greater use of risk factors as predictors of future outcomes, and an emphasis on early intervention strategies.
- These approaches can be criticised for further marginalising and criminalising young people, failing to take into account the personal biography.
- Young people are not mere risk 'dupes', framed entirely by policy and unable to exercise personal agency in the construction of their own lives and identities.
- Workers bring their own values and ideologies to bear on policy interpretation and delivery, and in the area of youth policy they present 'firewalls' to the direct impact of current policies.

Introduction

Youth and risk are increasingly intertwined in contemporary social policy, with young people characterised as either 'at risk' or as the site of risk(s) to others (Kelly 2003; Sharland 2006; France 2007). Life for young people in contemporary society is both challenging and uncertain. The individual life course is no longer mapped out and predictable (Giddens 1991, 2001), and the 'risk society' is described as inherently uncertain (Giddens 1991, 1998a, b; Beck 1992) within which risks are individually framed and experienced and negotiated individually. This is particularly acute for young people who are the first generation to 'grow up' in the risk society (Wyn and Dwyer 1999). Biographies are no longer 'normal' or standard, but are experienced by social actors as complex and ambivalent (Kelly 1999; Lopez and Hernandez 1999; EGRIS 2001; Furlong and Cartmel 2007). Thus, individuals are framed as shapers of their own worlds 'making decisions according to calculations of risk and opportunity' (Petersen 1996: 47), but risking blame and punishment if they get their choices wrong.

This chapter will explore the evolving role of risk in youth social policy, with particular reference to the increased 'problematisation of youth' (Kelly 2000) and state driven interventions to regulate and control youth. In this context, social policy is interpreted more broadly than 'mere' welfare, but as the strategic state organisation of social provision in its many forms and its use within broader public policy – for example, to regulate youth transitions into adulthood (Lavalette and Pratt 1997). Following Power (2004) the ambiguity of risk and its ability to elide precise definition is taken as a starting point. This enables a focus on how risk is framed by youth social policy for attention, and how risk has been used as a key driver in the framing of the 'crisis of youth' (Eckersley 1988, 1992, 1995) and the subsequent state controlled interventions (Kelly 2000).

This discourse of risk – whether 'at risk' or 'dangerous' youth – individualises risk and responsibilises youth and their families for its effective management (Kelly 2001). Individualisation reconstitutes social risks as individual ones, e.g. unemployment as personal skill deficit and hence amenable to human agency and choice. Risks are the product of individual decision making and individuals are responsible for their avoidance and for the exercise of prudential choice (e.g. skill training and life-long learning) (Rose 1996b). This is what Rose has termed responsibilisation (Rose 1996b, 2000). Rose (1996a, b) argues that governance in neo-liberal societies is carried out at the 'molecular level' in which the active citizen is required to self-regulate towards the pre-set norms of society. Those who fail to exercise the prudential risk choice are excluded, marginalised and demonised.

From a broader perspective, the drive towards responsibilisation and the creation of 'active citizens' (Rose 1996a, b) is seen as compounding existing inequalities rather than addressing them (Walklate 1998). In brief, some sections of the population (and perhaps disadvantaged youth most of all) do not have the resources to become expert risk managers of their fate, and these less active citizens are heavily constrained in their risk choices by poverty, social exclusion, and geographical location (Stenson 2001). Risk is not necessarily an equitable business, and is enmeshed in wider processes of social regulation (Kelly 2000).

To what extent is youth policy led by risk?

'Risk society' and the issues of governance in post modern neo-liberal societies have been seen as crucial to recent social policy changes (Culpitt 1999) although the extent to which risk has been a key driver is contested (see Kemshall 2002a for a review). In brief, the contention is that the State has increasingly devolved responsibility for the management of risks (e.g. ill health, unemployment, etc.) to the individual and that social responsibility has been eroded (Rose 1996a). This reduces the costs to the State, but as importantly reduces dependency and moral hazard (Parker 1982), and encourages a more flexible and risk-taking attitude to the navigation of the life course and the changes that will inevitably take place (Giddens 1991, 1998b). The 'active' rather than the 'passive' citizen is seen as desirable, both morally and economically, particularly in an era of rapid social and technological change, an issue explored by Jason Wood in Chapter 12. The contention is that social policy is no longer about the alleviation of individual needs or about the pursuit of a collective good. Rather it is about the prevention of risk and the displacement of risk management responsibilities onto the 'entrepreneurial self' who must exercise informed choice and self-care to avoid risks (Castel 1991; Petersen 1996, 1997).

The concepts of risk and responsibilisation also raise questions about new techniques of social regulation (although there is some debate about how transformative present conditions currently are, see Garland 2001). This trend can be discerned in the following areas: policy responses to social exclusion (MacDonald and Marsh 2001); the transformation of welfare needs to risks (Kemshall 2002a); and the reframing of youth social policy into criminal justice policy (see Chapter 14). Within this context, dealing with 'troubled' or 'troublesome' young people is now a major policy concern (Goldson 2000).

It is, however, tempting to make grand claims about the ubiquitous nature of risk, particularly at the policy level, although such claims can often be difficult to empirically evidence (Dingwall 1999; Kemshall and Maguire 2001; O'Malley 2004). Similarly, general claims about responsibilisation and individualisation have been subject to much scrutiny, particularly with reference to youth (Engel and Strasser 1998; Green et al. 2000; Cote 2002; Furlong and Cartmel 2007). As Kelly argues (1999) youth have long occupied the 'wild zones' of 'deviancy', 'delinquency', and 'ungovernability', but the key difference now is the 'institutionalised mistrust' of youth, all youth (Kelly 2003), resulting in this mistrust becoming:

> increasingly governmentalized – rationalized, instituionalized and abstracted under the auspices of a constellation of State agencies, quasi-autonomous non-government organizations, and non-government organizations … This governmentalization energizes processes of surveillance-surveillance that is targeted and focused, in the interests of economy, at those populations that pose, or face, the greatest dangers and risks. (Kelly 2003: 167)

This risk based surveillance extends itself into numerous areas of young peoples' lives – examination and surveillance at school, CCTV of public spaces and the 'street', 'outreach' with 'at risk populations', regulation of behaviours (drug taking, etc.) and the criminalisation of problematic activities (e.g. ASBOs); ably supported by research, risk tools and formalised procedures to identify 'early risk factors', 'at risk populations', and those likely to pursue criminal careers (Farrington 2000). Two specific areas will now be considered:

- Identification and regulation of 'at risk' youth.
- The criminalisation of youth who 'pose a risk'.

Identification and regulation of 'at risk' youth

Located within the risk prevention paradigm (Farrington 2000) preoccupation with 'at risk' children and youth permeates much youth policy, and is concerned with a cost-effective and unproblematic transition from youth to adulthood, and most particularly into active citizenship and productive labour (see Batten and Russell 1995; Withers and Batten 1995 for a full review). Identifying 'at risk' youth has spawned an industry, with Swadener and Lubeck (1995) arguing that in the United States between 1989 and 1995 over 2500 articles on at risk children and families were published (see also Tait 1995 for the framing of the 'at risk'discourse). Policies and interventions also proliferated in the 1990s, ranging (in the UK) from early interventions (Farrington 1995) including Sure Start (Glass 1999), assessing children in need (*Every Child Matters* DfES 2003), those in danger of a 'Mis-spent Youth' (Audit Commission 1996), and those at risk of developing a criminal career (Farrington 2000).

While the ensuing interventions are often presented in the discourse of care, protection and support (DoH/DEE 2000; Garrett 2003), ensuring social cohesion and economic performance are also key considerations (Kelly 2006). As Evans contends, the 'more insecure and flexible system' of the English labour market 'necessitates greater proactivity and the maintenance of the positive approach to 'opportunities'' (2002: 265). In addition, the economic discourse of risk has also permeated social policy itself, with considerations of cost and benefit in policy formation (Kemshall 2002a) – what are the societal and economic benefits of pursuing a particular policy? The costs of not pursuing policies are also pertinent, for example in the costs of social exclusion (Social Exclusion Unit 2000b, c), the perpetuation of a dependent (and potentially criminal) underclass (Murray 1990), and the social dislocation of 'sink estates' (Campbell 1993).

These risk prevention policies have the following in common:

- A focus on the individual and family as the site of risk and regulation.
- A formal, calculable and probabilistic approach to risk.

Families and individuals have long been the site of social engineering and social regulation, not least through the 'soft policing' of the welfare state, education, and the informal controls of the labour market (Donzelot 1979). In recent decades increasing attention has focused on 'breaking the cycle of dependence' and dysfunction, and in the alleviation of accumulated risk factors through the life course (Schoon and Bynner 2003). This has been particularly acute under New Labour, with its emphasis upon 'rights as well as responsibilities' (Blair 1998) and the alleviation of inequality through the labour market rather than through welfare (see Kemshall 2002a for a full review). Central to this position has been the early identification of 'problematic' children and families for early interventions, and programmes targeted at the alleviation of risk factors at particular points during the life course, for example *Sure Start*, literacy programmes, school inclusion projects, and assistance in the transition from school to work, for example *Connexions* (Atkinson and Hills 1998; Glass 1999; Schoon and Bynner 2003). Fundamental to this approach is the identification of risk factors and risk trajectories in which one risk factor 'reinforces another, leading to increasingly restricted outcomes in later life (Rutter 1990)' (Schoon and Bynner 2003: 23). Children and their families are then constructed as repositories of risk factors, with predetermined risk trajectories ripe for intervention. As Schoon and Bynner put it:

> Risk factors therefore provide targets for policy in the sense that they help to identify populations at risk – those in disadvantaged neighbourhoods, those growing up in adverse circumstances, ... together with related components of children's experience that may be directly susceptible to intervention (e.g. children falling behind at school, parents showing no interest in their children's education). (2003: 22)

While constructed within an agenda concerned to address social exclusion and to provide more inclusionary strategies, this approach has been critiqued for its potential to compound existing exclusion and marginalisation by stigmatising disadvantaged groups and in some cases criminalising them (Scraton 2004). A clear example is the Youth Inclusion Projects (YIPs), targeted at the 50 most 'at risk' children in communities (usually disadvantaged communities) for early preventative intervention and aimed primarily at the prevention of offending. YIPs are a Youth Justice Board initiative and while couched in the language of 'at risk' and need, their objectives are crime prevention (Youth Justice Board undated). It is perhaps no coincidence that the 50 most needy and 'at risk' children are also the 50 deemed most at risk of offending (often defined as the most problematic children in the neighbourhood and often from the most problematic families (Yates 2006)). In this way social policy concerns reveal themselves as social regulation ones, and social policy elides into criminal justice policy (Stenson 2001).

The risk prevention paradigm has also been critiqued on the grounds that risk prediction remains difficult. The linkage of risk factor(s) to risk trajectory(s) has been empirically difficult. This is due in large part to the difficulty in establishing the relationship between risk factor(s) and subsequent outcomes, well expressed by Farrington who asks how we distinguish between causal relationships and mere correlations, how we can attribute weight to different factors when causes may be multi-factorial, and how levels of risk can be calculated when risk 'scores' are not merely additive? (2000: 7). For Farrington the greater challenge is in establishing 'processes or developmental pathways that intervene between risk factors and outcomes, and to bridge the gap between risk factor research and more complex explanatory theories' (p.7). This may require the recognition that risk trajectories are social processes that have multiple causes, and that such causes are not merely additive; and that subtle differences in initial conditions may over time produce large differences in outcomes (Byrne 1998: 2–28). This would help to explain why children initially risked marked similarly (e.g. by individual and family risk markers) actually go onto have different risk trajectories, and why a proportion of 'high risk' children go on to have positive outcomes (see also Schoon and Bynner 2003). This makes targeting with certainty inherently difficult, and the identification of those children and youths able to risk navigate successfully despite adverse circumstances has been less well researched and is less evident in policy responses (see Kemshall et al. 2006).

The criminalisation of youth who 'pose a risk'

As argued above, social policy responses can quickly elide into criminal justice ones. As Goldson expresses it:

> policy formation is conditioned within the context of wider political priorities. In this respect the government's steadfast resolve to be seen to be 'tough' on crime, social disorder and 'anti-social behaviour' is especially significant ... Indeed when the children of the poor behave in such a way as to disturb moral sensibilities, or worse still to transgress the law, the humane logic of progressive welfare oriented anti-poverty responses is eclipsed by disciplinary measures encoded within an increasingly repressive and responsibilizing correctionalism. (2002: 685)

This transposes structural issues into individual ones, and responsibilises children and their families for their solution (Bandalli 2000; Goldson 2002). Crime is not a response to structural disadvantage or even a rational choice for dealing with daily survival on Britain's 'sink estates' (Yates 2006), it is simply a matter of moral degeneracy and faulty thinking. Such risk based correctionalism has resulted in what Goldson has called a 'schism' between the '"deserving" troubled child' and the '"undeserving" troublesome one' (2002: 685), the former deserving of a 'hand up' and the latter deserving of remoralisation and correctional programmes (Kemshall 2002b). This latter position was clearly reflected in the Home Office document *No More Excuses* (Home Office 1997), and reflects what Muncie has called an 'institutionalised intolerance' to youth offending (1999b).

Children (and their families) are now subject to a wide range of interventions (some only subject to civil standards of proof) such as the Anti-Social Behaviour Orders, the Child Safety Order, Child Curfews, and the Parenting Order; imposed 'whether or not the child has been prosecuted, or even committed an offence' (Goldson 2002: 692; see also Brown 2004; Burney 2005; and Yates, Chapter 14), supported by inter-agency interventions through Final Warning schemes and Referral Orders for preventative actions (for a full review see Goldson 2000).

With young offenders, and particularly youth 'at risk' of offending, this has resulted in increased attention to 'developmental careers' (Loeber and LeBlanc 1990; Robins and Rutter 1990; Loeber et al. 1991) and the formation of 'interventions designed to prevent the development of criminal potential in individuals' (Farrington 2000: 3). This approach is attractive because it promises a more effective focus for policy, better targeting of programmes and practitioner resources, and an emphasis on prevention and pre-custodial programmes is seen as both morally and economically desirable for dealing with youth crime. This approach has also extended itself to 'communities at risk' (Hawkins and Catalano 1992; Catalano and Hawkins 1996), prey to anti-social behaviour, crime, disadvantage and social exclusion (Utting 1999; Social Exclusion Unit 2000b, c). Such communities have been targeted for multi-agency interventions such as 'zero tolerance' of crime and incivility (Home Office 2003), 'building social capital' and resilience to crime (Halpern 2005), and informal surveillance through information collection and exchange by key agencies and formal surveillance through CCTV (Yates 2006). A strategy not only to tackle social exclusion, but also to reclaim Britain's 'dangerous places' (Campbell 1993).

This creeping criminalisation of youth has been instrumental in a significant 'Othering' of youth (Kelly 2003, 2006), using a discourse of risk to place youth on the margins of mainstream society and in need of normalisation (Rose 1996a). In this process both the discourse of 'posing a risk' and being 'at risk' have been significant labels (Goldson 2000; Kelly 2000). This 'Othering' of youth has become such a powerful and pervasive discourse it has extended to all children, for example the statement that *Every Child Matters* (DfES 2003), and the framework for assessment of children in need and their families (DoH/DEE 2000). Potentially all children can be 'at risk' and on this basis state intervention is justified.

Conclusion: is it as risky as all that?

There is considerable evidence that social policies aimed at youth are risk driven, especially in the area of key life transitions; avoiding crime, delinquency and dependency; and in regulating families and individuals towards greater entrepreneurship and responsibilisation. However, it is important not to caricature young people as mere risk 'dupes', framed entirely by policy and unable to exercise personal agency in the construction of their own lives and identities. Recent studies have shown young people as proactive risk takers (Green et al. 2000; Essau 2006), capable of constructing alternative selves to those framed by policy (Yates 2006), and capable of negotiating risk and adverse circumstances contrary to current risk prevention predictions (Evans 2002; Schoon and Bynner 2003). It is also important to recognise that policies are also mediated by the workforces tasked with implementing them. Workers bring their own values and ideologies to bear on policy interpretation and delivery, and in the area of youth policy they may for example present 'firewalls' to the direct impact of current policies (O'Malley 1996). They may for example focus on resilience rather than risk, care rather than control, and empowerment rather than marginalisation.

Grand theoretical claims for the power of individualisation and globalisation to transform all concerns into risk may be overstated and remain open to empirical contestation (O'Malley 2004). Yeates for example states that we need a more 'nuanced' understanding of globalisation that takes into account 'the enduring power of local forces', culture and ideology to mediate the impact of and reaction to globalisation (1999: 372). As she states: 'The 'constraints' that are placed on social policy development are primarily ideological and thus susceptible to political manipulation' (1999: 389). They are a matter of political will and choice, and are not merely ordained by factors totally beyond our control. Similar criticisms have been levelled at individualisation, with Furlong and Cartmel (2007), among other commentators (e.g. Engels and Strasser 1998) doubting the extent to which individualisation has subsumed structure as a major determinant in the lives of young people. While more negotiation of the complexities of post modern life may be called for, it is still a truism that disadvantaged youth is also high risk youth (Goldson 2002), and that ethnicity, class and to some extent gender remain major precursors of the life course (Evans 2002; Furlong and Cartmel 2007). Paradoxically, individualisation is posed as a key driver for the risk society, and yet the uncertainties inherent in individualisation are subsumed by policy to the general predictions of the risk prevention paradigm. This conundrum and challenge is perhaps the most hopeful 'firewall' to risk policy – for policy based on predictability and probabilistic certainty is likely to be strained by individualisation. Personal biography may yet triumph over risk prediction.

Reflective questions for practice

- In what ways do you think social problems have become classified as individual risks?
- In what ways are the young people you work with categorised as either 'at risk' or likely to 'pose a risk' to others?
- How do 'risk factors' influence your approaches to work with young people?
- Do you act as a 'firewall' in mediating risk policy? If so, in what ways do you think you do this?

Further reading

Furlong, A. and Cartmel, F. (2007) *Young People and Social Change: individualization and risk in late modernity* **2nd edn, Buckingham: McGraw-Hill/Open University Press.** This is seminal work on the relative impact of late modernity on youth. The authors draw on extensive empirical work to evaluate whether 'youth' is indeed presented with more wide ranging risks that previously, and interestingly conclude that the roles of class and gender are still pertinent to the lives of youth as well as new risks arising from late modernity.

Kemshall, H. (2008) 'Risks, rights and justice: understanding and responding to youth risk', *Youth Justice***, 8 (1): 21–37.** This article reviews the current challenges to youth arising from both social and criminal justice policy, and explores some recent policy and practice responses to 'problem youth'. The gradual erosion of 'youth rights' is posed as a particular concern as policy responses continue to focus on the control of problematic youth.

Sharland, E. (2006) 'Young people, risk taking and risk making', *British Journal of Social Work***, 36 (2): 247–265.** An interesting article that reviews the current perspectives on youth risk taking that are embedded in current social policy and social work responses to youth. The author presents a wide range of literature and empirical studies in an well argued presentation of the key issues.

14

YOUTH JUSTICE: MOVING IN AN ANTI-SOCIAL DIRECTION

Joe Yates

Key arguments

- Since 1998 Youth Justice in England and Wales has undergone significant change and rapid expansion. Anti-Social Behaviour powers offer one of the starkest examples of this expansion and these now play a central role in the regulation and social control of youth.
- Anti-social behaviour is an elastic concept and defining it is inherently problematic. This has allowed anti-social behaviour powers to be used in a wide range of ways targeting a wide range of behaviours.
- While concerns about young people are nothing new, there is now a concerted 'total panic' about youth, particularly those who do not fit with middle-class notions of childhood.
- In the current context youth work is increasingly under pressure to play a central role in responding to and managing 'anti-social' youth and managing the 'risks' that youth are constructed as posing.

Introduction

Anti-social behaviour has become a focus of New Labour criminal justice policy and powers introduced to 'tackle' it now play a central role in the regulation and social control of youth. Since the Anti-Social Behaviour Order first appeared on the statute books in 1998 there has been a raft of legislation which has further extended these powers. In any text aimed at professionals working with young people, a critical appraisal of the importance afforded to 'anti-social behaviour' in governmental discourses and the powers designed to tackle it is of central importance. Brown (2005) argues that anti-social behaviour legislation has created a new domain of professional and power and knowledge. This chapter offers a critical appraisal of this new domain, which has massively extended criminalising modes of social control, and explores some of the implications that anti-social behaviour powers have had for marginalised young people. The chapter begins by exploring the genesis of these powers and attempts to locate them within the broader remit of New Labour crime control and youth justice strategies. It then goes on to identify the problems inherent in defining what represents anti-social behaviour. Anti-social behaviour powers and the legislation which underpins them are briefly identified outlining the anti-social legislative framework and discussing the extent to which the drive to tackle anti-social behaviour has focused on marginalised young people. The chapter then moves on to consider historical and contemporary concerns about youth. The chapter concludes by identifying the limits of the anti-social behaviour paradigm and offering an analysis of the challenges this presents for youth work professionals.

New Labour and youth justice

> Youth justice systems are dynamic and ever-changing sites of contestation and change, the settlements of competing and/or intersecting thematic concepts including: 'welfare'; 'justice'; 'informalism'; 'rights'; 'responsibilities' and 'retribution/punishment'. (Goldson and Muncie 2006: 204)

In any attempt to critically appraise New Labour youth justice policies it is important to consider the context out of which the New Labour project emerged so as to understand why the thematic priorities of 'responsibility' and 'retribution/punishment' gained ascendancy in shaping youth justice policy over other arguably more progressive 'priorities' (Goldson and Muncie 2006). Youth justice in England and Wales has recently undergone a number of significant changes, which commenced with the implementation of the 1998 Crime and Disorder Act. These changes have radically altered the rationale and focus of the youth justice system. They have included the abolition of *doli incapax* (the presumption that young people under the age of 14 were incapable of criminal responsibility), which has effectively reduced the age of criminal responsibility from 14 to 10 (see Bandalli 2000); the development of multi-agency Youth Offending Teams (YOTs) (see Burnett and Appleton 2004); the setting up of the Youth Justice Board (YJB); the introduction of a range of new orders (including the anti-social behaviour order and local child curfews, see R. Smith 2003); and the promotion of early criminal justice interventions as an effective way of working with young people in trouble (see Goldson 2001).

A number of commentators have been critical of these changes in relation to the extent to which they represent a process of net-widening, exposing greater numbers of young people to the stigmatising and criminalising effects of criminal justice processes (Muncie 1999b; Goldson 2001; Pitts 2003; Goldson and Yates 2008). Indeed, even those who adopt a more favourable analysis have noted concerns regarding worryingly high levels of youth custody (D. Smith 2003) which currently stand as the highest in Western Europe. This concern was expressed by a recent chair of the Youth Justice Board of England and Wales who voiced concerns regarding the high number of young people being drawn into the system for relatively minor acts of youthful transgression and worryingly high levels of child custody. Thus, New Labour's 'New Youth Justice' (Goldson 2000) is argued to represent a punitive and unnecessary authoritarian interventionist approach to young people in trouble (Jamieson 2005). A system which since 1993 has seen a 90 per cent increase in the number of children imprisoned. The United Nations Commissioner on Human Rights observed – albeit in a more diplomatic tone – that it was difficult for him 'to avoid the impression that (in the UK) juvenile trouble-makers are too rapidly drawn into the criminal justice system and young offenders too readily placed in detention' (Gil-Robles 2005: 27).

It has been suggested that the emergence of a distinctive New Labour position in relation to youth crime can be traced to 1993, 'when a perceived political imperative of challenging Tory dominance in this area of policy began to be translated into a coherent strategy' (R. Smith 2003: 49). The 1970s, 1980s and 1990s represented a period when the Conservative right established a hegemony in the field of law and order and challenging this became a key element of the electoral strategy of the New Labour opposition (Pitts 2000). Challenging this hegemony clearly presented a contest to the Labour party for whom law and order was seen as something of an 'Achilles heel' (Morgan 2000). Indeed as Morgan (2000) observes, the Labour party stance had historically asserted the need to consider socio-economic and broader structural issues in order to understand criminality, however this was often interpreted as providing excuses for offending and not reflecting the publics 'real' concerns about crime. In the quest to wrestle the mantle of law and order from the right, New Labour utilised the tools of 'punitive rhetoric' (Goldson 2005: 16) to gain political ground in the law and order debate (Goldson 2005; Jamison and Yates 2009; Tonry 2004). Indeed in both opposition and in government, New Labour actively sought to make political capital out of populist concerns around youth and crime. In doing this it has been argued that they were 'talking up the problem' of law and order and 'anti-social behaviour' in order to appear 'tough' (Tonry 2004). This reflects the extent to which law and order became a key electoral priority for New Labour (Brownlee 1998) as it became seen as the space where the demons of the Labour movement's 'idealist' past would be exorcised through the enforcement of a rigorously authoritarian agenda. Nowhere was this more evident than in the area of youth justice which became the site of intense 'toughness jousting' between the two major parties (see Jamieson and Yates 2009).

The New Labour administration's desire to give the 'impression that something is being done – here now, swiftly and decisively' (Garland 2001 cited in Jamieson, 2005) about youth, crime and more recently anti-social behaviour has subsequently led to an unprecedented expansion of the system of social control (Scraton 2004). Anti-social behaviour powers perhaps offer the starkest example of net-widening in the field of criminal justice processes as they have played a key role in the expansion of the youth justice system and led to a dispersal of discipline (Cohen 1985), which has effectively exposed ever younger children to criminalising processes for behaviours which are not in themselves criminal. Thus at the 'shallow end' of prevention, younger children are exposed to what Goldson (2005) has termed 'criminalising modes of social control' for behaviour which – historically – would not have fallen within the remit of the criminal justice system. Correspondingly at the 'deep end', the number of children held in custodial environments has increased leaving Britain as Western Europe's child jail capital. Processes which the introduction and enforcement of anti-social powers have arguably contributed to.

Defining the 'anti-social'

As noted in the introduction 'anti-social behaviour' has become a key term in the lexicon of the social control industry. However, defining actually what is anti-social behaviour is a problematic exercise. Garside (2005) argues that the definition provided by the Crime and Disorder Act 1998, which defines anti-social behaviour as behaviour which 'caused or was likely to cause harassment, alarm or distress', could mean anything and what can be anti-social for one individual or group may not for another. The Home Office White Paper, *Respect and Responsibility* (2003) acknowledges this stating, 'Anti-social behaviour means different things to different people'. The Home Office (2006) website identifies examples of anti-social behaviour which not only provide insight into the scope of behaviours which can fall into the remit of the 'anti-social' but also the lack of clarity around what is anti-social, what is crime and what is both, as shown in the box below:

Box 14.1   Examples of anti-social behaviour

- nuisance neighbours
- rowdy and nuisance behaviour
- yobbish behaviour and intimidating groups taking over public spaces
- vandalism, graffiti and fly-posting
- people dealing and buying drugs on the street
- people dumping rubbish and abandoning cars
- begging and anti-social drinking
- the misuse of fireworks

Source: www.homeoffice.gov.uk/anti-social-behaviour/what-is-asb/?view=Standard

These very different forms of behaviour which fall into the remit of anti-social behaviour, as Burney argues, reveal 'the inherent logical flaws in an overarching concept of "anti-social behaviour" which embraces perceptions of such varied phenomena' (Burney 2005: 60). In addition as R. Smith (2003) argues they also dilute the burden of proof otherwise required to justify a coercive intervention. This has led Burney to describe the Anti-Social Behaviour Order as an 'emblem of punitive populism' (2002: 469) which effectively blurs the boundaries between civil and criminal law. Millie et al. go as far as to argue that there has been an unwillingness on behalf of government to offer a clear definition of what constitutes anti-social behaviour, so as not to 'curb artificially the range of uses to which the new measures for tackling ASB could be put' (2005: vii). This has allowed anti-social behaviour powers to be used in a wide range of ways targeting a wide range of behaviours. Indeed behaviours as diverse as spitting, associating with friends and family, travelling on buses in a specific area, going into shops, committing suicide, being sarcastic, being on the street, political protesting, and visiting family members have all been prohibited by anti-social behaviour powers (www.asboconcern.org.uk).

On a national and a local level this level of 'elasticity' can lead to a confused understanding among professionals of what constitutes anti-social behaviour and has implications in relation to the discretionary manner in which anti-social behaviour powers are used (Yates 2006). This 'elasticity' has also facilitated a level of flexibility in how different agencies in different localities have approached both identifying and responding to 'anti-social behaviour' (Yates 2006). It has also meant that the use of anti-social behaviour powers has varied across authorities posing the very real risk of a form of injustice by geography – clear evidence of which can be seen in the discrepancies in the use of anti-social behaviour orders in comparable authorities (see Hancock 2006 and Koffman 2006). It is also apparent that these powers on a national and a local level have been consistently and purposefully targeted at young people (Koffman 2006; Squires and Stephen 2005; Yates 2006) and they have 'borne down hard on Britain's most disadvantaged communities' (Millie et al. 2005: 38). As Hughes and Follett argue, 'the seemingly newly "discovered" problem of anti-social behaviour appears to be increasingly recoded as a problem of young people in deprived and marginalised communities and neighbourhoods' (2006: 157).

Anti-social powers

The roots of anti-social powers theoretically can be found in right 'realist' theory such as Wilson and Kelling (1982) and politically in the policy proposals emerging from right-wing policy think tanks in the early 1990s. However, it was the New Labour administration which made tackling anti-social behaviour a priority in their 1997 electoral strategy and it was with the Crime and Disorder Act 1998 that the Anti-Social Behaviour Order was introduced; arguably reflecting the extent to which they were influenced by 'realist' criminologies from both the right and the left (see Muncie 2000). In line with its earlier stated aims that there will be *No More Excuses* (Home Office 1997) for young offenders and to be 'tough on crime and the causes of crime', anti-social behaviour powers have been heralded by New Labour as evidence that the 'state means business' (Cohen 1985: 234). It is important to note here that anti-social behaviour powers should not be seen as only being related to anti-social behaviour orders, rather the full range of anti-social powers should be considered. While there is not space within this chapter to explore all of these powers (see Burney 2005; Squires and Stephen 2005; and Millie 2008 for a thorough appraisal), the key pieces of legislation and powers which have had the most tangible impact on youth are set out in the box below.

Box 14.2   Key anti-social behaviour powers

Crime and Disorder Act 1998	Section 1 introduces the *Anti-Social Behaviour Order* Section 1(a) offers a *definition of anti-social behaviour* as behaving 'in a manner that caused or was likely to cause harassment, alarm or distress to one or more persons not of the same household as himself'
Police Reform Act 2002	Section 65 Introduced the *interim Anti-Social Behaviour Order*, which can be sought in the lead up to an application for a full Anti-Social Behaviour Order.

Anti Social Behaviour Act 2003	Section 30 *Dispersal of groups and removal of persons under 16 to their place of residence* – Introduces powers to disperse groups in 'dispersal zones', which are designated on application by the police and the local council. Within these zones groups can be dispersed if the police believe members of the public have been, or are likely to be, harassed, intimidated, alarmed or distressed as a result of the presence or behaviour of groups of two or more people.

While recent figures identify nationally that 43 per cent of Anti-Social Behaviour Orders (ASBOs) – have been made on juveniles, Koffman's (2006) empirical study into the use of anti-social behaviour orders in East Brighton identifies the extent to which these powers have been targeted at children and young people. Here he identified that more applications are made for ASBOs on under 21 year olds than any other age group. When introduced by the Crime and Disorder Act 1998 youths were not the paradigmatic target of anti-social powers. Indeed the powers were identified in Home Office guidance as 'normally applying to adults except where young people have been involved with adults in anti-social behaviour' (Home Office 1998: 4 cited in Burney 2002). However, it is apparent that these powers have been systematically targeted disproportionately at young people (Squires and Stephen 2005). In addition to the Anti-Social Behaviour Order, Section 14 of the Crime and Disorder Act also introduced the Local Child Curfew which enabled the police in conjunction with the local authority to impose a local curfew over all children in a designated area. However, these were not taken up in any numbers by local authorities (Jamieson 2005) – arguably due to the resource implications for local police services which effectively made them unworkable. While the original provisions of the Crime and Disorder Act 1998 in relation to Local Child Curfews were extended by the Criminal Justice and Police Act, 2001 (Walsh 2002 cited in Jamieson 2005), they were still not extensively used. As a result of the continued reluctance of Local Authorities to employ these powers the Local Child Curfew was re-configured as dispersal powers in the 2003 Anti-Social Behaviour Act. These provide similar powers but factoring in discretion for the police made them more manageable. Thus rather than having a curfew on all children in a local area the police could use their discretion regarding who they considered might cause nuisance, alarm and distress and order them to disperse. Failure to do so, or if an individual returned to the zone within 24 hours, would constitute a breach of the order and would be a criminal offence. In addition the Police Reform Act 2002 introduced the interim Anti-Social Behaviour Order, which Koffman argues 'proved controversial, with critics claiming that it enables a temporary order to be imposed on the flimsiest of evidence and without proper safeguards for the recipient' (Koffman 2006: 607).

The introduction of these powers has been presented as dealing with the 'real' concerns of ordinary citizens which centre on low-level quality of life offences which in turn impact on the quality of life of local communities. In this way anti-social behaviour powers are presented as evidence that government is on the side of the ordinary citizen providing tools which enable local authorities to respond to their concerns. In doing this anti-social behaviour powers have been configured in a manner which enables them to circumnavigate judicial due process as they require only a civil burden of proof. Thus, anti-social behaviour powers have served to widen the net of social control while also thinning the mesh extending control over behaviours which previously would not be made subject to criminalising modes of social control. Consequently, anti-social behaviour powers could be argued to both reinforce and extend the nets of social control (Brown 2005).

Contemporary and historical concerns about youth

New Labour has presented its criminal justice reforms as reflecting the 'real' concerns of 'communities' and as dealing with the problems which blight the lives of ordinary citizens. In contemporary British society there are highly publicised concerns about the 'criminal' (see Brown 2005 for a discussion of recent trends) and more recently the 'anti-social' behaviour of young people (Squires and Stephen 2005). Brown (2005) has reminded us that youth serves as the 'prism' through which fears are refracted, arguably reflecting the historical view of youth as a 'barometer' of social ills (see France, Chapter 2). Concerns around youth are not new; both Pearson (1983) and Clarke (1985) chart complaints regarding juvenile delinquents back to at least the seventeenth century and it is apparent that throughout history there has been a level of continuity in discourses around youth and crime, which have focused on youth as the target of societies' 'respectable fears' (Pearson 1983). Thus contemporary concerns around anti-social behaviour can be argued to reflect the extent to which British society remains, as Smith argues, 'beset by a perennial sense of threat, notably from the young who become caricatured and demonized as a result' (R. Smith, 2003: 153–154).

However, while continuity is evident in discourses around youth and crime, change is also evident. Indeed the targeting of youth as the prime locale of anti-social behaviour in the late twentieth and early twenty-first centuries appears to represent a concerted 'total panic' around youth (Brown 2005). Arguably this process has gained renewed vigour under the New Labour administration (Brownlee 1998; Scraton and Haydon 2002) as it has sought to exploit fear of crime and anti-social behaviour for electoral advantage (Pitts

2000) in a manner unprecedented in the history of the Labour party (Brownlee 1998). This has served to re-politicise the issue of youth crime (Muncie 1999b) and has legitimised new mechanisms to control and regulate them (Squires and Stephen 2005; Jamieson and Yates 2009). However, fear of crime and anti-social behaviour appears to be somewhat at odds with what we know about crime rates. Indeed it is apparent that while there is evidence that crime rates have continued to fall, increasing percentages of the population believe it is rising (see Tonry 2004 for a discussion). Similarly in relation to juvenile crime the United Nations Human Rights Commissioner noted 'a curious contradiction in policy', which 'reflects a broader disparity between the reality of juvenile crime and the perception of it' (Gil-Roble 2005: 27). Thus rather than reflecting (and emerging from) the actual risk of being the victim of crime, or an increased rate of juvenile offending, fear of crime, as Tonry (2004) suggests, may well be linked to the centrality afforded to crime and anti-social behaviour in electoral politics, and the political capital that can be made from exploiting these fears (Pitts 2000). As Jamieson observes:

> A paradoxical outcome of New Labour's continued preoccupation with 'respect' is that it is likely to increase public fear and anxiety in relation to young people, a group who already occupy the perennial role of 'society's folk devil' (Muncie, 2004). (2005: 186)

As noted earlier in this chapter anti-social behaviour it is clear that young people are singled out and blamed for the perceived rise in anti-social behaviour. Indeed as Burney observes the category of 'anti-social' has become 'synonymous with youth' (2005: 64). While there are concerns expressed regarding the behaviour of youth, as evidenced in the British Crime Survey (see Millie et al. 2005 for an overview of this in terms of anti-social behaviour), it is apparent that these concerns have been compounded by a negative media portrayal of young people (and in particular working-class youth) as the archetypal anti-social 'folk devil' (Cohen 1972). Indeed a relatively recent study identified that three in four articles in the media about young people had a negative tone and that one in three discussed young people in relation to contexts of anti-social behaviour or violence (MORI 2004). In many ways concerns around the anti-social behaviour of young people can be understood as the latest manifestation of the 'respectable fears' around youth (Pearson 1983) which punctuate British history.

In this context particular contingencies of youth, which do not fit with middle-class notions of childhood, have been identified as particularly problematic and 'anti-social' and have become the target of criminalising modes of social control (Goldson 2005). As Haines and Drakeford argued, 'attitudes towards young people remain at best ambivalent and, at worst, characterised by outright hostility' (1998: 2). However, whether certain groups of young people are singled out as being of particular concern and for particularly 'hostile' treatment has historically followed racial (Hall et al. 1978) and class-based lines (Pearson 1983; Goldson 2005), and as such reflect structural hierarchies and social inequalities in society (Jamieson and Yates 2009).

This is clearly evident in discourses around anti-social behaviour as the threat of the 'anti-social' has been primarily located as lying with marginalised young people who are presented as 'constituting a particular type of *moral category*' who are 'morally corrupt' and 'needing to be disciplined' (White and Cuneen 2006: 21). As White and Cuneen argue 'It is the most disadvantaged and structurally vulnerable young people who tend to receive the most attention from youth justice officials at all points of the system' (2006: 19). In terms of anti-social behaviour, the targeting of particular groups of young people is a clear example of this as is the disproportionate use of anti-social behaviour powers against them. As Koffman observes in his research examining the case files of Anti-Social Behaviour Order applications, many of the young people had serious educational, behavioural and other health related problems and came from severely disadvantaged backgrounds (2006: 612). Thus many of the young people targeted by anti-social behaviour powers are themselves vulnerable and suffer multiple disadvantage including disabilities. Indeed the British Institute for Brain Injured Children (2005) identified that up to 35 per cent of Anti-Social Behaviour Orders were imposed on children with a diagnosed mental disorder or accepted learning difficulty.

In a perverse logic, these young people are criticised and held responsible for holding back the regeneration of their own communities. In this way they become culpable and responsible for their own marginalisation and the structural disadvantages they face. Thus the structural inequalities which shape their lived experience of adolescent transition are the result of their own activities. Echoing right 'realist' perspectives, and in particular Wilson and Kelling (1982), the Home Office website argues:

> Anti-social behaviour doesn't just make life unpleasant. It holds back the regeneration of disadvantaged areas and creates an environment where more serious crime can take hold. (www.homeoffice.gov.uk/anti-social-behaviour/what-is-asb/?view=Standard)

Thus not only do discourses around 'anti-social' behaviour serve to mask the 'criminogenic social contexts bearing down upon the "delinquent"' (Squires and Stephen 2005) and the failings of public service provision in respect of this (Burney 2005) they also identify anti-social behaviour and its 'perpetrators' as being the cause. Thus young people themselves become seen as the author of their own circumstances, held responsible for their own disadvantaged position in society and as such legitimate targets for the 'Contemporary armoury of urban crime control paraphernalia' (Coleman et al. 2005: 2513).

The limits of the 'anti-social behaviour' paradigm

While acknowledging that there is a level of confusion, flexibility and 'elasticity' (Scraton 2004) about what constitutes anti-social behaviour, a hegemonic orthodoxy can be identified regarding the groups which are being identified as being the main perpetrators. This orthodoxy draws heavily on enduring domain assumptions regarding the 'deserving' and 'undeserving' poor (Byrne 2005) and as noted earlier focuses on certain contingencies of young people residing in Britain's 'throw away places' (Campbell 1993).

Anti-social behaviour powers are presented as tools to ensure that 'hard working decent families' or the 'deserving poor' can be protected from the behaviour of the undeserving dangerous 'others' in their midst (White and Cuneen 2006). There is a raft of research which identifies that marginalised communities are most likely to suffer from crime (Dorling 2005) and social harm (Hillyard and Tombs 2005) and that some of the problems faced by these communities do involve young people. However, as youths have become 'the universal symbol of disorder' (Burney 2002: 473), other groups and in particular more powerful groups have avoided scrutiny (Tombs and Yates 2008).

Therefore, it is here that the 'elasticity' (Scraton 2004) of the construct of anti-social behaviour reaches its limits, as it has been largely confined to a myopic focus on the behaviour of marginalised and disadvantaged young people. Thus despite claims by government that the definition of anti-social behaviour is intentionally wide-ranging to allow the orders to be used in a variety of circumstances, there is little evidence to suggest that they are routinely being used to tackle the 'anti-social activities' of the powerful, which undoubtedly cause social harm in marginalised communities (Hillyard and Tombs 2005). Thus harmful and anti-social activities of powerful groups, despite undoubtedly causing nuisance, alarm and distress, are largely ignored in mainstream 'community safety' initiatives (Coleman et al. 2005; Tombs and Yates 2008) and avoid being picked up on the 'radar' of the 'anti-social behaviour industry' (Squires and Stephens 2005). This is evidence that that what is defined as anti-social and subsequently targeted is not a 'neutral reactive force but an active process that selectively defines deviance (in this case anti-social behaviour) in line with the particular interests of controlling agents and institutions' (Coleman et al. 2005: 18). Louise Casey (national director of the Home Office anti-social behaviour unit), in an exchange with Shami Chakrabarti (Director of the campaign group Liberty) argued, that 'most people living with anti-social behaviour would not, I think, thank us for filling these pages with a discussion about its definition. They know only too well what is meant by it and they want something done about it' (Casey and Chakrabarti 2005).

However, what is clear is that anti-social powers are targeted at the behaviour of some groups and not others. Therefore it is apparent that whether behaviour is successfully labelled anti-social depends not on the extent to which the behaviour causes nuisance, alarm or distress but 'on how certain acts are labelled and who is doing the labelling' (Hall and Scraton 1981: 488). Thus, when we hear politicians talk of the concerns of local citizens we need to think critically about how what we know becomes 'knowable' and why one set of actions become labelled as anti-social whereas another set of actions do not. This requires an understanding of the politics of knowledge production. For example the work of Pearce (1990) identified that people self-reported being the victims of commercial crime (crimes committed by business) in greater numbers than traditional forms of street crime. This was because people were asked specifically about being the victim of these types of crime, which is often not the case in criminology which invariably focuses on the crimes, or anti-social acts, committed by powerless groups (Tombs and Yates 2008). Therefore, as the work of Kare and Wall (2006) illustrates, the public views certain white collar crime offences as equal to, or more serious than, certain traditional street crimes. In the UK these concerns do not seem to be reflected in academic, policy or practice discourses around anti-social behaviour and subsequently avoid the radar of the anti-social behaviour industry.

Conclusion

The changes to youth justice implemented by New Labour, as argued throughout this chapter, have been characterised by the promotion of net widening, early intervention, and prevention, framed within the criminal justice systems (Goldson and Yates 2008). Thus, what were once viewed as youthful transgressions are problematised and young people criminalised in ever increasing numbers. Anti-social behaviour powers have played a central role in this process as they have been disproportionately targeted at youth. As the youth justice system has expanded and discipline has become more dispersed (Cohen 1985) a range of agencies, which historically have not seen themselves as being central players in the youth justice system, have become co-opted to participate in the formal processes of social control in the form of anti-social behaviour initiatives. If they do not as the quote from Scraton illustrates they risk censure, 'As with the global war on terror, in the local war on 'terror' agencies and their workers are expected to sign up and participate or endure the public criticism of being apologists for crime and anti-social behaviour' (2004: 22).

However, this new 'domain' of the anti-social behaviour 'industry' (Squires and Stephen 2005), with the development of anti-social behaviour powers, their increasing use, and the targeting of these powers at marginalised youth, presents particularly acute challenges not only to young people but also to the professionals working with them. In some respects these challenges are nothing new as 'there are fundamental structural continuities that make the basic challenges for youth work in the next decade much the same as those of the last several decades' (Poynting and White 2004: 39). However, it is also apparent that 'historical changes and conjectural circumstances mean that tensions within youth service provision present themselves in a new guise, with unique and original problems for youth workers to confront in the new millennium' (Poynting and White 2004: 39). This chapter contends that one of the greatest challenges to professionals working with youth, at this historical juncture, is the extent to which coercive methods of social control, in the form of anti-social behaviour initiatives, are being targeted at marginalised youth. Arguably in the current context youth work is under increasing pressure to play a central role in responding to and managing 'anti-social' youth and to manage the 'risks' that youth are constructed as posing. In this context youth workers' relationship with the young person becomes a resource in the social control of youth, facilitating the targeting of anti-social behaviour initiatives in order to remoralise 'underclass', 'dangerous' and 'undeserving' youth.

Reflective questions for practice

- Reflecting on this chapter, and Hazel Kemshall's Chapter 13, consider the changes in youth justice, risk and anti-social behaviour debates over the past ten years. What do you think has driven this change?
- Does the organisation you work for attempt to reduce or tackle anti-social behaviour, or youth crime?
- Are these attempts located at the 'shallow end' or the 'deep end' of crime control?
- What does it define as anti-social behaviour? What do you?

Further reading

Brown, S. (2005) *Understanding Youth and Crime: Listening to Youth?*, **2nd edn, Buckingham: Open University Press**. This text offers a thorough overview of criminological approaches to understanding youth and crime.

Burney, E. (2005) *Making People Behave: Anti-Social Behaviour, Politics and Policy*, **Cullompton: Willan**. A thorough appraisal of how anti-social behaviour powers have been employed on a local level.

Squires, P. (2008) *ASBO Nation: The Criminalisation of Nuisane*, **Bristol: Policy Press**.

Squires, P. and Stephen, D. E. (2005) *Rougher Justice: Anti-Social Behaviour and Young People*, **Cullompton: Willan**. An extremely useful text which provides a detailed appraisal of anti-social behaviour powers.

15

GOOD PRACTICE IN GUIDANCE: LESSONS FROM CONNEXIONS

Scott Yates

Key arguments

- **Research that evaluated the impact of the Connexions service provides lessons for welfare, advice and guidance services more generally.**
- **Young people's needs are varied and complex and present with widely differing needs and risks, at different times in their lives. The impact that services can have with young people is multi-faceted and is not always addressed in the pursuit of targeted outcomes.**
- **Achieving positive impact depends on the relationship between the young person and their key worker. Trusting relationships involve attention, sensitivity and appropriate responses to young people's previous experiences, opinions, attitudes, needs and desires.**
- **Other key elements of good practice included taking a person-centred approach, working in settings where young people feel comfortable and striking a balance between assessing needs and building rapport over time.**

Introduction

The rolling out of the Connexions service began in England in 2001, with the aim of meeting a policy vision for the new millennium (DfEE 1999; Social Exclusion Unit 1999; DfEE 2000a). This vision was based upon ideals of replacing the previously 'patchy,' 'fragmented' and 'inconsistent' (DfEE 1999) system of services aimed at young people with a 'radical approach' that would bring together the systems for delivery of help and support and provide a comprehensive, socially inclusive full-service advice and support function to all 13–19 year olds (Social Exclusion Unit 1999). Connexions thus began with the aim of providing a universal service of advice and guidance for all young people, and also ensuring that those with specific problems received the intensive, targeted support they need.

Connexions worked through partnerships with a range of other agencies (social services, youth offending teams, drugs action teams, etc.) to provide a holistic, integrated service. The key personnel were Personal Advisers (PAs) based in a variety of settings (including secondary schools, further education colleges, Connexions centres and youth and community centres) whose role was to 'identify individuals' needs, supply directly or broker the services they need' and monitor their progress to ensure they receive the necessary support (National Audit Office 2004). This mix of advice and guidance with intensive support would, it was envisioned, 'contribute to greater stability in the lives of young people' (DfEE 2000a:12) in general and tackle widescale problems linked with an identified cycle of deprivation, dependency and social exclusion, such as long-term unemployment, lack of post-16 education and training, poor health and criminal behaviour.

In 2005, however, the Green Paper, *Youth Matters* (DfES 2005) noted that, while there had been some local successes, overall the service was not effectively meeting its broad remit, and not enough was being done to ensure that young people received appropriate advice, guidance and support or to prevent many young people from drifting into a life of poverty, crime and social exclusion (DfES 2005). At the time of writing, the future of Connexions is somewhat uncertain. Although Youth Matters contained proposals to maintain Connexions in areas where it is performing well, there are also indications that support and guidance services currently provided by Connexions should 'go local' where possible, and that responsibility for co-ordinating the focus of services working with young people into a coherent and holistic response should lie in the future with Children's Trusts.

Whatever the future of the service, the challenges it faced and the successes and failures it achieved hold lessons not only for the nascent Children's Trusts which will take on some of their roles, but for all services working with children and young people. This chapter will draw on in-depth research that was carried out into Connexions to illustrate some of the key lessons that can be derived from Connexions for other services concerned with welfare, guidance and advice for young people.

The evidence that this chapter will draw on comes from the Connexions Impact Study (Hoggarth and Smith 2004), which, in 2003 and 2004, carried out almost 1300 interviews with young people, Connexions Personal Advisers (PAs) and other services' workers. The overall findings of the study were very expansive, and it would not be possible to touch on them all here, even briefly. However, many of these findings related specifically to particular operations of Connexions and do not have an immediate wider relevance.

This chapter will consider and expand upon research findings in two key areas that are most relevant for providing some general lessons for services providing welfare, advice and guidance to young people. First is the multi-faceted nature of young people's needs and the potential impact that services can achieve with them, and the challenges to working effectively with these needs presented by the target-driven environment in which many services operate. Second is an examination of the style of work with young people that is most successful and that they find most appropriate – notably the importance of establishing trust and rapport between a young person and key worker – and the challenges this can present. In exploring these dimensions, the chapter aims to highlight good practice in developing effective welfare, advice and guidance services for young people.

The multi-faceted nature of impact and working in a target-driven environment

The main focus of the Connexions research (and a central concern for work with young people in general) was with evaluating the *impact* that the service had with young people. Impact can be defined as a positive change in a young person's circumstances, reasoning and/or behaviour that can be attributed to the interactions (s)he had with the service.

Measuring impact effectively and fully is more complex than might first appear. Connexions, for instance, uses specific performance indicators to assess its impact. These focus specifically on ensuring that young people successfully move from pre-16 education into further education, training or employment. It thus has specific targets to reduce the number of young people not in employment, education or training (NEET) in their partnerships' areas. The Green Paper indicates that future services will retain such performance indicators (including the continued reduction in number of NEET young people) to asses their impact (DfES 2005).

A key point to emerge from the Connexions research, however, was that young people's lives are varied and complex and they present to services with widely differing needs and priorities. Measurements of services' impact, by their nature, tend to focus on a limited number of pre-defined parameters – such as facilitating the movement of NEET young people into education, training or employment (EET). Given the complexity of young people's situations, though, such a focus risks missing the varieties of ways that services can achieve impact with them. It should be recognised that the impact that services can have with young people is multi-faceted, and can involve outcomes in a number of areas of their lives, including such things as personal development or dealing with underlying risks or issues, as well as what might be considered a service's primary area of impact (such as movement into an EET destination for Connexions). Different types of interventions might be needed to achieve these different types of impact, and the varied forms of impact might become more or less important at different times in the life of a young person. It is important for services to recognise this complexity and to respond so as to achieve the appropriate impact at the appropriate time.

This point can be illustrated by examining the case of one particular young person who was in contact with Connexions when the research took place. He was involved in heavy substance misuse and offending behaviour, and had recently been homeless, as well as being NEET. He describes the impact that Connexions had with him thus:

YP: *G__[Connexions PA] was explaining to me if I kept on going the way I was … smoking drugs, then it was speed, pills, coke and whatever … then in about 5 years I am just going to be a smack-head and a thief. The way I see it, that was the way I was heading, so he straightened me out a bit.*

[…]

I: So, out of all the things you have spoken to G__ about, what would you say is the most important?

YP: *I would say my lifestyle. My drugs and being homeless, he has helped me with them and I think they are more important than anything else I can think of.*

[…]

I: So, in terms of careers, what is on the horizon?

YP: *I have agreed that I am going to try and sort out my housing and my drugs before I try and sort out a job. When I was trying to find a job before, I came to see him about it and then when this popped up, we both agreed that it was more important to sort my life out than to have money in my pocket.*

This young person was typical of many who were interviewed by researchers in having numerous 'risks' (factors or conditions that put him at risk of remaining NEET in the long-term and of becoming socially excluded) and issues in his life that warranted intervention. Each of these is an area around which impact could potentially be achieved. This young person explicitly states, however, that the impact for which Connexions is primarily assessed (moving young people like this to EET destinations) is not as high a priority for him as impact in other areas of his life (substance misuse and homelessness) at this time, although it will become more important to him in the future.

The lesson from this illustration is that with the great complexity in young people's lives and the variety of risks that they face comes a variety of potential forms of impact that services can achieve with them. It is important for services to recognise this multi-faceted nature of impact, and to respond to the presenting needs of young people in a way that impacts on the area of their lives that consider the most urgent. However, measurement and targeting systems which take account of specific, pre-determined hard targets – such as moving NEET young people into education, employment or training – often do not encourage this broad, holistic focus. Both Hazel Kemshall (Chapter 13) and Jean Hine (Chapter 3) have illustrated problems with reliance on neat policy targets at the expense of paying attention to the personal biographies of young people.

Target–centred working can tend to reduce the focus on important areas of impact with young people that are not reflected in measured targets, and encourage instead work on areas of measured impact at times when the young person may not hold such outcomes as an urgent priority. As the young person first cited above commented, he viewed impact in areas of his life other than employment, education or training as '*more important than anything else I can think of,*' and he valued his relationship with Connexions more highly as a result. As was stated, work on other areas of impact, such as a move into an EET destination would likely not have been as productive with this young person at this particular time. Indeed, young people are very sensitive to target-driven environments, and can quickly develop negative opinions of a service and withdraw from it if they feel they are being given a generic, target-meeting response rather than an individually-tailored one that addresses the issues they perceive as most pressing.

However, whilst there was evidence of good practice and positive outcomes when this focus was taken (as in the case of the young person referenced), concentrating on such 'soft outcomes' is not encouraged when the prime focus is on 'hard outcomes' (those which are measured and around which targets are set). Indeed, a recurring theme in the Connexions research was that a too-early or heavy-handed focus on EET destinations without due attention first being paid to the needs that the young person considers most important was wholly counter-productive, often leading to mistrust, irritation, and withdrawal from contact. These feelings are summed up by the one young person describing his experiences of meeting a Connexions PA: '*They just, I don't know, try to persuade you into things you don't want to do in a way. They just, you know what I mean, just talk about it and keep talking about it, and keep talking about it, to try to get you into it, like.*' Similarly, another young person with difficulties around offending behaviour lamented the heavy-handed focus on changing his NEET status, complaining that important issues were overlooked because '*She [his Connexions PA] is only … banging on with trying to get me into a placement*' (see Yates and Payne 2006).

These findings illustrate the point, also noted by Spence (2004) and Bessant (2004), that work with young people functions most productively through processes of participative engagement, flexibility and tailored responses to presenting needs, and this can be undermined by pressures to meet specific hard targets (such as reducing the numbers of NEET young people), which are apt to become crudely applied. Jordan and Jordan (2000) even argue that this situation can lead to workers taking on an 'enforcement counsellor' role, in which the primary concern becomes ensuring compliance with a particular social policy regime and upholding specific targets, rather than meeting clients' real needs.

The target-driven environment in which services often operate can present challenges to the necessary flexibility of focus of work with young people in a number of ways, and there were observed in Connexions a range of problems attributable to the time- and resource-limited, target-driven environment in which it existed.

As well as encouraging inappropriate, target-focused responses to the complexity of young people's needs (as seen above), this can also cause attention to become disproportionately focused on young people who can relatively easily be supported to achieve measured target outcomes, often at the expense of others who would also benefit from intervention, and who, in some cases, are in more urgent or greater need of it. In Connexions, this manifested as PAs focusing time and attention on those young people who could fairly assuredly and quickly be moved into an EET destination. One PA summed up the impact that these targets had on her work as follows:

> A: Maybe we have got 20% who are very much not involved in things and need a lot of input or who need a lot of input to keep them in place. They are the ones who perhaps through illness, pregnancy, caring responsibilities, other reasons, aren't actually able to be part of the employment market. So it is about saying to them "Well we are here if you need us but at the end of the day there is not an awful lot we can offer while you are in that position."[...] It's a sad fact that what gets measured gets done.

While it may be justified in some cases for professional workers to close the cases of some young people and cease contact, there will also inevitably be a pressure to close the cases of others who would benefit from contact merely because they could make only slow, if any, progress towards EET destinations. As the above Connexions worker continued: '*There has to come a point at which you say, "look in order to make most effective use of your time we have got to pull the plug on that one and move on"*'.

The young people most affected by this focus of attention in response to targeting are those whose circumstances mean that it will not be easy to move them into EET destinations, either because of other problems or risks they face which will affect their ability or willingness to do so (as in the case of the young man in the first extract above), or because they have made a conscious decision not to pursue such a destination for some time (this often happens due to parenting or caring responsibilities). This was a problem often encountered with young parents in particular. Over 40 per cent of young parents contacted by researchers had seen a Connexions PA on only two or fewer occasions. Many of the young people in this position, as well as having parental responsibilities, lived very isolated lives, often with very little in the way of visible social support networks. Such young people would benefit from contact with services such as Connexions to provide such support networks, to maintain motivation and confidence during the time that they are caring for their children, and to provide ongoing help and support with planning and managing a future return to employment, education or training. However, they do not represent an efficient use of limited resources within the current system of target-centred priorities for services.

Another ill-desired, and (one would imagine) unintended, side-effect noted by a number of PAs, connected to this issue, is that the emphasis on meeting targets discourages potentially important *preventative* work with young people. Simply put, there is a concentration of effort aimed at making positive impact that meets targets at the expense of working with young people who might be *at risk* of adverse outcomes, but who do not currently exhibit them. In Connexions, this was manifested as a concentration of effort around moving NEET young people into an EET destination at the expense of work providing support to those who might be at risk of becoming NEET or developing other problems, *before* they actually do so. Many young people currently in education, employment or training still exhibit the same sorts of multiple and profound risks seen with some of the young people above. However, 45 per cent of the young people encountered who could be defined as being in this 'high-risk-but-EET' (Yates and Payne 2006) situation had either had no contact with Connexions at all, or only one or two meetings with a PA and no further contact. One Connexions PA summed up the frustration that is felt around the issue of having to work towards targets in this way: *'You can't measure the negative, you can't prove how many people* didn't *become NEET because of our intervention'*.

The importance of trust and rapport

Another key finding to emerge from the research study was that, while services like Connexions have a number of interventions available to them to work with young people, the key to success in achieving positive impact lies in the relationship between the young person and their key worker in the service – the Connexions Personal Adviser (PA). The interaction between young people and their adult worker(s) and the establishment of an effective rapport between them is crucial for achieving impact. Its importance cannot be overstated. It was identified in the research as *the* key mechanism through which impact with young people is achieved, and one that is essential if changes in reasoning and behaviour are to be encouraged, and interventions made successfully (Hoggarth and Smith 2004). Indeed, this realisation was made in the landmark publication *Bridging the Gap* (Social Exclusion Unit 1999), where it was acknowledged that a key aspect of 'what works' in engaging young people who are currently disengaged is 'staff with the ability to build up a rapport with often quite difficult individuals, to facilitate the developmental process' (1999: 115). However, it is often a challenge to build an effective, trusting relationship with young people, especially those with multiple and profound risks or difficulties who may already possess negative perceptions of professional services, and it can be a challenging process with young people who have had frequent previous contact with services for a variety of problems (one service worker commented that such young people often feel 'over social-worked' and they can be initially very resistant to new services and particularly difficult to establish trust and rapport with).

Establishing an effective, trusting relationship with young people does not happen automatically. It is an ongoing process involving attention, sensitivity and appropriate responses to young people's previous experiences, opinions, attitudes, needs and desires.

It is particularly important that service workers do not over-step the bounds of trust in the early stages of a relationship. One of the most common causes of failure to establish an effective relationship between young person and key worker occurs when service workers use official assessment tools (such as Connexions' Assessment, Planning, Implementation and Review framework – APIR) or ask questions that are perceived as too personal or intrusive before the appropriate level of trust has been developed. A number of young people in the Connexions research – young people who often had a number of sensitive, personal issues that they are wary about discussing with strangers, especially adults in apparent positions of authority – commented that they experienced early contact with PAs as intrusive, insensitive or unpleasant for these very reasons.

Such damage to the relationship between young person and key worker may be irreparable, and impact from the service will suffer as a result, as evidence from a number of young people testifies. For instance, young people commented that their early impressions of a PA were of 'a busybody' or 'someone who sticks her nose in too much'. A frequent complaint was that in general Connexions workers tended to 'go […] too far' or dig 'too deep' early on in their contact with a young person. For such young people, the feeling is that 'some things are just too personal to talk about' and assessment with them must be undertaken in a sensitive and flexible manner alongside awareness of the need to build trust and rapport and potential to be seen as inappropriately intrusive.

There are some challenges here for services. On the one hand, there is the need to make accurate assessments of young peoples situations as early as possible in order that appropriate, and sometimes urgently needed, responses and interventions can be put in place, and many services have working protocols to adhere to in this regard. On the other hand, though, this need must be balanced against the very real possibility of such assessment being negatively perceived as too intense or personal and damaging the vital fledgling young person-adult worker relationship.

Another issue negatively impacting on the development of trust and rapport with young people was young people perceiving that promises made to them by workers had not been kept, or that they have been provided with information that they believe is inaccurate, unhelpful, or not appropriately tailored to their needs. These issues need special attention, as it was observed that even one such negative experience, especially early in the relationship, was often magnified in young people's minds and negatively coloured their future perceptions of the service. The case of one young woman serves as an illustration. She met with a Connexions PA in her final year of school to discuss her future options, about which she said she was '*a bit confused.*' However, rather than offering her advice about her range of options, as she was expecting, she maintained that the PA instead pushed her towards one specific option – A-levels at the local college – based upon incorrect details about her predicted GCSE grades. This resulted in the young woman in question staunchly refusing any further contact with Connexions, having thought to herself, she said, '*what's the point? She's got it wrong once*'. Similarly, an incident as simple as a PA failing to turn up for an arranged meeting without explanation led one young man to comment that he was no longer comfortable visiting Connexions, saying that '*it's weird now*' having him as PA after two broken appointments.

Another point where the building of a trusting relationship between young people and service workers can be hampered is when workers are not in tune with things that young people find socially and culturally important and, for instance, dress or behave in ways that mark them out as culturally or demographically very different from the young people in the environment in which they work. They thus become perceived as less approachable, less likely to understand the situations of the young people they work with, and thus less likely to earn their trust. For example, comments made about Connexions PAs included complaints that they seemed '*posh*' that they '*wore suits,*' and that consequently, '*you think they're just like your school teachers.*' One young person stated quite straightforwardly that PAs would be more likely to engage young people if '*they dress down to their level,*' and another commented that '*they [PAs] have got to help young people with personal problems … [but they are] alien to your environment*'.

Good practice

While the issues discussed thus far have been characterised largely by illustrations of challenges to good practice and things that can go wrong in working with young people, they should not be taken as blanket criticisms of Connexions or of any other service. Indeed, much of what was observed was notable not for what went wrong or for where working practices created problems, but for the dedication and professionalism of the workers involved, and the sometimes quite remarkable impact they achieved in the lives of very troubled young people. The points made above, then, are intended as potential pitfalls to be aware of, and as lessons that should be heeded for good practice to emerge.

In contrast to these situations, however, were cases in which Connexions was achieving remarkable positive impact with young people. The most important factors bearing on this positive impact were consistently identified as the focus of the work that was undertaken with young people, and the relationship between them and their PAs.

A common characteristic of instances in which good practice were noted was flexibility of approach by workers early on in the interaction. Where PAs took a 'person-centred' approach and worked flexibly on issues that young people themselves considered most pressing, a solid foundation could be laid for developing a productive relationship. Other factors included working in settings in which young people felt most comfortable, at times that suited them, taking a non-judgemental, engaged and responsive approach to young people's problems, and striking a balance between making assessments of needs, providing support and building trust and rapport over time.

In instances where this occurred, young people greatly valued their relationships with their PAs, and typically commented that they were '*easy to get on with*', someone who '*listens to you*', '*solves your problems*', and also someone who '*treats you like an equal*' and '*doesn't talk down to you*' or '*doesn't judge you*'. As Reina and Reina (1999) predicted, young people in these trusting situations were more likely to share important personal information, make and keep positive arrangements, and to admit and face their past mistakes.

The impact achieved that could thus be achieved was extremely noteworthy. One PA was described, for instance, as '*a lifesaver*', and young people made such comments as '*I don't know where I'd be without her*', '*I'd probably be on the streets*' or even, '*I don't think I'd be here now [without the support of a particular PA]*'.

Conclusion

A number of points can be taken from the Connexions research as general lessons for good practice. First there is the importance of recognising that young people's lives are complex, that their experiences, attitudes, presenting issues, needs and desires will differ markedly, and as such the forms of impact that services can achieve with them is multi-faceted in nature. It is important if young people are to be engaged in the service for workers to respond to these differing characteristics of their lives effectively, and adopt a flexible approach, listening for the urgency of needs and desires from young people, and tailoring their work to appropriate forms of impact at appropriate times.

Also crucial is the issue of trust and rapport. The relationship between young person and key worker is *the* key mechanism through which impact is achieved, and that the establishment of trust and rapport is essential for this relationship to develop successfully. Characteristics most conducive to establishing trust and rapport were flexibility of working, and an engaged, non-judgemental approach that avoids personal questions or formal assessment procedures too early in the relationship. It is important that workers respect young people's sensitivity to intrusion, keep any early promises that are made, provide accurate and appropriate information, and act and present themselves in a way that enables young people to feel at ease.

Despite the importance of these factors, the environment in which many services operate – characterised by limited time and resources, pressure to establish credibility and meet specific hard targets, and the structural formalisation of assessment procedures – can add to the challenge of already difficult work, and can actively discourage the flexible support, relationship-building and preventative interventions through which work with young people most productively operates.

These challenges need to be recognised at managerial and policy-setting levels, and attempts made to mitigate some of the pressures that undermine some of the more effective aspects of work with young people. The challenge remains for practitioners to work in difficult institutional and political contexts with troubled young people in a way that upholds the principles of good work with young people – something that, despite the difficulties involved, a number of Connexions PAs were managing very well.

Reflective questions for practice

- **Reflect on the different ways in which you measure the impact of your work. What would you consider to be your key 'hard targets' and 'soft outcomes'? Is the balance between these two measures right?**
- **What has helped you to support young people in your advice or guidance role?**
- **What do you believe are the key elements in building trusting relationships with the young people who you work with?**
- **What steps do you take to ensure that you maintain these relationships?**

Further reading

Hoggarth, L., Smith, D.I. et al. (2004) *Understanding the Imapact of Connexions on Young People at Risk*, **London: DfES**. The government funded research report that examined the implementation and impact of the Connexions service. Notable for involving a large sample of young people in the study.

Yates, S. and Payne, M. (2007) '"Minding the gap" between policy visions and service implementation: lessons from Connexions', *Youth & Policy*, **95: 25–40**. A critical article that considers the findings from the evaluation of Connexions, discussed within this chapter.

16

YOUTH WORK AND THE YOUTH SERVICE

Bernard Davies

Key arguments

- The youth service has traditionally been identified as a home for the delivery of youth work.
- As part of its wider 'modernisation' of services, New Labour has significantly reformed youth services introducing targeted approaches, measurable outcomes and integrated support services often directed by child care and welfare professionals.
- Social and personal education, a long-standing aim of youth work, was sidelined in favour of a focus on the provision of positive activities.
- Youth workers have also been required to contribute to other policy priorities such as the drive to tackle anti-social behaviour and to secure entry into employment.
- All of this means that the future of the Youth Service as the provider of youth work is uncertain.

Introduction

Youth workers have long seen the Youth Service as the Cinderella of public provision: struggling alone in the back room, left with the tatters of other agencies' premises and equipment, spending its time picking up the pieces of their youth failures and rejects. With despondency and anger often lurking beneath these perceptions, a willing embrace of victimhood has at times not been far behind: 'Why are they treating the Youth Service so badly?'

In a world of ambitious empire-builders, youth workers' determination to defend what is distinctive about their practice is understandable – indeed essential. Too easily however this can turn them inwards. And, once there, they can fail to notice that, as always, powerful political imperatives are driving wider social policy agendas – that 'they', far from just picking on 'us', have other services in their sights, too; that 'we' are in fact simply being caught up in a much bigger strategy.

This has certainly been true since 1997. Though the waves have taken time to surge, New Labour's relentless 'modernisation' tsunami has eventually washed over public service providers as marginal as the Youth Service. Some of the initiatives have been quite specific to it and therefore unmissable – *Transforming Youth Work* (DfEE 2001); *Resourcing Excellent Youth Services* (DfES 2002); the Green Paper *Youth Matters* (DfES 2005); and its follow up *Youth Matters – The Next Steps* (DfES 2006); Section 6 of the 2006 Education and Inspections Act (DfES 2007). Other, wider policy initiatives, though not directed at the Service per se, have nonetheless had major implications for it – for example the original planning documents for the Connexions Service (see DfEE 2000a: 52); the *Every Child Matters* strategy (DfES 2003) and the establishment of local authority children and young people's services; and the Treasury's 2006–7 Comprehensive Spending Review, its associated review of children and young people's services (HM Treasury/DfES 2007) and its ten year strategy paper *Aiming high for young people* (HM Treasury/DCSF 2007). By 2007 youth workers could hardly have failed to notice how national policy requirements, both directly and more generally, were shaping the overall direction of their work and substantially determining their access to resources.

This chapter starts by highlighting the core features of these wider New Labour social policy imperatives post-1997. It then traces their increasing application to the Youth Service and their impact on its priorities, management and practice. Finally, it addresses the question: where does all this leave the Youth Service – particularly its remit, unique among public services over the past 60 years, to sustain and develop that distinctive practice known as youth work?

New Labour social policy: from a public service ethic to 'contestability'

Many of what came to be regarded as the distinguishing features of New Labour's approach to social policy had their roots in the Thatcher governments' onslaught on the welfare state of the 1980s and 1990s. This – purposefully, often ruthlessly – broke the 'welfare settlement' which for three decades had assumed the need for some (modest) wealth distribution underpinned by 'cradle-to-the-grave' forms of material, social, health and educational support and provision.

The Thatcher governments viewed this 1940s and 1950s inheritance as both morally and economically debilitating, creating a 'dependency culture' among individuals and families and draining Britain's capacity for wealth creation. Starting from the proposition that 'there is no such thing as society', the Thatcherite solutions focused on freeing up 'the market' from the constraints of government bureaucracy and trade union power and 'encourag(ing) families – in the widest sense – to resume responsibilities taken on by the state, for example … for … unemployed 16 year olds' (Guardian, 1983).

New Labour's embrace of the Thatcherite doctrines was never total: after an initial two-year moratorium, it increased spending on public services and committed itself to eliminating child poverty by 2020, reducing youth unemployment and substantially increasing levels of child care, especially for poor families. Nonetheless, its underlying presumption was that: 'The twentieth century traditional welfare state that did so much for so many has to be re-shaped as the opportunity society capable of liberation and advance…' (Blair 2004).

Here, 'liberation' and 'advance' again emphasised the economic, leaving 'market forces' as unencumbered as possible. It also gave a new priority to responsibilities over rights – to promoting a '"something for something" society' with 'the family' being required increasingly to take on roles previously seen as collective and particularly as falling to the state. In all this the overriding policy goal was meritocratic: '… not equal incomes … But true equality – equal worth, an equal chance of fulfilment, equal access to knowledge and opportunity … The class war is over' (Blair 1999).

New Labour policy-makers were clear too that, in their actual operation, welfare state institutions remained seriously flawed: often cumbersome and fragmented in their delivery, inefficiently managed and offering poor value for money. In the new consumerist climate, they particularly challenged what they saw as their outdated and obstructive ideologies and the priority given to providers' (especially professionals') interests over users' choices.

Labour's 'new model public service' particularly looked to private business to provide relevant models for action. Part of some services – within health, education, the prisons – were moved into the private sector, commercial as well as non-profit. In order to improve quality, increase diversity and reduce costs, those that remained 'public' were exposed to greater competition ('contestability') – for example through commissioning and forms of payment-by-results. Increasingly, too, public sector organisations were required to adopt business practices: to be 'evidence-based' in their planning, to meet often 'hard' statistical 'targets', to introduce computerised information systems and to monitor progress towards 'measurable outcomes'. In the process users – patients, social work clients, pupils and their parents – became 'consumers' who had to be offered the widest possible personalised 'choices'.

To achieve New Labour's goals of efficiency, effectiveness and accountability, services were (in some cases repeatedly) restructured in the name of improved 'co-ordination' and greater 'integration' – of 'joined up solutions to joined up problems'. In the process, instrumental, managerial and indeed commercial imperatives increasingly squeezed out the professional and public service ethic which – with all its faults and failures – had shaped the welfare state from its foundation, including underpinning the person-centred approaches so central to the youth work practice at the heart of Youth Service delivery.

Youth service policy under New Labour

Transforming youth work

Though Labour took until 2001 to publish its first formal policy statement on the Youth Service, its first 'minister for youth', Kim Howells, quickly teased out the Service's lack of 'fit' with this New Labour's social policy template. As early as 1998, he had concluded that:

> 'It's the patchiest most unsatisfactory of all the services I've come across. I've never met such down-at-heart, 'can't do' representatives as I've met of youth services throughout Britain.' (cited in Henman 2007: 7)

This off-the-cuff judgement soon became firmly embedded in official thinking. In a foreword to the 1998 Youth Service audit, Howell's successor, George Mudie, pointed to, '… the great variation in … the quality of provision and (in) the relationships and interaction with other services for young people' (cited in Marken et al. 1998).

Few objective observers would have contested this assessment which, as ministers were never slow to point out, was subsequently confirmed by numerous Ofsted reports. However, from then on it became the leitmotif of ministerial statements on the Service, often to the exclusion of any acknowledgement of positive qualities. It was for example reiterated with even greater authority in *Transforming Youth Work*, published in March 2001 which determined provision as 'at least, patchy …[it is] all too often not properly integrated into mainstream provision' (DfEE 2001: 5).

And it reappeared in the 2005 green paper:

> Where Local Authorities value and prioritise the Youth Service, it can be excellent. However, we know – not least from recent Ofsted inspections – that there are highly variable levels of provision and quality. (DfES 2005: 22)

Some of these statements also revealed how the wider New Labour critique of welfare state institutions was being applied to the Youth Service. Here 'fragmentation' was a special concern: in this case the need for youth workers to, as yet another youth minister

(Margaret Hodge) was later to put it: '…*rather than adopting a "silo" approach … They must think children and young people, not services'* (cited in Barrett 2004: 15).

New Labour's emphasis on 'joined up' services was only one of its wider social policy preoccupations to impinge on the Service. Here *Resourcing Excellent Youth Services* which followed *Transforming Youth Work* in December 2002 turned out to be a landmark paper, particularly in its much more 'hard-edged' determination to bring order to the Service's historic messiness. It sought to impose some clarity on its traditionally imprecise 'outcomes' by setting it 'measurable' targets: for 'reach', accredited outcomes and user satisfaction. A four page annex laid down 22 'standards for youth work provision' and performance indicators focused on, for example, spending per head of the relevant population and 'development opportunities' (DfES 2002).

Youth Matters and its aftermath

By the time the green paper *Youth Matters* was published in 2005, the New Labour social policy agenda had apparently hardened still further to the point that it was no longer clear a Youth Service was needed at all. Despite some token nods towards past policy positions, its at least implicit message was that the strategy embodied in *Resourcing Excellent Youth Services* was not working well enough. Speaking during the Labour Party conference three months after the green paper appeared, Phil Hope, a junior education minister and former youth worker, put into words what the drafters of *Youth Matters* never quite brought themselves to set down in black and white: that '… youth services in that 60s sense are not part of the agenda and they've been proved not to work' (cited in Lloyd and Barrett 2005).

And so, amidst all the green paper's talk of 'a revised statutory duty on Local Authorities in relation to activities for young people' and of 'new national standards' (DfES 2005: 65), youth workers found themselves leafing in vain through its 70-plus pages for encouraging and *integrated* references to the Youth Service. Any (usually passing) positive comment – 'Youth Services can make a crucial contribution' – was once again instantly qualified by reminders of its patchiness – 'but they are not doing this everywhere' (p. 11). Local Authority Youth Services were defined as 'the only publicly-funded and nationwide service focused on the personal and social development of young people' (pp. 14–15). However, references to these were at best small walk-on parts for the Service in case studies or mentions in the cast lists of services expected to deliver its recommended improvements:

> Some of the activities will be delivered by schools; others will be delivered in partnership with the community, the Youth Service and other children's services. (DfES 2005: 35)

> … practitioners from within the teams are able to work with and provide support for young people in settings where the young people are comfortable – schools, colleges, mainstream youth services and at home. (DfES 2005: 59)

Subsequently ministers also made explicit one other message left implicit within the green paper: the very limited view of youth work with which they were working. In December 2005, Beverley Hughes, the latest of six 'youth' ministers in eight years, explained:

> Primarily [youth work is] about activities rather than informal education. Constructive activities, things that are going to enhance young people's enjoyment and leisure … I want activities to be the main focus. (cited in Barrett 2005: 14–15)

By the start of 2006, therefore, for youth work and the Youth Service it was back to the future. Social and personal education – the commitment to young people which youth workers had spent the previous 40 years-plus refining and developing – was to be sidelined. According to the New Labour canon, only out-of-touch professionals would hold such highfalutin expectations of young people, while the young themselves – the new 'tech-sussed' service consumers – would, in exercising their 'choice', dismiss these more stretching aspirations as outside their interests or even, the green paper sometimes seemed to imply, beyond their capacity. Dressed up as 'positive activities', recreation – indeed, if the proposed youth opportunity card was any guide, market-driven off-the-peg consumerist recreation – was once again to be goal.

In all this, New Labour's application to its own policy development of another of its high profile market-oriented principles – the need for 'evidence-based' planning (DfEE 2000b: 29) – was, at best, highly selective. The green paper failed to make any reference to directly relevant recent research studies, two of which were DfES-funded (Crimmens et al. 2004; Hoggarth and Smith 2004; Merton et al. 2004, see also Hoggarth and Payne 2006 and Chapter 18). Prominence was given instead to another study (Feinstein et al. 2004) which, with considerable media effect, was highlighted by Hodge prior to the green paper's publication. 'Baldly' if 'with caution' she used this to suggest that rather than attending youth clubs '… young people would have been better off at home watching television' (Ward 2005). What was also left unacknowledged publicly by ministers was that, when Feinstein and his colleagues reworked their findings, they emphasised a need for 'the very great skill of youth workers who make day to day judgments about appropriate levels of risk and support …' (Davies 2008).

Nor was this the only example of political imperative overriding objective evaluation. Largely in response to a questionnaire blatantly phrased to get 'desirable' answers, *Youth Matters* generated 19,000 contributions from young people as well as a further 1000 from organisations, professionals and parents. In the Government's response to this consultation exercise (DfES 2006), some marginal shifts in perspective from the green paper were discernible. Gay, lesbian, bisexual and transgender young people got a mention as did the wider difficulties faced by Black and Minority Ethnic (BME) groups 'because of poverty and poor education and employment outcomes' (para 2.16). The arts were endorsed as well as sport as a form of positive activity while the centrality of affordable transport to young people's ability to access them was also acknowledged.

Some key green paper ideas had also obviously received a reality check – particularly the youth opportunity card which originally ministers had seen as the way of embedding consumer choice in youth provision but which, it turned out, was first to be extensively piloted. On the other hand, by the time *Next Steps* appeared, the money available for the youth opportunity fund and the youth capital fund – both to be substantially controlled by young people themselves though with a strong targeting edge – had risen to £115m.

In crucial ways however the document left the core policy super-structure outlined in the green paper unchanged, not least with its emphases on commissioning, the pooling of budgets and (discussed in more detail below) the integration of local Youth Services into the new children's trusts. Indeed, though repeatedly invoking the importance of 'youth services', references to the Youth Service as such were again most notable for their absence.

Next Steps did identify youth work skills as 'vital' (DfES 2006, para 8.24) – an endorsement which was perhaps (if only implicitly) underpinned by the extension of its strap line to include 'someone to talk to'. However, with this not appearing until four paragraphs from the end of the document, youth work was still left substantively unintegrated into its overall vision, particularly for delivering the other high priority elements of the strap line: 'things to do, places to go'.

The 2006 Education and Inspections Act and the Treasury review of children and young people's services

Unsurprisingly given this context (and *its* title), when the relevant clause in the 2006 Education Bill was first published, its focus on 'functions in respect of recreation etc.' did nothing to contradict such interpretations (House of Commons 2006: 4–6). In legislating for local authorities' future role and contribution, the word 'must' did appear a number of times – including in relation to securing 'educational leisure-time activities' for 13–19 year olds. However, these were at no time described as 'youth work' or explicitly designated as a Youth Service function.

By the time the Bill became law in November 2006, substantial lobbying by Youth Service interests had succeeded in filling this gap. As the DfES's guidance made clear, the leisure-time activities outlined in the Act had to meet national standards. Though still picking out sport for special endorsement, these also laid down that every young person must be offered two hours a week of 'other constructive activity in clubs (and) youth groups' (DfES 2007: 6). A 'sub-set' of these activities, focused on young people's personal and social development, was explicitly defined as 'activities (to be) delivered using youth work methods and approaches' (DfES 2007, para 9 and 13).

This shift of official stance was ground-breaking – the first time a state paper of this kind had 'named' youth work in this way. Moreover, youth work's sudden emergence into the light of official approval seemed to be confirmed by the review of services for children and young people undertaken by the Treasury during 2006–2007 as part of its Comprehensive Spending Review. One of the most striking features of its discussion paper on the evidence it had received, published in January 2007, was an often taken-for-granted assumption that youth work had an important role to play in young people's personal and social development. Moreover, in making this argument the Treasury explicitly distanced itself from Margaret Hodge's simplistic view of youth clubs as damaging to this development (Ward 2005). 'Unstructured settings can', the paper noted, 'be effective in attracting disadvantaged young people and may offer a means both to engage and deliver support for vulnerable groups' (HM Treasury/DfES 2007 para 4.16). Indeed, the paper displayed a quite sophisticated understanding of the tensions involved in achieving and sustaining such engagement – particularly of the delicate balancing practitioners often need to strike between on the one hand starting where young people are and on the other challenging them in ways which help raise aspirations and stretch achievement (HM Treasury/DfES 2007 paras 4.33, 4.37).

However, welcome though this recognition of their practice was to youth workers, within the legislation it was hedged round by two significant qualifications. Firstly, in requiring a local authority to fulfil its duty to provide youth work only 'so far as is reasonably practicable', the Act allowed it to 'take into account its resources, capabilities and other priorities' (DfES 2007, para 17). In other words, it seemed – crudely put – 'No money, no youth work'.

Secondly, the Act did not require local authorities *themselves* to provide youth work. It merely gave them a duty to 'take all reasonable steps' to *secure* this provision, where appropriate by commissioning it from the private as well as from the voluntary and community sector (DfES 2007, paras 3, 64–75). In effect therefore the Act could be seen – and indeed, by some local authorities, was almost immediately treated – as a mandate for dismantling the only publicly funded body, the local authority Youth Service, with an explicit remit for sustaining and developing youth work practice. Indeed, even before it became law, the Act had encouraged a local authority like Northamptonshire (albeit, ministers claimed, unintentionally) to plan to make all its youth work staff redundant and transfer what was left of its youth work services to private and voluntary sector agencies (Rogers 2006a; Rohrer 2006).

The Youth Service and wider New Labour youth 'agendas'

Legislation, underpinned by documents such as *Transforming Youth Work, Resourcing Excellent Youth Services* and *Youth Matters*, were clearly crucial to shaping the Youth Service in the decade after 1997, even if often only by acts of omission. In these years however, as they made clear, these papers were often merely vehicles for tying the Youth Service into wider youth policy agendas. Driven by offers of some additional (if usually time-limited) funding, those – separately but especially cumulatively – with the most far-reaching effects included:

- *Young people's health needs* focused on substance misuse (including smoking and alcohol), sexual health, healthy eating especially to combat new epidemics such as obesity and diabetes and, in a period when teenage self-harm and suicide rates were climbing, mental health issues.
- *Teenage pregnancy and support for young parents*
- *Youth volunteering*, especially following the Chancellor of the Exchequer's high-profile endorsement of the Russell Commission's recommendations (Russell 2005).
- *Young people's 'participation' in governance and service delivery,* as a response particularly to the 'democratic deficit' amongst 18–24 year olds as evidenced by the dramatic fall in their turn out at general elections – from 68 per cent in 1997 to 37 per cent in 2005 (see Wood, Chapter 12).
- *'Social and community cohesion'*, especially following the 2001 'race riots' in which young people were seen to have been particularly involved (see Cantle 2001).

However, though Labour raised expectations of the Youth Service's role in all these areas, its responses to three other 'youth issues' proved to be the most critical for the Service's development, nationally and locally. One was what in Labour's third term came to be called its 'respect' agenda for tackling 'anti-social behaviour'. The second flowed from its determination to re-engage 'NEET' young people – those not in education, employment or training. And, following the murder of nine-year-old Victoria Climbie in 2000, the third was its sweeping reform of the structures and systems for protecting children and young people from abuse and exploitation. Labour initiatives and legislation in these areas not only added significantly to the recasting of youth work as the core practice delivered through the Youth Service. They also, step-by-step, radically reconfigured the institutional frameworks through which this was delivered, to the point where it was not clear that local Youth Services as separate entities could survive. Each of the areas therefore requires detailed attention.

Respect, respect, respect ...

Though it was often hard to see, the Blair Governments' mission to eradicate 'anti-social behaviour' from public places was part of a much wider strategy for tackling 'crime and disorder' and was aimed at a range of population groups. Nonetheless, as Joe Yates indicates in Chapter 14 both in the public perception and in its effects, the term came increasingly to stand as a metaphor for 'disreputable youth' – a 'central role in the regulation and social control of young people' and so had significant consequences for the Youth Service. Widespread anecdotal evidence, in part confirmed by the Joseph Rowntree Foundation's study of detached and outreach youth work (Crimmens et al. 2004) and other unpublished research, suggested that the Respect campaigns greatly intensified pressures on the service – from politicians, the media, services such as the police and housing, parents and the wider public – to douse constantly erupting youthful 'hot spots'. In a private email one principal youth officer vividly captured this demand for 'firefighting' anything youthful that moved on the streets: 'When I come into the office on a Monday morning to find yet another demand from a councillor to get youth workers into her or his area to sort out groups of young people, the one answer that is not allowed is "No"!'.

It was not New Labour's style, however, to leave such momentous matters to informal hit-and-miss procedures. *Resourcing Excellent Youth Services* gave explicit 'direction' on 'the contribution the youth service can make to … tackling anti-social behaviour and crime'. A repeating theme in *Youth Matters* was the need for 'positive' activities of the kind available through Youth Services as a way of preventing 'anti-social behaviour' (see for example para 79). The Prime Minister himself, in his Labour Party Conference speech in September 2005, called for more such activities 'so that [young people] are off the streets' (Blair 2005) while in the 'Respect Action Plan', launched personally by Blair in January 2006, he emphasised the 'enormous benefits for young people' of 'constructive and purposeful activities' (Respect Task Force 2006: 8).

Most concretely, the 1998 Crime and Disorder Act placed a duty on local authorities to ensure that *all* their services (including therefore the Youth Service) contributed to preventing crime in their areas. As one of a raft of other measures, it created youth offending teams (YOTs) to which 'youth and community work departments' were 'encouraged to contribute resources' – which in practice often involved seconding a youth worker to the local YOT. With 'punishment proportionate to the seriousness and persistence of (the) offending' as one of the required provisions (Every Child Matters 2005), the 'youth work' then on offer could begin to take some unfamiliar – and contradictory – directions.

Re-educating the young for work

As a way of restructuring the Youth Service and its practice, however, this turned out to be minor in comparison with what was subsequently attempted through New

Labour's efforts to get to grips with 'NEET' young people. For well over a century, the inability or unwillingness of a youth underclass to engage in the (legitimate) labour market had been a recurring source of official anxiety. For post-1997 Labour Governments, its existence went far to explain 'social exclusion' (DfEE 1999; Social Exclusion Unit 1999) – a concept used as a proxy for more critical forms of structural analysis of social inequality. Like many previous twentieth century predecessors, they also saw these virtual emigrants from the labour market as undermining Britain's industrial and commercial competitiveness in a new global economy requiring a highly skilled workforce.

Indirectly, Labour responded to this problem by endorsing what were in effect 'pre-NEET' preventative approaches, including the deployment of youth workers in schools to work with 'failing' and 'disaffected' pupils. Its 'big idea' however was its Connexions Strategy, and in particular its creation of a Connexions Service (Yates, Chapter 15). This was promoted initially as the provision of seamless 'youth support arrangements' for all 13–19 year olds to be delivered by teams of 'Personal Advisers' (DfEE 2000a). However, with 'NEET' reduction set as its most explicit, measurable and so eventually dominant target, from the start the Service had to look to other services to put it in touch with these so-called 'hard-to-reach' groups.

It was this need above all which particularly helped to prise the Youth Service out of the policy shadows. 'Over many years and in many places', it was recognised, the Service had employed:

> ... detached workers ... active on the streets and in places where young people congregate, working to establish rapport (outside the confines of 'officialdom') with young people who may have had a negative experience of school or other formal contacts. (DfEE 2000b: 32)

Connexions was thus given the 'important role' of ensuring youth service activity is effectively co-ordinated and coherent, with the youth service being instructed to '... incorporate their outreach and detached youth workers within the [Connexions Service's] multi-disciplinary teams of Personal Advisers [to be] created at local level' (DfEE, 2000a: 52).

As they were forced increasingly to tack to the strong philosophical and ideological winds blowing from the Connexions Service's national unit and its local partnership boards, Youth Services found themselves shifting still further towards the more targeted forms of work which other youth policies were also demanding. However, though a few Youth Services were fully or substantially merged into Connexions, within three or four years it became clear that the New Labour goal of fully joined up services for young people was not being achieved. When the Government next set out in search of this nirvana, therefore, its approach was much more full-frontal and uncompromising.

Protecting the young from abuse

From the 1980s onwards, as child abuse became an increasingly high-profile social policy issue, youth workers had struggled to reconcile their informal styles of work with the stringent managerial procedures which came to frame the practice of all those working with children and young people. Local child protection committees – some more responsive than others – needed to be persuaded to adapt agreed protocols for application to youth workers' relatively unstructured relationships with their 'clients'. As repeated child abuse tragedies and the enquiry reports they generated brought tighter and tighter controls, even this room for manoeuvre was narrowed.

However, the Laming report on the death of Victoria Climbie, the subsequent green paper *Every Child Matters* (DfES 2003) and the 2004 Children Act which flowed from this had implications for the Youth Service which went well beyond their impact on its practice methodology. Three elements of the new policy framework were particularly significant.

One was the increasing pressure the Service found itself under to frame its aims within the five outcomes for children and young people specified by the Act – to be healthy, stay safe, enjoy and achieve, contribute to community and society and achieve economic well-being. As a statement of aspirations, these presented few problems for youth workers or their managers: indeed they were seen and used by many as balances against the narrower focuses on child protection and 'community safety' which national and local policies were prioritising. However, the legislative force behind them and their constant reiteration in policy statements and guidance documents added to the pressure on youth workers to turn 'the five outcomes' into specific goals for their work *in advance* of meeting any group of young people. They thus had the effect of pushing still further to the margins a youth work methodology and process which sought to give young people the first say on what the focus and aims of their involvement might be.

Secondly, youth work as a distinctive practice and body of skills was put under further pressure by the inclusion of youth workers in 'workforce development' plans set in motion by the *Every Child Matters* policy initiative. Despite reassurances on the preservation of such specialist expertise, the plans were rooted in the notion that generic competences existed which were applicable to all work with children and young people. Simply on the basis of lessons from history – for example, the failed attempt in the 1970s to make all social workers 'generic' – this was a questionable exercise, though the principled questions remained largely under-explored. More immediately, it again left youth workers within the new structures defending their specialist skills as a small minority among much more powerful professional groups whose appreciation of youth work, its timescales and complexities was often limited.

Finally, the primary preoccupation of the new services was *children*, with young people often appearing only as a tacked-on after-thought. This however was only a marker of a deeper problem for Youth Services: that *Every Child Matters* had been developed for, and was being substantially implemented by, 'partners' whose professional identity and preoccupation was child care, which in practice often meant child protection. It was they for example who had the decisive control over policy development, priority-setting and the resource allocation. More single-mindedly than in any of its previous attempts, New Labour policy – makers this time really did seem to mean what they said: that 'silos' were to be dismantled, professional boundaries erased, provision joined up to the point where identifiable local Youth Services would no longer be visible – or tolerable.

Where Youth Services were clear about their distinctive mandate, where they had worked hard to win the support of local politicians and senior officers and of course where they were well used by young people, they appeared to be emerging from the restructuring still as discernible entities. Even here however Youth Service managers were liable to caution; in the words of one, 'We're doing OK – for now'.

Where Youth Services were starting from a weak base, however, and with limited leverage on local power structures their future seemed very uncertain. For them, the disappearance of a dedicated Youth Service budget stream in combination with the Children Act requirement that authorities consider 'outsourcing' provision meant that many free-standing local Youth Services committed to youth work as a distinctive practice were in effect facing emasculation. Thus by May 2006 the Association of Principal Youth and Community Officers was flagging up the loss of PYO posts within the restructured departments (*Young People Now* 2006; Rogers 2006b). By early 2007 the Community and Youth Workers Union was pointing to eliminated youth work posts and, even where nominally they were surviving, to their incorporation into generic children and young people teams (Henman 2007). At least two authorities were reported to be planning merging their Youth Service with their Youth Offending Team (See for example *Young People Now* 2007).

Conclusion: Is this closure?

As this chapter is being completed (in July 2008) it isn't possible to predict with total confidence where, in the longer-term, the constantly shifting but inter-locking youth policy developments set in motion by New Labour since 1997 will leave the Youth Service and youth work (see Davies 2008). Two trends – of profound significance for both – were however well established.

One was the uncompromising and unremitting emphasis of all New Labour youth policies on 'targeting' – in the case of young people, on those broadly, and variously, explained as 'disaffected', 'anti-social', 'disengaged', 'vulnerable'; or more specifically named as NEET, offenders, drug abusers, teenage parents. Starting from such adult-imposed labels was not only putting serious strain on what youth workers (rather optimistically) called their 'universal' or (more reasonably) their 'open-door' approaches (see Merton et al. 2004: 117–121; Crimmens et al. 2004: 73–74). It was also marginalising one of youth work's defining features: its reliance on a process through which young people's expectations of their encounters with a youth worker, rather than being pre-determined by adults, emerged from within the dynamic of those encounters (see Davies 2005a). New Labour policies may well have served the instrumental needs of managers and politicians for greater accountability and ensuring 'value for money'. However, notwithstanding the new verbal endorsements of youth work by the 2006 Education Act, from the Treasury review and in *Aiming High*, what these policies were generating was a practice, from which the very features so many agencies had come to value were being evacuated.

The second major trend in New Labour youth policies since 1997, including but also crucially beyond those directed specifically at the Youth Service, was the radical reconfiguration of the specialist institutional 'home' within which historically such practice had been delivered. This – the local authority Youth Service – had in many respects been deeply flawed: weakly rooted in legislation; too loosely structured to guarantee coherent policy-making, and – as politicians and inspectors never tired of repeating – patchy in its delivery and impact. However, for 60 years it had been the only state-financed institution with an explicit and primary *remit* to provide youth work, to seek its long-term sustenance and development and, in bad times, to help it to survive. As this practice disappeared into the new amorphous children and young people's departments, it was very far from clear who – which interest groups – would have the leverage or, ultimately, the commitment and incentive to reassert this remit and insist that such a practice was still needed.

All of which suggests that a chapter such as this could, in five or ten years time, read more like an obituary than a mere effort at policy analysis.

Reflective questions for practice

- **How is youth work organised, delivered and funded in your local area?**
- **Have the changing policy priorities for youth work had a measurable impact on your practice? If so, in what ways?**
- **What leverage do youth workers have in local partnership arrangements?**
- **Comparing Chapters 16 and 18, reflect on the professional identity of a youth worker. How has it changed? What do you think are the benefits and problems associated with this change?**

Further reading

Davies, B (2008), *The History of the Youth Service in England Volume 3 1997–2007: The New Labour Years,* **Leicester: National Youth Agency.** A more detailed account of and commentary on the development of the Youth Service and youth work in the period covered by this Chapter, located within a critical analysis of wider New Labour social policies.

Spence, J. and Devanney, C. (2006) *Youth Work: Voices of Practice,* **Leicester: National Youth Agency.** A research report, written mainly from the perspective of practitioners, which offers revealing evidence on the impact of the developing tension between New Labour policies and key youth work principles and practice.

Williamson, H. (2006) *Youth Work and the Changing Policy Environment for Young People,* **Leicester: National Youth Agency.** Sets the development of youth work within the context of 'youth transitions' and the changing policy goals and priorities for dealing with these, particularly since 1997.

17

YOUTH WORK AND THE VOLUNTARY SECTOR

Tom Wylie

Key arguments

- Youth work has long been delivered by voluntary agencies, and there continues to be great range and diversity of voluntary sector provision for young people.
- Since the Second World War this work has been increasingly professionalised with a state-sponsored youth service and more intensive work with particular categories of young people.
- As a result of the state being the largest funding body, voluntary sector youth work is drawn into issues which affect the voluntary sector as a whole including funding and sustainability.
- Government contracts for the delivery of defined services have gradually replaced open grants in a climate of contestability and competition between different providers. These developments may favour big charities at the expense of local neighbourhood projects.

Introduction

This chapter will discuss how youth work in the voluntary sector has developed from the nineteenth century to the present day. It explores some of the contemporary policy pressures on the sector and the tensions associated with establishing a close relationship with the state in service delivery.

In common with much British social welfare provision, the roots of contemporary youth work lie in voluntary endeavour in the late nineteenth and early twentieth centuries. What marks youth work apart from other forms of social welfare such as schooling or health services is that the state has not intervened directly or consistently to take up or promote youth work as a state or universal service. In consequence, voluntary sector youth work continues to diversify, flourish and engage itself with a wide variety of need, though increasingly it has been drawn into partnership with government, both at a local and national level.

The legacy shapes the landscape

Although times have changed, many current purposes in voluntary youth work can be traced back to, and still resonate with, the kind of inspiration which Davies (1999a) identified in their philanthropic predecessors:

> Some of their founders – often charismatic, not to say idiosyncratic, individuals – were far from uncritical of a society shaped by such self-interest. Many were openly appalled at how young people were being treated by its usually ruthless economic system. As upper and middle-class philanthropists, they sought to offer some at least ameliorating experiences and opportunities. … These youth work motives and aims did not emerge out of a social and ideological vacuum. Underpinning them was a conception of charity as the proper and indeed only framework for responding in a very 'targeted' way to those who were regarded as in need – and as deserving help. (Davies 1999a: 8)

Much of this inspiration, and some of the mindset, continues to the present day both in the sector itself and in policy makers. It has resulted in a great diversity of voluntary sector provision for young people. A substantial proportion remains very local, responding to needs in a neighbourhood or community, including an ethnic or faith community. Many such bodies are not only voluntary in the sense of having lay governance but also have a predominantly voluntary workforce, albeit some also have a slender professional national cadre of administrators and trainers: this is the pattern, for example, of Scouts and Girl Guiding. Other voluntary sector bodies such as federations of youth clubs and some faith-based organisations, including YMCA and YWCA, often have professional workers in charge of larger neighbourhood centres as well as having national development staff but still have a substantial volunteer workforce. The pattern of a growing professionalisation has been most evident since the Second World War and particularly after the Albemarle Report (HMSO 1959) and the consequent development of a more systematic, arguably state-sponsored, Youth Service, characterised at least in theory as a partnership between voluntary bodies and local authorities. Such professionalisation is also a consequence of the development of more intensive work with particular categories of young people, particularly those who are disadvantaged and perceived as having various vulnerabilities, notably towards offending but also in respect of risk-taking in respect of their health (teenage pregnancy, alcohol or drug misuse), or having insecure accommodation, or poor educational attainment (see Davies, Chapter 16). The response to such social concerns has led to the creation of various youth-serving agencies specialising in particular themes such as Crime Concern; Foyers and Centrepoint (housing); and Brook Advisory Centres (sexual health). Some voluntary bodies, for example Fairbridge, Rainer, Rathbrone, and The Prince's Trust, focus on disadvantaged young people and provide a range of programmes particularly concerned with their personal and social development and with encouraging them to rediscover their capacity for learning. All of these types of organisation tend to have a substantial professional workforce and management and their 'voluntariness' thus lies more in their governance and associated charitable status.

The gradual engagement of the state and changes in social attitudes in providing children's services – notably for those who could not be looked after by their natural parents – has resulted in sharp changes in emphasis by such long-established children's charities as Barnados, The Children's Society (of the Church of England) and its Methodist equivalent, NCH. The change of name by the latter first to 'NCH' then to 'Action for Children', as its title rather than its original 'National Children's Homes' symbolises a general move away from the provision of orphanages into national campaigning about, and local project work with, vulnerable young people. Such developments also illustrate a gradual encroachment into the later adolescent years which were the traditional territory of youth-serving rather than children's charities.

Shifts in the nature of provision in respect of new needs (and, on occasion, in responding to government funding) are evident across the voluntary sector. Hence the YMCA has consciously built on its strengths in sport and inter-generational work (Jeffs and Gilchrist 2005); the YWCA, prompted by changes in housing finance, has adjusted its focus from providing hostels to campaigning on issues affecting young women. New bodies have emerged – Youthnet, Groundwork, Muslim HelpLine – and more established youth organisations have declined. The Boys Brigade, for instance, appears to be in a long-term retreat to its Scottish and Northern Irish heartlands; the Guides are increasingly a pre-adolescent movement. Some voluntary organisations, have responded to market pressures by merging – as in the case of the Royal Philanthropic Society and Rainer. Mergers may be easier to accomplish once the founders have departed from the scene, but deep-seated if arcane ideological positions can provide intractable barriers to what, to an outsider, can seem obvious cases for merger: for example, in the national support structures for what were once defined as 'boys clubs' and 'youth clubs' or between Scouts and Guides, which is resisted in the UK and USA but common in continental Europe.

Faith groups have long engaged with young people for various reasons – 'give me a child until he is seven and I will give you the man' is a well-known saying attributed to the Jesuits. A tradition remains of evangelism – 'the extension of Christ's Kingdom among boys' to quote the old Boys Brigade mission; or at least of an effort to deepen the faith of the home (including in Jewish and Muslim communities). This tendency has been replaced or complemented in many organisations by a wish to serve also the more temporal needs of the young – for housing or just friendship – as well as their spiritual development (Green 2005). Not all those who engage in such faith-based work would define themselves as 'youth workers' and some of the wilder claims of church organisations concerning the scale of their workforce can be viewed with some scepticism when a more precise definition is used. As with sport or recreation, not all those engaged in faith-based work with young people are doing youth work, if by that is meant subscribing to a particular set of purposes, methods and values.

Youth work and New Labour

The arrival of a Labour government in May 1997 provided a much-needed boost to work with young people. The main foci for action by the new government were youth unemployment via the New Deal, changes to the youth justice system (see Yates, Chapter 14) and actions intended to improve standards in schools (Coles 2000).

The creation of the Social Exclusion Unit, reporting directly to the Prime Minister, heralded attention to socio-economic disadvantage and led to a set of actions concerned with neighbourhood renewal as well as towards specific disadvantaged groups (Social Exclusion Unit 2004). Much of this policy attention was on young people and those voluntary bodies which benefited most were those flexible enough to offer programmes which connected directly with the government's policy concerns, notably on youth unemployment and in the renewal of particular communities. More general, or traditional, forms of youth work were slower to advance into the warming rays of policy attention and consequential funding.

A notable, if contentious, element in the new approach to young people was the creation of a fresh organisational creature – Connexions – which arose from concerns about the position of those young people not in education, employment and training as reflected in a major report, *Bridging the Gap* (Social Exclusion Unit 1999). To deal with this issue, the DfES created Connexions with its own national civil service unit, 47 regional partnerships and established a nation-wide service built on the model of a personal adviser for each individual. Connexions can be seen as the apotheosis in youth policy of the two complementary mantra that dominated the discourse on policy-making in the 1990s – 'joined-up government' and 'partnership working'. The first expressed the need to break down departmental silos in central and local government; the second the desirability of drawing together a range of organisations across the public, private and voluntary sectors to achieve common goals. In Chapter 16, Davies sets out a critique of some of these developments.

Many in the field had accepted that there needed to be a radical re-configuration of local services with and for the young for which the Social Exclusion Unit's PAT12 report had also provided a compelling case (Social Exclusion Unit 2000c). But they saw limits to the capacity of information and advice – the core activity of Connexions – to produce changes in individuals, never mind in their peer groups and communities. They argued that it needed the full range of youth work including detached work and work with small groups to be deployed, not simply a personal adviser role.

After some early difficulties, most Connexions partnerships found themselves involving Youth Services, local authority and voluntary sector, in their governance and contracting them to supply particular services, such as detached work. Indeed, various voluntary organisations benefited from a modest 5 per cent of finance which was nominally ring-fenced to support their contribution to Connexions activity (Hoggarth, Smith 2004).

Meanwhile, from 2001, general youth work itself benefited from a whole set of governmental interventions designed to build its capacity, reform its organisational arrangements and specify standards for local provision. These developments were branded as *Transforming Youth Work* and represented a bold new architecture for youth work with a national framework establishing the basis for local co-ordination and delivery in both the local authority's direct youth work and its partnership with the voluntary sector.

But, as Davies has suggested, the arrival of a New Labour Government with a relatively clear, if narrow, youth policy agenda and a determination to push this through promised to sharpen the debate about the state's role and power (Davies 1999b: 190). It was, in practice, creating a national youth policy in an arena which had, by and large, been left to voluntary providers. The relationship between government and the voluntary sector was a theme which was increasingly evident across the welfare state, not simply within youth services.

The voluntary sector context

By the beginning of the twenty-first century, the government had become the largest single funder of voluntary and community organisations (but disproportionately so – the top 2 per cent of charities accounted for 60 per cent of the sector's income). Voluntary sector youth work is, in consequence, drawn into issues which affect the voluntary sector as a whole. The relationships between government and the wider sector have been transformed since 1997, symbolised by the introduction of a 'Compact' intended to regulate the relationships between government and voluntary sector on a range of matters. These matters generally hinge on arrangements for funding: will any contracts be long enough to allow the recruitment and retention of skilled staff? Will the full costs be met? Will the voluntary sector be enabled to compete on a level playing field with both public and private sectors? Will engaging in a policy campaign place a grant in jeopardy?

Such concerns reflect a deeper issue: the very nature of the relationship between the voluntary sector and the state. In earlier generations, this issue was often obscured by the provision of grants to voluntary organisations for their general work whether nationally or locally. From the 1980s onwards such grants were increasingly replaced by contracts for the delivery of defined services, particularly in the social care and welfare fields but increasingly encompassing youth work including that by national voluntary youth organisations. By 2006, various community groups – often very local in nature – were pointing to the difficulties of these new arrangements. One survey reported that:

> More than half of the community groups that responded say that the number of grants available to them has dropped in the last three years. ... Of those, 56 per cent had themselves had grants replaced by contracts, 73 per cent said the cut in grants would make it harder for them to survive in the long term, 50 per cent said their independence had been compromised by the switch to contracts, and 42 per cent said the shift is forcing them to provide services that are less geared to local community needs. (Carpenter 2006)

The chief executive of one representative body of community settlements warned that the shift to contact culture at a local level could mean a 'lot of local community organisations will go to the wall ... reducing the type of work community organisations are able to carry out.' He said that the shift to contracts meant community groups are increasingly becoming 'service delivery agents designed to fulfil the Government's target driven priorities' (Hughes cited in Bassac 2006).

Youth work was not sheltered from such forces. Even before Connexions and *Resourcing Excellent Youth Services* could properly bed in, government was engaged in an even greater upheaval. This was the reconfiguration of all local services for children and young people consequent on new arrangements established by The Children Act (2004). The process established by this Act and by the subsequent green paper 'Youth Matters' (DfES 2005) emphasised how important it was that the new local arrangements for governance – local authorities acting through Children's Trusts and Children and Young People's Partnerships – acted as the securers of services, not primarily their providers:

> We expect children's trusts to draw on the experience and expertise of voluntary and community youth organisations as strategic partners in all aspects of planning, developing and delivering services for young people. Local Authorities, through children's trusts, will want to invest in building the capacity of voluntary and community organisations in the locality as part of their strategy for shaping and developing the market for young people's services to ensure greater contestability. We expect them to follow current good practice guidance in their funding relationships with these organisations, including minimising monitoring and reporting requirements, and adopting the principle of full cost recovery. (DfES 2005)

This explicit recognition of the growing place of the voluntary sector was an acknowledgement of a role claimed both by the sector itself and by some academic researchers. Coles, for example, has written, perhaps a little generously, of the significant role of the voluntary sector in innovation to meet new needs and also to treat young people holistically and not simply on a specific presenting issue such as homelessness or drug misuse. It may also, he commented, be more willing to extend provision beyond statutory age ranges:

> One of the strengths of the voluntary sector is that it is adept at recognising gaps in services, and failures to meet need. Given such a widespread and rapid re-configuration of services, this monitoring role must be carried out even more vigilantly ... There is a wealth of experience within the voluntary sector in doing such work and avoiding disciplinary or professional blinkers, and bickering. The voluntary sector is in a strong position to take the lead on this as well as to monitor the problems that lie ahead. (Coles 2000)

Whether based on such evidence or not, politicians have become quick to praise the role of the voluntary sector. In early 2006, the then Prime Minister said:

> The Government is committed to bringing public services closer to our citizens. And what's clear is what matters to people is not who delivers these public services but that they are high-quality and accessible to all. It's why the country's third sector, with all its expertise and experience, is playing an increasing role – in giving a voice to the excluded, in championing the ambitions of communities and in providing services themselves. We need to make better use of its skills and deep roots in our communities to improve service delivery. (Blair 2006)

And, of course, the voluntary sector itself has not been slow to trumpet its skills and success and to seek to extend both of its influence and direct provision. The Association of Chief Executives of Voluntary Organisations (ACEVO) has been in the forefront of arguing this case. In a typical example it urged the Government to reform Jobcentre Plus, allowing the voluntary sector to compete on a level footing with the private and public sectors under better contractual conditions: '[We are] proposing the removal of employment and training services from Jobcentre Plus in favour of contracting them out to external providers – including voluntary sector bodies' (Thomas 2006). Such proposals fitted well with the governmental agenda for youth provision as its 'Youth Matters' proposals took shape:

> Mapping existing services from the voluntary, private and public sectors – including the Local Authority itself – against young people's needs would enable children's trusts to improve the quality of existing services and commission new services to fill any gaps. We would expect there to be a focus on the best available services from the public, private and voluntary sectors and will be issuing guidance and practical help on how to do this ... The voluntary and community sector is often best placed to reach and engage with the most vulnerable and disadvantaged young people, and offers a rich seam of innovation.... (DfES 2005)

Under the mantra of what was now called 'contestability', the government was urging local authorities that they should seek to give private and voluntary sector providers a fair crack at displacing what were previously run as public services. As one of New Labour's principal advocates noted, 'Used judiciously, contestability sent a powerful message that if you won't do the job properly, we can find someone who will (Denham 2005).

But such proposals by government need back-up if they are to advance beyond rhetoric. One immediate issue is that of the sector's capacity. Some politicians are quick to endorse particular work in the voluntary sector, and it has a tendency itself to overclaim for its potential contribution. The consequence can be a naïve assumption that highly successful projects, often led by a charismatic individual in a particular community, can be easily scaled up nationwide. But the Social Exclusion Unit has identified some 4,000 housing estates which need major social initiatives. How would projects in all of these be secured, staffed and funded in a sustainable way, not least as sustainability is a key feature of success with disadvantaged young people?

Moreover, voluntary sector bodies – notably in fields such as housing and justice – are not averse to competing with each other, as well as with the local authority. It remains to be seen whether the Trusts can be sufficiently intelligent in their role as commissioners to be able to judge competing providers against consistent standards of quality. As Denham observed:

> The new model public service can't survive its first encounters with the real world. Policies produced to this simplistic template come up against unavoidable problems. Few services can be provided effectively by autonomous institutions competing for their attention. Even the simplest health problem may involve more than one professional. If we fall ill we may well want a choice about where we go, and the time of our treatment. But we don't want the effectiveness of our healthcare to depend on our choices. We need someone to ensure that the system is in place long before we know we will need it. (2005)

Similar considerations apply to youth work, although less sharply perhaps than for health needs.

A claim by the voluntary sector – and those who champion it – that it could replace the State's role is not only unrealistic, it may be positively harmful. As one writer has suggested:

> the five giants, which the last century bred and Beveridge sought to slay: want, idleness, ignorance, disease and squalor … Was it not the state with its anti-poverty, unemployment, education, health and housing programmes that at least disabled if not slew them? (Dean 2005)

Similar considerations apply in youth work. Some voluntary sector bodies, and their local and national leadership, appear quick to underline the distinctive place of the sector and to downplay any partnership with local authorities. In one notorious example in 2006, where a local authority not only reduced spending on its direct youth services but sought to replace these with voluntary providers, the spokesperson for the local council of voluntary youth services was quoted as saying 'this could be good news for the voluntary sector' (Young People Now 2006). The impression given was that the consequences for young people did not come first.

There are deep roots to such mutual ambivalence about partnership working in the youth field:

> Particularly following the Albemarle Report in 1960, the statutory sector took on the role of direct provider with increasing vigour and considerably more resources than the voluntary organisations could command. More and more over this period these organisations in effect became clients of the state as, locally and nationally, they came to rely on public funds to develop – even often just to maintain – their core facilities and activities. (Davies 1999b: 186)

Such a role, as a kind of junior partner to the state, was never comfortable. Now it brings with it other kinds of expectations and responsibilities.

Targets – themselves a form of micro-management increasingly used across the public sector – was an aspect of the youth work agenda from 2000. They were seen by some as inimical to the process of youth work and were accompanied by other regulatory frameworks. Indeed, the growth of regulation – criminal records, outdoor safety – has been particularly notable in the youth sector in view of concerns about child protection and personal safety, both prompted by tragic incidents (see Davies, Chapter 16). Commentators claimed that:

> Regulatory frameworks designed to guarantee minimum levels of service from public bodies and protect the most vulnerable from the free market are often inappropriate for those whose primary motivation is simply to help out. Legislation forces regulators to replace individual initiative and goodwill with rigid rules and procedures. Although public bodies should be looking to reduce risk for the public, they end up reducing their officials' exposure to risk. ... red tape is having a negative impact on public willingness to volunteer and the sector's ability to deliver. Government bodies must therefore be prepared to take more risk in the way they work, to ensure that the voluntary core qualities of flexibility, individualism and compassion are properly appreciated, rather than ungratefully bound in the standard-issue straitjacket of bureaucracy. (Slack 2006)

And such commissioners in securing provision other than that of the local authority may turn, not to the voluntary sector, but to the private sector. Bureaucracy may also favour the larger provider – the national body, albeit with local units, which can provide some assurances about quality control, financial management and contract compliance. Big charities compete with smaller, neighbourhood organisations and grants that were once given to local groups are converted into awards and contracts through competitive tendering (Curley 2006).

The Chair of the Council of Ethnic Minority Voluntary Sector Organisations has drawn attention to the baleful consequences of such arrangements for minority ethnic bodies:

Success has mostly been the domain of large mainstream organisations with skilled workforces and considerable corporate capabilities. Membership of this charity super-league remains the preserve of mainstream white-led organisations ... In contrast, their minority ethnic counterparts preside over an impoverished reality inhabited by cash-strapped local service providers struggling to meet the needs of the country's most deprived communities ... Most of the organisations provide support to vulnerable individuals. They offer culturally sensitive services and lend a voice to groups nobody else speaks for. But their causes do not attract funding. It is not the sector's new contract culture that is the problem, but the deep-seated culture of inequality and disadvantage still pervading British society. (Sarda 2006)

Recognising the capacity weaknesses of the general voluntary sector and of youth services, government has increasingly sought to develop its infrastructure. An important step in 2006 was to reshuffle responsibility for the voluntary and community sector away from the Home Office and into a new subdivision of the Cabinet Office with its own Minister. The Office of the Third Sector quickly began to flex its muscles on longstanding issues concerned with the development of the voluntary sector, including its increasingly important 'social enterprise' role. In his role as the then Chancellor of the Exchequer, Gordon Brown noted that new not-for-profit organisations needed access to finance:

We established Futurebuilders to help existing charities adapt to the modern world. We need to examine how we might do more to encourage new charities and social enterprises, locally and nationally, to start up, develop and flourish – perhaps with a fund for seedcorn finance. (Brown 2006)

By early 2006 this government-backed fund had agreed a total of £36m in loans and grants with 102 organisations. These included such youth-oriented bodies as the Ariel Trust, a radio training agency for young unemployed people in Manchester which received a £14,000 development grant in 2005, and a £120,000 loan and a £50,000 grant to help it expand its training across the north west of England.

The practical implementation of the government's grand rhetoric has been assessed also by the House of Commons' Committee of Public Accounts. Its Chairman said

Whitehall's lack of expertise at working with the sector is compounded by the scarcity of information on how funding is distributed between voluntary organisations. My Committee is concerned that the poorest communities might be getting a rough deal from the way funding is distributed. The voluntary organisations themselves can hardly be encouraged by bureaucratic procedures for applying for funding and the uncertainty which goes together with having to renew contracts annually (Edward Leigh cited in Focus 2006: 22).

Conclusion

Voluntary sector youth work has continued to diversify, professionalise and flourish. It looks likely to remain a favourite of politicians for the foreseeable future as it gives the impression that at least some parts of it can go further and faster (and perhaps more cheaply) than those who are more directly the servants of the state. But this position of rhetorical advantage comes at a price. The sector's increasing dependence on government funding can challenge traditional ways of working and values. It may also bring with it approaches to managerial, administrative and professional practice with which some in the sector will be uncomfortable and a challenge to independence of thought and action. There will certainly be a challenge to its capacity as it seeks to scale up individual approaches into more systematic, nation-wide provision for the young.

Reflective questions for practice

- What voluntary sector organisations are you aware of that work with young people?
- Consider your own work in a voluntary sector organisation. What are the sources of funding?
- What specific or general needs must the organisation address in order to fulfil its funding obligations?
- How were these needs identified?

Further reading

Davies, B. (1999a; 1999b) *A History of the Youth Service in England*, **Leicester: National Youth Agency**. This three volume history does not simply provide a magisterial chronology to 2007 but threads through the narrative a set of themes, including the place of the voluntary sector.

Coles, B. (2000) *Joined Up Youth Research, Policy and Practice*, **Leicester: National Youth Agency**. Coles marshals his account around particular themes – unemployment, crime, etc. – and analyses policies and research in each theme as well as providing case studies of relevant practice.

18

MODERN YOUTH WORK: 'PURITY' OR COMMON CAUSE?

Malcolm Payne

Key arguments

- **Youth work has always been difficult to define in a 'pure' way and has tended to be too aligned in academic literature to youth services.**
- **There is a tension between educational and welfare purpose that does not help in defining new forms of work with young people.**
- **Practitioners need to negotiate between adherence to practice principles, the contexts or situations they work in and the priorities of local and national social policy.**
- **The territory to be claimed by modern youth work needs to be broad and inclusive. That will mean joining forces across the spectrum of work with young people; to find common cause and to construct a practice model across welfare and education dimensions.**

Introduction

The central concern of this chapter is the occupational identity (Tucker 2005) of what we call youth work in the UK. While this is not a new concern, it has nonetheless become more pressing in a policy climate that seeks *integration* of services at local level as the way forward in what Davies (Chapter 16) sees as 'the new amorphous children's and young people's departments' with the potential loss of youth work's remit this is felt to threaten. In parallel with these developments, there is much discussion of 'work with young people', particularly as integrated youth support services become more prominent. This might signal either a recognition of some kind of 'genericism' within the work, or perhaps, its opposite: that youth work is now expected to perform a host of highly specialised (and arguably, competing) tasks so that differentiation within such work becomes increasingly difficult. As Harrison et al. contend (2007: 1), the term 'work with young people' indicates 'a wide range of practices, traditions, contexts and roles; taking account of current breadth and diversity of this professional field'. To make sense of modern youth work then is a difficult challenge: we must account for the complexities and ambiguities inherent in its practice(s); to test the models claimed or assumed in order to explore what many have asserted as its distinctiveness when compared with other forms of work with young people.

Practitioners and researchers have offered a wide array of social policy arenas in which youth work appears successfully to deploy itself. These include claims for its positive impact on 'social cohesion', mental health and social inclusion among others. For example, Sarah Banks (Chapter 5) explores the contribution of youth workers in youth offending teams. Yet there has been an equally strong contention (see for example Young 1999) that what this illustrates is either a diversion from youth work's core purpose – even indeed a corruption of that purpose – or perhaps, that what is unique about youth work is in danger of being lost. Given that position, the contention by Beverley Hughes, then the minister with responsibility for youth services, that 'youth work is about activities rather than informal education' (Barrett 2005: 14–15) received a predictably disapproving response among practitioners. It confirmed what some had thought all along: that the state's interest in youth work (at least since 1997) has been purely instrumental. Such a view, it is argued, values it only for its impact on specific policy goals: educational achievement, inclusion, health, crime reduction and employability, rather than youth work's own broader concerns for the personal and social development of young people. More recently, the emphasis on so-called positive activities, seen in the government's 10 year youth strategy (HM Treasury/DCSF 2007) appears to confirm the state's view of what youth work has to offer.

Against this background, and given the wide range of agencies, programmes and approaches intended to have an impact on the behaviour and well-being of young people, the relationship between what has come to be known as 'youth work', and a range of other kinds of work with young people, needs careful consideration.

This chapter seeks to consider some of the questions which arise. In particular, it explores:

- The ways in which youth work seeks to distinguish itself from other work with young people
- The nature of key elements of youth work practice theory that this draws upon
- Whether the claimed distinctions hold up and indeed are in youth work's or young people's interests.

In order to consider these issues the chapter takes what has sometimes been referred to as a 'constructionist' approach (Berger and Luckmann 1967), arguing that the practice of youth work, and other forms of work with young people, are constructed out of the interaction between a number of 'social' (including political) forces. These include at their heart what have been referred to as 'practice theories' and 'practice ideologies' (Payne 1997: 38) which, in this case, seek to explain and lay claim to what 'youth work' is, what 'youth workers' do, and how these relate to young people's worlds and the social policy terrain they find themselves in. The chapter argues that, first, youth work has tended to overlook the differences and ambiguities within it in order to lay claim to distinctiveness. Second, that practice principles associated with these theories must be seen in the context of the socio-political situations youth workers find themselves in. The interplay between context and practice is critical to an understanding of the work. Third, what is often depicted as youth work, it is argued, is frequently derived from a particular, and narrow, contextual arena in which specific forms of the work have taken place. As a result, youth work has become over-identified with what has been provided by youth services. Valuable as those services may be, the benefits to young people of working with them according to a broadly understood practice model applicable to a wide range of settings, risks being lost or diminished. A critical practice model is needed which recognises and enhances forms of work with young people beyond the purely educational – not to exclude that from the equation but to be able to *include* other settings and arenas, and to assert the value of an approach based on personal and social development within them.

This is not intended as an argument against the importance in young people's lives of youth clubs, projects and activities which are open to all (universal), or of workers meeting young people on their own territory (as in detached youth work). Instead, it is to argue that such provision should be seen as making a valuable contribution alongside, and in close association with, other forms of work. Furthermore it is to assert that youth workers have a distinctive role to play across the spectrum of work with young people.

Situating work with young people

Any discussion of modern youth work must include a close examination of the influence of the state. And, in turn, it must acknowledge the factors to which the state itself is responding – popular opinion, media pressure, concerns for international (or local) competitiveness, research and other knowledge, legal requirements and so on. While a reading of any history of youth work quickly demonstrates there was never a form of the work entirely free of political intent, the importance of gaining an understanding of how practice is constructed now has never been greater – or perhaps, more complex. The time is long gone when the state could be seen as a relatively benign influence – content to allow practitioners, agencies and services to get on with the job with little interference. The past 20 or more years has witnessed intrusion into the processes of youth work and other forms of work with young people on a scale and in ways which were unimaginable at the time of the Albemarle Report 1960 and only perhaps glimpsed in the Thompson Report 1982.

The state's determination to intervene – increasingly devising and managing mechanisms to 'bend' practice towards political imperatives – has not simply been directed towards youth work. The technology of state management of work with young people extends in all directions: work with young offenders, health, employment and training, community development and regeneration, and of course, schools. State influence and regulation has been experienced by most human professions: teaching, social work and probation for example. So youth work is not alone in finding its identity to be a 'site of struggle' (Foucault 1991 cited in Tucker 2005: 211) The national state provides a significant mandate for the work, sets its parameters, provides much of the funding and, through its management and accounting mechanisms, a regulatory framework. Local authorities have significant powers too, but are in many ways subservient to an increasingly interventionist national state. The stance that practitioners take in response to this scenario is critical to the practice models which emerge.

Where youth work and other work with young people is concerned, it is now far from clear what that mandate might be. The state's concerns about the behaviour, lifestyle or condition of particular groups of young people, has been enacted through an increasing range of agencies and programmes (for example, Youth Offending Teams, Connexions, Drug and Alcohol Action Teams, extended schools, Pupil Referral Units). This has served to challenge and perhaps blur the boundaries between 'traditional' youth work and these newer areas of work. Where youth work may have been seen, by definition, as primarily that work which was delivered by youth services (made up of both statutory and voluntary sectors), youth work from 1997 onwards has been expected increasingly to contribute to overarching policy objectives for work with young people (see Davies, Chapter 16 for a review). This has three distinctive features. First, youth *services* have been expected to adjust their priorities to take account of these policy objectives – to direct their attention to particular groups in order, for example, explicitly to contribute to their social inclusion or towards crime reduction. Second, youth *workers* have also been expected to work in particular ways, including with other agencies, to help them to achieve their objectives. As a result, youth workers may be directly involved in providing these new services in fields such as advice and guidance, or youth justice. And third perhaps, newly emerging agencies have adopted some of the informal education approaches which were sometimes felt to be the preserve of youth work as they have sought to take on new forms of work or to reach those who had not been reached hitherto.

Youth work and youth services

Youth work in the UK is usually closely identified with local youth services. The introduction to *Transforming Youth Work: Resourcing Excellent Youth Services* (DfES 2002) is an example. Recognising their inherent 'diversity', youth services are nonetheless 'underpinned by having in place a shared set of youth work values and by the use of distinctive methods' (p. 6). Although the difficulty associated with this lack of distinction has been well rehearsed (see Jeffs and Smith, 1988; Smith 1988), it is surprisingly pervasive.

Attempts to offer a definition of youth work through forms of categorisation of the work itself are, to say the least, problematic, whether by the different forms the work takes, the perspectives adopted, the setting, organisational arrangements, or even ideology. Different historical traditions and sheer complexity militate against easy explanation. Pedagogical, philosophical, sociological, psychological and other theories are drawn upon to attempt to capture role and purpose; and symbolism (associated with for example, membership of a particular movement or 'club') is used to mark out the boundaries between one form of work and another since it 'allows workers with seemingly conflicting orientations to be located in the same tradition' (Smith 1988: 63).

Bradford (2005: 58) suggests that youth work 'has remained an ambiguous set of practices, pushed in different directions at different times by different interests'. He argues that it takes on various 'guises' and 'shifts its identity in response to varying conceptions of youth need' (ibid: 58). Such a conception of what youth work is, and does, requires youth work's 'territory' to be defined in qualitative terms – by the nature of the relationship between worker and young person; by the processes which guide it – if it is to retain some sense of professional identity. The purpose of the work becomes defined by its values and practice principles. As Davies acknowledges (Davies 2005a: 8), neither is this position easily sustained. Hence his attempt, in the face of current policy directions, to defend the practice of youth work by offering a manifesto to make explicit what its defining characteristics might be.

But there are inherent risks even in this approach. While the presence of competing practice theories is inevitable (and healthy) the status we attach to the notion of 'theory' itself and its associated practice, may lead us to believe that the 'reality' of youth work can be explained in terms of a particular and perhaps consensual theoretical or ideological position. The complexity of the ideas that 'youth work' represents, and the apparent confusion about where it is actually located, suggests otherwise. Theory-building, particularly in the face of what are felt to be threats emanating from state youth policy, may have led us to believe that there is – conceptually at least – a youth work which is in some way 'pure' – free from the interests which may be pushing it hither and thither – and which can act as a reference point for the work.

This is not surprising: youth work has always represented a philosophical view of one kind or another of young people's position in the world; and those who argue for their view of youth work to prevail are, in so doing, arguing for their view of broader youth social policy (and indeed, society) also to prevail. So, for example, if one's view of the state's past interventions in youth training is that it has been used primarily to prepare young people 'for a life of low skilled, insecure work and inter-mittent periods of unemployment' (Mizen, in Banks 1999: 25), for youth work to be in any way engaged in such a project could be seen as a corruption of purpose. This may have led to a tendency for youth work theorists, in examining critically each new area of work with young people, to argue that any youth work associated with it is either not 'pure', or indeed, not youth work at all. In this conception, youth work defined by its practice principles and values, could be backed into a corner. Only when it is free of the expectations directly to deliver particular social policy objec-tives (reducing youth crime, reducing the proportion of 'NEET' young people by providing youth support services, or improving educational attainment for example) is it really doing what its heart and soul dictate.

This is not to suggest that youth work does not claim to be delivering benefits which underwrite those policy objectives. The position offered in the evaluation of its impact in England (Merton et al. 2004: 29), that it has two inter-related purposes: personal and social development, and social inclusion, was uncontroversial. What is less clear perhaps was the question of function. That study did not seek to make a clear distinction between youth work per se, and the services which provide it. Yet what evidence there is (see for example Crimmens et al. 2004; Merton et al. 2004) points to some of the ways in which youth workers, involved in a variety of ways with young people, achieve what has come to be known as 'impact'. Thus, while youth work's purpose is personal and social development, it can serve the function *inter alia* of reducing social exclusion when it is deployed in particular ways. But if this is seen to be achieved by deploying youth workers to new tasks (e.g. reducing youth crime) – and thereby, new purposes, or redirecting the resources of youth ser-vices to different forms of work, then the result will be to marginalise 'pure' youth work. We could, so the argument goes, end up with youth workers (and even youth services) but no youth work.

Kerry Young's position offers a further illustration of this argument: she sees youth work as having been 'remodelled' to fit the funding criteria of different bod-ies and, as a result, to have 'obscured its fundamental purpose.' (Young 1999: 78) When youth work's heart is defined as being the Socratic question: *How should I live?* – that is, to be primarily if not solely concerned with 'discussing, understand-ing and mediating values' (ibid. p. 80) then any departure from that agenda will be seen as a youth work that has 'lost its way'.

In fact, such an argument begs as many questions as it answers. By decontextualising purpose it tempts us to believe that it can be answered in the abstract and without recourse to the situations that youth workers, or young people, find ourselves in. It thus serves to confuse. For the question 'How should I live?' cannot be answered without reference to context: of the youth work role; or, of young people with whom they work, the social structures they inhabit and their lived experiences. It takes on a different meaning for someone experiencing homelessness, compared with the same question when basic needs are not at issue. For the worker, discussion, understanding and mediation of values has not become absent where she or he is operating in a hostel. The pressing priority – to address the young person's housing situation – provides the context in which that mediation takes place and the practice becomes constructed. Put simply, in this example, the worker will (rightly) be judged on whether the immediate problem has been addressed *and* whether the solution is sustainable in the longer term for the young person. That will demand attention both to their housing situation and to any underlying (personal) or wider (social) issues in the young person's life.

In truth, and as many studies have shown, young people's issues do not arrive in single file. Instead, they are interlinked, complex and contingent (see for example, Social Exclusion Unit 1999; Hoggarth and Smith 2004; Merton et al. 2004). Any response to them will need to work with such complexity and the ambiguities this may present. What then should be youth work's stance?

An international comparison may serve to further elucidate this question. If we look at what 'youth services' mean in other European countries what we see is usually a collection of different approaches and services which, as in the UK, have arisen from particular historical traditions. They are often constituted by broad functional categories: cultural and leisure services, welfare and support, counselling, advice and guidance, residential care and so on. Together, these constitute services for youth (see for example, Becsky et al. 2004). Those different aspects of services are delivered by different agencies, both statutory and voluntary. Some will be delivering what in the UK has come to be recognised as youth work – for example through youth clubs, projects or detached work. Some are 'open to all' (universal); while others are provided for specific categories of young people – those who are excluded from school, or who are involved with youth justice for example. Socio-cultural and leisure services – the nearest equivalent perhaps to what we call youth services in the UK – take their place alongside the more targeted provision for young people. Social pedagogues or socio-cultural workers working with young people – the nearest equivalent to youth workers in the northern European tradition – work in all or most of these agencies in many European countries.[1] Social pedagogy as a practice is to be found across the range of functions (and beyond). But importantly, there is no service which defines itself in these terms. The professional group which goes by that name will not find a 'home' in which some 'pure' form of its work – social pedagogy or socio-cultural work – takes place. There is usually no single

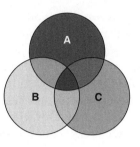

Figure 18.1   Youth work in the UK

youth service which does *only* youth work. Of course, there is considerable debate and exploration of social-pedagogical (and socio-cultural) practice principles but, for the most part, such debates are located in particular practice arenas and are concerned as much with the translation of those principles into practice as with an abstraction of the underlying practice principles.

In contrast, youth work in the UK has come to be identified with, or at least to be embodied by, what youth services and (some) youth organisations do – typified and perhaps defined by – traditional open access forms of the work with young people in their leisure time. The consequence may be that *other* work with young people becomes seen in the UK as in some way different: it is not youth work because 'pure' youth work defines itself in ways which exclude those other forms of work with young people. In contrast, the social pedagogue or socio-cultural worker expects (and indeed is trained) to locate her or himself by applying practice principles in a wide range of settings and contexts. Some of those emphasise 'welfare', others learning and leisure. All however, would lay claim to an educative function.

The UK position can be illustrated diagrammatically as in Figure 18.1. 'A' in the diagram represents the youth service – the range of activities and programmes it provides. Not all of what youth services do, according to this conception, is youth work. So, providing one-to-one mentoring support for young people leaving care, may not be seen to constitute youth work even when it is provided by the youth service. Neither might the deployment of some youth service staff to work within other agencies, e.g. Connexions: they may be youth workers but they are not necessarily 'doing youth work'. In both cases, because they depart from the precepts associated with informal education as it is usually understood, youth work's role is seen to be compromised.

'B' represents other services to young people including perhaps the work of Connexions, Youth Offending Teams (YOTs) and Drug and Alcohol Action Teams (DAATs). Their primary agendas – reducing the number of NEET young people; diversion from crime; or reducing drug misuse, are seen to mark them out as having a different purpose to the youth service whose 'primary purpose is the personal and social development of young people' (DfES 2002: 6). Some of these services will include youth workers in their workforce and indeed, may even be doing some 'youth work' but this will not be their primary objective. It is in this arena perhaps, that 'work with young people', and more recently, 'integrated youth support' is most often located.

'C' represents what youth workers are engaged in doing. They may be 'doing youth work' when they work within YOTs (as above) for example, but only if certain conditions are fulfilled. Even in their work in the youth service, they will only be 'doing youth work' if that work is seen to conform to a set of principles, values and critically, purposes and methods. According to this analysis, youth work, at the heart of the Venn diagram, only takes place when its service objectives (functions) *and* its core purpose (personal and social development) coincide – and fulfil the practice principles, methods and values which youth work has set for itself. The range of work will still be quite diverse, but it is seen to be quite distinct from the more welfarist agendas associated with what is provided within 'B'. It is primarily, if not exclusively educational: attempting to reconcile the tensions between Rousseau's 'learning for freedom' and 'learning for life' – the personal and the social if you like.[2]

The contention of this chapter is that such a conception, while apparently protective of 'real' youth work, is neither that, nor necessarily in young people's interests. The problem is that it fails to distinguish between practice principles, values and purpose on the one hand; and the organisational and socio-political context (including mandate) within which that practice is enacted.

The argument here is that practice itself is always constructed from three elements: the daily interactions between workers and young people; the agencies which set policy and objectives within the social policy landscape; and the practice theories which guide the work. It is explained in the negotiation of purpose, methods, principles and values *and* their context. That context may be the religious or spiritual purposes associated with the youth work of a religious movement, the objectives of a secular youth organisation, or the mandate provided by the state for a particular service. But when practice principles and values become intrinsically linked to, and identified with a *particular* context and mode of delivery – open access youth work within the youth service for example – the effect is to set the practice in a form which reifies one context and serves to divorce it from others.

Principles can guide practice but can only be expected to define it if 'youth work' is understood as an ideal type: constructed only of chosen elements rather than any empirical, contextualised reality.

Youth workers in 'other' agencies

Many agencies working with young people employ professionally qualified youth workers. This is not a new phenomenon. Although there is no statistical evidence to measure its scale, most of us who have contact with such agencies can confirm it. Anecdotal evidence suggests that at least a third and probably more of the present Connexions workforce for example, is made up of youth work professionals. YOTs, DAATs and Entry to Employment (E2E) schemes also employ youth workers although the scale here is probably different. The range of agencies employing youth workers beyond these high profile examples is bewilderingly wide: regeneration schemes, hospitals, libraries, teenage pregnancy agencies, community safety projects, women's refuges, hostels, leaving care projects, community development initiatives, mediation schemes, outdoor education – to name but a few. Tellingly, many agencies employing untrained staff to work with young people sponsor their attendance on professional youth work training courses, seeing this route as directly relevant to the work they are being asked to do.

Roles and approaches

There is an absence of robust research evidence about the roles and work methods adopted by such staff. The Connexions service provides a useful case example because it has been cast in the role of undermining youth work (Smith 2000, 2007) and has received considerable negative attention as a result. Guidance on the role of Personal Advisers (PAs) emphasises notions of individualised support (DfEE 2000) and this is one of its features which has given rise to concern among promoters of youth work (see for example, Cisse 2001; Smith ibid.). The Connexions Impact Study (Hoggarth and Smith 2004), while not scrutinising the role in these terms, nonetheless offered some assessment and insight: examples abound of PAs interacting with young people at risk, counselling, advising, supporting them in such arenas as schools, colleges, drugs advice agencies and youth projects (see for example pp. 40–41). Personal development, alongside practical support, in the words of one young man, 'to really get things sorted out' (p. 36) is central to the practice of PAs. As the study makes clear, Connexions does not claim the personal development of young people as its sole territory but PAs nonetheless see it as central to what they do (p. 37). Yates (Chapter 15) explores the role of the Connexions personal adviser in greater detail.

Neither is such one-to-one work all that Connexions does. There is evidence too of groupwork with for example, young carers, those resisting school, refugees and asylum seekers and others – either undertaken directly by the service, or supported by it. And there is a considerable amount of work going on to promote young people's participation – although perhaps only, to date, a relatively narrow version of this. There is also evidence of some Connexions services making concerted efforts to redistribute resources towards those whose access to services may be restricted – Black and minority ethnic young people, refugees and asylum seekers, young parents for example.

Conceptually however, such work, when seen from the perspective of youth work, is found wanting: it is seen to represent for example, a 'welfarist' casework approach and is held by some to run counter to the 'openness' of youth work's orientation (Smith 2000: 1). Its preoccupation with those 'at risk' is seen to carry with it the attendant danger that the broader structural considerations which give rise to individual young people's social conditions are ignored or down-played (Kemshall, Chapter 13) – as Williamson has argued, that social policy is 'recasting public issues as private troubles', resulting in 'pathological' approaches (Williamson 1993: 35). Targeting the work is thought to bring with it attendant dangers, particularly those associated with labelling young people: for example as NEET (not in employment, education or training); anti-social; or drug users.

Putting to one side the social policy issues (which are dealt with briefly later) at the level of practice and practice theory, what is it that is being compared here? The danger is that again, a reductive 'pure' form of youth work is claimed as the legitimate youth work comparator. It is 'open door' youth work, or detached or project work perhaps, which is held up as the 'standard' against which other work is to be judged. By this token, youth work's involvement for example in supporting young people leaving care (Merton et al. 2004: 64) is in danger of being relegated to second class status; its fundamentally educational aims seen as inevitably marginal to, or in conflict with, its statutory responsibility for the young person's welfare.

Voluntary participation

The tendency to have in mind only a narrow version of youth work is illustrated in Davies' manifesto (Davies 2005a: 13). Here, the 'voluntary principle' for example, ('perhaps the ... defining feature of youth work' he suggests), and acknowledging the caveats offered, is explored primarily in the context of youth work's engagement in traditional leisure time youth service activity: young people choosing to go to youth provision. Similarly, Jeffs (2007: 97) asserts 'the inalienable right of young people to refuse to engage with the worker'. This is a tough condition to meet when it is cast in absolute terms. It implies that the young person has free (though not necessarily informed) choice. It suggests that there is *either* voluntary engagement, *or* compliance, control and compulsion. Yet the graduations between these states are subtle, contested and frequently, highly subjective. 'Voluntary engagement' is not quite so easy to detect as a principle in the realities of young people's lives. Freedom to walk away there might be, but that choice may well also have consequences: losing access to valued friends or facilities, or, more subtly, bringing with it the disapproval of adults. For sure, young people have the right, but that right might not always be easily exercised. And the worker, as Jeffs and Banks (1999: 101) readily acknowledge, even in the open setting finds themself having to exert control which to say the least, confuses the apparent simplicity of the principle. (You are free to come here provided that you have the entrance fee. Or, you will have to leave if you do not comply with our rules on smoking/ alcohol/dope/bullying. Of course, you are also free *not* to come. But if you do, these are the ground rules.)

Examples are offered in Merton et al. (2004: 126–128), of youth work beginning with young people whose choice to engage is constrained. These complexities cannot be left to one side in order to lay claim to the principle. Voluntary engagement is an important element of practice, but not in a 'pure', unalloyed or decontextualised form. Youth workers' practice can be seen to interpret it to have relevance in those settings in which there may also be compulsion or sanction – they 'used their skills of negotiation and persuasion, and – gently and gradually – gave the young people incremental choice and control' (Merton et al. 2004: 127). The Thompson Report acknowledging young people's choice to participate, saw it thus:

> Youth workers have of course a certain authority but their authority has to be of a different kind from that which young people are likely to have experienced from their teachers, parents and other caring (or non-caring) adults. In brief, young people find with the right sort of youth worker that their views and attitudes are treated with respect. (Review Group on the Youth Service in England 1982: 34)

Workers in other agencies see the principle to be important too – not simply as an absence of compulsion, but the pursuit of the young person's active willingness to take part. As we said in the Connexions Impact Study (Hoggarth and Smith 2004: 33) 'The crucial issue is that early contact needs to bring young people to the point of seeing Connexions as a viable source of support … early contacts, even a first meeting, can also determine whether or not a young person will ever voluntarily use the service again'. This is a complex ethical arena but the point here is that if we 'purify' the principle in the youth work context in order to claim distinctiveness, we endanger the broader ethical principle – that the way in which work with young people is pursued should maximise their ability to make informed choices and respect the decisions they take. The National Youth Agency's statement of ethical principles (National Youth Agency 2001) elucidates the importance of these broad principles. But they can never be pure in youth work – nor in any other form of work with young people. There are strong echoes here of old (but nonetheless important) discussions about social education versus social control, of Rousseau's domains of learning mentioned earlier. Ethical cautiousness and critical uncertainty about the extent of choice and control we can (and do) offer young people in all settings is a healthier position than claiming the presence of free choice in one form of work and its absence in another.

Conversation and the role of the worker

A parallel argument can be made in relation to the role that youth workers adopt. Again, role cannot be distanced from context. Young's discussion is instructive, seeing as it does, the youth worker's role, in conversation with young people, to be that of 'guide, philosopher and friend' (Young 1999). Just so. But, as its interpretation in the Evaluation of the Impact of Youth Work made clear,

> youth workers tend to take on multiple roles … for example, friend, teacher, counsellor, coach, advocate and mentor. The most effective youth workers adopt and adapt roles according to the demands and needs of the young people … and the requirements of the moment. (Merton et al. 2004: 41)

Youth workers have always taken on roles which enable the 'guidance, philosophy and friendship' they wish to offer to be taken up. To do so they have sought vehicles to carry those concerns, and been prepared to 'get their hands dirty' – whether through organising an activity, helping in gaining access to housing, or offering first aid training. Youth work has focused its attentions on particular groups of young people and sought new arenas within which to operate. Yes, the activity, location or service must have intrinsic worth but, as Davies readily acknowledges, it is still the process which really matters: 'that its hidden curriculum of inter-personal interaction is as important for generating the desired outcomes as its declared and overt content' (Davies 2005a: 8).

The recognition that conversation lies at the heart of youth work practice (Smith 1996; Young 1999: 84) should not obscure the complexity of the role: conversation is necessary but not sufficient in most forms of work with young people. There is evidence in Merton et al. (2004), Hoggarth and Smith (2004) and Crimmens et al. (2004) in relation to detached youth work, of the critical importance that young people attach to being listened to: the warmth, friendship, respect and acceptance offered by workers. Conversely, if the worker is felt to have been intrusive, or to have paid insufficient attention to the pressing needs and concerns of the young person (Hoggarth and Smith 2004), this is seen as much to be poor practice in the Connexions field as it might be in youth work. Equally, there is evidence in all of these studies and elsewhere (e.g. Williamson 1997) of the value placed on practical assistance, activity and, however this is defined, some sort of progress – 'sorting out a problem', dealing with a health issue, or trouble with friends, parents, school or the law. All of these indicate that there is a premium on conversations taking place within a relationship between young person and worker. Whatever the context in which such conversations and relationships take place, it seems that it will be youth workers' qualities which are the primary determinants of the benefits they bring to young people. The evidence suggests that trusted adults who can guide, advise, assist, stimulate, question or reflect; who are tuned to the needs and concerns of young people and who act in their interests (i.e. do not *just* talk), make a difference to their lives.

The contention here is that such approaches do not exist – nor should they – only within what we call 'youth work'. Nor indeed do they exist in a pure form within youth work itself.

While arguing here for a wider understanding of work with young people, this is not intended to close down legitimate debate of youth policy or different approaches to providing services. We will wish to weigh the relative merits of providing advice and guidance, and the particular form that this takes within Connexions; or the nature of service which works with young offenders in the form of YOTs (see Chapter 14). Equally, we might debate the precepts and approaches of the Sea Cadets or the Woodcraft Folk; or the range of services provided by local authority youth services. And inevitably, the roles and emphases adopted by workers within these different contexts will be different. However, what we might wish to try to ensure is that practice within all of these settings conforms to what we believe to be both good and effective work. The common ground is more important than the differences: all should act ethically; adhere to broadly agreed principles (such as those associated with human rights); and bring to their encounters with young people intentions and roles that they judge will bring benefit to them and society more generally. We seek, as Young states, a practice which 'develops the potential for excellence in each individual, while also serving the 'common good' (Young 1999: 121). Young people's interests will best be served by ensuring that, in whatever encounters they have with adults who work with them, their choices are promoted, respected and understood. This should apply equally in those contexts where they encounter youth justice, where they seek advice and guidance about their welfare, education and work, and in the traditional youth work arena. In all of these, young people can be confronted by caring adults with difficult and challenging choices – about who they are, what they believe, how they behave and the journey they are on. There is no avoiding conversation and learning here if potential is to be realised. And equally, there is no avoiding the need to go beyond, to *do* something if we, and they, judge that to be required.

Questions of purpose and benefit

Another arena in which youth work has sought to distinguish itself from other forms of work with young people is focused on the question: why are we doing this work? What is it for?

The dominant discourse among youth work commentators runs along the following lines. The fundamental purpose of youth work is educational; its benefits lie in the personal and social learning that young people gain. Its distinctive methods, associated with *informal education*, enable young people to gain skills, knowledge and attitudes which result in personal growth and which have wider social benefits. As a result, young people are able to take, individually and collectively, increasing and informed control of their own lives, and make a contribution to society. While acknowledging its normative function associated with the socialisation of young people, youth work's educational purposes also lead to beneficial social change and in turn, can contribute to social justice (see for example Davies and Gibson 1967; Davies 1999a, b; M.K. Smith 1981, 1988).

Youth work claims for itself that it is able to straddle, more or less, the competing social horses of education and control. It does so by asking of itself the critical question: to what end? What higher purposes are served by our educational interventions? *Cui bono?* (Who benefits?) At one level of course, youth work cannot claim distinctiveness in such questions. They have, for example been central to philosophical enquiry as applied to education since the time of Socrates, and to modern social work theory for more than 100 years. If youth work was not asking such questions of itself we might be justified in saying 'Why not?'.

But while youth work has laid claim to educational purposes, and considered its potential benefits over many years, it is perhaps only in comparatively recent times that it has sought to claim that its educational purposes distinguish it from other forms of work with young people. Now, it appears to wish to claim welfare benefit but to *disclaim* explicit or conscious welfare intention (see Smith 2000, 2007). This argument is often, though not exclusively, focused on the question of casework – by which is usually meant that the 'client' who is the recipient of the 'service' is seen as in need of individual help or possibly reform (Payne 1997). The underlying model referred to here is what Jeffs and Smith (2002) have characterised as individualisation – in other words, a focus on 'targeting interventions at named individuals' to the exclusion of the social or economic conditions which will be seen as giving rise to their situation. This is a familiar argument, long debated in social work. But, as so often, it is couched in terms of 'either or' rather than 'both and'. To claim that all work with young people which has a casework element is, by definition, ignoring social and economic determinants is as much a fallacy as claiming that all youth work takes full account of them.[3] The truth is that 'individualist-reformist' (Payne 1997: 4) models of practice exist across the spectrum of work with young people, alongside more radical 'collectivist' models. Casework-based approaches can and do take place hand-in-hand with approaches designed to recognise, respond to and attempt to change the social and economic environment by 'tipping the balance of power in favour of young people' (Davies 2005a). Rather than turning their backs on casework or other forms of more individualist approaches, youth workers will wish closely to examine the context within which they work in order to draw out – and critically, to act upon – the underlying power imbalances if they seek to work from a collectivist viewpoint. To do this, they frequently seek to 'reframe' the issues posed to them.

A case example (Box 18.1), drawn from the Evaluation of the Impact of Youth Work (Merton et al. 2004) serves to illustrate this approach.

Box 18.1   Hospital youth work

Research undertaken in a city hospital showed that many young people arrived at Accident and Emergency with symptoms of self-harm or overdose but, after the admissions procedure, did not wait to be treated. This was seen as a 'cry for help' which was going unheard. Feedback from young people was that they were being treated as 'cases' rather than as individuals. The report argued for a young person's advocate to provide them with information and support during clinical encounters so that they were able to take responsibility for their health. Discussion led to the recognition that the hospital was too heavily focussed on medical intervention, failing to take account of the other issues in young people's lives: their family situation, housing, emotional stability – and therefore, their ability or readiness to engage with medical professionals.

Three youth workers now form the Hospital Youth Work Team and, after initial cynicism about what was an untried approach, this has now become an integral part of the hospital's service to young people. All young patients aged 11 upwards are contacted by youth workers. They offer support, information and activities, including taking young people out for a break, to the shops, or for a game of pool. Frequently they are involved intensively with young people who are distressed and fearful. Alongside such casework support, a central concern is to be advocates on behalf of young people, to 'de-mystify' medical language so that they can understand and be more actively involved in their own health care. The team runs training sessions with medical staff about communicating with young people, and about young people's issues and perspectives.

Youth workers have made a significant difference within the hospital:

I can see the transition of the young people. They are healthier; they are taking responsibility for themselves; they are empowered; they are able to vocalise their views; elements of contentment/satisfaction in their lives – you can see that in the way they engage with professionals (Member of Hospital Staff)

The point to make here is that the workers have not abandoned an educational approach in order to pursue a welfare agenda. The two dimensions are intrinsically linked. Intensive casework support takes place alongside and, indeed involves more educative interventions. Each serves to reinforce the other in a symbiotic relationship. And, if there is a distinctive youth work element in the approach (and perhaps there is not) it lies in the ability and commitment of the workers to engage with young people's worlds: as individuals with pressing needs; as 'patients' whose needs may previously have gone unnoticed and whose power was muted; and, as situated in a complex and potentially disempowering social (and institutional) context. As with the earlier example of young people and housing, success in the end, is judged in terms of the outcome: they are healthier, they take more responsibility for themselves and so on. But take away any of its elements: the case work support, the activities, the advocacy, or the training of medical staff, and arguably, the approach is much weakened – and the outcomes less likely to be attained. The relationship with young people (and others) sustains the work – but is not enough on its own.

At another level of analysis, workers make choices about the agencies in which to locate themselves. In doing so they are *inter alia* choosing roles, functions, purposes, methods, organisational values and styles of work with young people. Those choices are deeply personal and values-based. Some choose the Connexions arena while others choose the youth offending service; yet others choose the open youth project. Each has their attendant and different roles (and tensions) but there is common cause. What is seen to be essential to the practice of the PA for example: to be able to take a 'holistic and non-stigmatising approach', using 'flexible means of working' (Hoggarth and Smith et al. 2004: 189), is fundamental also to the youth worker who must be 'welcoming, flexible, responsive to their starting points …' (Davies 2005a: 16). Each of us will find constraints within the contexts we work and, it is to be hoped, interrogate our own values and approaches, and the context of our organisation and its practices; but neither of us needs to dismiss the work of the other as alien or of lesser import. The argument here is not that what we call youth work, and other forms of work such as that of the PA, are one and the same; each is contextualised, complex and ambiguous, each is orientated to the needs of young people in particular settings; and both can coexist and inform the other. Properly practiced, they have more in common than they are different.

Conclusion

The central contention of this chapter is that a false dichotomy has emerged within the discourse about youth work in the UK. In attempting to claim the distinctiveness of its approach compared with other forms of work with young people, and in the face of what is felt to be a threat to its continued existence, it has first, tended to mask the internal differences which have always been present within its ranks. This can be seen in the differences between for example, the work of very diverse voluntary and charitable organisations, or the wide range of approaches taken by local authorities. Perhaps because it has relied upon very few writers to develop its theoretical basis, it has allowed itself to be informed principally by models derived from liberal educationist views which eschew and consciously compete with what tend to be dismissed as 'welfarist' models. In the process, elements of youth work practice theory have tended to become reified and idealised.

The importance of practice principles and values associated with youth work are not intended to be dismissed here. What has become known as the 'voluntary principle' for example, is a central tenet. It is concerned with respecting young people's rights to opt in or opt out as they choose, rather than enforcing compliance by institutional, legal or personal means. But, in constructing our practice in the complex arenas in which we operate, we negotiate between our adherence to the principle and wider needs – of the situation in which we find ourselves and our assessment of the young people with whom we work. We do not, for example, put their safety or the safety of others in jeopardy for the sake of the principle. At times, youth workers also find themselves working with young people who have little choice but to be involved. Again, we construct a practice, informed by the principle and in the light of their (and our own) situation. Workers in other agencies can do the same in the contexts in which they work: the relationship may 'not be entirely voluntary' for example, when providing for young people leaving care (Merton et al. 2004: 64).

> The key to securing voluntary engagement is not necessarily the conditions under which the young people first come to the project but how they are received and treated when they arrive. If they are accorded respect and responsibility, and if they are given choices, their attitudes and behaviour can change. (ibid. 128)

A second and connected feature of the way that youth work has been constructed in the UK – particularly in England and Wales – has been the over-identification of youth work with youth services. As a result, there is a tendency to see 'youth work' as only taking place in traditional youth work settings. The concomitant of this is that where youth workers undertake work in very different settings they are thought not to be 'doing youth work'. The chapter argues for a different and more inclusive model where those working with young people across the spectrum of leisure, cultural, youth justice, health and educational settings are able to sign up to practice principles which are just as relevant to their work as they are to those working in more traditional youth work settings. In all these arenas it is argued, practice is constructed by workers and agencies out of a complex set of interactions between purposes, methods, principles, values and ideologies. Consigning youth work (and 'youth work' principles) to only one arena is neither in the interests of young people nor does it serve to support the ways of working that youth work values. While not wishing to argue for the professional identity of social pedagogy itself to become a model for the future of work with young people in the UK, there is nonetheless, strength in there *being* such a model – whatever we choose to call it.

Finally, there is a thread running through the chapter concerning the state's social policy intentions towards young people. Although this has not been a specific focus it has nonetheless been present as a shadow throughout. The argument that emerges here is that all those who work with young people will wish to interrogate how their practice, and the principles upon which it is based, relate to what they see to be the state's (and others') intentions. In constructing that practice they will negotiate their own roles and relationships with young people *and* negotiate within and beyond the agencies which employ them, the beliefs, approaches and methods in use – and the potential for young people to influence these. Some of these questions are explored further in Mary Tyler's analysis of the tensions in work with young people (Chapter 19). That leaves us with a different youth social policy question: what should be the make-up of local services for young people – the balance between their components, how they should interact, and on what tenets should they be based? Such a question implies a search for common practice principles and methods and, critically, a broadly understood view of young people's social conditions rather than a defence of 'purity'.

In the climate of integrated services provided through Children and Young People's Services, there is some danger that locally based projects and open access work will be squeezed out as local authorities seek to meet the targets associated with new Public Service Agreements. The benefits of open access work are more difficult to evidence. Equally, the strong emphasis on 'positive activities' may endanger important practice principles, values and methods – a central focus on personal and social development, voluntary participation or informed consent, young people's influence, experiential approaches – as some agencies seek crude measures of positive impact. A failure to understand or value the youth work process and its benefits could (and arguably has already begun to) lead to a narrowing and increasingly instrumental youth policy and practice agenda.

The territory to be claimed by youth work in these circumstances needs to be broad and inclusive. That will mean joining forces across the spectrum of work with young people; to find common cause and to construct a practice model across welfare and education dimensions. They are not separate in young people's lives; neither should they be in our practice.

Reflective questions for practice

- In what setting do you currently work with young people?
- What do you define as the purpose of this work?
- What outcomes or benefits for young people do you strive to achieve in your work? Are these outcomes distinct to the work in this setting or are they similar to work done in other settings?
- Are there broader ethical principles that guide your work, and if so what do you believe these to be?

Further reading

Merton, B., Payne, M. and Smith, D. Youth Affairs Unit, De Montfort University (2004) *An Evaluation of the Impact of Youth Work*, **Nottingham: DfES Publications**. Referred to throughout this chapter, this report is based upon an extensive empirical study of the impact of youth work in various different contexts.

(Continued)

(Continued)

Payne, M. (2005) *Modern Social Work Theory*, **3rd edn, Basingstoke: Palgrave**. Examines the theories of social work practice and addresses the issues of competing social constructions of social work theory.

Davies, B. (2005) 'Youth work: a manifesto for our times', *Youth and Policy*, **88: 5–28**. This article sets out some defining youth work values, processes and contributions in order to describe what is unique to what we call 'youth work'.

Notes

1 There are quite complex differences between European countries in this respect, and distinctions made also between socio-cultural and socio-pedagogical approaches.
2 This idea is central to Rousseau's philosophy as, for example in *Émile or On Education* (Rousseau 1979).
3 This could be seen in philosophical terms as an extension of the 'straw man' fallacy: setting up an opposing position in order to dismiss it when the position itself is not in fact true. The extension is 'my straw man can beat up your straw man': neither is actually true, but one is inherently better than the other!

19

MANAGING THE TENSIONS

Mary Tyler

Key arguments

- The government has recognised the capacity of youth work to address a range of social problems that impact upon young people. This had led to increased expectations that youth workers will make a contribution to policy objectives.
- Youth workers are also subject to expectations from their professional values, the young people they work with and the wider community. These are often complementary to their expectations of other workers.
- These expectations can cause conflict and overlapping tensions. Practitioners need to interpret these policy tensions and develop their work in their own and context specific ways.
- This approach relies on being a 'principled pragmatist': being both practical and realistic and committed to professional values and principles.
- Youth workers and managers need to be clear about and stand up for their approach and values and ensure that youth work is understood and used appropriately.

Introduction

This chapter outlines the inherent tensions between the demands of targeted social policy initiatives and the values of work with young people, and identifies qualities, skills and knowledge practitioners need to help them manage these tensions. The focus is on youth work specifically where these tensions are especially sharp due to its particular purpose, methods and values.

Most people enter work with young people, especially youth work, with a desire to 'make a difference', to be 'helpful', to 'pay something back' and use their experience positively. They want to play a positive part in the lives of people who are on the journey from childhood/dependence to adulthood/interdependence. They believe this will provide job satisfaction. This career choice reflects key elements of what those workers believe to be important in the way they live their lives. There is a level of altruism – this work is not chosen if making big money is a driving force. Through upbringing, life and relevant work experience, and possibly faith or spirituality, practitioners develop a set of values which then become more conscious, professional and explicit through education and training for work with young people and further work experience. For the purpose of simplicity this chapter later looks especially at youth work undertaken by those in professional level roles which are often full time because these roles are pivotal in a context where a huge percentage of practice is undertaken by part time and volunteer staff.

Those who work with young people do not do so in a vacuum as is clear from the preceding chapters. They work in organisations. They are in most cases agents of government policy directly or indirectly by virtue of who pays their wages (Newman 2002: 83) and this includes much of the more intensive voluntary sector work with young people. Nowadays there is a very clear connection between such policy intention and its implementation at the front line. This connection is made significantly through performance measurement of work with young people. To make this possible 'outputs' have been developed such as the number of young people who gain accreditation through their contacts with the youth service, or the number of NEETS entering education or work through Connexions. The work climate is target driven, as Bernard Davies (Chapter 16) has illustrated.

This chapter argues that practitioners can benefit from developing their abilities as 'principled pragmatists', an approach outlined by Davies (2005a) with reference to youth work. This approach reflects the strength of the practitioner's value base, and their competence as a manager of their work, and can help to steer them through the daily tensions of their target driven work climate. The chapter first discusses the differing expectations made of youth work practitioners by government policy and their professional values. It then explores the nature of the tensions so caused and the strategies practitioners can pursue to manage them, informed by this principled pragmatist approach.

The expectations

What are the expectations made of youth workers by the government?

The government of New Labour has increasingly recognised youth work's role in its social policy intentions especially in relation to social inclusion and the children's agenda

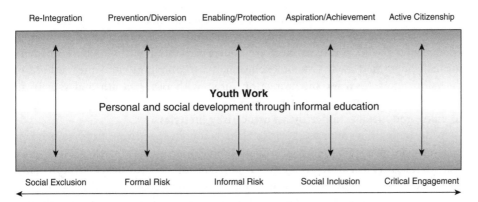

Re-Integration   Prevention/Diversion   Enabling/Protection   Aspiration/Achievement   Active Citizenship

Youth Work
Personal and social development through informal education

Social Exclusion   Formal Risk   Informal Risk   Social Inclusion   Critical Engagement

Figure 19.1   Youth work contribution to policy objectives
Source: Merton et al. 2004: 36

for change. Government intentions reflect the fact that it is made up of politicians who get involved because they wish to influence our society and improve it. They have different beliefs about what that improvement might look like, partly distinguished by their political party membership. Politicians are significantly influenced by the media because this reflects and influences popular public opinion and it publicises their intentions to the citizens who vote them in and out of power. Governments usually wish to remain in power and so are liable to be influenced by the views reflected most in media coverage which recently have tended to be dominated in relation to young people by, for instance, those supporting the 'respect'/anti-social behaviour agenda (National Youth Agency 2006b; Yates, Chapter 14), and those with high levels of concern about protection (DfES 2003).

Youth work is clearly one of the spades in the policy garden. It is not at the centre of public order and public safety agendas but it has been drawn increasingly in that direction by government expectations. Drawing on a major evaluation of its impact (Merton et al. 2004), youth work can be seen to contribute to five key social policy themes on a spectrum from re-integration through to active citizenship (Figure 19.1). Policy is based on a view of young people as both a problem (needing more control or remedies) and a solution as future adult citizens.

Youth services have often employed teams of workers to work on the streets in 'hot spot' areas of tension and conflict including multi-ethnic inner city areas, complementing police and criminal justice work. This reflects the reintegration and prevention/diversion themes above. Reintegration involves often intensive work with young people significantly marginalised from society due, for example, to their lack of engagement in work or training (NEET) or due to their 'health-risky' behaviour such as their sexual activity or drug use. This work can enable young people to access local services especially through mediation and advocacy with those agencies to ensure they are more responsive. Other activity at the 'harder' targeting end of the continuum includes for instance work with those young people who youth workers are concerned about but who have not been formally identified as at risk of exclusion. This contribution to prevention and diversion refers to work on protection often with other health and social care agencies and offering diversionary opportunities to young people to enable them to enjoy good health rather than pursue risky lifestyles.

At the same time youth work is also facing a set of expectations from government that emanate from a softer concern for both young people's welfare, seen more recently in *Every Child Matters* (DfES 2003), and the need to develop future active and effective citizens as expressed for instance in *Youth Matters* (DfES 2005). These are the enabling/protection, aspirational/achievement and active citizenship themes. Youth work that enables and protects offers safe environments and is about 'equipping young people with the relationships, skills, knowledge and understanding that help them steer a safe course in the world' (Merton et al. 2004: 132). Aspiration and achievement is about ensuring young people get the most out of life and develop broad skills for adulthood by extending opportunities for them to achieve and enjoy doing so. Active citizenship includes youth work that involves young people in making a positive contribution to the community and society. It engages young people in their local community and local structures such as planning and helping to run their own activities, campaigning for a local skate park and being involved in the local Youth Council. This research report (Merton et al. 2004) identifies youth work's strengths in building social capital (see also Boeck, Chapter 8).

Kemshall argues (Chapter 13) that youth social policy is significantly based on notions of young people as 'at risk' or 'risky' which justifies substantial state intervention. Davies provides a detailed analysis of relevant policy under New Labour in Chapter 16 arguing that the impact of the various and conflicting targets on youth work and the new joined up structures of Children's Trusts could lead to the disappearance of 'identifiable' local Youth Services. As this has been its chief publicly funded provider he is seriously concerned for the future of youth work. This risky situation for youth work has developed in a climate that has been affected by huge changes in the way that public services are organised as well as what government expects of them. This 'managerialism' is now having a major effect on youth work which is progressively more directed and more closely controlled particularly as it has become increasingly finance led.

Managerialism or New Public Management (NPM), as it has been labelled more recently, is both an ideology and a way of managing public services. It first had an impact in the UK during Thatcher's government in the 1980s and has continued in various forms. There was a renewed belief that professionals were too powerful and too bureaucratic leading to inefficiency, rigidity and poor quality in the public services where they were employed. The New Right argued for a smaller role for government, and therefore public services, and a larger role for consumer style relationships between society and its citizens. The assumption was that *good* management practice from the commercial world applied to the public sector would help to reduce the problems these services are designed to tackle through more efficient provision (Pollitt 2003).

Management became '*the* solution of our times' in public policy (Thrupp and Willmott 2003: 3). The language and realities of the market place (competition, tendering, cost centres), contracts, and partnerships became the norm. The intention was to increase accountability by giving managers more independence to manage but with clear measurable outcomes to be met (performance management). However this delegation increasingly separated public services from their political bosses, national and local. It also tended to value the manager rather more than the professional be they the doctor, the teacher, the social worker, the planner, the housing officer, or the youth worker.

New Labour's Third Way social democracy then adapted this managerial agenda at the end of the 1990s recognising that some aspects of private sector management are not workable or appropriate when applied to the public sector. For example, local authorities were now expected to achieve quality via 'best value' rather than the Conservative's cheapest via compulsory competitive tendering. Labour's modernisation agenda gave greater recognition to the democratic base of public services and therefore put increased emphasis on not just accountability to the tax paying citizen but also the involvement of citizens and service users in decision making. It reduced the emphasis on competition which had been found to reinforce organisational boundaries and encourage professional rivalry and 'silo' thinking. However, New Labour emphasised ever firmer targets and standards to control 'activities previously within the sphere of professional judgement' (Banks 2004a: 40). The emphasis was also placed on innovation, 'evidence-based' practice' and 'joined-up policy and solutions, where partnership and collaboration are dominant themes' (Haynes 2003: 14).

Managers in the public sector need to achieve targets successfully for their organisations and work collaboratively with other organisations on 'cross-cutting' themes (Newman 2002). Youth workers and their managers employed by local authorities have had to contribute in particular to their employer's corporate aims; Resourcing Excellent Youth Services (REYS) targets (DfES 2002); Best Value Performance Indicators (BVPIs) for youth work; ECM outcomes and Joint Area Review (JAR)/OFSTED inspection standards (OFSTED 2004, NYA 2006a). In many cases they have to meet other funders' standards and targets too. They also have to work together with other professionals to foster community cohesion and meet broader youth policy demands for instance in teenage pregnancy reduction strategy groups and Drug and Alcohol Action Teams. At the time of writing youth work looks as though it will also be affected by the expectation that trusts will commission services for young people (see Davies, Chapter 16 and Payne, Chapter 18). Contracts for these services will be based on outcomes for young people and will in some cases involve competition between different youth work providers (National Youth Agency 2006c; HM Treasury 2007) a situation new to local authority youth services but more familiar to the voluntary sector (Wylie, Chapter 17).

Youth work is now suffused with management language illustrating a level of change that newer recruits will not really appreciate. This has arrived later in youth work than related professional areas like health or probation. This language of inputs and performance indicators can be traced back a century to the impact of influential scientific management theorists like Frederick Taylor and his obsessive desire to control and measure pig-iron handling and earth shovelling (Morgan 2006). This approach has proved appropriate for routinised work with pre-determined goals in organisations like fast food restaurants but is often not appropriate in human services and especially in youth work where process and working with what concerns and interests young people is a distinctive feature. Youth work has had to be increasingly presented in tidy curriculum terms, be recorded and measured, and is often short term due to the nature of funding regimes.

It can be argued that this emphasis on outcomes has been to the detriment of process (Ord 2004), and has caused distortion leading to delivery of performance indicators rather than a focus on learning and development processes. This result is an example of what de Bruijn argues is the inevitable perverse effect of assigning too much importance to performance measurement (de Bruijn 2002: 116), a point well illustrated in Scott Yates' analysis of the impact of Connexions (Chapter 15).

What are the expectations made of youth workers by their professional values?

As accountable professionals, youth workers expect of themselves to do their job well thereby gaining job satisfaction. However, it also needs to be the *right* job to provide job satisfaction. The rightness of the job is identified by the congruence of its purpose with the profession's values.

Sarah Banks considers professional ethical values in youth work in depth in Chapter 5 which emphasises the way in which concepts integral to these values, like 'welfare', 'respect' and 'social justice', are 'open to interpretation'. These professional values emanate from the worker's personal values, their notion of the 'ideal' society, and the nature and purpose of the work which is ultimately about personal and social development through relationships (Merton et al. 2004) and informal education (Jeffs and Smith 2005).

These values mean that youth work is expected to be about voluntary or self-chosen engagement of young people, about working with their needs and agendas, enabling their decision making and empowerment through conversation, trusting relationships, activity, and exposing them to experiences and perspectives which are new to them. It is holistic, putting the young person or group of young people (since much of the work is through the medium of the group) and their interests and concerns at the centre. Youth work potentially can involve relationships through which young people build meaningful, impactful self-knowledge, reflect, explore their doubts and dilemmas and come to their own decisions about for instance morally responsible behaviour (individually made but often in a context together with others). Youth work values are about being alongside young people, being consistent in being there and making the right expectations at the right time for each individual, consistently believing in their potential and making sure they know they are valued as individuals.

Youth work values lead practitioners to wish to achieve more at the critical engagement end of the above continuum where young people can play a part in changing society at local and wider levels. Jeffs and Smith (2005) see youth workers as informal educators and explain the purpose of informal education as 'fostering democracy'. Youth work therefore is about enabling young people to learn:

> to engage with each other in ways that display mutual respect, a concern for others needs, and a belief in community. For without this, such democracy as we have will be subverted, and oppression will flourish. (Jeffs and Smith 2005: 56)

An example of youth work values presented by government is in the REYS document (DfES 2002) about local authority youth services. It reflects much of the above but with less explicit emphasis on democracy, social justice and social capital (Merton et al. 2004). Because youth work values include a strong commitment to social justice and anti-oppressive practice (Chouhan, Chapter 6), a significant long-term outcome of such youth work is a critical understanding by young people of themselves and their world, the impact of divisions in society like age and race and how many issues and problems are the 'outcome of processes which are largely outside of the control of individuals' (Furlong and Cartmel 2007: 144). This is especially significant in the context of the increasingly individualistic society in which young people grow up which, as Kemshall argued earlier, leads to individual blame for problems which need resolving collectively. Mark Smith argued for youth workers to make the values that inform their work explicit. He also stated that 'personal problems and experiences can only be fully understood and acted upon when they are seen as both private "troubles" and public issues' (Smith 1982: 56).

Young people appreciate and expect from youth workers the opportunity to have fun; a space to chill; and safety through the negotiation and holding of boundaries of behaviour that youth workers engage in. They expect a personal interest in them to be demonstrated through listening and the creation of opportunities to talk in reflective ways; friendliness and care; empathy, honesty and trust; not being judged; challenge and support (physical, mental and emotional); and advice and information.

These expectations of youth work are important and legitimate, overlapping but often complementary to those of a range of other practitioner roles with young people such as teaching, social work, and mentoring. Most young people's lives are busy and demanding. They have vast study and examining expectations on them, family pressures, peer group pressures, and those of the consumer culture which 'is central to the shaping of young people's identity in the modern world' (Furlong and Cartmel 2007: 86). Some young people have few adults showing a caring interest or providing positive feedback, some have tight protective and cultural limitations on their leisure, many experience daily discrimination at some or all of Thompson's (2006) personal, cultural and structural (PCS) levels. Some are seriously exploited and some have created significantly different and very risky lifestyles from the majority society (e.g. substantial illegal drug use, prostitution or gun crime).

'Practice is an interpretive act in which flexibility and openness are crucial' (Spence 2004: 265). Youth work values lead to the necessity for flexibility and considerable time and care to be invested in order to partner young people on their journeys of discovery and development. This is especially so when working with those young people who have already experienced considerable discrimination and damage from their families, communities and society.

As well as the expectations from government and their professional values youth workers face similar and also different ones from the communities in which they work, their local politicians, and other local agencies with which they work. It is not the intention to explore these expectations but to observe that these add further levels of complexity to the context of youth work practice and therefore the tensions it experiences.

The tensions and their implications

These often conflicting expectations made of youth workers are experienced as a range of different and overlapping tensions. Youth workers need to work sensitively with the most marginalised young people who may want nothing to do with structures and 'officialdom', but also those workers have to find ways to structure and measure this work. They are expected to be responsive to young people's agendas but also meet government agendas measured through achieving politically set targets for young people's achievements. They need to be innovative but also achieve previously set targets through previously planned activities. They need to be efficient but also effective, achieving both quantity and quality on limited resources. They have to work to short-term deadlines when some more sustainable results true to young people and their future development will only be achieved with a longer-term framework. They also have to act as conduits for enabling the presentation of young people's experiences and perceptions, concerns and needs to those with the power *as well as* interpreting a variety of adult perceptions and government concerns and policy intents to young people on behalf of those with power.

These tensions for youth work illustrate very sharply the tension in government policy that Haynes argues 'asks public service workers to be innovative and enterprising, while at the same time increasing regulation and imposing potentially narrow definitions of performance' (2003: 84). 'Accountability versus flexible, responsive services' (Haynes 2003: 12) for youth work may mean time spent completing monitoring forms versus time spent preparing an activity newly requested by young people for their next session. 'Standardization versus creativity and innovation' (Haynes 2003: 12) may mean potentially limiting young people's progress and development to fit it into an accreditation scheme versus taking some risks and letting the buzz and unpredictable group process follow its own developmental path.

Using rather risky language each of the above tensions is like a tightrope. The youth worker has to balance on some of them simultaneously and each worker will find that a slightly different place achieves the best balance for them. Each worker (and each team of workers and youth work managers) has to find their way of interpreting these policy tensions and developing their work in their own and context specific ways.

Alongside these tensions youth workers are getting mixed messages about the value of their work as on the one hand many agencies want a 'piece of the action' while at the same time these agencies want to shape youth work until its very creativity and its responsive quality has been squeezed out. They can feel that success is constantly out of their reach, or regularly moved beyond their reach, as the goalposts move again as target numbers increase. Their skills can become diminished and devalued as they find themselves employed alone or in very small numbers in contexts where other professionals are the majority and continue to dominate the style of the work and the organisation's culture e.g. youth work in schools with extended services, or in a Youth Offending Team. The emphasis on targets rather than learning and development processes can lead to youth workers reducing their work with those most in need because it is more difficult to evidence outcomes (see Scott Yates, Chapter 15).

Haynes discusses both social work and teaching as examples of work where process should be seen 'as part of the outcome agenda, not separate from it' (2003: 154) arguing that such processes will always create spontaneous outcomes. Due to youth work's essential focus on process these tensions are especially sharp for its practitioners.

Managing the tensions – approaches and strategies

In order to manage these daily tensions youth workers need firstly to recognise and understand them for what they are, appreciating the interlinked social policy and 'modern management' agendas and their impact. So they need to be reflective, analytical and critical thinkers. They also need to actively manage themselves and their work, ensuring their values and young people's needs and expectations remain at the centre, informing what they do. Professional workers need to maintain a focus on being good quality practitioners. They need to feel that they are doing the *right* job *and* doing it *well* – managing the tension.

In order to do this, workers can benefit from building their abilities as principled pragmatists. For the purposes of this chapter a *pragmatist* is someone who takes a practical approach, who is realistic about what they can achieve in a given context. A *principled* pragmatist is someone whose pragmatism is informed by principles meaning that they will take care, in pursuing success, that their actions are not significantly compromising their values of for example equity, consistency and honesty and they can live with their actions. In other words their focus on practical day to day achievement will not overtake their overall purpose. Their practice will be critical and political. Critical because it is informed by a key understanding of the government policy intent and how youth work can be both maintaining the status quo and changing it by operating 'in and against the state' (Davies 2005b: 13), and political because it remains focused on democracy as an aim.

The abilities the principled pragmatist needs to have are grouped under five headings: purpose; creativity; power and influence; nurturing capacity; and demonstrating and promoting. Some are largely skills focused while others are more about knowledge and understanding.

A principled pragmatist has a clear understanding of the *purpose* of their work with young people. They know why they have chosen this work and broadly what they hope to achieve. They are able to call up the 'big picture' at least once a working day, know what aspects of it they can have any influence upon and understand how their every interaction is part of this bigger picture. They are clear about what they are trying to achieve with any given young person at any moment whether it be simply getting them to notice that you are interested in them which may help improve their self-esteem, or sustaining a group negotiated game for 20 minutes that rewards less swearing or smoking and therefore provides an opportunity to develop some self-chosen self control. They value their contribution, confident that what they contribute in terms of for instance time, empathy and practical help with young people is rarely wasted even if it is not them that see any outcomes.

Principled pragmatist know they are enabling young people to understand the position they find themselves in as well as supporting them to improve their circumstances. For instance a homeless young person has a problem for which their society, their community, their family and themselves may all have some responsibility. They are not wholly responsible but can play their part to change the situation which the worker can support them to do practically and emotionally. However, the youth worker may be able to inform and campaign for the need for more provision, change in the law or other necessary reform to reduce youth homelessness.

242

A principled pragmatist is *creative* in the way they plan their work and then interpret it. They know that their project may not survive if they do not work with sufficient young people and find ways to record outcomes and accredit some of them. However, they know there is plenty of room for creativity. Government and the various bodies it funds are often on the lookout for examples of good practice and often these show that there are many different ways to achieve results. Workers can interpret their organisation's brief in different ways influenced by what the young person or 'customer' wants and using the policy expectation to be 'responsive' to their advantage. They can use other principles of policy to their advantage as well. For instance with respect to active citizens and communities and their participation and consultation, youth workers can work on any issues (and in many ways) that have been identified with young people through their active engagement.

Achieving outcomes prescribed by others does not prevent youth workers from meeting their own expectations and those of the young people they work with – they are not usually mutually exclusive. Principled pragmatists are able to construct their own objectives so they portray what they believe they can achieve and which are appropriate to youth work values. These should also achieve some of the externally prescribed targets by making links between the two. For instance engaging in lively debate for ten minutes about whether the legal driving age should be raised or cooking a meal are both fun, popular and involve key social and life skills which can also move young people in the long-term direction of education and work. Evidence of this learning can be recorded (see Comfort et al. 2006 for useful advice on recording outcomes).

Principled pragmatists will be straight with young people about what their project is being funded to achieve with them. While the young people are choosing to engage with a music workshop offered in response to their interests the worker will want to understand and challenge their attitudes to their drug use or criminal activity during the workshops. The worker may take opportunities to use this explanation of their project's funding objectives as another source of debate and learning. Workers are also able to manage their resources so they meet external and immediate expectations. A team has discussed and planned its capacity and adaptability so, while the planned activity continues, any team member can respond immediately and confidently to whatever emerges in a project session.

A principled pragmatist understands their personal, professional, political and organisational *power and influence* and uses it ethically and effectively. This power will vary depending on a worker's experience, confidence, the nature of their job role and hierarchical position, and their employing agency. Not recognising, or recognising but denying this power is dangerous. Youth work is less authoritarian than youth offending work or social work as there are few formal sanctions in most youth work jobs. However good youth work can have a powerful impact on young people especially given they are engaged in self-chosen relationships with workers. Workers can be powerful role models for young people and for less experienced colleagues.

Recognising power, sharing what is appropriate, and using it to achieve resources for young people as well as ensuring those they manage are working at their best is the responsible way for youth workers to use it – informed by their values.

In terms of their workplace each youth worker is what Thompson calls an 'organisational operator' (see 2003: 209–217) who understands how organisations work and how to change aspects of their structures, procedures and their culture or ways of doing things. They work to ensure youth work values remain central to their organisation's practice by influencing it upwards. So they might start by providing their manager with evidence of the needs of particular marginalised groups with whom they have sought contact which the organisation has not previously identified. They can also argue for what they can do or have done to meet this need, using their position in the middle, between young people, part time staff and volunteers *and* managers and the organisation. They can also identify and work with allies, influence the practice of partnerships and strive to ensure their values are echoed at policy level locally or more nationally for instance through trade unions, professional associations, local and national politicians. Unlike many other workers in the public and voluntary sector, youth workers may be in contact with local politicians as part of their legitimate work supporting young people's voice and/or advocating for young people when they are subjected to local complaints.

A principled pragmatist consistently *nurtures* capacity, their own and colleagues. If youth workers are to create the opportunities for support, personal growth, reflection and analysis for young people then they have to achieve this for themselves and workers they are responsible for. Therefore they ensure they get and use supervision well and in turn provide good quality supervision and support to staff and volunteers. If they cannot increase paid youth work time they reduce face to face time a little to ensure sufficient time is spent discussing the session and outcome recordings so they are fruitful to future good practice and not merely 'box ticking'. They use these opportunities and others with the teams they manage and their peers to discuss the inherent tensions they face. They ask questions regularly about the nature of the work and its quality thereby playing their part towards developing a learning organisation. They can use their performance indicators as 'tin-openers' to this process (Everitt and Hardiker 1996: 83). They engage with professional support networks to sustain youth work's identity and values, particularly crucial for youth workers based in multi-agency/disciplinary teams.

A principled pragmatist gains support for their work and motivates others by *demonstrating* their principles and *promoting* their work. 'Their most convincing supporting evidence will come through practising in ways in which the quality and impact speak for themselves' (Davies 2005a: 10). They develop good working relationships with key stakeholders like funders, local community groups, local businesses, the police and politicians. They communicate honestly and effectively with young people, with colleagues, with partners, with their managers and other decision makers. This includes presenting credibly what they do and achieve through events and case studies of good practice, and communicating government policy intentions to those delivering alongside them. Youth workers mirror the same values in the way they work with staff and volunteers they manage as they do with young people.

Principled pragmatists promote their work. They know it is very important to ensure stakeholders understand what youth work can achieve, and also what it cannot achieve without additional resources. They know time is well spent preparing clear informative and attractive presentations and annual or project reports for local politicians, funders, potential staff and actual employees. These reports are clear about the values, intentions and nature of their youth work practice, about participation and voice. Funders then cannot legitimately express dismay when for example young people decide to take on their local councillor for their lack of support for them over an issue.

Conclusion

A principled pragmatist is clear about the purpose and nature of their practice and realistic about what they can achieve. Being a professional is about 'realising values' (Thompson 2003: 211). In the context of complex and conflicting expectations explored in this chapter youth workers need to be optimists, self-confident in their youth work and their abilities as principled pragmatists. Youth workers are not only often at the front line in the policy garden working on the stony ground with some of the vulnerable seedlings and complex weeds, but they can influence the fertilising and planting plans or policy process. They need to be clear about and stand up for their approach and values and ensure that youth work is understood and used appropriately. Since youth work is now being utilised in so many settings it is its values and principles which need to be the key guide to action rather than previous actions themselves. They work in a climate in which past youth work delivery patterns may or may not be the right or politically acceptable ones. They need to aim for what will work best for the young people concerned based on their current interests, needs and expectations.

The latter part of the chapter has focused on the professional youth worker but there is no intention to absolve the manager of responsibility. Managers of youth work, wherever they are located, should be creating space for their youth workers to develop their principled pragmatism. They should be acting as shock absorbers, allowing youth workers to take risks where this may be best for the young people concerned, and acting as interpreters of young people's experiences and effective youth work to the policy makers influencing changes to policy.

On 'judgement day' a principled pragmatist can argue with confidence that their work with young people was legitimate and authentic. They can wear their youth work principles as a crown rather than a hood to hide under, and be strategic, prioritising the various expectations made of them according to their congruence with these principles. They have to choose which plates to juggle while they walk the tightropes! They cannot be all things to all people and ultimately it is young people who will miss out if youth workers do not learn to live with and manage these tensions.

Reflective questions for practice

- Reflect on this chapter, and on the chapters by Sarah Banks, Malcolm Payne and Bernard Davies. Consider what you think the different expectations are of you in your role as a youth worker.
- Who are you accountable to and what is expected of you?
- Are there identifiable tensions in these different expectations?
- What strategies do you use to manage the tensions?
- Using the discussion in this chapter, how could you apply the notion of the 'principled pragmatist' to your everyday work?

Further reading

Banks, S. (2004) *Ethics, Accountability and the Social Professions*, Basingstoke: Palgrave Macmillan. For a full discussion on professionalism and accountability.

Haynes, P. (2003) *Managing Complexity in the Public Services*, Berkshire: Open University Press. For a full exploration of the impact of Managerialism on professionals and public services, see especially the first chapter.

20

WORKING WITH YOUNG PEOPLE: EMERGENT THEMES

Jean Hine and Jason Wood

The chapters in this book offer reflections on some current issues and developments in theory and policy debates that have direct and indirect implications for the practice of those who work with young people. The issues are wide ranging, highlighting the complexity and subtlety of the inter-relationships between theory, policy and practice, and the inherent tensions and contradictions within and between them. Although coming from different perspectives a number of common themes emerge from the chapters: (1) the impact of the wider economic and social context within which work with young people takes place; (2) the centrality of issues of governance and social control; (3) the importance of issues of 'identity'; and (4) participation and citizenship and the value of working *with* young people.

Economic and social context

The current historical period has been called variously 'post-modernity' (Armstrong, Chapter 7), 'late modernity' (France, Chapter 2) or 'high modernity' (Giddens 1991). Whichever term is used it indicates a move away from 'modernity', a period which it is argued began with the enlightenment and the industrial revolution. These terms are used to indicate both a way of thinking about the world, the organisation of production and social and political relationships. Modernity was/is the age of science and reason, which led to innovation and invention and the development of capitalist consumer society.

In late modernity, 'predictabilities and certainties characteristic of the industrial era are threatened and a new set of risks and opportunities are brought into existence' (Furlong and Cartmel 2007: 3). It may be that the certainties of the modern industrial era were an illusion, but there was certainly a dominant view that human ingenuity, through science, would find a solution to all problems. That belief is now less prevalent, and 'the world is perceived as a dangerous place in which we are constantly confronted with risk' (Furlong and Cartmel 2007: 3). As the apparent certainties of modernity are stripped away late modernity offers a range of new opportunities for individuals as well as uncertainty. However, these opportunities and uncertainties are not equally distributed:

> Like wealth, risks adhere to the class pattern, only inversely: wealth accumulates at the top, risks at the bottom. ... Poverty attracts an unfortunate abundance of risks. By contrast, the wealthy (in income, power or education) can purchase safety and freedom from risk. (Beck 1992: 35)

This suggests a shift in the balance between structure and agency (see France, Chapter 2), that is the extent to which the actions of an individual are acts of free will and agency, and the extent to which they are determined by the structures within which they live. Most authors accept that reality is a mix of the two, with terms such as 'bounded agency' (Evans 2002) and 'structured individualism' (Hodgson 1986) being used to describe the relationship. Furlong and Cartmel argue that late modernity gives young people the impression that they have substantial choice and agency, but that they are suffering from an 'epistemological fallacy' that masks the reality of the substantial impact of the structural factors that mediate and limit their choices (2007: 138). This is clear from much of the research which seeks to understand young people's lives from their perspective (e.g. MacDonald and Marsh 2005, Schoon and Bynner 2003).

Such research shows that one of the major constraints on young people's lives is their economic circumstances, with the opportunities and life chances available to those from lower income families being much less than for those with more. This is not merely a matter of money, but includes features such as the schools that they attend, space at home to do homework, and even language competence (Snow and Powell 2007). Importantly, place is very much related to life chances, with young people living in socially deprived neighbourhoods being less likely to do well in life.

Most of those who work with young people are working with young people from this latter group, often termed the socially excluded. There is debate about what term should be used to describe people living in this position of relative deprivation, with many using the term 'social exclusion' as it indicates more than just lack of financial resources. This is certainly the preferred term of policy makers. However, this too is fraught with confusion, with different understandings and definitions in use. Levitas (2006) describes three discourses of social exclusion: the redistributive discourse (RED) with a focus on reducing inequality; the social integration discourse (SID) with a focus on paid employment; and the moral underclass discourse (MUD) with a focus on morality. The latter two discourses are the most prevalent in policy, where 'the emphasis is on opportunities for individuals to escape from poverty, not on the abolition of poverty itself' (2006: 48). This is apparent in the dual and ambiguous strands of policy which on the one hand seek to intervene to prevent problem behaviour (SID) and at the same time use sanctions to respond strongly to those who deviate too far from such norms (MUD).

Youth is seen as a stage of transition between childhood and adulthood (Hine, Chapter 3), the markers of which are social and economic. Many writers argue that this transition has undergone significant change over the last quarter of a century. One marker of the achievement of adulthood is obtaining employment. High rates of youth unemployment in the 1970s and 1980s led to a delay in achieving such status and was one of the contributors to the notion of 'extended transition'. Research shows that generally young people are now older when they achieve many of the markers of adulthood, such as a job, independent accommodation and a stable relationship (Valentine 2003). However, this research also shows substantial differences in transition between young people with an affluent background and those with a poorer one, acknowledging the impact of space and time in framing those transitions (Webster et al. 2004; Pais 2007). Young people with a more affluent background have more protected and extended transitions than young people with less affluent backgrounds, who are more likely to leave education, leave the parental home, obtain employment, and start a family in their teens and early twenties (Bynner 2005). At the same time, the very notion of 'transition' from child to adult is questioned arguing that the notion of 'adulthood' too has undergone significant change (Skelton 2002) and that adults 'struggle to hold onto what they see as the positive characteristics of youth into middle and old age' (Jeffs and Smith 1999b: 8). Understandings of 'adulthood' and how this has changed are rarely addressed, but are crucially important if one accepts the notion of young people as in a stage of transition to adulthood.

The emphasis on young people for what they might be in the future, as 'becomings', as adults of the making, is a relatively recent focus of UK government policy, though as France (Chapter 2) says, this has often been a feature of theorising about young people and their development. One impact of this focus on young people as the future is a failure to acknowledge the importance to young people of 'being'.

Governance and social control

The modernity belief in the ability to control events has given way to the late modern view that events, and people, can and should be managed. This is particularly true of measures designed to manage and control young people, who have been described as 'expensive nuisance, slave, and super-pet' (Holt, quoted in James et al. 1998: 210) and are viewed with a mistrust that is institutionalised (Kelly 2003). This management takes a variety of guises, including education (Armstrong, Chapter 7; Wood, Chapter 12), youth work (Davies, Chapter 16), information, advice and guidance (S. Yates, Chapter 15) and youth justice (J. Yates, Chapter 14).

Many of the chapters in this book refer to the importance of socialisation and education as mechanisms of social control (Chouhan, Chapter 6; Armstrong, Chapter 7; Wood, Chapter 12; Kemshall, Chapter 13), and the importance of self-governance which requires individuals to internalise the dominant beliefs and customs of a society in order for that society to run smoothly. There are always individuals and groups that do not conform to those social norms and these pose a problem for governance, a problem that requires resolution. Ideally that resolution should be through socialisation and acceptance and internalisation of those norms (Chouhan, Chapter 6), often delivered through programmes of early intervention and prevention, but where these informal mechanisms of control fail there is a need for strong formal control mechanisms through the criminal justice system and imprisonment. It is paradoxical that current policy in England has resulted in considerable funding for a wide range of projects and programmes for children and young people at the same time as having record numbers of children and young people in custody.

Work with young people is framed within this context of late modernity. While those that do this work can mediate between policy and young people (Banks, Chapter 5; Kemshall, Chapter 13) they themselves are subject to those same pressures.

> … professional discourses reflect the interests of professionals … as much as the interests of young people. As a result such professional discourses are implicated in the surveillance of young people and the social construction (or rather narrow archetypes) of what it is to be a young person in contemporary societies. (Cieslick and Pollock 2002: 15–16)

Identity

A theme running through much of the debate about young people is the notion of identity – how individuals see themselves, present themselves to others and are perceived by others. It's a topic that has been the focus of some key modern thinkers (e.g. Giddens 1991; Bauman 2000) and central to those discussions is how the changing economic and social context has affected all three aspects, essentially because the nature of the relationships between individuals has changed dramatically. Identity is a complex topic, described by Buckingham as 'a very broad and ambiguous concept' (2008: 18). Many of those who work with young people will recognise this ambiguity; 'our identity is something we uniquely possess: it is what distinguishes us from other people. Yet on the other hand, identity also implies a relationship with a broader collective or social group of some kind' (Buckingham 2008: 1).

Identity is multi-faceted, with a wide range of different aspects of identity being explored by theorists and researchers. Many people have written about cultural, ethnic and racial identities and its relevance to minority groups and experience of oppression (e.g. Dominelli 2007). Young people tend to invest considerable effort into creating and maintaining an identity. An essential part of that identity formation, and socialisation, is consumption, both directly through individuals, and indirectly through parents and families (Kenway and Bullen 2005). Identity and image is a key aspect of marketing and increased segmentation of the market has seen youth as a distinct marketing segment rise considerably in importance and value since the end of the Second World War. Kenway and Bullen argue that, driven by advertising and the media, this was linked to a general acceptance of the so-called 'generation gap', and associations of youth with 'autonomy and rebellion' (2005: 209). At the same time they acknowledge the role of young people in their assimilation of consumerism:

> ... products alone do not make identity; gender, race, class and location are major factors in the manner in which consumer products are taken up, reinvented and used as sources of identity, empowerment and subversion. (Kenway and Bullen 2005: 221)

Bauman (2000) suggests that identities are 'fluid' in this age of 'liquid modernity', and new technology has certainly made it easier for everyone, not just young people, to create a range of identities. However, an understanding that each of us maintains a range of different identities in different contexts of our lives is not new (Goffman 1969). Legitimate identity however is crucially important in the modern world as it provides access to the benefits of citizenship, and is a key element of a new system of governance (Rose 2000).

Citizenship and participation

People are frequently required to confirm their identity, be that with passports and driving licences, bank cards or store cards. These and many other systems store data about individuals; data which is accessed by the providers of services to confirm our legitimacy. Identity has become a means of social control which generates vast amounts of data at the same time as providing access to privileges such as mortgages, insurance and utility services. It is within this context that 'identity theft' has become such a major issue because of its consequences for both the service providers and the legitimate identity owner. Much depends on virtual 'networks of surveillance' that are 'pre-emptive and preventive, denying access to benefits on the basis of what one might do rather than apprehending one after the act ... the securitization of identity' (Rose 2000: 326).

Rose describes this as control 'through conditional access to circuits of consumption and civility' (2000: 326) with working and shopping being the fundamental components of citizenship, though not citizenship in the terms that are promoted through citizenship education (Wood, Chapter 12). In Rose's model access to the benefits of citizenship become conditional upon maintaining a good record within these systems, and thus upon controlling our own behaviour. In this way individuals and organisations are required to act responsibly and prudently, not by the imposition of external controls, but by the subjective acceptance of this approach as morally and ethically correct (see also Chouhan, Chapter 6). Within such a system expert advice becomes important and generates a market of goods and services to assist that prudence. With these developments has come the 'risk thinking' that permeates life today: the notion that risks are endemic to all spheres of life and that they need to be assessed and managed if not avoided. It frames the actions of many policy makers and practitioners with individuals, organisations and communities being required to take responsibility for their own risk management. Active citizenship requires self-motivation, self-responsibility and self-reliance (Rose 2000: 329). Those that do not take up this mantle are seen as a threat that must be managed and the threat neutralised. They are the 'non-citizens, failed citizens, anti-citizens' (Rose 2000: 331). Young people are routinely excluded from these systems by reason of their age and lack of income, and thus automatically are 'non citizens' in this model. Those who come from disadvantaged backgrounds are less likely to have these identity trappings and more likely to be NEET (Not in Education, Employment or Training) and thus are 'failed citizens', and those that refuse to conform, perhaps by being involved in problematic, anti-social or criminal behaviour, will be Rose's 'anti-citizens'. These are the very groups of young people that will be accessing or targeted by professional or voluntary services.

Young people are then to a great extent outside this identity net of citizenship, much of which is not available to them until they achieve some of the markers of adulthood. This in turn makes them appear more dangerous as their risk cannot be assessed in the same way. They must be managed accordingly, with childhood being 'the most intensively governed sector of personal existence' (Rose 1989: 121). This management focuses on the creation of the good active citizens of the future (Wood, Chapter 12) and involves both protection and control through the wide range of professionals and organisations that impinge upon their lives. Fundamental to this exercise is the notion of 'normality':

> criteria of normality are elaborated by experts on the basis of their claims to scientific knowledge of childhood and its vicissitudes. And this knowledge of normality has not, in the main, resulted from studying normal children. (Rose 1989: 131)

The search for normality and its concomitant risk factors is one that tends to 'homogenize' normality (Armstrong 2006). It is based on middle-class norms and lacks cultural sensitivity (Ungar 2004). Interventions based on such assumptions can have unforeseen negative consequences for young people (Kelly 2000). There is considerable potential for collusion between policy makers and researchers, seeking to improve the tools and

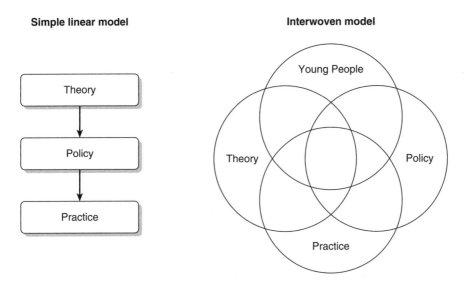

Simple linear model

Interwoven model

Figure 20.1   The relationship between theory, policy and practice

techniques for identifying, reshaping and controlling problematic young people. One way to minimise this collusion is the participation of young people themselves in these processes (Fleming and Hudson, Chapter 10). Research is a political activity, and methods socially constructed: it serves the ends of the powerful, but can also be a means of exposing unacceptable and shifting policy and practice (Mayall et al. 1999).

Evidence, policy and practice: the missing link

The relationship between theory policy and practice is often presented as a simple, linear model, particularly by politicians and policy makers promoting evidence led practice. However, the notion of evidence led or even evidence informed policy and practice is open to dispute (Hine 2008). There is no simple top down linear relationship of theory/research (evidence) to policy to practice. Rather there is an impalpable interweaving of these three dimensions, together with the one key aspect that emerges as important within each of the chapters – the general public and users of these services, which in the context of this book is the lives as lived and understood by young people themselves. The difference between these two relationships can be represented in Figure 20.1.

The involvement of young people in decision making as in the interwoven model is increasingly promoted by policy makers (DfES 2001), though there is some scepticism about the extent to which such involvement is allowed to impact on policy (see Davies,

Chapter 16). At the same time there is a growing body of evidence that involving young people and genuinely taking account of their perspective on issues that affect them can provide insights that can make a valuable contribution to both policy and practice (see Hine, Chapter 3; Perkins, Chapter 9; Fleming and Hudson, Chapter 10).

Working with young people: the importance of *with*

Many of those who work with young people, especially in spheres such as education, social work, youth justice and youth work, are aware that they act as agents of social control, and while the ways in which they are able to work is increasingly controlled and technicised by policy directives, many of them attempt to work in ways within that framework that mediate those policy requirements (Banks, Chapter 5; Chouhan, Chapter 6; Kemshall, Chapter 13), ways that involve working with the young person as a participant. This is not a comfortable position to take (Tyler, Chapter 19). These workers are managing the tensions between young people and adult fears and anxieties about young people. As acknowledged in many chapters in this book, recent times have seen a recognition of the rights of children and young people and calls for their greater participation in public life (DfES 2001), there has been a simultaneous increase in calls for them to be responsible (Blair 2006), in the same way as the demand for a balance of rights and responsibilities has been levelled at adults.

The discourse of risk permeates all spheres of work with young people, be it health, education or criminal justice, and in all areas the role of those working with young people is to assess and manage that risk, frequently using tools and techniques developed by experts and based on 'evidence': what Kelly describes as 'processes of individualization and standardization' (2001: 26). These dominant discourses of risk do not acknowledge other aspects of risk, such as the positive role that it can play in young people's lives (Perkins, Chapter 9) and the way in which constructions of risk are dynamic and change over time (Lupton 2006). Research with young people has revealed that the behaviour of young people categorised as problematic or as an indicator of risk can actually indicate a rational and resilient response to risk on the part of the young person (Ungar 2004). Young people are not merely passive recipients of risk but actively confront it and collude with notions of risk (Miles 2002). They are very aware of the risks that confront them on a day-to-day basis and make choices between competing risks (France 2000). Those who work with young people have a difficult job in acknowledging these different understandings of risks, assessing them in the context of the real lives of young people, and avoiding negative unintended consequences for the young people.

Jeffs and Smith (1999b) argue that the distinction between children, young people and adults is artificial as they share the same underlying problems, and they propose that these should be the framework for organising support and intervention rather than age. Current policy focus on young people suggests that will not happen any time soon, and in the meantime those who work with young people will have to manage these tensions, together with those created by any dissonance between their own values and policy directives about their work. There has been considerable diversification of work with young people since the 1990s, as the title of this book, working with young people, reflects. There has been a move away from education and youth work being the most numerous and significant professions working with young people (Davies, Chapter 16) to a wide range of statutory and voluntary organisations (Wylie, Chapter 17; Payne, Chapter 18) within which work with young people is being undertaken.

This book did not set out to be a call to arms or argument for traditional youth work, and yet it is amazing how frequently different chapters refer to the need to work with young people in ways that can be attributed to the principles of traditional youth work, even when there is some dispute about these (see Perkins, Chapter 9; Davies, Chapter 16 and Payne, Chapter 18). Paradoxically the evaluation of success/ effectiveness of youth work has been inconclusive, yet as this book shows, reflections on theoretical debates and evaluations of policy and alternative practices with young people are providing evidence of the value of these principles for working with young people. Indeed Payne (Chapter 18) argues that these principles should be embedded in all work with young people in whatever context. All those who work with young people, whether in a statutory or voluntary capacity, in whatever organisation, and no matter how tightly prescribed by policy that work might be, have some degree of autonomy in respect of the delivery of that practice.

It is in the *how* of practice, if not in the *what*, that the greatest impact on young people's lives will be achieved. It is here that practice should be informed by a knowledge of the context, within which practitioners work and the dilemmas that they, as well as young people, face. The principled pragmatist (Tyler, Chapter 19) understands the macro, exo, meso and micro systems that impact on young people's lives (Bronfenner 1989; Klein and Kozlowski 2000) and their own practice. They work within that and *with* young people for their benefit; in the here and now as well as in their future.

REFERENCES

Aapola, S., Gonick, M. and Harris, A. (2005) *Young Femininity: Girlhood, Power and Social Change*, London: Palgrave.

ACOP (1989) *Surviving Poverty: Probation Work and Benefits Policy*, London: Association of Chief Officers of Probation.

Adebowale, V. (1999) *Meeting the Needs of Disadvantaged Young People: A Report to the New Deal Task Force*, London: Department for Education and Employment.

AGC (Advisory Group on Citizenship) (1998) *Education for Citizenship and the Teaching of Democracy in Schools (The Crick Report)*, London: Qualifications and Curriculum Authority.

Arches, J. and Fleming, J. (2006) 'Young people and social action: youth participation in the United Kingdom and United States', *New Directions for Youth Development Theory Practice Research*, Fall: 81–91.

Aristotle (1954) *The Nichomachean Ethics of Aristotle*, translated by Sir David Ross, London: Oxford University Press.

Aristotle (1992) *The Politics*, London: Penguin Classics.

Alderson, P. and Morrow, V. (2004) *Ethics, Social Research and Consulting with Children and Young People*, London: Barnardos.

Armstrong, D. (2006) 'Becoming criminal: the cultural politics of risk', *International Journal of Inclusive Education*, 10 (2–3): 265–278.

Atkinson, A. B. and Hills, J. (1998) *Exclusion, Employment and Opportunity, CASE Paper 4*, London: Centre for Analysis of Social Exclusion, London School of Economics.

Audit Commission (1996) *Mis-spent Youth*, London: Audit Commission.

Back, L. (1996) *New Ethnicities and Urban Culture*, London: UCL Press.

Badham, B. (2005) *So, What's Changed? An Evaluation of the External Impact of Ask Us*, London: The Children's Society.

Badham, B. and Wade, H. (2005) *Hear by Right: Standards for the Active Involvement of Children and Young People*, Leicester: National Youth Agency.

Bailey, R. and Williams, B. (2000) *Inter-Agency Partnerships in Youth Justice: Implementing the Crime and Disorder Act 1998*, Sheffield: University of Sheffield Joint Unit for Social Services Research.

Ball, S. J. (2003) *Class Strategies and the Education Market: Middle Classes and Social Advantage*. London: RoutledgeFalmer.

Bandalli, S. (2000) 'Children, responsibility and the new youth justice', in B. Goldson (ed.), *The New Youth Justice*, Lyme Regis: Russell House Publishing.

Banks, S. (1996) 'Youth work, informal education and professionalisation: the issues in the 1990s', *Youth and Policy*, 54: 13–25.

Banks, S. (1999) 'Ethics and the youth worker', in S. Banks (ed.), *Ethical Issues in Youth Work*, London: Routledge, pp. 3–20.

Banks, S. (2001a) 'Professional values in informal education work', in L. Richardson and M. Wolfe (eds), *Principles and Practice of Informal Education: Learning Through Life*, London: Routledge.

Banks, S. (2001b) *Ethics and Values in Social Work*, 2nd edition, London: Macmillan.

Banks, S. (2004a) *Ethics, Accountability and the Social Professions*, Basingstoke: Palgrave Macmillan.

Banks, S. (2004b) 'Professional integrity, social work and the ethics of distrust', *Social Work and Social Sciences Review*, 11 (2): 20–35.

Banks, S. and Imam, U. (2000) 'Principles, rules and qualities: an ethical framework for youth work', *International Journal of Adolescence and Youth*, 9: 61–78.

Barber, B. (1992) *Jihad versus McWorld*, New York: Times Books.

Barnes, C. and Mercer, G. (2005) 'Disability, work, and welfare: challenging the social exclusion of disabled people', *Work, Employment & Society*, 19 (3): 527–545.

Baron, S., Field, J. and Schuller, T. (2001) *Social Capital: Critical Perspectives*, Oxford: Oxford University Press.

Barrett, S. (2004) 'Youth services are part of the package', *Young People Now*, 1–7 December: 15.

Barrett, S. (2005) 'Youth work must lift its sights', *Young People Now*, 7–13 December: 14–15.

Barry, M. (1996) 'The empowering process', *Youth and Policy*, Autumn.

Barry, M. (2001) *Challenging Transitions: Young People's Views and Experiences of Growing Up*, London: Save the Children.

Bassac (2006) 'Contract Culture Threatens Community Groups, Research Finds', press release 05.02.2006.

Batten, M. and Russell, J. (1995) *Students at Risk: A Review of Australian Literature 1980–1994*, Melbourne: Australian Council for Educational Research.

Bauman, Z. (1990) *Thinking Sociologically*, Oxford: Blackwell.

Bauman, Z. (2000) *Liquid Modernity*, Cambridge: Polity.

Beck, U. (1992) *Risk Society: Towards a New Modernity*, London: Sage.

Beck, U. and Beck-Gernsheim, E. (2002) *Individualization*, London: Sage.

Becsky, S., Dreber, M-L., Freitag, C. and Hänisch, D. (2004) *Child and Youth Policy, Child and Youth Services in the Federal Republic of Germany*, Bonn: IJAB.

Beechey, V. (1986) 'Women and employment in contemporary Britain', in V. Beechey and E. Whiteleggs (eds), *Women in Britain Today*, Buckingham: Open University Press.

Beinhart, S., Anderson, B., Lee, S. and Utting, D. (2002) *Youth at Risk? A National Survey of Risk Factors, Protective Factors and Problem Behaviour among Young People in England, Scotland and Wales*, London: Communities that Care.

Bennett, A. (2005) *Culture and Everyday Life*, London: Sage.

Benson, P. L. (2003) 'Developmental assets and assets-building community: conceptual and empirical foundations', in R. Lerner and P. Benson (eds), *Developmental Assets and Asset-building Communities: Implications for Research, Policy, and Practice*, New York: Springer Publishers.

Berdan, K., Boulton, I., Eidman-Aadahl, E., Fleming, J., Gardner, L., Rogers, I. and Solomon, A. (eds) (2006) *Writing for a Change: Boosting Literacy and Learning through Social Action*, San Francisco, CA: Jossey-Bass.

Beresford, P. (2002) 'User involvement in research and evaluation: liberation or regulation?', *Social Policy and Society*, 1 (2): 95–105.

Beresford, P. and Evans, C. (1999) 'Research note: research and empowerment', *British Journal of Social Work*, 29: 671–677.

Berger, P. L. (1966) *Invitation to Sociology: A Humanistic Perspective*, Harmondsworth: Penguin.

Berger, P. L. (1991) *Invitation to Sociology*, London: Penguin.

Berger, P. L. and Luckmann, T. (1967) *The Social Construction of Reality*, Harmondsworth: Penguin.

Berger, P. L. and Luckmann, T. (1995) *Pluralism and the Crisis of Meaning*, translated by J. A. Tooze, Gütersloh: Bertelsmann Foundation Publishers.

Bernard, B. (2004) *Resiliency: What Have we Learned?* San Francisco: WestEd.

Berridge, D., Brodie I., Pitts J., Porteous, D. and Tarling, R. (2001) *The Independent Effects of Permanent Exclusion from School on the Offending Careers of Young People*. RDS Occasional Paper No 71, London: Home Office.

Bessant, J. (2004) 'Risk technologies and youth work practice', *Youth and Policy*, 82: 60–76.

Bilton, T., Bonnett, K., Jones, P., Skinner, D., Stanworth, M. and Webster, A. (1996) *Introductory Sociology*, 3rd edn, London: Macmillan.

Blair, T. (1993) 'Why modernisation matters', *Renewal* 3 (4).

Blair, T. (1998) *The Third Way*, London: Fabian Society.

Blair, T. (1999) Speech to Labour Party Conference, Bournemouth, 28 September.

Blair, T. (2000) 'Values and the power of community', speech to the Global Ethics Foundation, 30 June.

Blair, T. (2004) Speech to Labour Party Conference, Brighton, 28 September.

Blair, T. (2005) Speech to Labour Party Conference, Brighton, 27 September.

Blair, T. (2006) 'Our nation's future: social exclusion', speech to Joseph Rowntree Foundation, York, 5 September.

Blunkett, D. (2003a) *Civil Renewal: A New Agenda, the CSV Edith Kahn Memorial Lecture*, London: Home Office Communications Directorate.

Blunkett, D. (2003b) *Active Citizens, Strong Communities: Progressing Civil Renewal*, London: Home Office Communications Directorate.

Boeck, T. and Fleming, J. (2002) 'Social Capital and the Nottingham Social Action Research Project, Nottingham Social Action Research Project', Nottingham City Primary Care Trust, SARP, Nottingham.

Boeck, T. and Fleming, J. (2005) 'Social policy: a help or a hindrance to social capital?', *Social Policy and Society*, 4 (3): 259–270.

Boeck, T., Fleming, J., Hine, J. and Kemshall, H. (2006) 'Pathways into and out of crime for young people', *Childright 2006*, July/August: 18–21.

Boeck, T., Fleming, J. and Kemshall, H. (2006) 'The context of risk decisions: does social capital make a difference?', *Forum: Qualitative Social Research* 7 (1).

Boeck, T., McCullogh, P. and Ward, D. (2001) 'Increasing social capital to combat social exclusion: the social action contribution', in A.-L. Matthies, K. Narhi and D. Ward (eds), *The Eco-Social Approach in Social Work*, Jyvaskyla: SoPhi.

Boss, J. (2007) *Ethics for Life: A Text with Readings*, 3rd edition, New York: McGraw-Hill.

Bourdieu, P. (1986) 'The forms of capital', in J. Richardson (ed.), *Handbook of Theory and Research for the Sociology of Education*, New York: Greenwood Press.

Bourdieu, P. (1991) *The Logic of Practice*. Cambridge: Polity.

Bradford, S. (2005) 'Modernising youth work: from the universal to the particular and back again', in R. Harrison and C. Wise (eds), *Working with Young People*, London: Sage/Open University.

Brendtro, L. K., Brokenleg, M. and Van Bockern, S. (1990) *Reclaiming Youth at Risk: Our Hope for the Future*, Bloomington, IN: National Education Service.

British Institute for Brain Injured Children (2005) *Young People with Learning and Communication Difficulties and Anti-Social Behaviour*, available at www.bibic.org.uk/newsite/general/campaigns.htm (accessed 02.01.2009).

Bronfenner, U. (1989) 'Ecological systems theory', in R. Vasta (ed.), *Annals of Child Development*, Greenwich CT: JAI Press.

Brookfield, S. D. (1987) *Developing Critical Thinkers: Challenging Adults to Explore Alternative Ways of Thinking and Acting*, San Francisco, CA: Jossey-Bass.

Brown, A. P. (2004) 'Anti-social behaviour, crime control and social control', *The Howard Journal*, 43 (2): 203–211.

Brown, G. (2006) Speech to the Fabian Society New Year Conference, London 14.01.2006.

Brown, P. (1987) *Schooling Ordinary Kids*, London: Tavistock Publications.

Brown, S. (2005) *Understanding Youth and Crime: Listening to Youth?*, 2nd edn, Maidenhead: Open University Press.

Brownlee, I. (1998) 'New Labour-new penology? punitive rhetoric and the limits of managerialism in criminal justice policy', *Journal of Law and Society*, 25 (3): 313–335.

Bryman, A. (2004) *Social Research Methods*, Oxford: Oxford University Press.

BSA (British Sociological Association) (2002) Statement of Ethical Practice for the British Sociological Association (March 2002), available at www.britsoc.co.uk/equality/Statement+ Ethical+ Practice.htm

Buckingham, D. (2008) 'Introducing identity', in D. Buckingham (ed.), *Youth, Identity, and Digital Media. The John D. and Catherine T. MacArthur Foundation Series on Digital Media and Learning*, Cambridge, MA: The MIT Press.

Burnett, R. and Appleton, C. (2004) 'Joined up services to tackle youth crime: a case study in England', *British Journal of Criminology*, 44 (5): 34–54.

Burney, E. (2002) 'Talking tough acting coy: what happened to the anti-social behaviour order?', *Howard Journal of Criminal Justice*, 41 (5): 341–356.

Burney, E. (2005) *Making People Behave: Anti-Social Behaviour, Politics and Policy*, Cullompton: Willan.

Bynner, J. (2001) 'British youth transitions in comparative perspective', *Journal of Youth Studies*, 4 (1): 5–23.

Bynner, J. (2005) 'Rethinking the youth phase of the life course: the case for emerging adulthood?', *Journal of Youth Studies*, 8 (4): 367–384.

Byrne, D. (1998) *Complexity Theory and the Social Sciences*, London: Routledge.

Byrne, D. (2005) *Social Exclusion*, 2nd edn, Maidenhead: Open University Press.

Bytheway, B. (1995) *Ageism*, Buckingham: Open University Press.

Calder, A. (1969) *The People's War: Britain 1939–1945*, London: Panther Books.

Campbell, B. (1993) *Goliath: Britain's Dangerous Places*, London: Methuen.

Cantle, T. (2001) *Community Cohesion: A Report of the Independent Review Team*, London: Home Office.

Carnegie Council on Adolescent Development (1995) *Great Transitions: Preparing Adolescents for a New Century*, New York: Carnegie Corporation.

Carpenter, J. (2006) 'Third sector claims grant cuts hinder work', in *Regeneration & Renewal*, 10 February: 9.

Carr, W. and Hartnett, A. (1996) *Education and the Struggle for Democracy: The Politics of Educational Ideas*, Buckingham: Open University Press.

Carter, A. (1988) *The Politics of Women's Rights*, London: Longman.

Casey, L. and Chakrabarti, S. (2005) 'Mob justice or yob rule?', *Guardian*, 19 March.

Castel, R. (1991) 'From dangerousness to risk', in G. Burchell, C. Gordon and P. Miller (eds), *The Foucault Effect: Studies in Governmentality*, London: Harvester Wheatsheaf.

Castles, S. and Kosack, G. C. (1973) *Immigrant Workers and Class Structure in Western Europe*, Oxford: Oxford University Press.

Catalano, R. F. and Hawkins, J. D. (1996) 'The social development model: a theory of antisocial behaviour', in J. D. Hawkins (ed.), *Delinquency and Crime: Current Theories,* Cambridge: Cambridge University Press.

CSA (Centre for Social Action) (2005) *Newsletter Autumn 05*, available at www.dmu.ac.uk/Images/CSA%20Newsletter1_tcm2-35456.pdf (first accessed 01.05.06).

Chawla, L. and Malone, K. (2002) 'Neighbourhood quality in children's eyes', in P. Christensen and M. O'Brien (eds), *Children in the City: Home, Neighborhood, and Community*, London: Routledge.

Checkoway, B. and Richards-Schuster, K. (2003) 'Youth participation in community evaluation research', *American Journal of Evaluation*, 24 (1): 21–33.

Chisholm, L. (2006) 'Youth research and the youth sector in Europe: perspectives, partnerships and promise', in M. Milmeister and H. Williamson (eds), *Dialogues and Networks: Organising Exchanges between Youth Field Actors*, CESIJE Youth Research Monographs, Luxembourg: Editions Phi.

Chouhan, J. (1991) 'The Communication Environment of the Gujarati Community in Leicester', thesis submitted for the award of PhD, University of Bradford.

Cieslick, M. and Pollock, G. (2002) 'Introduction: studying young people in late modernity', in M. Cieslick and G. Pollock (eds), *Young People in Risk Society: The Restructuring of Youth Identities and Transitions in Later Modernity*, Aldershot: Ashgate.

Cisse, T. (2001) *Beyond Connexions. Issues in constructive engagement.* The informal education forum: www.infed.org/personaladvisers/cisse-connexions.htm (accessed 28.07.07).

Cixous, H. and Clement, C. (1996) *The Newly Born Woman*, London: I.B. Tauris.

Clarke, D. (1996) *Schools as Learning Communities: Transforming Education*, London: Cassell.

Clarke, J. (1985) 'Whose justice? the politics of juvenile control', *International Journal of the Sociology of Law*, 13 (4): 407–421.

CLRAE (1992) *European Charter on the Participation of Young People in Municipal and Regional Life*, Strasbourg: Council of Local and Regional Authorities in Europe.

Coffey, A. (2004) *Reconceptualizing Social Policy*, Maidenhead: Open University Press.

Cohen, P. and Ainley, P. (2000) 'In the country of the blind?', *Journal of Youth Studies*, 3 (1): 79–96.

Cohen, S. (ed.) (1971) *Images of Deviance*, Harmondsworth: Penguin.

Cohen, S. (1972) *Folk Devils and Moral Panics*, London: Paladin.

Cohen, S. (1985) *Visions of Social Control*, London: Polity Press.

Coleman, J., Catan, L. and Dennison, C. (2004) 'You're the last person I'd talk to', in J. Roche, S. Tucker, R. Thomson and R. Flynn (eds), *Youth in Society*, 2nd edn, London: Sage.

Coleman, J. and Warren-Adamson, C. (eds) (1992) *Youth Policy in the 1990s: The Way Forward*, London: Routledge.

Coleman, J. S. (1997) 'Family, School and Social Capital', in L. J. Saha (ed.), *International Encyclopedia of the Sociology of Education,* New York: Elsevier Science, pp. 623–627.

Coleman, R. (2004) *Reclaiming the Streets: Surveillance, Social Control and the City*, Cullompton: Willan.

Coleman, R., Tombs, S. and Whyte, D. (2005) 'Capital, crime control and statecraft in the entrepreneurial city', *Urban Studies*, 42 (13): 2511–2530.

Coles, B. (2000) *Joined Up Youth Research, Policy and Practice*, Leicester: National Youth Agency.

Coles, B. (2001) *Joined-up Youth Research, Policy and Practice: a new agenda for change?*, Leicester: Youth Work Press.

Colley, H. with P. Boetzelen (eds) (2006) *Social Exclusion and Young People in Europe*, Strasbourg: Council of Europe Publishing.

Collier, R. (1998) *Masculinities, Crime and Criminology*, London: Sage.

Comfort, H. with Merton, B. and Payne, M. (2006) *Capturing the Evidence: Tools and Processes for Recognising and Recording the Impact of Youth Work*, Leicester: The National Youth Agency.

Community and Youth Workers' Union (1999) 'Code of ethics', *CYWU Part-time Youth Workers' Handbook*, Birmingham, CYWU, pp. 21–29.

Connell, R.W. (2000) *The Men and the Boys*, Cambridge: Polity.

Connell, R. W. and Messerschmidt, J. W. (2005) 'Hegemonic masculinity: rethinking the concept', *Gender & Society*, 19 (6): 829–859.

Cote, J. (2002) 'The role of identity capital in the transition to adulthood: the individualization thesis examined', *Journal of Youth Studies*, 5 (2): 117–134.

Council of Europe Youth Directorate (2003) *Experts on Youth Policy Indicators: Final Report*, Strasbourg: Council of Europe Youth Directorate.

Council of Europe (2005) *Advanced Training for Trainers in Europe: Volume 1 – Curriculum Description*, Strasbourg: Council of Europe Publishing.

Council of the European Union (2005) *Conclusions by the Council (Education/Youth/Culture) on Youth in the Framework of The Mid-Term Review of the Lisbon Strategy*, Brussels: European Commission.

Craig, R., Kerr, D., Wade, P. and Taylor, G. (2004) *Taking Post-16 Citizenship Forward: Learning from the post-16 citizenship development projects*, London: DfES (Research Brief 604).

Crimmens, D., Factor, F., Jeffs, T., Pitts, J. Pugh, C., Spence, J. and Turner, P. (2004) *Reaching Socially Excluded Young People: A National Study of Street-based Youth Work*, Leicester: National Youth Agency/Joseph Rowntree Foundation.

Crompton, R. and Scott, J. (2005) 'Class analysis: beyond the cultural turn' in F. Devine, M. Savage, J. Scott and R. Crompton (eds), *Rethinking Class: Culture, Identities and Lifestyle*, London: Palgrave.

Csikszentmihalyi, M. (1997) *Finding Flow: The Psychology of Engagement with Everyday Life. The Masterminds Series*, New York: Basic Books.

Culley, L., Hudson, N. and Rapport, F. (2007) 'Using focus groups with minority ethnic communities: researching infertility in British South Asian communities', *Qualitative Health Research*, 17 (1): 1–11.

Culpitt, I. (1999) *Social Policy and Risk*, London: Sage.

Cunningham, S. and Lavalette, M. (2004) '"Active Citizens" or "Irresponsible Truants?" School student strikes against the war', *Critical Social Policy*, 24 (2): 255–269.

Curley, K. (2006) Letters – 'Contract culture is a threat to local bodies', *Third Sector*, 22 February: 25.

Cutler, D. and Frost, R. (2002) *Taking the Initiative: Promoting Young People's Involvement in Public Decision-Making in the UK*, London: Carnegie UK Trust.

Dalrymple, J. and Burke, B. (2006) *Anti-Oppressive Practice, Social Care and the Law*, Buckingham: Open University Press.

Darder, A. (2002) *Reinventing Paulo Freire: A Pedagogy of Love*, Boulder, Co: Westview Press.

Davies, B. (1999a) *A History of the Youth Service in England. Volume 1, 1939–1979: From Voluntaryism to Welfare State*, Leicester: Youth Work Press.

Davies, B. (1999b) *A History of the Youth Service in England. Volume 2, 1979–1999: From Thatcherism to New Labour*, Leicester: Youth Work Press.

Davies, B. (2005a) 'Youth work: a manifesto for our times', *Youth and Policy*, 88: 5–28.

Davies, B. (2005b) 'Threatening youth revisited: youth policies under New Labour', *The Encyclopaedia of Informal Education*, www.infed.org/archives/bernard_davies/revisiting-threatening_youth.htm

Davies, B. (2008) *The History of the Youth Service in England, Volume 3, 1997–2007: The New Labour Years*, Leicester: National Youth Agency.

Davies, B. and Gibson, A. (1967) *The Social Education of the Adolescent*, London: University of London Press.

Davies, D. and Neal, C. (eds) (1996) *Pink Therapy*, Buckingham: OUP.

Davies, J. (2004) 'Negotiating femininities online', *Gender and Education*, 16 (1): 35–49.

De Bruijn, H. (2002) *Managing Performance in the Public Sector*, London: Routledge.

Dean, M. (February 2005) 'Charities are not the answer to everything', *Guardian*.

DEA (Development Education Association) (2005) *Global Youth Work: Training and Practice Manual*, London: DEA.

DeFilippis, J. (2001) 'The myth of social capital in community development', *Housing Policy Debate*, 12 (4): 781–806.

Denham, J. (2001) *Building Cohesive Communities: A Report of the Inter-Departmental Ministerial Group on Public Order and Community Cohesion*, London: Home Office.

Denham, J. (2005) 'This rigid market model won't survive the real world', *Guardian*, 21 December.

DfEE (Department for Education and Employment) (1997) *Excellence for All Children: Meeting Special Educational Needs*, London: DfEE.

DfEE (Department for Education and Employment) (1999) *Learning to Succeed: A New Framework for Post-16 Learning*, London: DfEE.

DfEE (Department for Education and Employment) (2000a) *Connexions: The Best Start in Life for Every Young Person*, London: DfEE.

DfEE (Department for Education and Employment) (2000b) *Connexions: The Connexions Service – Prospectus and Specification*, London: DfEE.

DfEE (Department for Education and Employment) (2001) *Transforming Youth Work: Developing Youth Work for Young People*, London: DfEE.

DfES (Department for Education and Skills) (2001) *Listening to Children and Young People*, London: DfES.

DfES (Department for Education and Skills) (2002) *Transforming Youth Work: Resourcing Excellent Youth Services*, London: DfES.

DfES (Department for Education and Skills) (2003) *Every Child Matters*, London, DfES.

DfES (Department for Education and Skills) (2005) *Youth Matters*, London: DfES.

DfES (Department for Education and Skills) (2006) *Youth Matters: Next Steps*, London: DfES.

DfES (Department for Education and Skills) (2007) *Statutory Guidance on Section 6 of Education and Inspections Act (Positive Activities for Young People)*, London: DfES.

DoH/DEE (Department of Health, Department of Education and Employment, Home Office) (2000) *Framework for the Assessment of Children in Need and their Families*, London: The Stationery Office.

Devine, F. and Savage, M. (2005) *The Cultural Turn, Sociology and Class Analysis*, London: Palgrave.

Dingwall, R. (1999) '"Risk society": the cult of theory and the millennium?', *Social Policy and Administration*, 33 (4): 474–491.

Dominelli, L. (2007) 'The postmodern "turn" in social work: the challenges of identity and equality', *Social Work and Society*, 5 (Festschrift for Walter Lorenz), available at www.socwork.net/2007/festschrift/arsw/dominelli (first accessed 13.08.07).

Donzelot, J. (1979) *The Policing of Families*, London: Hutchinson.

Dorling, D. (2005) 'Prime suspect: murder in Britain', in P. Hillyard, C. Polantzis, S. Tombs, D. Gordon and D. Dorling (eds), *Criminal Obsessions: Why Harm Matters More than Crime*, London: Crime and Society Foundation.

Doyle, C. (1997) 'Protection studies: challenging oppression and discrimination', *Social Work Education*, 16 (2): 8–19.

Dwyer, P. (2004) 'Creeping conditionality in the UK: from welfare rights to conditional entitlements?', *Canadian Journal of Sociology*, 29 (2): 265–287.

Dwyer, P. and Wyn, J. (2001) *Youth, Education and Risk: Facing the Future*, London: Routledge Falmer.

Dyhouse, C. (1981) *Girls Growing Up in Late Victorian and Edwardian England*, London: Routledge and Kegan Paul.

Eccles, J. and Gootman, J. A. (2002) *Community Programs to Promote Youth Development*, Washington, DC: National Academy Press.

Eckersley, R. (1988) *Casualties of Change: The Predicament of Youth in Australia*, Carlton South Australia's Commission for the Future.

Eckersley, R. (1992) *Youth and the Challenge to Change*, Carlton South Australia's Commission for the Future.

Eckersley, R. (1995) 'Values and visions', *Youth Studies Australia*, 14 (1): 13–21.

Education Committee (1998) *Disaffected Children*, 5th report of the House of Commons Education Select Committee, London: The Stationery Office.

Edye, D. (2002) *Young People and Citizenship in the European Union*, London: CiCe.

EGRIS (2001) 'Misleading trajectories: transition dilemmas of young adults in Europe', *Journal of Youth Studies*, 4 (1): 110–118.

Engel, U. and Strasser, H. (1998) 'Global risks and social inequality: critical remarks on the risk-society hypothesis', *Canadian Journal of Sociology*, 23: 91–103.

Erben, R., Franzkowiak, P. and Wenzel, E. (1999) 'People empowerment vs social capital: from health promotion to social marketing', *Health Promotion Journal of Australia* 9 (3): 179–182.

Essau, C. A. (2006) 'Risk-taking behaviour amongst German adolescents', *Journal of Youth Studies*, 7 (4): 499–512.

Etzioni, A. (1993) *The Spirit of Community: The Reinvention of American Society*, New York: Touchstone.

Evans, K. (2002) 'Taking control of their lives? agency in young adult transitions in England and the New Germany', *Journal of Youth Studies*, 5 (3): 245–269.

Evans, K. and Furlong, A. (1997) 'Metaphors of youth transitions: niches, pathways, trajectories or navigations', in J. Bynner, L. Chisholm and A. Furlong (eds), *Youth, Citizenship and Social change in a European Context*, Aldershot: Ashgate.

Everitt, A. and Hardiker, P. (1996) *Evaluating for Good Practice*, Hampshire: Macmillan.

Everitt, A., Hardiker, P., Littlewood, J. and Mullender, A. (1992) *Applied Research for Better Practice*, London: Macmillan.

Evers, A. (2003) 'Social capital and civic commitment: on Putnam's way of understanding', *Social Policy and Society*, 2 (1): 13–22.

Every Child Matters (2005) 'Youth offending teams', available at http://www.every childmatters.gov.uk/youthjustice/yot/ (first accessed 01.03.06).

Farias, L. (2006) 'Changing our world', in K. Berdan, I. Boulton, E. Eidman-Aadahl, J. Fleming, L. Gardner, I. Rogers and A. Solomon (eds), *Writing for a Change Boosting Literacy and Learning though Social Action*, San Francisco: Jossey-Bass.

Farrington, D. P. (1995) 'The development of offending and antisocial behaviour from childhood: key findings from the Cambridge study in delinquent development', *Journal of Child Psychology and Psychiatry*, 36: 929–964.

Farrington, D. P. (1996) *Understanding and Preventing Youth Crime*, York: Joseph Rowntree Foundation.

Farrington, D. P. (2000) 'Explaining and preventing crime: the globalization of knowledge – the American Society of Criminology 1999 Presidential Address', *Criminology*, 38 (1): 1–24.

Faulks, K. (2000) *Citizenship*, London: Routledge.

FCDL (2003) 'Federation of Community Development Learning, National Occupational Standards for Community Development Work', http://fcdl.org.uk/ publications/documents/nos/StandardsSummaryA4.pdf (accessed 26.07.07).

Feinmann, J. (2006) 'Body dysmorphia: the tyranny of thin', *Independent*, 19 September.

Feinstein, L., Bynner J. and Duckworth, K. (2004) *Leisure Contexts in Adolescence and their effects on Adult Outcomes*, London: Centre for Research on the Wider Benefits of Learning, Institute of Education, University of London.

Field, J. (2003) *Social Capital*, London: Routledge.

Finch, J. (1984) *Education as Social Policy*, London: Longman.

Fish, J. (2006) *Hetrosexism in Health and Social Care*, Basingstoke: Palgrave Macmillan.

Fitzpatrick, T. (2005) *New Theories of Welfare*, Basingstoke: Palgrave.

Fleming, J. (2003) 'Youthbank Evaluation Report' (unpublished), Leicester: De Montfort University Centre for Social Action.

Fleming, J. and Ward, D. (2004) 'Methodology and practical application of the Social Action Research model', in F. Rapport (ed.), *New Qualitative Methodologies in Social Care Research*, London: Routledge.

Focus (2006) 'VCS Funding "Failing" the Poorest', *Focus: The electronic newsletter of the Society of Local Authority Chief Executives and Senior Managers*, London: SOLACE.

Foley, P., Roche, J. and Tucker, S. (eds) (2001) *Children in Society: Contemporary Theory, Policy and Practice*, Basingstoke: Palgrave.

Fook, J. (2002) *Social Work: Critical Theory and Practice*, London: Sage.

Forbes, A. and Wainwright, S. P. (2001) 'On the methodological, theoretical and philosophical context of health inequalities research: a critique', *Social Science & Medicine,* 53 (6): 801–816.

Foucault, M. (1967) *Madness and Civilization: A History of Insanity in the Age of Reason*, London: Tavistock.

Foucault, M. (1977) *Discipline and Punish*, Harmondsworth, Penguin.

Foucault, M. (1979) *The History of Sexuality, Vol. 1; An Introduction*, London: Allen Lane.

Foucault, M. (1991) *Discipline and Punish: the Birth of the Prison*. Harmondsworth: Penguin.

France, A. (2000) 'Towards a sociological understanding of youth and their risk taking', *Journal of Youth Studies*, 3 (3): 317–331.

France, A. (2004) 'Young people', in S. Fraser, V. Lewis, S. Ding, M. Kellett and C. Robinson (eds), *Doing Research with Children and Young People*, London: Sage.

France, A. (2007) *Understanding Youth in Late Modernity*, Basingstoke: Open University Press.

France, A. (2008) 'Risk factor analysis and the youth question', *Journal of Youth Studies*, 11 (1): 1–15.

Frazer, E. (1999) *The Problems of Communitarian Politics: Unity and Conflict*, Oxford: Oxford University Press.

Freire, P. (1996) *Pedagogy of the Oppressed*, London: Penguin.

Freire, A. M. A. and Macedo, D. (eds) (1998) *The Paulo Freire Reader*, New York: Continuum.

Friedmann, J. (1992) *Empowerment: the Politics of Alternative Development*, Oxford: Blackwell.

Frith, S. (2004) 'Afterword', in A. Bennett and K. Kahn-Harris (eds), *After Subculture*, Basingstoke: Palgrave.

Fromm, E. (1997) *The Fear of Freedom*, London, Routledge.

Fromm, E. (2001) *The Fear of Freedom*, Abingdon: Routledge.

Frosh, S., Phoenix, A. and Pattman, R. (2002) *Young Masculinities*, London: Palgrave.

Furlong, A. and Cartmel, F. (1997) *Young People and Social Change: Individualisation and risk in late modernity*, Milton Keynes: Open University Press.

Furlong, A. and Cartmel, F. (2007) *Young People and Social Change*, 2nd edn, Berkshire: Open University Press.

FEFC (Further Education Funding Council) (2000) *Citizenship for 16–19 Year Olds in Education and Training: Report of the Advisory Group to the Secretary of State for Education and Employment*, London: DfEE.

Galloway, D. (1985) *Schools, Pupils and Special Educational Needs*, London: Croom Helm.

Gamble, A. (1988) *The Free Economy and the Strong State*, London: Macmillan.

Garland, D. (2001) *The Culture of Crime Control: Crime and Social Order in Contemporary Society*, Oxford: Oxford University Press.

Garland, D. (2002) 'Of crimes and criminals: the development of contemporary criminology', in M. Maguire, R. Morgan and R. Reiner (eds), *The Oxford Handbook of Criminology*, Oxford: Oxford University Press.

Garrett, P. M. (2003) 'Swimming with dolphins: the assessment framework, New Labour and new tools for social work with children and families', *British Journal of Social Work*, 33: 441–463.

Garrett, P. M. (2004) 'The electronic eye: emerging surveillant practices in social work with children and families', *European Journal of Social Work*, 7 (1): 57–71.

Garrett, P. M. (2007) '"Sinbin" Solutions: the "Pioneer" Projects for "Problem Families" and the Forgetfulness of Social Policy Research', *Critical Social Policy*, 27 (2): 203–230.

Garside. R. (2005) *Are Antisocial Behaviour Strategies antisocial?* London: Crime and Society Foundation available online at www.crimeandsociety.org.uk (accessed 16. 10. 2006).

Gearon, L. (2003) *How do we Learn to Become Good Citizens? A BERA Professional User Review*, Southwell: British Educational Research Association.

Gewirtz, S. (2000) 'Bringing the politics back in: a critical analysis of quality discourses in education', *British Journal of Education Studies*, 48 (4): 352–370.

Giddens, A. (1973) *The Class Structure of the Advanced Societies*, London: Hutchinson.

Giddens, A. (1991) *Modernity and Self-Identity: Self and Society in the Late Modern Age*, Cambridge: Polity Press.

Giddens, A. (1998a) *The Third Way*, Cambridge: Polity Press.

Giddens, A. (1998b) 'Risk society: the context of British politics', in J. Franklin (ed.), *The Politics of Risk Society*, Cambridge: Polity Press.

Giddens, A. (1999) Reith Lectures, lecture 1, available at www.bbc.co.uk/radio4/reith1999/

Giddens, A. (2001) *The Global Third Way Debate*, Cambridge: Polity Press.

Giddens, A. (2002) *Runaway World*, London: Profile.

Gilchrist, A. (2003) 'Community development in the UK: possibilities and paradoxes', in *Community Development Journal*, 38 (1): 16–25.

Gil-Robles, A. (2005) Report by Commissioner for Human Rights on His Visit to the United Kingdom, Strasbourg: Office of the Commissioner for Human Rights.

Gilroy, P. (1987) *There Ain't No Black in the Union Jack*, London: Routledge.

Giroux, H. A. (2003) *Public Spaces, Private Lives: Democracy Beyond 9/11*, Oxford: Rowman and Littlefield.

Glass, N. (1999) 'Sure Start: the development of an early intervention programme for young children in the United Kingdom', *Children and Society*, 13: 257–264.

Gleeson, D. (1994) 'Wagging, bobbing and bunking off: an alternative view', *Educational Review*, 46 (1): 15–19.

Goes, E. (2004) 'The Third Way and the politics of community', in S. Hale, W. Leggett and L. Martell (eds), *The Third Way and Beyond: Criticisms, Futures, Alternatives*, Manchester: Manchester University Press.

Goffman, E. (1969) *The Presentation of Self in Everyday Life*, London: Allen Lane.

Goldson, B. (ed.) (2000) *The New Youth Justice*, London: Russell House.

Goldson, B. (2001) 'A rational youth justice? some critical reflections on the research, policy and practice relation', *Probation Journal*, 4 (2): 76–85.

Goldson, B. (2002) 'New Labour, social justice and children: political calculation and the deserving-undeserving schism', *British Journal of Social Work*, 32: 683–695.

Goldson, B. (2005) 'Taking liberties: policy and the punitive turn' in H. Hemdrick (ed.), *Children and Social Policy: An Essential Reader*, Bristol: The Policy Press.

Goldson, B. and Chigwada-Bailey, R. (1999) '(What) justice for black children and young people?', in B. Goldson (ed.), *Youth Justice: Contemporary Policy and Practice*, Aldershot: Ashgate.

Goldson, B. and Muncie, J. (2006) 'Critical anatomy: towards a principled youth justice', in B. Goldson and J. Muncie (eds), *Youth Crime and Justice*, London: Sage.

Goldson, B. and Yates, J. (2008) 'Youth justice policy and practice: reclaiming applied criminology as critical intervention', in B. Stout, J. Yates and B. Williams (eds), *Applied Criminology*, London: Sage, pp. 103–134.

Goldson, G. (2000) '"Children in need" or "young offenders"? Hardening ideology, organizational change and new challenges for social work with children in trouble', *Child and Family Social Work*, 5: 255–265.

Goldthorpe, J. H., Lockwood, D., Bechhoffer, F. and Platt, J. (1968) *The Affluent Worker: Industrial Attitudes and Behaviour*, Cambridge: Cambridge University Press.

Gomm, R. (1993) 'Issues of power in health and welfare', in J. Walmsley, J. Reynolds, P. Shakespeare and R. Woolfe (eds), *Health, Welfare and Practice*, London: Sage.

Granovetter, M. S. (1973) 'The Strength of Weak Ties', *American Journal of Sociology*, 78 (6): 1360–1380.

Green, E., Mitchell, W. and Bunton, R. (2000) 'Contextualising risk and danger: an analysis of young people's perception of risk', *Journal of Youth Studies*, 3: 109–126.

Green, M. (2005) *Spirituality and Spiritual Development in Youth Work*, Leicester: The National Youth Agency.

Green, S. (2002) 'Ideology and community: the communitarian hi-jacking of community justice', *British Journal of Community Justice*, 1 (2): 49–62.

Griffin, C. (1993) *Representations of Youth*, Cambridge: Polity Press.

Guardian (1983) 'The family policy debate', 17 February.

Guardian (2006) 'More help needed for the disadvantaged, says Blair', 5 September.

Guinness Housing Trust (2000) *Youthagenda: A Good Practice Guide to Working with Young People on their Home Ground*, High Wycombe: Guinness Trust Group.

Haines, K. and Drakeford, M. (1998) *Young People and Youth Justice*, London: Palgrave.

Hall, G. S. (1904) *Adolescence, its Psychology and its Relations to Physiology, Anthropology, Sociology, Sex, Crime, Religion and Education*, New York: Appleton.

Hall, S., Critcher, C., Jefferson, T., Clarke, J. and Roberts, B. (1978) *Policing the Crisis: Mugging, the State, and Law and Order*, London: Macmillan.

Hall, S. and Jefferson, T. (eds) (1975) *Resistance through Rituals*, London: Routledge and Kegan Paul.

Hall, S. and Scraton, P. (1981) 'Law, class and control', in M. Fitzgerald, G. McLennan and J. Pawson (eds), *Crime and Society: Readings in History and Theory*, London: Routledge and Kegan Paul.

Hallet, C., Murray, C. and Punch, S. (2003) 'Young people and welfare: negotiating pathways', in A. Prout and C. Hallett (eds), *Hearing the Voices of Children: Social Policy for a New Century*, London: Routledge Falmer.

Hallsworth, S. (2000) 'Rethinking the Punitive Turn: economies of excess and the criminology of the other', *Punishment & Society*, 2 (2): 145–160.

Halpern, D. (2001) 'Moral values, social trust and inequality: can values explain crime?', *British Journal of Criminology*, 41 (2): 236–251.

Halpern, D. (2005) *Social Capital*, Cambridge: Polity Press.

Hancock, L. (2006) 'Urban regeneration, young people, crime and criminalisation', in B. Goldson and J. Muncie (eds), *Youth Crime and Justice*, London: Sage.

Hanley, B., Bradburn J., Gorin, S., Barnes, M., Evans, C., Goodcare, H., Kelson, M. and Kent, A. (2000) *Involving Consumers in Research and Development in the NHS: briefing notes for researchers*, Hampshire: INVOLVE.

Haralambos, M. and Holborn, M. (2004) *Sociology: Themes and Perspectives*, London: HarperCollins.

Hargreaves, D. H. (1972) *Interpersonal Relations and Education*, London: Routledge and Kegan Paul.

Harrison, R., Benjamin, C., Curran, S. and Wise, C. (eds) (2007) *Leading Work with Young People*, London: Sage/Open University.

Hawkins, D. J. and Catalano, R. F. (1992) *Communities that Care*, San Francisco, CA: Jossey-Bass.

Hayes, M. (2002) *Taking Chances: The Lifestyles and Leisure Risk of Young People*, London: Child Accident Prevention Trust.

Haynes, P. (2003) *Managing Complexity in the Public Services*, Berkshire: Open University Press/McGraw Hill.

Hazel, N., Hagell, A. and Brazier, L. (2002) *Young Offenders' Perceptions of their Experiences in the Criminal Justice System*, Swindon: ESRC.

Heater, D. (1999) *What is Citizenship?*, Cambridge: Polity Press.

Heater, D. (2004) *Citizenship: the Civic Ideal in World History, Politics and Education*, Manchester: Manchester University Press.

Hendrick, H. (1990) *Images of Youth: Age, Class and the Male Youth Problem*, Oxford: Clarendon Press.

Hendrick, H. (2003) *Child Welfare: Historical Dimensions, Contemporary Debate*, Bristol: Policy Press.

Henman, K. (2007) 'What future for youth work?', *Rapport*, January.

Hillyard, P. and Tombs, S. (2005) 'Beyond criminology?,' in P. Hillyard, C. Polantzis, S. Tombs, D. Gordon and D. Dorling (eds), *Criminal Obsessions: Why Harm Matters More than Crime*, London: Crime and Society Foundation.

Hine, J. (2004) *Children and Citizenship* (Online Report 08/04), London: Home Office.

Hine, J. (2006) 'Risky business', *Safer Society*, Summer, pp. 25–27.

Hine, J. (2007) 'Young people's perspectives on final warnings', *Web Journal of Current Legal Issues*, 2, http://webjcli.ncl.ac.uk/2007/issue2/hine2.html

Hine, J. (2008) 'Applied criminology: research, policy and practice', in B. Stout, J. Yates and B. Williams (eds), *Applied Criminology*, London: Sage.

HM Treasury/Department for Children, Families and Schools (2007) *Aiming High for Young People: A Ten Year Strategy for Positive Activities*, London: HM Treasury.

HM Treasury/Department for Education and Skills (2007) *Policy Review of Children and Young People: A Discussion Paper*, HM Treasury/DfES.

HMSO (1959) *The Youth Service in England and Wales (Albemarle Report)*, London: HMSO.

HMSO (2003) *Social Trends No 33*, London: Stationery Office.

Hodge, M. (2005) 'The youth of today', Speech to Institute of Public Policy Research, 19 January.

Hodgson, G. (1986) 'Behind methodological individualism', *Cambridge Journal of Economics*, 10 (3): 211–244.

Hoggart, L. (2007) Young women, sexual behaviour and sexual decision making', in B. Thom, R. Sales and J. J. Pearce (eds), *Growing up with Risk*, Bristol: Policy Press.

Hoggarth, L., Smith, D. I. (2004) *Understanding the Impact of Connexions on Young People at Risk*, London: Department for Education and Skills.

Hoggarth, L. and Payne, M. (2006) 'Evidence based or evidence buried: how far have the implications of the national impact study of the work of Connexions with young people at risk informed the Green Paper?', *Youth & Policy*, 90: 43–58.

Hoghughi, M. (1978) *Troubled and Troublesome*, London: Burnett Books.

Holland, J. (2005) 'Fragmented youth: social capital in biographical context in young people's lives,' in *Whither Social Capital: Past, Present and Future*, London: London South Bank University.

Holland, J., Reynolds, T. and Weller, S. (2007) 'Transitions, networks and communities: the significance of social capital in the lives of children and young people', *Journal of Youth Studies*, 10 (1): 101–120.

Hollands, R. and Chatterton, P. (2003) 'Producing nightlife in the new urban entertainment economy: coporatization, branding and market segmentation', *International Journal of Urban and Regional Research*, 27 (2): 361–385.

Hollin, C. (2002) 'Criminological psychology', in M. Maguire, R. Morgan and R. Reiner, *The Oxford Handbook of Criminology*, Oxford: Oxford University Press.

Home Office (1997) *No More Excuses: A New Approach to Tackling Youth Crime in England and Wales*, London: HMSO.

Home Office (2003) *Respect and Responsibility: Taking a Stand Against Anti-Social Behaviour*, London: Home Office.

Home Office (2006) 'What is anti-social behaviour', www.homeoffice.gov.uk/anti-social-behaviour/what-is-asb/?view=Standard (accessed on 16. 10. 2006).

hooks, b. (1981) *Ain't I a Woman: Black Women and Feminism*, London: Pluto.

Hoskins, B. and Williamson, H. with P. Boetzelen (eds) (2005) *Charting the Landscape of European Youth Voluntary Activities*, Strasbourg: Council of Europe Publishing.

House of Commons (2006) *Education and Inspections Bill*, London: Stationery Office.

Howard, M. (1993) Speech to Conservative Party Conference, 6 October.

Hughes, D. M. and Curnan, S. P. (2000) 'Community youth development: a framework for action', *CYD Journal*, 1: 7–13.

Hughes, G. and Follett, M. (2006) 'Community safety, youth and the "anti-social"', in B. Goldson and J. Muncie (eds), *Youth Crime and Justice*, London: Sage.

Hursthouse, R. (1999) *On Virtue Ethics*, Oxford: Oxford University Press.

Husband, C. (ed.) (1987) *'Race' in Britain: Continuity and Change*, London: Hutchinson.

Hyman, P. (2005) *1 out of 10: from Downing Street Vision to Classroom Reality*, London: Vintage.

Istance, D., Rees, G. and Williamson, H. (1994) *Young People Not in Education, Training or Employment in South Glamorgan*, Cardiff: South Glamorgan Training and Enterprise Council.

Jackins, H. (1979) *The Upward Trend*, Seattle: Rational Island Publishers.

Jackson, S. and Scott, S. (2004) 'Sexual antinomies in late modernity', *Sexualities*, 7 (2): 233–248.

James, A. and James, A. L. (2004) *Constructing Childhood: Theory, Policy and Social Practice*, Basingstoke: Palgrave.

James, A., Jenks, C. and Prout, A. (1998) *Theorizing Childhood*, Oxford: Blackwell.

James, A. and Prout, A. (1998) *Constructing and Reconstructing Childhood*, London: Falmer Press.

Jamieson, J. (2005) 'New labour, youth justice and the question of "Respect"', *Youth Justice*, 5 (3): 180–193.

Jamieson, J. and Yates, J. (2009) 'Young people, youth justice and the state', in R. Coleman, J. Sim, S. Tombs and D. Whyte (eds), *State, Power, Crime*, London: Sage.

Jeffs, T. (1979) *Young People and the Youth Service*, London, Routledge and Kegan Paul.

Jeffs, T. (2007) 'Crossing the divide: school-based youth work', in R. Harrison, C. Benjamin, S. Curran and R. Hunter (eds), *Leading Work with Young People*, London: Sage.

Jeffs, T. and Banks, S. (1999) 'Youth work and social control', in S. Banks (ed.), *Ethical Issues in Youth Work*, London: Routledge.

Jeffs, T. with Ruth Gilchrist (2005) *Newcastle YMCA 150 Years: Mind, Body, Spirit*, Leicester: The National Youth Agency.

Jeffs, T. and Smith, M. (eds) (1988) *Welfare and Youth Work Practice*, Basingstoke: MacMillan Education.

Jeffs, T. and Smith, M. (1999a) *Informal Education: Conversation, Democracy and Learning* 2nd edn, Ticknell: Education Now.

Jeffs, T. and Smith, M. K. (1999b) 'The problem of "youth" for youth work', *Youth and Policy* 62: 45–66. Also available in The Informal Education Archives, www.infed.org/archives/youth.htm

Jeffs, T. and Smith, M. K. (2002) 'Individualization and youth work', *Youth and Policy*, 76: 39–65.

Jeffs, T. and Smith, M. K. (2005) *Informal Education: Conversation, Democracy and Learning*, 3rd edn, Nottingham: Educational Heretics Press.

John, G. (2006) *Taking a Stand*, Manchester: The Gus John Partnership.

Jones, A. (2004) 'Involving children and young people as researchers', in S. Fraser, V. Lewis, S. Ding, M. Kellett, C. Robinson (eds), *Doing Research with Children and Young People*, London: Sage.

Jones, G. (2002) *The Youth Divide: Diverging Paths to Adulthood*, York: Joseph Rowntree Foundation.

Jordan, B. with Jordon, C. (2000) *Social Work and the Third Way: Tough Love as Social Policy*, London: Sage.

Kane, J. and Wall, A. D. (2006) *The 2005 National Public Survey on White Collar Crime*, Fairmont, WV: National White Collar Crime Centre.

Kant, I. (1964) *Groundwork of the Metaphysics of Morals*, New York: Harper Row.

Kelly, P. (1999) 'Wild and tame zones: regulating the transitions of youth at risk', *Journal of Youth Studies*, 2 (2): 193–211.

Kelly, P. (2000) 'Youth as an artefact of expertise: problematising the practice of youth studies', *Journal of Youth Studies*, 3: 301–315.

Kelly, P. (2001) 'Youth at risk: processes of individualisation and responsibilisation in the risk society', *Discourse: Studies in the Cultural Politics of Education*, 22 (1): 23–33.

Kelly, P. (2003) 'Growing up as risky business? risks, surveillance and the institutionalised mistrust of youth', *Journal of Youth Studies*, 6 (2): 165–180.

Kelly, P. (2006) 'The entrepreneurial self and "youth at risk": exploring the horizons of identity in the twenty-first century', *Journal of Youth Studies*, 9 (1): 17–32.

Kemshall, H. (2002a) *Risk, Social Policy and Welfare*, Buckingham: Open University Press.

Kemshall, H. (2002b) 'Effective probation: an example of "Advanced Liberal" responsibilisation', *Howard Journal of Criminal Justice*, 41 (1): 41–58.

Kemshall, H. (2003) *Understanding Risk in Criminal Justice*, Buckingham: Open University Press.

Kemshall, H., Marsland, L., Boeck, T. and Dunkerton, L. (2006) 'Young people, pathways and crime: beyond risk factors', *Australian and New Zealand Journal of Criminology*, 39 (3): 354–370.

Kenway, J. and Bullen, E. (2005) 'Inventing the young consumer', in C. Jenk (ed.), *Childhood: Critical Concepts in Sociology*, Abingdon: Routledge.

Kerr, D., Ireland, E., Lopes, J., Craig, R. with Cleaver, E. (2004) *Citizenship Education Longitudinal Study: Making Citizenship Education Real*, London: DfES.

Kimberlee, R. (2002) 'Why don't young people vote at general elections?', *Journal of Youth Studies*, 5 (1): 85–97.

Kirby, P. (1999) *Involving Young Researchers: How to Enable Young People to Design and Conduct Research*, London: Joseph Rowntree Foundation.

Kirby, P. (2004) *A Guide to Actively Involving Young People in Research: For Researchers, Research Commissioners and Managers*, Hampshire: INVOLVE.

Klein, K. J. and Kozlowski, S. W. J. (2000) 'From micro to meso: critical steps in conceptualizing and conducting multilevel research', *Organizational Research Methods*, 3 (3): 211–236.

Knepper, P. (2007) *Criminology and Social Policy*, London: Sage.

Koffman, L. (2006) 'The use of anti-social behaviour orders: an empirical study of a new deal for communities area,' *Criminal Law Review*, 593–613.

Kundnani, A. (2007) *The End of Tolerance: Racism in 21st Century Britain*, London: Pluto Press.

Laming, H. (2003) *The Victoria Climbié Inquiry*, London: The Stationery Office.

Lauritzen, P. and Guidikova, I. (2002) 'European youth development and policy: the role of NGOs and public authority in the making of the European Citizen', in R. Lerner, F. Jacobs and D. Wertlieb (eds), *Handbook of Applied Developmental Science 3*, London: Sage, pp. 363–382.

Lavalette, M. and Pratt, A. (eds) (1997) *Social Policy: A Conceptual and Theoretical Introduction*. London: Sage.

Lerner, R. M. (2002) *Adolescence: Development, Diversity, Context, and Application*, Upper Saddle River, NJ: Prentice-Hall.

Lerner, R. M. (2004) *Liberty: Thriving and Civic Engagement among America's Youth*, Thousand Oaks, CA: Sage.

Lerner, R. M., Fisher, C. and Weinberg, R. (2000) 'Toward a science for and of the people. Promoting civil society through the application of developmental science', *Child Development*, 71: 11–20.

Levitas, R. (2004) 'Let's hear it for humpty: social exclusion, the Third Way and Cultural Capital', *Cultural Trends*, 13 (2): 41–56.

Levitas, R. (2006) 'The concept and measurement of social exclusion', in C. Pantazis, D. Gordon and R. Levitas (eds), *Poverty and Social Exclusion in Britain*, Bristol: Policy Press.

Lister, R., Middleton, S., Smith, N., Vincent, J. and Cox, L. (2002) *Negotiating Transitions to Citizenship*, London: ESRC.

Lister, R. (2003) *Citizenship: Feminist Perspectives*, 2nd edn, Basingstoke: Palgrave.

Lloyd, T. (2006) 'Police send 500 young people home under dispersal powers', *Young People Now*, 8–14 February, p. 2.

Lloyd, T. and Barrett, S. (2005) 'Blair pledges commitment to youth services at conference', *Young People Now*, 5–11 October, p. 2.

Loeber, R. and LeBlanc, M. (1990) 'Toward a developmental criminology', in M. Tonry and N. Morris (eds), *Crime and Justice, Vol. 12*, Chicago: University of Chicago Press.

Loeber, R., Stouthamer-Loeber, M., Van Kammen, W. and Farrington, D. P. (1991) 'Initiation, escalation and desistance in juvenile offending and their correlates', *Journal of Criminal Law and Criminology*, 82 (1): 36–82.

Lopez, B. and Hernandez, A. J. (1999) *Jovenes en una sociedad segmentada*, Valencia: Nau Llibres Col. Edad y Sociedad.

Lupton, D. (2006) 'Sociology and risk', in G. Mythen and S. Walklate (eds), *Beyond the Risk Society: Critical Reflections on Risk and Human Security*, Maidenhead: Open University Press.

Lyon, J., Dennison, C. and Wilson, A. (2000) *'Tell Them so They Listen': Messages from Young People in Custody*, London: Home Office.

MacDonald, R. and Marsh, J. (2001) 'Disconnected youth?' *Journal of Youth Studies*, 4 (4): 373–391.

MacDonald, R. and Marsh, J. (2005) *'Disconnected Youth': Growing Up In Poor Britain*. Basingstoke: Palgrave.

MacIntyre, A. (1985) *After Virtue: A Study in Moral Theory*, 2nd edn, London: Duckworth.

Macionis, J. J. and Plummer, K. (1997) *Sociology: A Global Introduction*, London: Prentice-Hall.

Malchacek, L. (2000) 'Youth and the creation of civil society in Slovakia', in H. Helve and C. Wallace (eds), *Youth, Citizenship and Empowerment*, Aldershot: Ashgate.

Mandelson, P. and Liddle, R. (1996) *The Blair Revolution: Can New Labour deliver?*, London: Faber and Faber.

Marken, M., Perrett, J. and Wylie, T. (1998) *England's Youth Service: the 1998 Audit*, Leicester, Youth Work Press.

Marshall, T. H. (1950) *Citizenship and Social Class*, New York: Cambridge University.

Marshall, T. H. (1992) *Citizenship and Social Class*, New York: Cambridge University Press.

Masten, A. S. (2001) 'Ordinary magic: resilience processes in development', *American Psychologist*, 56: 227–238.

Mayall, B., Hood, S. and Oliver, S. (1999) 'Introduction', in S. Hood, B. Mayall and S. Oliver (eds), *Critical Issues in Social Research: Power and Prejudice*, Buckingham: Open University Press.

McAra, L. and McVie, S. (2005) 'The usual suspects? street-life, young people and the police', *Criminal Justice*, 5 (1): 5–36.

McCulloch, G. (1994) *Educational Reconstruction: the 1944 Education Act and the Twenty-first Century*, Ilford: Woburn Press.

McCulloch, T. (2006) 'Reviewing "what works?": a social perspective', *British Journal of Community Justice*, 4 (1): 19–32.

McFadyen, I. (1992) *GYM: The Phenomenon of Global Youth Marketing*. Available at http://ozemail.com/au~imcfadyen/gym.htm (accessed 01. 09. 06).

McGuigan, J. (1992) *Cultural Populism*. London: Routledge.

McKenzie, N. (2005) 'Community youth justice: policy, practices and public perception', in J. Winstone and F. Pakes (eds), *Community Justice: Issues for Probation and Criminal Justice*, Cullompton: Willan.

McLaughlin, H. (2006a) 'Service user involvement in research: panacea or pretence?', Conference presentation at INVOLVE conference, September.

McLaughlin, H. (2006b) 'Involving young service users as co-researchers: possibilities, benefits and costs', *British Journal of Social Work*, 36: 1395–1410.

McRobbie, A. (1980) 'Settling accounts with subculture': a Feminist critique' in *Screen Education*, Spring (34): 37–50.

McRobbie, A. (1994) *Post Modernism and Popular Culture*. London: Routledge.

Merton, B., Comfort, H. and Payne, M. (2005) *Recognising and Recording the Impact of Youth Work*. Leicester: The National Youth Agency.

Merton, B., Payne, M. and Smith, D. (2004) *An Evaluation of the Impact of Youth Work*, Research Report 606, Nottingham: DfES Publications.

Merton, R. K. (1957) *Social Theory & Social Structure*, Glencoe, IL: Free Press.

Miles, S. (2002) 'Victims of risk? young people and the construction of lifestyles', in M. Cieslick and G. Pollock (eds), *Young People in Risk Society: The Restructuring of Youth Identities and Transitions in Later Modernity*, Aldershot: Ashgate.

Mill, J. S. (1972) *Utilitarianism, On Liberty, and Considerations on Representative Government*, London: Dent.

Millie, A. E. (2008) *Anti Social Behaviour*, Maidenhead: Open University Press.

Millie, A., Jacobson, J., McDonald, E. and Hough, M. (2005) *Anti-Social Behaviour Strategies: Finding a Balance*, London: Joseph Rowntree Foundation.

Ministry of Education (1960) *The Youth Service in England and Wales (The Albemarle Report)*, London: HMSO.

Mintel (2003) *Teenage Shopping Habits*. www.reports.mintel.com/sinatra/reports (accessed 5. 12. 05).

Mizen, P. (1999) 'Ethics in an age of austerity: "work-welfare" and the regulation of youth', in S. Banks (ed.), *Ethical Issues in Youth Work*, London: Routledge.

Mizen, P. (2004) *The Changing State of Youth*, Basingstoke: Palgrave Macmillan.

Moore, H. (1994) 'Divided we stand: sex, gender and sexual difference', *Feminist Review*, 47: 78–95.

Morgan, G. (2006) *Images of Organization*, 3rd edn, London: Sage.

Morgan, R. (2000) 'The politics of criminological research' in R. D. King and E. Wincup (eds), *Doing Research on Crime and Justice*, Oxford: Oxford University Press.

Morgan, R. (2007) *The Insider: Cashing in the Hoodies*, Channel 4, 22 June.

MORI (2004) *Media Image of Young People*, London: MORI.

Morley, L. (1991) 'Towards a pedagogy for empowerment in community and youth work training', *Youth and Policy*, 35: 14–19.

Morrison, D. (2004) 'New Labour, citizenship and the discourse of the Third Way', in S. Hale, W. Leggett and L. Martell (eds), *The Third Way and Beyond: Criticisms, futures, alternatives*, Manchester: Manchester University Press.

Morrow, V. (1999) 'Conceptualising social capital in relation to the well-being of children and young people: a critical review', *Sociological Review* 47 (4): 744–765.

Morrow, V. (2001) 'Young people's explanations and experiences of social exclusion: retrieving Bourdieu's concept of social capital', *International Journal of Sociology and Social Policy*, 21 (4/5/6): 37–63.

Morrow, V. (2002a) 'Children's experiences of "community" implications of social capital discourses', in C. Swann (eds), *Social Capital and Health – insights from Qualitative Research*, London: HDA.

Morrow, V. (2002b) 'Improving the Neighbourhood for Children', in P. Christensen and M. O'Brien (eds), *Children in the City: Home, Neighborhood, and Community*, London: Routledge.

Morrow, V. (2004) 'Children's "social capital": implications for health and well-being', *Health Education*, 104 (4): 211–225.

Morrow, V. (2005) 'Invisible children? Towards a reconceptualization of childhood dependency and responsibility', in C. Jenks (ed.), *Childhood: Critical Concepts in Sociology*, Abingdon: Routledge.

Mulgan, G. and Wilkinson, H. (1997) 'Freedom's children and the rise of generational politics', in G. Mulgan (ed.), *Life After Politics*, London: Fontana.

Mullender, A., Hague, G., Iman, U., Kelly, L., Malos, E. and Regan, L. (2003) '"Could have helped but they didn't": the formal and informal support systems experienced by children living with domestic violence', in A. Prout and C. Hallett (eds), *Hearing the Voices of Children: Social Policy for a New Century*, London: Routledge Falmer.

Muncie, J. (1999a) *Youth and Crime: A Critical Introduction*, London: Sage.

Muncie, J. (1999b) 'Institutionalized intolerance: youth justice and the 1998 Crime and Disorder Act', *Critical Social Policy*, 19 (2): 147–175.

Muncie, J. (2000) 'Pragmatic realism? Searching for criminology in the new youth justice', in B. Goldson (ed.), *The New Youth Justice*, London: Russell House Publishing.

Muncie, J. (2004) *Youth and Crime*. London: Sage.

Muntaner, C., Lynch, J. and Smith, G. D. (2000) 'Social capital and the third way in public health', *Health Inequalities* 10; Part 2: 107–124.

Murray, C. (1990) *The Emerging British Underclass*, London: IEA Health and Welfare Unit.

Mythen, G. and Walklate, S. (2007) (eds), *Beyond the Risk Society: Critical reflections on risk and human security*, Maidenhead: Open University Press.

National Assembly for Wales (2000) *Extending Entitlement: Supporting Young People in Wales*, Cardiff: National Assembly for Wales.

National Audit Office (NAO) (2004) *Connexions Service: Advice and Guidance for All Young People*, National Audit Office, London.

National Youth Agency (1990) *Recommendations of 2nd Ministerial Conference of the Youth Service (England and Wales)*, Leicester: National Youth Agency.

National Youth Agency (2001) *Ethical Conduct in Youth Work: a Statement of Values and Principles from the National Youth Agency*, Leicester: National Youth Agency.

National Youth Agency (2004a) *Ethical Conduct in Youth Work: Statement of Values and Principles from the National Youth Agency*, Leicester: The National Youth Agency.

National Youth Agency (2004b) *Ethical Conduct in Youth Work: A Statement of Values and Principles from The National Youth Agency*, Leicester: The National Youth Agency (reprint).

National Youth Agency (2005) *Professional Validation*, Leicester: The National Youth Agency.

National Youth Agency (2006a) *Demonstrating the Impact of Youth Work*. Spotlight 33, Leicester: The National Youth Agency.

National Youth Agency (2006b) *Every Child Matters: Change for Children Joint Planning and Commissioning Local Youth Service Briefing*, Leicester: The National Youth Agency.

Nava, M. and Nava, O. (1992) 'Discriminating or duped? Young people as consumers of advertising', in M. Nava (ed.), *Changing Cultures: Feminism, Youth and Consumption*, London: Sage.

Nelson, J., Wade, P., Kerr, D. and Taylor, G. (2004) *National Evaluation of the Post-16 Citizenship Development Projects: Key Recommendations and Findings from the Second Year of Development*, London: DfES.

New Opportunities Fund (2003) *Engaging Young People in Evaluation and Consultation*, London: New Opportunities Fund.

Newman, J. (2002) 'The new public management, modernization and institutional change: disruptions, disjunctures and dilemmas', in K. Mclaughlin et al. (eds), *New Public Management: Current Trends and Future Prospects*, London: Routledge.

Noguera, P. A. (2005) 'The trouble with black boys: the impact of social and cultural forces on the academic achievement of African American males', in O. S. Fashola (ed.), *Educating African American Males: Voices from the Field*, Thousand Oaks, CA: Corwin Press.

Nursing and Midwifery Council (2004) *The NMC Code of Professional Conduct: Standards for Conduct, Performance and Ethics*, London: NMC.

Obijiofor, C. (2006) 'Community action in a summer writing institute', in K. Berdan, I. Boulton, E. Eidman-Aadahl, J. Fleming, L. Gardner, I. Rogers and A. Solomon (eds), *Writing for a Change Boosting Literacy and Learning though Social Action*, San Francisco: Jossey-Bass.

O'Brien, M. and Whitmore, E. (1989) 'Empowering Women Students in Higher Education', *McGill Journal of Education*, 24: 305–320.

OFSTED (2004) *Local Authority Youth Services: A Framework for Inspection*, London: OFSTED.

Oliver, M. (1990) *The Politics of Disablement*, Basingstoke: Macmillan.

Oliver, M. (1996) *Understanding Disability: From Theory to Practice*, Basingstoke: Palgrave Macmillan.

O'Mahoney, D. and Haines, K. (1996) *An Evaluation of the Introduction and Operation of the Youth Court*, London: Home Office.

O'Malley, P. (1996) 'Post-social criminologies: some implications of current political trends for criminological theory and practice', *Current Issues in Criminal Justice*, 8 (1): 26–39.

O'Malley, P. (2004) 'The uncertain promise of risk', *The Australian and New Zealand Journal of Criminology*, 37 (3): 323–343.

ONS (2003) 'Social capital project work plan 2003–4', vol. 2004.

Ord, J. (2004) 'The youth work curriculum and the transforming youth work agenda', *Youth and Policy*, 83: 43–59.

Osler, A. and Starkey, H. (2003) 'Learning for cosmopolitan citizenship: theoretical debates and young people's experiences', *Educational Review*, 55 (3): 243–254.

O'Sullivan, R. and D'Agostino, A. (2002) 'Promoting evaluation through collaboration', *Evaluation*, 8 (3): 372–387.

Pais, J. M. (2007) 'The multiple faces of the future in the labyrinth of life', *Journal of Youth Studies*, 6 (2): 115–126.

Parker, H. (1974) *View From the Boys*, Newton Abbot: David & Charles.

Parker, H. (1982) *The Moral Hazard of Social Insurance*, London: Institute of Economic Affairs.

Parsons, T. (1964) *Essays in Sociological Theory*, Chicago: Free Press.

Parton, N. (2006) *Safeguarding Childhood: Early Intervention and Surveillance in Late Modern Society*, Basingstoke: Palgrave Macmillan.

Payne, M. (1997) *Modern Social Work Theory*, 2nd edn, Basingstoke: Macmillan Press.

Pearce, F. (1990) *The Second Islington Crime Survey: Commercial and Conventional Crime in Islington*, Middlesex: Middlesex Polytechnic and Queens University, Ontario.

Pearson, G. (1983) *Hooligan: A History of Respectable Fears*, London: Macmillan.

Pensions Commission (2006) *Implementing an Integrated Package of Pension Reforms: the Final Report of the Pensions Commission*, London: HMSO.

Perkins, D. F. and Borden, L. M. (2003) 'Risk factors, risk behaviors, and resiliency in adolescence', in R. M. Lerner, M. A. Easterbrooks and J. Mistry (eds), *Handbook of Psychology: Vol. 6 Developmental Psychology*, New York: Wiley.

Petersen, A. (1996) 'Risk and the regulated self: the discourse of health promotion as politics of uncertainty', *Australian and New Zealand Journal of Sociology*, 32 (1): 44–57.

Petersen, A. (1997) 'Risk, governance and the new public health', in A. Petersen and R. Bunton (eds), *Foucault, Health and Medicine*, London: Routledge.

Piaget, J. and Inhelder, B. (1969) *The Psychology of the Child*, New York: Basic Books.

Pirie, M. and Worcester, R. M. (2000) *The Big Turn-Off: Attitudes of Young People to Government, Citizenship and Community*, London: Adam Smith Institute.

Pittman, K. J. (2000, March) 'Grantmaker strategies for assessing the quality of unevaluated programs and the impact of unevaluated grantmaking'. Paper presented at Evaluation of Youth Programs symposium at the Biennial Meeting of the Society for Research on Adolescence, Chicago.

Pittman, K., Irby, M. and Ferber, T. (2001) 'Unfinished business: further reflections of a decade of promoting youth development', in P. Benson and K. Pittman (eds), *Trends in Youth Development: Visions, Realities and Challenges*, Boston, MA: Kluwer Academic Publishing, pp. 3–50.

Pitts, J. (2000) 'The new youth justice and the politics of electoral anxiety', in B. Goldson (ed.), *The New Youth Justice*, Lyme Regis: Russell House Publishing.

Pitts, J. (2003) *The New Politics of Youth Crime: Discipline or Solidarity*, 2nd edn, London: Russell House Publishing.

Pollitt, C. (2003) *The Essential Public Manager*, Buckingham: Open University Press.

Portes., A. and Landolt, P. (2000) 'Social capital: promise and pitfalls of its role in development', *Journal of Latin American Studies*, 32 (2): 529–548.

Power, M. (2004) *The Risk Management of Everything: Rethinking the Politics of Uncertainty*, London: Demos.

Poynting, S. and White, R. (2004) 'Youth work: challenging the soft cop syndrome', *Youth Studies Australia*, 23 (4): 39–46.

Pritchard, D. G. (1963) *Education and the Handicapped 1760–1960*, London: Routledge and Kegan Paul.

Putnam, R. (2000) *Bowling Alone: The Collapse and Revival of American Community*, New York: Simon & Schuster.

Raffo, C. and Reeves, M. (2000) 'Youth transitions and social exclusion: developments in social capital theory', *Journal of Youth Studies*, 3 (2): 147–166.

Rantanen, T. (2005) *The Media and Globalisation*, London: Sage.

Reina, D. and Reina, M. (1999) *Trust and Betrayal in the Workplace*, San Francisco, CA: Berrett-Koehler.

Respect Task Force (2006) *Respect Action Plan*, London, Home Office.

Review Group on the Youth Service in England (1982) *Experience and Participation* (The Thompson Report), Cmnd 8686, London: HMSO.

Rhodes, J. E. (2002) *Stand by Me: The Risks and Rewards of Mentoring Today's Youth*, Cambridge, MA: Harvard University Press.

Richardson, D. and Robinson, V. (1997) *Introducing Women's Studies*, Basingstoke: Palgrave Macmillan.

Roberts, K. (2001) *Class in Modern Britain*, Basingstoke: Palgrave.

Robins, L. and Rutter, M. (1990) *Straight and Devious Pathways from Childhood to Adulthood*, Cambridge: Cambridge University Press.

Rogers, E. (2006a) 'Northamptonshire cuts could lead to redundancies for staff', *Young People Now*, 11–17 January, p. 2.

Rogers, E. (2006b) 'Who will stand up for youth work?', *Young People Now*, 24–30 May.

Rohrer, F. (2006) 'The nothing to do generation', *BBC News*, http://news.bbc.co.uk/1/hi/uk/4693674.stm (first accessed 01. 06. 07).

Roker, D. and Eden, K. (2002) '...*Doing Something': Young People as Social Actors*, Leicester: National Youth Agency.

Roker, D., Player, K. and Coleman, J. (1999) 'Young people's voluntary and campaigning activities as a source of political education', *Oxford Review of Education*, 25 (1/2): 185–198.

Ronan, F. and Cooper, N. (2005) *Young People as Police Trainers*, Norfolk: Norfolk County Council.

Rose, N. (1989) *Governing the Soul: The Shaping of the Private Self*, London: Routledge.

Rose, N. (1996a) 'Governing "advanced" liberal democracies', in A. Barry, T. Osborne and N. Rose (eds), *Foucault and Political Reason: Liberalism, Neo-liberalism and Rationalities of Government*, London: UCL Press.

Rose, N. (1996b) 'The death of the social? Re-figuring the territory of government', *Economy and Society*, 25 (3): 327–356.

Rose, N. (1999) *Powers of Freedom*, Cambridge: Cambridge University Press.

Rose, N. (2000) 'Government and control', *British Journal of Criminology*, 40: 321–339.

Roth, J. and Brooks-Gunn, J. (2003) 'What exactly is a youth development program? Answers from research and practice', *Applied Developmental Science*, 7: 94–111.

Roth, J., Brooks-Gunn, J., Murray, L. and Foster, W. (1998) 'Promoting healthy adolescents: synthesis of youth development program evaluations', *Journal of Research on Adolescence*, 8: 423–459.

Rousseau, J. (1979) *Émile or On Education*, New York: Basic Books.

Russell, I. M. (2005) *A National Framework for Youth Action and Engagement*, Norwich, HMSO.

Russell, R. and Tyler, M. (2002) 'Thank heaven for little girls: "girl heaven" and the commercial context of feminine childhood', in *Sociology*, 36 (3): 619–637.

Rutter, M. (1990) 'Psychosocial resilience and protective mechanisms', in J. Rolf, A. S. Masten, D. Chiccetti, K. H. Nuechterlein and S. Weintraub (eds), *Risk and Protective Factors in the Development of Psychopathology*, Cambridge: Cambridge University Press.

Sallah, M. (2008) 'Global youth work: is it beyond the moral and green imperatives', in M. Sallah and S. Cooper (eds), *Global Youth Work: Taking it Personally*, Leicester: National Youth Agency.

Sallah, M. and Cooper, S. (eds) (2008) *Global Youth Work: Taking it Personally*, Leicester: National Youth Agency.

Sanders, B. (2004) 'Childhood in different cultures', in T. Maynard and N. Thomas (eds), *An Introduction to Early Childhood Studies*, London: Sage.

Sarda, K. (2006) Letters: 'Inequality, not contract culture, is the real problem', in *Third Sector*, 22 February, p. 25.

Sardar, Z. and Wyn Davies, M. (2002) *Why do People Hate America?*, Cambridge: Icon Books.

Save the Children (2004) *On the Right Track: What Matters to Young People in the UK*, London: Save the Children.

Schaefer-McDaniel, N. J. (2004) 'Conceptualizing social capital among young people: towards a new theory', *Children, Youth and Environments* 13 (1):153–172.

Schoon, I. and Bynner, J. (2003) 'Risk and resilience in the life course: implications for interventions and social policies', *Journal of Youth Studies*, 6 (1): 21–31.

Scraton, P. (2004) 'Streets of terror: marginalization and criminalization, and authoritarian renewal', *Social Justice*, 31 (1–2): 130–157.

Scraton, P. and Haydon, D. (2002) 'Challenging the criminalization of children and young people: securing a rights based agenda', in J. Muncie, G. Hughes and E. McLaughlin (eds), *Youth Justice: Critical Readings*, London: Sage.

Sharland, E. (2006) 'Young people, risk taking and risk making', *British Journal of Social Work*, 36 (2): 247–265.

Shaw, C. R. and MacKay, H. D. (1942) *Juvenile Delinquency and Urban Areas*, Chicago: Chicago University Press.

Simon, R. (1991) *Gramsci's Political Thought: An Introduction*, London: Lawrence and Wishart.

Sivanandan, A. (1991) *A Different Hunger*, London: Pluto Press.

Skellington, R. (1996) *'Race' in Britain Today*, London: Sage.

Skelton, T. (2002) 'Research on youth transitions: some critical interventions', in M. Cieslick and G. Pollock (eds), *Young People in Risk Society: The Restructuring of Youth Identities and Transitions in Later Modernity*, Aldershot: Ashgate.

Slack, B. (2006) 'Would like to meet…', *Charity Times*, January–February, p. 22.

Smith, D. (2003) 'New labour and youth justice', *Children and Society*, 17: 226–235.

Smith, M. K. (1981) *Creators not Consumers: Rediscovering Social Education*, Leicester: National Association of Youth Clubs.

Smith, M. K. (1982) *Creators not Consumers*, Leicester: Youth Clubs UK.

Smith, M. K. (1988) *Developing Youth Work: Informal Education, Mutual Aid and Popular Service*, Milton Keynes: Open University Press.

Smith, M. K. (1996) *Local Education: Community, Conversation, Praxis*, Buckingham: Open University Press.

Smith, M. K. (2000, 2007) *The Connexions Service in England*. www.infed.org/person aladvisers/connexions.htm (accessed 04. 01. 08).

Smith, R. (2003) *Youth Justice: Ideas, Policy and Practice*, Cullompton: Willan.

Smith, R., Monaghan, M. and Broad, B. (2002) 'Involving young people as co-researchers: facing up to the methodological issues', *Qualitative Social Work*, 1 (2): 191–207.

Snow, P. C. and Powell, M. B. (2007) 'Oral language competence, social skills and high risk boys: what are juvenile offenders trying to tell us?', *Children & Society*, pp. 1–13.

Social Exclusion Unit (1998) *Truancy and Social Exclusion*, London: HMSO.

Social Exclusion Unit (1999) *Bridging the Gap: New Opportunities for 16–18 Year olds Not in Education, Employment or training*, London: HMSO.

Social Exclusion Unit (2000a) *National Strategy for Neighbourhood Renewal: A Framework for Consultation*, London: Cabinet Office.

Social Exclusion Unit (2000b) *Report of Policy Action Team 8: Anti-social Behaviour*, London: Stationery Office.

Social Exclusion Unit (2000a) *National Strategy for Neighbourhood Renewal: Report of Policy Action Team 12 – young people*, London: The Stationery Office.

Social Exclusion Unit (2004) *Breaking the Cycle: Taking Stock of Progress and Priorities for the Future*. London: The Stationery Office.

Solomos, J. and Back, L. (2003) *Racism and Society*, London: Macmillan.

Spence, J. (2004) 'Targeting, accountability and youth work practice', *Practice. A Journal of the British Association of Social Workers*, 16 (4): 261–272.

Spence, J. (2005) 'Concepts of youth', in R. Harrison and C. Wise (eds), *Working with Young People*, London: Sage.

Spilsbury, J. C. and Korbin, J. E. (2004) 'Social capital from the perspective of neighborhood children and adults', in P. B. Pufall and R. P. Unsworth (eds), *Rethinking Childhood*, New Brunswick, NJ: Rutgers University Press.

Springhall, J. (1986) *Coming of Age: Adolescence in Britain 1860–1960*, London: Gill and Macmillan.

Squires, P. and Stephen, D. E. (2005) *Rougher Justice: Anti Social Behaviour and Young People*, Cullompton: Willan.

Stenson, K. (2001) 'The new politics of crime control', in K. Stenson and R. R. Sullivan (eds), *Crime, Risk and Justice: The Politics of Crime Control in Liberal Democracies*, Collumpton: Willan.

Storrie, T. (2004) 'Citizens or what?', in J. Roche, S. Tucker, R. Thomson and R. Flynn (eds.) *Youth in Society*, 2nd edn, London: Sage.

Sutherland, E. (1939) *Principles of Criminology*, Philadelphia: Lippincott.

Swadener, B. B. and Lubeck, S. (1995) 'The social construction of children and families "at risk": an introduction', in B. B. Swadener and S. Lubeck (eds), *Children and Families 'at promise': Deconstructing the Discourse of Risk*, New York: State University of New York Press.

Swain, J., Finkelstein, V., French, S. and Oliver, M. (eds) (1993) *Disabling Barriers: Enabling Environments*, London: Sage.

Swain, J., French, S. and Cameron, C. (2003) *Controversial Issues in a Disabling Society*, Milton Keynes: Open University Press.

Swanton, C. (2003) *Virtue Ethics: A Pluralistic View*, Oxford: Oxford University Press.

Swedish Ministry of Integration and Gender Equality (2007) *The End of the Beginning – Report of the Council of Europe's Final Event of the 'All Different – All Equal' Youth Campaign on Diversity, Human Rights and Participation*, Stockholm: Swedish Ministry of Integration and Gender Equality.

Sydney Bisexual Network (2000) *Bisexuality: Why would Lesbian and Gay Organisations include Bisexual?* Available at http://sbn.bi.org/brochures/wwlagoib.pdf (accessed 26. 07. 07).

Taft, J. (2001) 'Defining girl power: the culture machine vs. the girl activist', unpublished presentation at A New Girl Order? Young Women and the Future of Feminist Inquiry Conference, London, 12–14 November.

Tait, G. (1995) 'Shaping the "At Risk Youth": risk, governmentality and the Finn report', *Discourse*, 16 (1): 123–134.

Tam, H. (1998) *Communitarianism: A New Agenda for Politics and Citizenship*, Basingstoke: Macmillan.

Teenage Pregnancy Prevention Partnership Board (2007) *Teenage Pregnancy Strategy*, Leicester: Leicester City Council.

Thom, B., Sales, R. and Pearce, J. J. (2007) 'Introduction', in B. Thom, R. Sales and J. J. Pearce (eds), *Growing up with Risk*, Bristol: Policy Press.

Thomas, N. (2006) 'Reform employment service – Acevo' in *Third Sector*, 26 January, p. 16.

Thomas, P. (2003) 'Young people, "community cohesion" and the role of young people in building social capital', *Youth and Policy*, 81: 21–43.

Thompson, N. (2003) *Promoting Equality*, 2nd edn, Hampshire: Palgrave Macmillan.

Thompson, N. (2006) *Anti Discriminatory Practice*, 4th edn, Hampshire: Palgrave.

Thompson, S. (2005) *Age Discrimination*, Lyme Regis: Russell House Publishing.

Thrupp, M. and Willmott, R. (2003) *Education Management in Managerialist Times*, Berkshire: Open University Press.

Tolman, J. and Pittman, K. (2002) *Toward a Common Vision: Naming and Framing the Developmental Imperative*, Washington, DC: Academy for Educational Development.

Tombs, S. and Yates, J. (2008) 'Who are the real nuisance neighbours?', paper presented to the European Study Group on Deviance Conference: *Capital, Culture,*

Power: Criminalisation and Resistance, hosted by Liverpool John Moores University and Liverpool University, 2–4 July 2008, Liverpool.

Tomlinson, S. (1981) *Educational Subnormality: A Study in Decision-making*, London: Routledge and Kegan Paul.

Tombs, S. and Williams, B. (2008) 'Corporate crime and victims', in B. Stout, J. Yates and B. Williams (eds), *Applied Criminology*, London: Sage.

Tonry, M. (2004) *Punishment and Politics: Evidence and Emulation in the Making of English Crime Control Policy*, Cullompton: Willan.

Tucker, S. (2005) 'Exploring youth work identities', in R. Harrison and C. Wise (eds), *Working with Young People*, London: Sage and Open University Press.

Turner, M. and Beresford, P. (2005) *User Controlled Research: Its Meanings and Potential*, Hampshire: INVOLVE.

Ungar, M. (2004) 'A Constructionist discourse on resilience: multiple contexts, multiple realities among at-risk children and youth', *Youth & Society*, 35 (3): 341–365.

Ungar, M. (2007) *Too Safe for Their Own Good: How Risk and Responsibility Help Teens Thrive*, Toronto: McClelland and Stewart.

UNICEF (2003) *World Youth Report*, New York: United Nations.

United Nations (1989) Convention on the Rights of the Child, http://untreaty.un.org/English/TreatyEvent2001/pdf/03e.pdf (accessed 01. 09. 07).

Utting, D. (1999) *Communities that Care: A Guide to Promising Approaches*, London: Communities that Care.

Valentine, G. (2003) 'Boundary crossings: transitions from childhood to adulthood', *Children's Geographies*, 1 (1): 37–52.

Villarruel, F. A., Perkins, D. F., Borden, L. M. and Keith, J. G. (eds) (2003) *Community Youth Development: Practice, Policy, and Research*, Thousand Oaks, CA: Sage.

Walker, J., Marczak, M., Blythe, D. and Borden, L. (2005) 'Designing youth development programs: toward a theory of developmental intentionality', in J. L. Mahoney, R. W. Larson and J. S. Eccles (eds), *Organized Activities as Contexts of Development: Extracurricular Activities, After-school and Community Programs*, Mahwah, NJ: Lawrence Erlbaum Associates.

Walkerdine, V., Lucey, H. and Melody, J. (2001) *Growing Up Girl*, London: Palgrave.

Walklate, S. (1998) *Understanding Criminology*, Buckingham: Open University Press.

Wallace, C. (2003) 'Introduction: Youth and Politics', *Journal of Youth Studies*, 6 (3): 243–245.

Wallace, C. and Kovatcheva, S. (1998) *Youth in Society: The Construction and Deconstruction of Youth in East and West Europe*, London: Macmillan.

Walther, A., Stauber, B. and Pohl, A. (2005) 'Informal networks in youth transitions in West Germany: biographical resource or reproduction of social inequality?', *Journal of Youth Studies*, 8 (2): 221–240.

Ward, D. and Mullender, A. (1991) 'Empowerment and Oppression: An Indissoluble Pairing for Contemporary Social Work', *Critical Social Policy*, 11 (32): 21–30.

Ward, L. (2005) 'Youth clubs can be bad for you, says report', *Guardian*, 20 January.

Waters, M. (ed.) (2002) *Globalisation*, London: Routledge.

Webster, C., Simpson, D., MacDonald, R., Abbas, A., Cieslik, M., Shildrick, T. and Simpson, M. (2004) *Poor Transitions: Social Exclusion and Young Adults*, Bristol: Policy Press.

Weller, S. (2007) '"Sticking with your Mates?" Children's friendship trajectories during the transition from primary to secondary school', *Children & Society*, 21 (5): 339–351.

Welsh Assembly Government (2003) *Children and Young People: Rights to Action*, Cardiff: Welsh Assembly Government.

Werner, E. and Smith, R. (1992) *Overcoming the Odds: High Risk Children from Birth to Adulthood, Ithaca*, NY: Cornell University.

Wertheim, M. (2002) in Z. Sardar and M. Wyn Davies (eds), *Why do People Hate America?*, Cambridge: Icon Books.

Westwood, S. (2002) *Power and the Social,* London: Routledge.

White, R. and Cuneen, C. (2006) 'Social class, youth and crime', in B. Goldson and J. Muncie (eds) *Youth Crime and Justice*, London: Sage.

Wilkinson, H. and Mulgan, G. (1995) *Freedom's Children: Work, Relationships and Politics for 18–34 year olds in Britain Today*, London: Demos.

Williams, R. (1989) *Resources of Hope: Culture, Democracy and Socialism*, London: Verso.

Williamson, H. (1993) 'Youth policy in the UK and the marginalisation of young people', *Youth and Policy*, 40: 33–48.

Williamson, H. (1997) 'So what for young people?', in I. Ledgerwood and N. Kendra (eds), *The Challenge for the Future*, Lyme Regis: Russell House.

Williamson, H. (2002) *Supporting Young People in Europe: Principles, Policy and Practice*, Strasbourg: Council of Europe Publishing.

Williamson, H. (2004) *Youth Policy in Norway*, Strasbourg: Council of Europe Publishing.

Williamson, H. (2005) 'Young people and social inclusion – an overview of policy and practice', in M. Barry (ed.), *Youth Policy and Social Inclusion: Critical Debates with Young People*, London: Routledge.

Williamson, H. (2008), *Supporting Young People in Europe: Volume 2*, Strasbourg: Council of Europe Publishing.

Willis, P. (1977) *Learning to Labour: How Working Class Kids get Working Class Jobs*, Farnborough: Saxon House.

Willis, P. (1990) *Common Culture: Symbolic Work at Play in Everyday Cultures of the Young*, Milton Keynes: Open University Press.

Wilson, A., Williams, M. and Hancock, B. (2000) *Research Approaches in Primary Care*, Abingdon: Radford Medical Press.

Wilson, J. Q. and Kelling, G. (1982) 'Broken windows', *Atlantic Monthly*, March: 29–38.

Withers, G. and Batten, M. (1995) *Programs for At Risk Youth: A Review of the American, Canadian and British Literature Since 1984*, Camberwell: The Australian Council for Educational Research.

Wood, J. (2003) 'A comparative analysis of rural based Connexions partnerships', *Rural Impetus* (No. 19), Leicester: National Forum for the Development of Rural Youth Work.

Wood, J. (2008) 'Young People and Active Citizenship' thesis submitted for the award of PhD. Leicester: De Montfort University.

Woolcock, M. (2001) 'Microenterprise and social capital: a framework for theory, research, and policy', *Journal of Socio-Economics*, 30 (2): 193–198.

Worrall, A. (1999) 'Troubled or troublesome? Justice for girls and young women', in B. Goldson (ed.), *Youth Justice: Contemporary Policy and Practice*, Aldershot: Ashgate.

Worms, J.- P. (2004) 'Old and new civic and social ties in France', in R. D. Putnam (ed.), *Democracies in Flux: The Evolution of Social Capital in Contemporary Society*, New York: Oxford University Press.

Wring, D., Henn, M. and Weinstein, M. (1998) 'Young people and contemporary politics: committed scepticism or engaged cynicism?', *British Elections and Parties Review*, (9): 200–216.

Wyn, J. and White, R. (1997) *Rethinking Youth*, London: Sage.

Yates, J. (2006) 'An Ethnography of Youth and Crime in a Working Class Community', thesis submitted for the award of PhD. Leicester: De Montfort University.

Yates, S. and Payne, M. (2006) 'Not so NEET? A critique of the use of "NEET" in setting targets for interventions with young people', *Journal of Youth Studies*, 9 (3): 329–344.

Yeates, N. (1999) 'Social politics and policy in an era of globalization: critical reflections', *Social Policy and Administration*, 33 (4): 372–393.

Young, J. and Matthews, R. (2003) 'New Labour, crime control and social exclusion', in R. Matthews and J. Young (eds), *The New Politics of Crime and Punishment*, Cullompton: Willan.

Young, K. (1999) 'Youth worker as guide, philosopher, friend', in S. Banks (ed.), *Ethical Issues in Youth Work*, London: Routledge.

Young, K. (2006) *The Art of Youth Work*, 2nd edn, Dorset: Russell House Publishing.

Young, K. and Chouhan, K. (2006) *Anti-Oppressive Practice: Module Guide*, Leicester: De Montfort University.

Young People Now (2006) 'Principal youth officers' group concerned over threat to role', 17–23 May.

Young People Now (2007) 'Camden confirms its service merger', 21–27 February.

Youth Justice Board (undated) *Youth Inclusion Project (YIP)*. London: YJB. www. youth-justice-board.gov.uk/YouthJusticeBoard/prevention/YIP (accessed 24. 3. 2006).

INDEX